# MANUAL

## OF

# CHRISTIAN

# ARCHEOLOGY

# MANUAL

## OF

# CHRISTIAN ARCHEOLOGY

By ORAZIO MARUCCHI

*Fourth Italian Edition*
*Revised by Giulio Belvederi, D. D., Ph. D.*

Secretary of the Pontifical Institute
of Christian Archeology

*Rome, 1933*

TRANSLATED AND ADAPTED BY

**HUBERT VECCHIERELLO, O. F. M., Ph. D.**

*Dean of Science of St. Bonaventure College*

ST. ANTHONY GUILD PRESS
FRANCISCAN MONASTERY
PATERSON, NEW JERSEY
MCMXXXV

STUDIO ADDICTUS
Province of Holy Cross

*Imprimi Potest*
FR. MATHIAS FAUST, O. F. M.,
Minister Provincialis.

*Nihil Obstat*
ARTHUR J. SCANLAN, S. T. D.,
Censor Librorum.

*Imprimatur*
✠ PATRICK CARDINAL HAYES,
Archbishop of New York.

New York, November 8, 1935.

# Preface*

DURING the past few years, a number of books have been published in the form of elementary courses or manuals for the purpose of popularizing the study of Christian archeology. But some of these are too extensive in their treatment of the subject, and hence of a relatively prohibitive price; others are too cursory, lacking those plates and reproductions of monuments which, in books of this nature, are absolutely indispensable; finally, the most important books dealing with this subject are, unfortunately, written in foreign languages and consequently unavailable for the majority of readers.

It was thought opportune to publish this *Manual of Christian Archeology* in order to fill a long-felt want. The favor with which it was received has convinced the author that there was a need for a volume of this kind. The materials for this volume were, in large measure, taken from my *Elements d'archéologie chrétienne*.[1]

The author was greatly assisted in the work of excerpting pertinent matter from the French edition by Dr. Enrico Iosi, a young and enthusiastic student of things archeological. Dr. Iosi has not only been of great assistance in compiling new sections

---

\* This preface appeared in the last two editions of this work. It was prepared by the late lamented author, Prof. Orazio Marucchi. The fourth edition, revised and rewritten according to the latest archeological studies, appeared after the death of Marucchi, which occurred January 21, 1931.—Translator.

1. This is a treatise on Christian archeology, edited by Desclée and published in three volumes: *Notions générales* (*General Ideas*), *Catacombes* (*The Catacombs*), and *Basiliques* (*Basilicas*).

of this and other volumes, but has also rendered excellent aid in the preparation of much material of great help to my readers.

This volume has been of great use to the author's students in Christian Archeology at the Roman University. When the first and second editions were exhausted, a third was prepared, modified in several respects. The text was enlarged and a greater number of reproductions was included.

The manual begins with a short treatise on the foundations of Christian archeology, followed by a compendium of the history of the persecutions viewed especially from the standpoint of our subject. A study of the ancient Christian catacombs is then taken up and general conclusions are given, including a synopsis in tabular form of all the ancient topographical documents which throw any light on the catacombs.

This was thought likely to be of great help to readers, because it would save them from the necessity of recurring to the large tomes of *Roma sotterranea* published by de Rossi. A brief description of the principal Roman catacombs, with a glance at those of Italy and of other countries, is also included.

A treatise on Christian inscriptions is given, as well as another on ancient Christian art, especially as portrayed in the catacombs. Finally, Christian basilicas are spoken of and particular emphasis is laid on their origin and ornamentation. This part concludes with a list of the principal basilicas.

The present manual is based almost entirely on the ancient Christian monuments of Rome. This was intentional, because these are the monuments which are considered by all to be of the greatest importance; moreover, they possess a sequence which goes back to the very origin of Christianity itself.

This manual was composed particularly for classroom use. For this reason the author has omitted many details and observations which it were best for the teacher to supply when dealing with the various topics merely hinted at throughout the volume.

O. MARUCCHI.

Rome, January, 1923.

# Contents

# Part One

## FOUNDATIONS OF CHRISTIAN ARCHEOLOGY

---

### Chapter I

### GENERAL SOURCES

CHRISTIAN archeology, like all other historical sciences, is based on documents. The documents which are indispensable for its study are classed as *general* and *special*. The general foundations consist of the history of the Church and the books or writings of the ancient ecclesiastical writers.

The most ancient history of the Christian Church is found in the book of the Acts of the Apostles, written by St. Luke, a disciple of St. Paul. It is true that this history, even though it embraces at first the entire early Church, and can therefore be said to be the beginning of every other ecclesiastical history, finally becomes a particular history of the apostolate of St. Paul, omitting to speak of the vicissitudes of the other apostles. Moreover, as has been noted, it is not complete even with reference to the life of St. Paul, because it comes to an end with his arrival in Rome in the year 61 of our era.

However, the study of the history of Christianity, which naturally has its foundation in the four Gospels, begins with the Acts of the Apostles. Their contents must be familiar to everyone desiring to occupy himself with Christian archeology. In them, in fact, will be found indications of all those developments which will appear in later writings, in the organization of the Church, in the usages and customs of the first Christians.

1

Another very ancient and very important document is the so-called *Testamentum Domini Nostri Jesu Christi* (*Testament of Our Lord Jesus Christ*), of which the Syrian text was translated and published recently by Monsignor Ignatius Rahmani, Patriarch of Antioch in Syria (Magonza, 1899).

The following paragraphs deal with the ecclesiastical writers and writings deserving of special mention.

Clement of Rome, a contemporary of the apostles, wrote a very precious letter to the Corinthians. More will be said of this later. Many apocryphal works were long attributed to Clement of Rome, among them the *Constitutiones Apostolicae* (Canons of the Apostles), the books of the *Recognitiones,* and the *Gesta* of St. Peter. All these works go under the name of Pseudo-Clement.[1]

After the Gospels and the Epistles of St. Paul, the oldest document which mentions the Eucharist is the work called the Διδαχὴ τῶν δώδεκα ἀποστόλων. Its title is known from the writings of Eusebius of Caesarea,[2] of St. Athanasius,[3] and other Fathers; but the text was rediscovered only in 1883 by the Greek Metropolitan Bryennios, in an eleventh-century manuscript. This document has two well-defined parts: that which is doctrinal and moral harks back to the Synoptics and certainly cites St. Mark; the other, liturgical and disciplinary, presents certain analogies with the Gospel of St. John.[4] This writing may therefore be called the oldest liturgical manual of the Church, incomplete though it is. It makes no mention of the Consecration, which is clearly indicated in the Epistle of St. Paul to the Corinthians and in the first *Apology* of St. Justin.[5] However, it refers to the *Fractio panis* (*Breaking of Bread*): Κατὰ κυριακὴν δὲ Κυρίου συναχθέντες κλάσατε ἄρτον καὶ εὐχαριστήσατε προσεξομολογησάμενοι τὰ παραπτώματα ὑμῶν, ὅπως καθαρὰ ἡ θυσία ὑμῶν ᾖ ("Gather together on the Lord's Day, break bread and give thanks after you have confessed your sins so that your sacrifice will be pure" — XIV, 1).

Hermas, a writer of the first half of the second century, was the author of a book entitled *The Shepherd,* held in great esteem by the early Christians and containing an account of certain visions and a number of precepts which are very important in understanding the usages and customs of the primitive Church.[6]

Papias was Bishop of Hieropolis in Phrygia, and the disciple of the Apostle John. We have only a few fragments of his works concerning the Gospels.[7]

St. Ignatius,[8] Bishop of Antioch, was seized and condemned there to be exposed to the beasts in the amphitheatre in Rome. He was taken as a prisoner along the coast of Asia, Macedonia and Greece. At every port of call, numbers of the faithful who were members of the churches in the nearby towns came to pay him honor and respect, for they had heard of his condemnation: meetings which gave the occasion for the writing of his letters to thank his fellow Christians. These letters are valuable for their information concerning the beliefs of the faithful and the Christian institutions of that age. The number of authentic epistles which have come down to us is seven; of these the most important is that written to the Romans, because it contains a testimony of the common apostolate of Peter and Paul in Rome.

St. Justin,[9] native of Samaria, outstanding philosopher converted to Christianity, wrote two *Apologies,* the first of which was composed in Rome before the year 150, and presented by the saint to the Emperor Antoninus Pius. This writing has a special importance because it contains a description of the Christian liturgy as it was practised during the second century. It appears from this that the agape had already been separated from the Eucharistic Communion. The second *Apology* of St. Justin, more abridged than the first, was presented by him to Marcus Aurelius about the year 166. Many writings of an absolutely apocryphal nature were also attributed to St. Justin.

Other apologetes of Christianity were: Quadratus,[10] Bishop of Athens, who sent his apology to Hadrian about the year 126; Aristides,[11] also an Athenian and a contemporary of Quadratus; Melito,[12] Bishop of Sardis, who composed an apologetic work about the year 170; Claudius Apollinaris,[13] Bishop of Hieropolis, who presented his work to Marcus Aurelius; and Tatian,[14] native of Syria and follower of Justin. He later became the leader of a heretical sect  From his hand we have a discourse against the Gentiles. Finally, we should make mention of Athenagoras,[15] of the Alexandrian school, author of an apology directed to Marcus Aurelius and Commodus in the year 177; of Theophilus of Antioch;[16] and of Hermias.[17]

One of the greatest writers of the second century was Irenaeus of Lyons,[18] disciple of the great Polycarp, Bishop of Smyrna. He was sent by the faithful of Lyons to Pope Eleutherius in Rome about the year 177; during the persecution of Marcus Aurelius he was elected Bishop of Lyons, and he died a martyr's death in the persecution of Septimius Severus, in the year 212. The principal work of Irenaeus is his treatise *Adversus haereses,* which is fundamentally directed against the Gnostics. Its importance lies in its defence of the principal dogmas of Catholicism impugned by those heretics — the Sacraments, the ecclesiastical hierarchy, the primacy of the Roman Church, which he attests to be already universally recognized even in his own day.

Toward the beginning of the third century comes that other great apologete, Tertullian,[19] a native of Carthage, who devoted his genius and eloquence to the defence of Christianity against its three enemies: Jews, heretics and Gentiles. But in spite of all this, Tertullian's excessive rigorism, and his spirit of sophistry, caused him to fall into the heresy of the Montanists; and later he founded a special sect which took its name from him. His chief works are: the *Apologeticum,* an inexhaustible mine of information for the study of the history of the early Church and Christian antiquities, since it contains the most vivid and authentic descriptions of the customs of the early Christians; another book similar to it, entitled *Ad nationes;* and the work *De praescriptionibus,* very important for its demonstration of the apostolic origin of the Catholic Church, the unity of its doctrine, and the apostolic succession of the Bishops of Rome. A number of other works of Tertullian have special importance and interest for Christian archeology, including *De idololatria, De corona, De spectaculis, Ad martyres, De baptismo, De poenitentia, De oratione, De pallio, De fuga in persecutione.*

Another author, concerning whom there still remains much
that is obscure, is St. Hippolytus,[20] who lived in the first half
of the third century — a contemporary of Alexander Severus.
The authentic list of his works is engraved in marble on his
famous statue in the Lateran Museum. This also records the
Canon of Easter, composed by him. His writings are based on
arguments taken from theology and the Bible.

About the middle of the same century comes St. Cyprian,[21]
the celebrated Bishop of Carthage, who died a martyr under
Valerian in 258. The more important writings of St. Cyprian
for our purpose are the treatises *De lapsis* and *De Catholicae
Ecclesiae unitate* and *De exhortatione ad martyrium.* His contemporary was Minucius Felix,[22] author of the dialogue entitled
*Octavius,* which pits the doctrines of Christianity against those
of paganism. This work is one of the most notable for the study
of the antiquity of Christianity, since it makes known the calumnies and prejudices regarding Christians which were most widespread among pagans.

To the illustrious Church of Alexandria of Egypt belong
Clement of Alexandria[23] and Origen,[24] both of whom flourished
in the third century. One of the principal works of Clement is
that called the *Pedagogue,* in which he instructs neophytes in
the manner of living according to the teachings of that illustrious Teacher Who is Christ. The great importance of this
work consists in this, that the author enters with minutest detail
into the rules governing the lives of all Christians, including
those dealing with their meals, their conversations, their manner of dress, the ornaments that should be worn, and especially
the clothes of women.

Origen was the most prolific of all the early Christian
writers; St. Jerome said of him that no one could ever read all
that Origen had written. One of his principal works is the
colossal biblical work known as the *Hexapla, Tetrapla,* etc.
His memory has often been calumniated but his name has been
vindicated by many critics who have shown that he was a very
uncompromising Catholic.

Near the beginning of the third century belongs that anonymous and malicious writing, attributed to Origen and known as the *Philosophumena* or the *Refutation of the Heresies,* which sheds much light on the history of the Roman Church during the times of Popes Zephyrin and Callistus (*Origenis Philosophumena, sive omnium haeresum refutatio, e codice Parisino nunc primum edidit Emmanuel Mueller,* Oxford, 1851).[25]

In the last period of the persecutions, and during the first intervals of peace, we have Lactanctius[26] and Eusebius.[27] The first, called in justice the Christian Cicero, was the teacher of Crispus, the son of Constantine. He wrote a remarkable work in seven books entitled *Divinarum Institutionum contra Gentes,* very important because of its demonstration of the divinity of Christianity and of Christian morality; it gives solemn proof of the Christian concept of the equality of all men in the sight of God and of the brotherhood of all men, whether free or slaves. One of the most beautiful phrases taken from his works is: "Apud nos inter servum et dominum interest nihil, quia pares esse nos credimus." To him is also attributed an important book of great historical value known as the *De mortibus persecutorum,* which is a valuable source of the history of the persecutions, especially those of the last period, and of the times of the peace of Constantine. Numerous critics, however, deny that this last book was written by Lactantius, although most of them admit that it is the work of a contemporary.

Eusebius, called the father of Church History, was a friend of the Emperor Constantine. His chief work, which is of special interest to us, is the *Historia ecclesiastica,* in which he has left us valuable fragments of ancient Christian literature as well as the writings of the most ancient authors, of whom we would have no certain evidence had he not incorporated them in his narrative. Eusebius' history begins with the origin of Christianity and continues to the end of the year 325, when, after the death of the pagan Licinius, the Emperor Constantine could freely and openly show himself a Christian. Many are the data that he gives us concerning the origin of Christianity, the principal churches of the early Christian world, the succession of bishops of the more important sees, and the various persecutions. It is important to note that, while he does not omit the West, he gives fuller details concerning these persecutions and the resulting martyrdoms as they refer to the Orient. This is but natural since he himself hailed from the Orient. He wrote likewise a book on the martyrs of Palestine which is valuable for the history of the persecution of Diocletian as it was carried out in that region; Eusebius was present in person at some of the condemnations and executions. One may finally consider his *Life of Constantine* as an appendix to the *Historia ecclesiastica*.

During the fourth century, the century of peace and triumph for Christianity, we find other important works which are of inestimable value for Christian archeology. The great doctor of the Church, Augustine,[28] among his numerous writings has left us many which are truly priceless; for example, the abstract of the acts of the religious conference held in Carthage in the year 411, entitled *Breviculus collationis cum Donatistis*. This work gives us an idea of the condition of the Church when the persecution of Diocletian broke upon it in all its fury, in 303. In it Augustine describes the possessions of the African Church, its movable and immovable goods, the domestic and liturgical furnishings, etc. His other writings against the Donatists are important because in all of them will be found valuable historical allusions and the details of many contemporary occurrences, or the mention of facts the memory of which was still vivid in his own day.

The works of St. Ambrose,[29] Bishop of Milan, give us interesting details of great value concerning the martyrs venerated by that ancient Church, their relics and also certain liturgical usages practiced in his day, as for example, the consecration of the holy virgins.

The writings of St. Jerome[30] are more important for their biblical than their archeological material; yet they will also afford us much valuable historical information concerning his contemporaries, and certain particular points relative to monuments which existed in his day. Here one might make special mention of his book entitled *De viris illustribus.* To this epoch belongs Pope Damasus, who is mentioned by St. Jerome because of the poems which he composed. Damasus has handed down to us priceless memories of the martyrs, especially those of Rome, but as these writings deal with inscriptions composed by him, we shall give them separate notice later.

We may close this brief list of writers by citing the poet Prudentius,[31] who wrote toward the end of the fourth century and the beginning of the fifth. Among the various compositions he has left us, the series of hymns composed in honor of the martyrs is of special importance for the study of Christian archeology. This series is the so-called Περὶ στεφάνων or *De coronis.* In these short poems Prudentius gives us most valuable information on the history of individual martyrs, especially those of Rome. Some of these poems also describe sepulchral monuments.

## Chapter II

## SPECIAL SOURCES

THE SPECIAL sources for the study of Christian archeology are: The Acts of the Martyrs, Martyrologies, Calendars, the *Liber pontificalis,* and the various Sacramentaries.[1] Concerning the Itineraries, we shall speak separately in Part III, which is reserved for the study of the Catacombs.

### 1.  The Acts of the Martyrs[2]

When the Christians were brought before the judges, the notaries public or lawyers jotted down the questions which were put to them and the answers given. The verbal process was later placed in the public archives where access could be had to it and copies of the depositions often be made. From these official documents numerous Acts of the Martyrs were made. On the other hand, as for example in the case of the *Passio* of the martyrs of Lyons, the Acts are the work of Christians themselves, or the accounts of others who had witnessed the sufferings of the martyrs.

These documents, had they come down to us in their original form, would be a source of inestimable value. But almost all the early contemporary and authentic Acts have been lost. Of those which have been saved and are known as the *Proconsular Acts,* we may mention the Acts of the Martyrs of Lyons for France, those of St. Polycarp for Asia Minor, and those of Sts. Perpetua and Felicitas for Africa. The Roman Church has none. The Acts of her martyrs were destroyed during the great persecution of Diocletian, when the archives of the Roman Church were burnt. The same thing occurred in Africa, as we know from St. Augustine.[3]

In the period of peace, new Acts were composed from memory or from such documents as were saved from destruction. Their authority or value varies greatly according to the date of their composition. The major portion of them do not antedate the sixth century, and very often they confuse legend with history. Those written after the eighth and ninth centuries are nothing more than scholastic exercises — tasks which the monks had to perform, drawing copiously from their imagination, applying to one martyr the story which belonged to another, and accentuating at all times the allegedly extraordinary occurrences rather than the actual known happenings.

It is very evident that such Acts have no value in a critical study of this nature. Still, they often contain a portion of historical truth: the name of the martyr, the approximate date of the occurrences, often the name of the prefect, the judge, the governor, and especially the place of burial, since at the time these Acts were composed the ancient cemeteries were still visited. This has been abundantly proved by the Acts of Sts. Nereus and Achilleus which have justly been rejected by the critics as among the most legendary: yet the monuments discovered in the Ardeatine Way have shown that they are verifiable in certain points; that the two martyrs bore some relation to Flavia Domitilla and were buried in a cemetery on her property, "in praedio Domitillae." Le Blant[4] has shown the positive value of the Acts. It is possible to separate the genuine elements from the legendary additions with which they are burdened.

The early Christians themselves recognized the presence of legends in the Acts, as is shown by the decree attributed to Pope Gelasius (end of the fifth century) which prohibits the reading of certain books in the churches because they contained accounts of miracles which could not be proved. An excerpt from this decree illustrates this fact:

"Gesta sanctorum martyrum, qui multiplicibus tormentorum ideo secundum antiquam consuetudinem singulari cautela in sancta Romana Ecclesia non leguntur, quia et eorum qui concruciatibus, et mirabilibus confessionum triumphis irradiant . . . scripsere nomina penitus ignorantur, et ab infidelibus aut idiotis superflue, aut minus apte quam rei ordo fuerit, scripta esse putantur. Propter quod, ut dictum est, ne vel levis subsannandi oriretur occasio, in Sancta Romana Ecclesia non leguntur."[5]

The place of the Acts of the Martyrs[6] has been taken by the Martyrologies, which may be called synopses of the Acts.

## 2.   The Martyrologies

The feasts celebrated each year were indicated in the local Calendar, and every church had to have its own. The most ancient of the Calendars still extant are those of Rome, Tours and Carthage. By uniting the Calendars of the different churches, especially those of the metropolitan cities, the so-called Martyrologies were formed. It appears that the earliest compilations of this kind were made in Africa and Asia Minor about the middle of the fourth century. These have not come down to us in their original form, but are known through the *Martyrologium Hieronymianum,* a compilation made in Italy about the middle of the fifth century, and later reissued in France. About 590, another revision was made at Auxerre, from which all existing manuscripts actually take their rise.[7] These different manuscripts have been classified and from them the essential text of de Rossi and Duchesne has been published in the second volume of November of the Bollandists.[8] The Martyrology of Asia Minor has come down to us in still another translation in Syrian. This was recently discovered by Wright in a manuscript dating from the year 412.

The so-called "historical" Martyrologies were compiled much later;[9] they contain for every saint a brief account taken from his Acts. The better known ones are those of Venerable Bede (eighth century),[10] of Rabanus Maurus,[11] of Ado, Bishop of Vienna in the ninth century,[12] and of Usuard.[13] This last was written at St. Germain-des-Prés about the year 875; the actual Roman Martyrology is nothing but a second edition, revised and completed by Cardinal Baronius (1598). Benedict XIV wisely observed that this official edition cannot be modified without the consent of the Holy See; it does not follow, therefore, that it has an incontestable historical value. ("Asserimus Apostolicam Sedem non indicare inconcussae esse et certissimae veritatis quaecumque in Martyrologium Romanum inserta sunt.") He cited several examples of errors which had crept in but which were corrected subsequently. Thus (to give an example), for January 25 there was listed the feast of the holy martyr Xynoris; but it was shown that the homily from which this name had been taken (St. John Chrysostom[14]) does not speak of a martyr, but of two saints (ξυνωρίς, meaning a pair), Juventinus and Maximinus, martyrs who suffered during the persecution of Julian.[15]

### 3. The Calendars

The oldest Calendar is that known as the Liberian, compiled at Rome in 354, during the pontificate of Pope Liberius. It is also called the Philocalian Calendar, because it was written by Furius Dionysius Philocalus, the celebrated writer of the Damasian inscriptions, and the Bucherian Calendar from the name of Father Bucher, who published it toward the middle of the seventeenth century in his work, *De doctrina temporum*. The manuscript was dedicated to a certain Valentine: "Valentine, vivas; Valentine, floreas." The original manuscript has been lost, but the Imperial Library of Vienna possesses a very beautiful copy.

This Calendar furnishes us with many valuable data. It contains diverse documents: an astronomical calendar with the Canon of Easter according to the computation engraved on the pedestal of the statue of St. Hippolytus; a table of the feasts of the emperors, "Natales Caesarum"; a portion of the series of consuls, extracted from the Roman consular holidays; a series of the prefects of Rome from 254 to 354, that is to Pope Liberius; the *Depositiones episcoporum,* which also run from the year 254 to 354; the *Depositiones martyrum,* along with topographical notes indicating the place of burial of the principal martyrs. The Calendar records only the principal feasts: Christmas, the Chair of St. Peter, "Natale Petri de Cathedra," and the more solemn feasts of the martyrs. It says nothing, for instance, of the commemoration of St. Cecilia, indicating that this saint had not been accorded the solemnity she received later on; but it does mention St. Agnes. The text will be given later. It is, in fine, a chronology of the popes, closing with Liberius, with a mention of the numerous churches and oratories built in the reigns of the various popes; for instance, the three basilicas constructed by Julius I, the first on the Portuan Way, the second on the Aurelian Way, and the third on the Flaminian Way. This catalogue is commonly considered as the nucleus of the *Liber pontificalis.*

## 4.   The *Liber pontificalis (Book of the Popes)*[16]

The work which goes under the name of the *Liber pontificalis* is a gathering of biographical notes on each of the popes from St. Peter to Nicholas I, who died in 867.

The *Liber pontificalis* has been attributed to Damasus or Anastasius Bibliothecarius. It was published by John Vignoli (eighteenth century) and by Bianchini (1735).[17] Duchesne has shown that this compilation is anonymous, and from the time of the publication of these facts, the book has been known by its true name, the *Liber pontificalis.*

The *Liber pontificalis* has had numerous redactions. The first was made toward the end of the fifth century or the beginning of the sixth.[18] The celebrated manuscript of Verona, published by Muratori in the third part of his works, *Rerum Italicarum Scriptores,* gives the biographies of the popes to Anastasius II (498), and it is evident that that of Symmachus, successor of Anastasius, is the work of a contemporary and an adversary of the pope. A second redaction, already noted by Bianchini, comes to a close with the death of Pope Felix IV (530). A third goes to 687; a fourth continues to the year 714, the time of Pope Constantine. Finally, the last compilation belongs undoubtedly to the ninth century. William the Librarian appended a continuation to the twelfth century. (Cf. Cod. Vat. Lat. 3762.)

In the various redactions, all parts have an equal value from the topographical standpoint, but not from the historical. The earliest biographies are based upon apocryphal documents. It is only from the beginning of the sixth century that this work becomes a true source of the history of the Church, both in Rome and in Italy. As for the remainder, it is necessary to distinguish, with Duchesne, numerous groups of manuscripts, some of which are more authentic, others more corrupt.

## 5. The Sacramentaries[19]

The Sacramentaries, or ancient missals, furnish much valuable information on the cemeteries, the tombs of the martyrs or their commemorations, and analogous references, after the fashion of the stations in our modern missals. Three Sacramentaries are usually enumerated — the Leonine, the Gelasian, and the Gregorian.

The *Leonine Sacramentary* is the most ancient. The date of its composition may be assigned toward the middle or the end of the sixth century. It was published for the first time by Bianchini (1735), later by the Ballerini brothers in their edition of the works of Leo,[20] finally by Muratori in his *Liturgia Romana vetus* (1748), according to a manuscript of the seventh century belonging to the library of the chapter of Verona. It is a collection of liturgical formulae compiled by private individuals who must have had access to the numerous official books in use in the various Roman basilicas. The formulae are of diverse periods; some may belong to the fourth century; others appear to be of the same period as Pope Vigilius. In spite of this, they are in fine accord with the period and the style of St. Leo I, and this explains why this compilation is known as the *Leonine Sacramentary*. There is no doubt as to the Roman origin of the collection. The note gives a few examples to prove this point.[21]

The *Gelasian Sacramentary*[22] represents the liturgical order in vogue in France from the sixth to the eighth century among a large number of churches desirous of conforming to Roman usage. John the Deacon,[23] and other testimonies of the ninth century, point to Pope Gelasius as the author of this work. The oldest copy is Ms. 316 in the Vatican Library. It was published by Tomasi in his *Codices sacramentorum* (1860), and by Muratori in Vol. I of his *Liturgia Romana vetus* (1748). There are no topographical references in this work, there is not even the name of a single basilica of Rome; the Roman formulae are manifestly adapted to the use of a foreign land.

The *Gregorian Sacramentary*[24] is not known from an original text, but only from one used at the time of Adrian I; only two manuscripts reproduce it without supplement or Gallican additions. Still, it is not a difficult task to figure out the original text. It involves only the elimination of certain feasts which we know were established later than St. Gregory, as for example, the feast of St. Gregory himself. These are more readily ascertained by a comparison of the Sacramentary with the *Liber antiphonarius,* in which the offices of the feasts of a more recent date may easily be recognized by the fact that they do not have any music which is proper to themselves. (A few exceptions in certain offices introduced under the Byzantine influence betray their foreign origin by their musical character.)

The *Sacramentarium Gregorianum* expressly indicates the place of the solemn stations on all those days on which the feast of the day does not designate it itself; as for example, the stations during Lent. If the station should be preceded by a general procession, the Sacramentary is careful to indicate the church where the procession will begin and the one where Mass will be celebrated.[25]

## 6. The *Capitularia Evangeliorum*

The *Capitularia Evangeliorum* are the rubrics indicating those passages of the Gospels which were to be read during Mass in every church every day of the year. These rubrics were placed at either the beginning or the end of the Gospel-books. The *Capitularia,* like the Calendars, contain a list of the feasts of the martyrs, and if they do not name the cemeteries themselves, they often make mention of the roads along which the venerated sanctuaries are to be found. These documents have been published by Frontone,[26] Martène,[27] Tomasi[28] and Giorgi.[29] The better manuscripts were produced during the Carolingian period; one of the most important is that known as the Palatino-Vatican No. 50, which came from the library of Heidelberg. The same points are found in the Gospel-book of Aix-la-Chapelle, which was probably taken from the tomb of Charlemagne and which certainly had been sent to this emperor from Rome along with the books of the Gregorian liturgy.

## 7. Modern Authors[30]

The study of Christian archeology had its origin and development after that of classical archeology, because at the time of the Renaissance, during the fifteenth century, the attention of the learned was turned exclusively to the arts and literature of the classics. The humanists and artists of that time not only obscured but also unjustly belittled and underestimated the monuments of Christian antiquity.

The first impulse toward the study of Christian archeology arose from the desire of learned Catholics to cite the testimony of ancient Christian monuments against the Protestant accusation that the Roman Church had strayed from the faith and discipline of the first centuries. One of the first to take advantage of these ancient proofs in defence of the Catholic Church was the learned Augustinian, Onofrio Panvinio. He was followed shortly by Ciaconus and De Winghe, and later by Antonio Bosio.

Onofrio Panvinio, who died at the early age of thirty-eight, published numerous works on Christian antiquities,[31] among which we may cite in particular *De ritu sepeliendi mortuos apud veteres Christianos et de eorum coemeteriis* (1568). In this work, he places the number of the catacombs at forty-three, while confessing that when he wrote, only four were known, namely, those of St. Sebastian, St. Pancratius, St. Lawrence and St. Valentine.

Shortly after this, St. Philip Neri gave a great impetus to archeological studies.[32] He was accustomed, out of devotion, to visit the ancient basilicas and catacombs at frequent intervals; and he suggested that his disciple Baronius write a history of the Church in answer to the Magdeburgh Centuriators. The resulting *Annales* mark a true advance in our knowledge of Christian antiquities.

During the same period, an important part of the *coemeterium Jordanorum* was rediscovered on the Salarian Way. This was an extensive cemetery, with paintings, situated between that of Priscilla and that of St. Felicitas. "On that day," says de Rossi, "was born the name *Roma sotterranea.*"[33] Unfortunately, nothing immediate came of this discovery; Bosio, then only three years of age, could not know of it.[34]

Toward the end of the sixteenth century, Ciaconus, the Belgian de Winghe and Jean l'Heureux ("Macarios") performed some archeological work, though they published nothing. All that resulted was the *Hagioglypta Macarii,* in which l'Heureux treats of the paintings of the catacombs and of Christian symbolism.[35] The designs of Ciaconus are preserved in the Vatican Library (Cod. Vat. Lat. 5409).

Pompeio Ugonio, professor of the Roman University, wrote the *History of the Stations* of Lent,[36] and seems to have imbued his friend Bosio, burdened with the affairs of the Order of

Malta,[37] with a love for Christian antiquities. They began their first explorations together in 1593. Bosio also received the counsels of, or at least was influenced by, St. Philip Neri. For more than thirty years he explored the catacombs, studying all his discoveries in a scientific manner, and making available a great quantity of documents. After his death the amount and the importance of the work he had done became evident. He copied inscriptions, and made drawings of paintings and sculptures. The lack of means prevented him from making excavations. "I succeeded," he writes in his great simplicity, "in penetrating the catacombs with much difficulty, finding my way by means of lamplight." He had been injured in the cemetery of Domitilla, and he feared, as he says with humility, to profane with his dead body the remains of the holy martyrs.[38] He discovered, by chance, a historical crypt — that one which holds paintings of Sts. Abdon and Sennen — on the Portuan Way, where later an ancient baptistery also was found. Bosio died in 1629. His work, *Roma sotterranea,* was published in 1632 at the expense of the Order of Malta, by Father Severiano of the Oratory. Another priest of the same congregation, Father Aringhi, made a Latin translation of the work under the title *Roma Subterranea Antonii Bosii* (1651). Although much inferior to the original, it enjoyed a greater success.

Toward the end of the seventh century, Msgr. Fabretti compiled a collection of pagan inscriptions in which he inserted a chapter (the eighth) on Christian inscriptions. The collection is entitled *Inscriptionum antiquarum quae in aedibus paternis asservantur explicatio* (1699).

Boldetti, called the "Keeper of the Cemeteries," wrote a book in an apologetic vein against the Protestants entitled *Osservazioni sopra i cimiteri de' santi martiri ed antichi Cristiani di Roma* (1720). It is a work of observations, but observations of little scientific worth. After Bosio, knowledge was less accurate, and the number of the martyrs was exaggerated. (In England, meanwhile, the opposite error led to the statement that the catacombs were not even Christian cemeteries.) Some Catholics, such as Mabillon (*De cultu sanctorum ignotorum*) did protest, it is true, the excessive homage given to the bones found in the catacombs. Boldetti wished to defend the sacred character of the cemeteries of which he had charge; but the main purpose of all the explorers of the catacombs was to see the relics of the martyrs.

Marangoni attempted to edit a new *Roma sotterranea,* making copies of many paintings and inscriptions. Although all his papers were destroyed in a fire in 1720, he subsequently published (1740) many important documents in his *Acta S. Victorini.*

The work of Msgr. Bottari, *Sculture e pitture sacre estratte dai cimiteri di Roma, pubblicate già dagli autori della "Roma sotterranea," ed ora nuovamente date in luce con le spiegazioni* (1734-1754), is rather a description in story form of the pictures and sculptures of Christian art than a history of the catacombs.

In no period were the catacombs despoiled more than during the eighteenth century. Under Boldetti a certain number of inscriptions were removed and placed in the churches of Rome; some of them may still be seen in St. Mary's in Transtevere and in other churches. Many of the inscriptions were also destroyed, or used as ordinary building materials, especially for pavement work. Benedict XIV, who was interested in science, began a collection of monuments taken from the catacombs and housed it in the small Christian museum in the Vatican Library, where he placed the gilded glass and the small collection of inscriptions gathered by Boldetti and Bottari. At the suggestion of Cajetan Marini, prefect of the Vatican, Pius VII founded the great collection of inscriptions in the Vatican from which Pius IX took some of the principal Christian inscriptions for the museum which he established in the Lateran.

The French archeologist d'Agincourt, in his *Histoire de l'art par les monuments* (1823), devoted much study to the catacombs, especially from the standpoint of art. In this he was followed by Raoul Rochette, whose *Tableaux des catacombes* (1837) contains, however, a topographical list of the cemeteries which is absolutely fantastic. Abbot Settele later published numerous scientific dissertations on the Christian cemeteries; but he is remembered, above all, as having given Father Marchi his start in archeology. It was Father Marchi who in turn became the teacher of the illustrious de Rossi.

John Baptist de Rossi (1822-1894) has merited, even more than Bosio, the name of being "the Christopher Columbus of subterranean Rome."[39] From his twentieth year he carried on the work in Christian antiquities which was only interrupted by his death. For the space of half a century he went from discovery to discovery, remaking the topography of subterranean Rome. He found many cemeteries which had been forgotten for centuries, and were in a state of ruin. He explained his discoveries with great erudition and wisdom; and above all, he formulated the true canons or norms of Christian archeology. The principal works published by him are, *Roma sotterranea cristiana* (1864-1877), *Inscriptiones Christianae urbis Romae VII saeculo antiquiores* (1861-1888), and *Bullettino di Archeologia cristiana* (1863-1894). These and other works attest the great sweep of his knowledge; they constitute a scientific monument of the first order as well as an inexhaustible source of information for the study of Christian archeology.[40]

And now a word on all those others who, like de Rossi, have devoted their time and energies to the study of Christian antiquities. A complete list would be too lengthy and arduous a task. Only those names which indicate the most important works for the study of Christian archeology have been appended to this volume. The author feels constrained, however, to mention his companions in study, Armellini and Stevenson, both indefatigable workers, archeologists of distinction, and too soon snatched by death from the pursuit of this important science. It is to be hoped that they will have many imitators: the catacombs will furnish material for further studies for centuries to come.

# Part Two

## A BRIEF SYNOPSIS OF THE
## HISTORY OF THE PERSECUTIONS

### Chapter I

### THE BEGINNINGS OF CHRISTIANITY IN ROME

THE CHRISTIANS, confused at first with the Jews, availed themselves of the liberty which the latter enjoyed in the exercise of their religion. They lived, as Tertullian remarks, in the shadow of the synagogue: "quasi sub umbraculo insignissimae religionis certe licitae."[1]

The first relations of the Romans and Jews had begun at the time of the Maccabees.[2] In 64 B. C., Pompey reduced the kingdom of the Seleucids in Syria to a province, and nominated Hircanus king of Judea in place of Aristobulus, whom he took back as a captive to Rome.

So many other Jews followed in 63 and 62 B. C. that they soon formed a veritable Jewish community in Rome. Shortly afterward, Anthony permitted Herod to take over the government of Jerusalem. Meanwhile, Jewish immigration continued with such force that Cicero could say that there was a "multitude of Jews"[3] in Rome. Caesar favored them; Suetonius[4] records that they mourned Caesar's death, accompanied his body to the Forum where it was cremated, and remained several nights near his ashes out of respect to his memory. They were unmolested under Augustus, but were expelled by Tiberius, who issued an edict prohibiting oriental cults: "Externas caerimonias, Aegyptios Iudaicosque ritus compescuit."[5] After the death of Tiberius, however, and especially when Philo visited Caligula, the Jews returned to Rome. Claudius expelled them anew. "Iudaeos, impulsore Chresto assidue tumultuantes, urbe expulit," writes Suetonius.[6]

This is one of the first allusions to the Christians. The "Chrestus" mentioned by Suetonius is not, as Duruy[7] pretends, a certain Greek converted to Judaism, who had created a disturbance in the community: "Chrestus" is a corruption of the word "Christus," a corruption which is met again in certain inscriptions where one reads "Chrestiani" instead of "Christiani." The name of Christian was already known; a pagan hand wrote in derision on the walls of Pompeii: "Audi Chrestianos saevos olores."[8]

After the fall of Jerusalem many Jews followed the victors to Rome, to swell the number of the Jewish colony already established there. Toward the end of the first century, they had a synagogue for religious purposes, presided over by an *Archisynagogus,* and a Synedrium for civil matters. Their habitations were found in three sections of the city. The oldest settlement was in the Transtevere near the Portuan gate; another was close to the Capena gate, between the Caelian hill and the Aventine; and the third was in the vicinity of the ancient Subura. These three quarters also had three distinct cemeteries. Bosio[9] has briefly described the one in Transtevere, which was discovered by him, and rediscovered in 1904; it was located on the first mile of the Portuan Way, under a hill now known as Monte Verde. The quarter situated at the Capena gate had its cemetery on the Appian Way, discovered in 1857 in the Randanini vineyard, opposite St. Sebastian's. Numerous inscriptions in Greek and Latin, and even some paintings, were found in it. The third cemetery, connected with the *Synagoga Siburensium,* was located on the Labican Way, near the Porta Maggiore;[10] and even a fourth was rediscovered in 1920 on the Nomentan Way in the Torlonia vineyard.[11]

These cemeteries show a great many points in common with the ancient Christian cemeteries, for they both had their origin in usages typical of the Orient. The Christian religion began to assert itself in the midst of these Jewish communities. The first preachers of Christianity were probably some soldiers of the *cohors Italica civium Romanorum voluntariorum*. This band, made up of Romans who wished to follow a military career, was stationed at Caesarea, the residence of the governor of Palestine. The centurion Cornelius, of whom the Acts of the Apostles speak,[12] belonged to this *cohors Italica*. Probably many soldiers imitated their leader and, after their conversion to Christianity, returned to Rome to spread the good news.

It was not long after this that the Apostle Peter himself first came to Rome, the capital of the Empire.[13] This was probably during the reign of the Emperor Claudius, between the years 41-44.[14] It is likely that this first sojourn of the apostle in Rome was prolonged until the time of the publication of the imperial edict against the Jews (49 A.D.). In the year 50, Peter presided over the Apostolic Assembly in Jerusalem, and did not return to Rome until about the year 63 or 64; he was certainly not in Rome in 61, during the period of St. Paul's voyage.

These particular dates are not absolutely incontestable; but the principal fact, of St. Peter's coming to Rome, is historical, and capable of the most rigorous and scientific proof. Numerous critics, especially Protestants, have tried to deny it; but it cannot be doubted without throwing into doubt the more readily proved facts of Roman history. The most ancient testimony which confirms this fact is the epistle of St. Clement to the Corinthians. This letter, recorded by Eusebius,[15] had been lost; but Patricio Giunio discovered an incomplete text of it in a manuscript of the fifth century, the *Codex Alexandrinus* of London, and published it in 1643. In 1875, the Greek Orthodox Bishop, Bryennios, found it again in its entirety in a manuscript of the eleventh century which likewise contained the Διδαχὴ τῶν δώδεκα ἀποστόλων.[16] This letter was written in 96 or 97. In it St. Clement records the death of the Apostles Peter and Paul, numbering them among the many elect who had given a wonderful example of courage "in our midst."[17] The death of St. Paul in Rome is an undeniable fact; hence this passage, if it does not give a direct affirmative proof of St. Peter's stay in Rome, it is at least an important reference.

We find a similar allusion in the epistle of St. Ignatius of Antioch, who, writing to the Romans, implored them not to intercede for him with the emperor, adding: "I beseech you, I do not command you as did Peter and Paul; they were apostles, I am nothing but a slave."[18]

From the beginning of the second century, the testimonies became more explicit. The first is that of Irenaeus, disciple of St. Polycarp: "Matthaeus apud Hebraeos propria eorum lingua conscriptum Evangelium edidit, dum Petrus ac Paulus Romae Christum praedicarent et Ecclesiae fundamenta iacerent."[19]

At the beginning of the third century, the priest Caius mentions the tombs of the two apostles in writing against the Montanists: "Ego vero apostolorum tropaea possum ostendere, nam sive in Vaticanum sive ad Ostiensem viam pergere licet, occurrunt tibi tropaea eorum qui Ecclesiam illam fundaverunt."[20] One could cite Dionysius of Corinth,[21] Tertullian,[22] Origen,[23] St. Optatus of Mileve,[24] St. Jerome,[25] Prudentius[26] and many others. On the other hand, no church has ever claimed the tomb of St. Peter, a tomb which could not but be an object of great veneration.

Of what avail is the negative argument of the silence of the Acts and the Epistles, advanced by many Protestants, against all this positive evidence? This silence may be explained from another angle. The Acts could not mention the presence of St. Peter at that period, because he had left Rome in 49 and was absent from it until 61. St. Luke would have had occasion to speak of him had he continued his book. Similarly, when St. Paul wrote his Epistle to the Romans, in 58, he did not salute St. Peter because St. Peter was not in Rome.

But St. Peter himself bears witness to his own presence in Rome. His first Epistle is dated from "Babylon"; and by Babylon the Christians, at that time, most certainly understood Rome.

The tradition of St. Peter's coming to Rome has been preserved down to our day by several monuments which are in part authentic and in part legendary. Thus, the tomb of the apostle in the Vatican is the most authentic monument. St. Jerome writes of it in the fourth century: "Totius orbis veneratione celebratur."[27]

The tradition that St. Peter joined the Christians in the home of Pudens on the Viminal is also very ancient. The legendary story upon which its title rests is based upon historical fact.[28]   The name of the church of Pudentiana or St. Pudentiana is very old, and many discoveries have proved that there was really some connection between this title and the home of Aquila and Prisca, two converted Jews, who were expelled from Rome with St. Peter in 49, but who returned under Nero.[29]  They lived on the Aventine. In 1776, there was unearthed near St. Prisca's a bronze tablet sent in 222 by a city in Spain to a certain Caius Marius Pudens Cornelianus, a personage of senatorial rank, selected by the above-mentioned city as its patron.[30]  There was therefore some connection between the *Gens Cornelia,* the family of Pudens, and that of Aquila and Prisca.  Hence there is nothing surprising in the remark that they had a common cemetery, namely that of Priscilla on the Salarian Way, "the center to which, like lines leading from different points, converge the memories of the title of Pudens and that of Prisca."[31]

Near the Salarian Way, in the Ostrian cemetery, there was another venerable memento of St. Peter, that is, the "sedes ubi prius sedit S. Petrus"; in fact the cemetery was known as the "Coemeterium fontis S. Petri," "Coemeterium ubi Petrus baptizaverat."[32]

Another testimony in favor of St. Peter's presence in Rome may be found in the numerous objects — paintings, sculptures, stained glass and sarcophagi — with his image engraved on them, often accompanied by the very name: "Petrus." The fact is worthy of note that the representations of St. Peter's imprisonment are often found on the sarcophagi. The Acts speak of him when they say, "Abiit in alium locum,"[33] referring to the period following his liberation. May not this "other place" have been Rome?

Along with these mementoes of undoubted authenticity there are others which are not clear, or are only partially clear.

The tradition of the Mamertine prison has not one positive argument against it, although it appears for the first time in the

Acts of Processus and Martinianus, which do not go back earlier than the sixth century. Thus something which may contain a shred of historical fact was amplified in the Middle Ages by the addition of legendary details.

An opinion which is absolutely without foundation places the martyrdom of St. Peter on the Janiculum. This idea arose only in the Middle Ages. The true Roman tradition is in favor of the Vatican. The *Acta Petri,* which are ancient although not original, tell us that the apostle was crucified near the obelisk of Nero, which is on the Vatican.[34]

The story of the separation of the two apostles on the Ostian Way is entirely legendary. The account relative to the "Domine, quo vadis?", even though it is very old, is legendary in its particulars.[35]

St. Paul's Epistle to the Romans was written in the year 58. He came to Rome shortly afterward, perhaps in September or October of 61. Accused by the Jews before the governor Festus, he had appealed to Caesar[36] and embarked for the capital. St. Luke, his disciple, gives us a detailed and very exact account of his voyage.[37] After suffering shipwreck, he landed at Puteoli, from which he immediately set forth toward the capital, undoubtedly following the Appian Way. The Acts record two stops along this road: the *Forum Appii* and the *Tres Tabernae.* Excavations carried out under Pius VI have enabled archeologists to locate the position of the *Forum Appii* between Velletri and Terracina. Nibby has been able to determine the geographical position of the *Tres Tabernae,* a station which subsequently became a place of importance and in the fifth century an episcopal see.

The apostle finally entered the city by way of the Capena gate. According to the Acts he remained there for two years in a private home which served as his prison, though he was allowed a certain amount of freedom. St. Luke does not give us any more precise information on this point. It has been supposed that St. Mary's *in via Lata* was erected in commemoration of this sojourn of St. Paul's but no document of antiquity confirms this opinion. The ruins visible beneath the church are probably those of the walls of the Comitium (*Septa Julia*). In the midst of these ruins there was built a church adorned with paintings of the seventh and eighth centuries. A large part of this structure has lately been brought to light, and the excavations have demonstrated that the origin of the veneration of St. Paul in that place arose from a fourth-century painting of him. It is probable that the apostle actually had lived in the region of *Alta Semita,* close to the *Castra Praetoria,* and for that reason he could say that he had preached Christ "in omni praetorio."[33]

The preaching of the two apostles made many proselytes among the various classes of the Roman populace, especially among its three principal elements: Jews, Greeks and Romans. The names of the different persons to whom St. Paul sends his greetings indicate these diverse racial origins. The greater number manifest a humble origin: slaves, freedmen who are greeted with the words, "Qui sunt de Aristobuli domo; de Narcissi domo."[39] Ampliatus, whose name may be seen inscribed on a cubicle in the cemetery of Domitilla adorned with very ancient pictures, was none other than a slave; Roman citizens were never addressed by one name. For what reason should a slave have been buried in a chapel of such splendor? De Rossi supposes that he was on intimate terms with St. Paul, that to him was directed the greeting in the Epistle to the Romans, "Salutate Ampliatum dilectissimum mihi in Domino,"[40] and that out of respect for the apostle, his beloved disciple was thus greatly honored.

In the cemetery of Domitilla there was discovered another inscription which may refer to Narcissus, also mentioned in the Epistle of St. Paul.[41]

We find occasionally great personages among the converts. Tacitus speaks of a noble matron, Pomponia Graecina, who observed in the midst of her family a perpetual sorrow, "non cultu nisi lugubri, non animo nisi mesto."[42] It has been deduced that she was a convert to Christianity and the hypothesis has been confirmed by excavations carried on in the cemetery of Callistus. In the crypt of Lucina, near the tomb of St. Cornelius, there was discovered in fact the epitaph of "Pomponios Grekeinos";

it belongs to the middle of the second century and probably commemorates a nephew of Pomponia Graecina who was also a convert to Christianity. De Rossi imagined that Pomponia Graecina might have been the owner of the cemetery and the name "Lucina" was the symbolic one (*lux* — *light*) which she had received in baptism. Moreover, several inscriptions of the cemetery bear the name of Pomponius, and the Pomponii must have been the relatives of the Cecilii. Thus the Christian community of the first century numbered all classes. We know that St. Paul praised the Christians of Rome for their faith.[43]

The Christian community of Rome lived in peace to the end of the year 64. St. Paul, freed from his chains, "liberatus de ore leonis,"[44] made numerous journeys. His voyage to Spain might be ascribed to this year; if it did not occur then, it certainly took place in the year 63. He had had this journey in mind and most probably he acted upon it at this time.[45] St. Peter returned to Rome about this same time. The period of the persecutions was about to begin.

## Chapter II

## THE FIRST PERSECUTIONS

### 1. The Persecution of Nero

THE ILLUSTRIOUS historian Allard has exposed much better than anyone else the true character of the persecutions against the Christians, and has entered into their juridical basis. In so doing he has not only refuted the exaggerations which speak of eleven million martyrs, but also those at the opposite extreme which, following the false theories of Dodwell, reduce the extraordinary number of heroes of the Christian faith to a few. His classical work, the *Histoires des persécutions,* is invaluable as a reference book.

During the month of July of 64, a frightful conflagration, which began at the Circus Maximus (XI region of Augustus), destroyed the entire quarter lying between the Palatine and the

Aventine.[1] Nero, if he had not actually ordered it himself, certainly enjoyed the spectacle. It fell in with his plans for rebuilding the city, which still had many irregular features, rather resembling, so Titus Livius says, a soldiers' barracks than a capital: "Formaque urbis sit occupatae magis quam divisae similis."[2] Nero had already prepared a new plan, from which Septimius Severus later drew his inspiration for rebuilding the city. The populace knew the intentions of the emperor, and immediately accused him of the disaster. Nero became frightened and in turn blamed the Jews, whose quarters, although very close to the Circus Maximus, remained untouched; the Jews claimed that the Christians were responsible, and thus the calumny arose.

At first there were only a few isolated arrests made; later on a veritable crowd was imprisoned.[3] The accusations against them alleged that they were "incendiaries and enemies of the human race." These were repeated and eventually gave rise to those horrible holidays of which the Vatican gardens were the theatre. Thus we see the Christians, exposed to the jeers of the populace, dressed as mythological characters, covered with the skins of wild animals and chased by dogs like beasts of the wild; then, loaded down with weights, they were crucified, or burned in the manner of torches.

Many authors allude to this terrible persecution; St. Clement (who was perhaps an eyewitness) speaks of "the wonderful example given by a large band of the elect, of those noble women . . . of those Danaids, of those Dirci!"[4] It appears that even St. Peter, who had returned to Rome, saw these horrible scenes; so much may be deduced from the words he uses in urging the faithful of Asia Minor to have patience in their sufferings. This epistle was written in Rome under the name of Babylon.[5] The same word, πύρωσις or "incendium," which he employs, serves, as Allard notes, as "un reflet des torches vivantes du Vatican."[6] There is no doubt that Seneca, the teacher of Nero, had these first heroes of Christianity in mind when he praises these men who died with joy, with serenity, amid such sufferings and torment.[7]

A recent writer, Pascal,[8] has put forth the strange opinion that the Christians were the authors of the burning of Rome and that this crime was the cause of the persecutions. Such a statement is not even worth the time it takes to contradict it, for it runs counter to all history. It suffices to repeat the words of the renowned Allard in reference to such a proposition: "Ignorée des quatre premiers siècles, l'idée de la culpabilité des chrétiens n'est née que de nos jours. Tant qu' on n'aura pas produit un témoignage antique qui lui donne quelque consistance, le devoir de l'historien sera de n'en pas tenir compte."[9] Profumo has published a weighty volume demonstrating that the Christians were innocent and that the true author of the conflagration was Nero. He has also sought to prove that there were proceedings instituted to prove the guilt of the incendiary, but that Christians were accused in virtue of the *Institutum Neronianum*.[10]

No matter how much or from what angle we view the fact, it is well known that the persecution extended throughout the length and breadth of the Empire.[11] The burning of Rome was but a pretext, for the Christians were to be considered as enemies of the human race — "odio humani generis convicti"; and it was thought sufficient to impute this to them in order to persecute and condemn them to death.

We do not know the names of the first to shed their blood for the faith, but we do know the two most illustrious victims of the persecution of Nero, St. Peter and St. Paul. Some idea of the large number of martyrs during the persecution of Nero (and mentioned by Tacitus) may be gained by referring to the enormous group of anonymous martyrs commemorated in the case of Rome, in the martyrology of St. Jerome, on June 29. The date of the martyrdom of the two apostles may be placed, in the opinion of many, in the year 67. This opinion is based first upon St. Jerome's assertion that Seneca's death took place two years before theirs,[12] and our knowledge that Seneca died in 65 A.D.; and secondly, upon the passage in the epistle of Clement stating that St. Paul suffered martyrdom "under the prefects" — ἐπὶ τῶν ἡγουμένων. We know positively that, in

67, Nero journeyed to Greece, first making the prefects of the Praetorian Guard rulers of Rome. The Philocalian Calendar gives us, it is true, the year 57 "consulatu Vinicii et Longini"; but this date was arrived at by making the pontificate of St. Peter last 25 years, beginning with the year of the death of our Saviour — a number that is merely traditional: it was reported for the first time by Eusebius, and in fact is not trustworthy.[13] An ancient tradition places the death of St. Peter and St. Paul on the same day; another, recorded by Prudentius, indicates a year between them. The first opinion is the one generally accepted; it is certain that from the beginning of the fourth century their common feast has been celebrated on June 29, especially in Rome.[14]

It is, however, very probable that the Apostle Paul was killed before Peter, and that Peter was crucified on the Vatican either at the same time as the protomartyrs under Nero or shortly afterward.

St. Paul was buried on the Ostian Way, St. Peter on the Vatican, near the spot where he suffered crucifixion; that is, near the Circus of Nero. Later the bodies of his successors for more than a century, from St. Linus to St. Victor (202), were laid to rest at the tomb of the first pope, "Juxta sepulcrum beati Petri."[15] After St. Victor, that is, about the beginning of the third century, the Roman Church secured a new cemetery, that of Callistus on the Appian Way, which then became the papal cemetery.

Thus much is certain: that the ancient tombs of the apostles were respectively on the Vatican and on the Ostian Way. Later on, as we shall indicate, their remains were placed temporarily on the Appian Way.

In the rebuilding of the foundations of the baldachin of the modern Vatican basilica, in the seventeenth century, pagan tombs were found which prove that this area was a cemetery near the gardens of Nero, but separated from them by the Cornelian Way. It was in this area that the Apostle Peter was buried.

The tomb of St. Peter remained visible, beyond doubt, until the ninth century. From that period it became necessary to hide the monument because of the invasion of the Saracens, and there is no further mention of it. Clement VIII saw it when the modern altar was built, and he believed that he was able to recognize the cross of gold placed on the sarcophagus by Constantine; but instead of bringing it to light, he had it walled in anew.[16]

The tomb of St. Paul was also open to view until the ninth century. The fire of 1823 did not damage it; the covering of the sarcophagus and the inscription of Constantine can still be seen under the high altar. Gregory XVI was inclined to open the sarcophagus, but was dissuaded from doing so by the example of Clement VIII.

To return to the persecution of Nero. It must be remembered that the mood of the populace soon was turned from the cruelties of the year 64 or 65, and hence these were not prolonged. The Christians were thereafter condemned to hard labor, and forced to work on the various public projects made necessary by the rebuilding and transformation of the city.

The immense public works begun under Nero were suspended after his death. His successors, more modest, were content to live on the Palatine. The persecution came to an end in 69, and for more than twenty years thereafter — that is, under Galba, Otho, Vitellius, Vespasian and Titus — the Christians lived in peace throughout the Empire.

With the onset of the first persecution, however, the Christian religion was legally separated from the Jewish synagogue, and therefore was looked upon as illicit. The Christians thus fell under the general provision of the Roman laws which prohibited the practice of strange religions not authorized or approved by a special decree. It is also probable that under Nero there was issued an edict against the Christians, though there is no actual proof of this.

## 2.  The Persecution of Domitian

Under Vespasian and Titus, the Church enjoyed an almost unbroken period of tranquillity.[17] Domitian (81-96) renewed what Tertullian calls the *institutum Neronianum*,[18] that is, the taking of rigorous measures against the Christians. Aubé and certain other modern writers deny that this persecution was ever inaugurated, but the fact is absolutely certain. St. John refers to it clearly in his Apocalypse which, according to most critics, was written toward the end of the reign of Domitian: "Vidi subtus altare animas interfectorum."[19] The existence of this persecution also naturally explains that passage in the epistle of St. Clement to the Corinthians wherein the pope says that he was unable to reply to the Church of Corinth because of the disasters which befell the Roman Church. It was during a momentary respite that he took advantage of the peace to address his letter to the Corinthians.[20] Finally, when Trajan, at a later date, told Pliny that he was no longer to condemn the Christians on anonymous accusations, he showed implicitly that such allegations had been employed previously. St. Clement refers to the time of Domitian when he speaks of some Christians who had become apostates about twenty years before.[21]

Over and above this, we have the explicit and formal testimony of both Christian and pagan authors: Eusebius;[22] Tertullian,[23] who recounts the martyrdom of St. John in Rome by immersion in boiling oil; Suetonius,[24] and Dion Cassius,[25] who record that a large number of distinguished persons were accused of practising strange rites, Jewish customs and atheism, and for that reason were condemned. One of the most illustrious of these martyrs was Flavius Clemens, son of Flavius Sabinus and cousin of the emperor. Flavius Sabinus, according to Tacitus a mild, pious individual with a horror of blood,[26] was probably converted, with his whole family, during the period of the first persecution. His son, Flavius Clemens, was arrested as a simple suspect during the year of his consulate (95), and later killed. His wife, Flavia Domitilla, was exiled to the island of Pontia.[27] In the cemetery of Domitilla on the

# GENEALOGY OF THE FLAVII

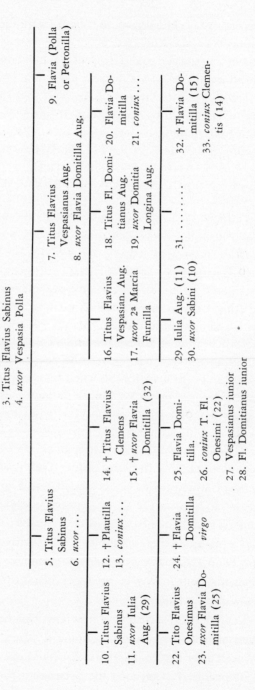

1. Titus Flavius Petronius
2. *uxor* Tertulla

3. Titus Flavius Sabinus
4. *uxor* Vespasia Polla

5. Titus Flavius Sabinus
6. *uxor* ...

7. Titus Flavius Vespasianus Aug.
8. *uxor* Flavia Domitilla Aug.

9. Flavia (Polla or Petronilla)

10. Titus Flavius Sabinus
11. *uxor* Iulia Aug. (29)

12. † Plautilla
13. *coniux* ...

14. † Titus Flavius Clemens
15. † *uxor* Flavia Domitilla (32)

16. Titus Flavius Vespasian. Aug.
17. *uxor* 2ª Marcia Furnilla

18. Titus Fl. Domitianus Aug.
19. *uxor* Domitia Longina Aug.

20. Flavia Domitilla
21. *coniux* ...

22. Tito Flavius Onesimus
23. *uxor* Flavia Domitilla (25)

24. † Flavia Domitilla *virgo*

25. Flavia Domitilla.
26. *coniux* T. Fl. Onesimi (22)
27. Vespasianus iunior
28. Fl. Domitianus iunior

29. Iulia Aug. (11)
30. *uxor* Sabini (10)

31. .........

32. † Flavia Domitilla (15)
33. *coniux* Clementis (14)

N. B. Crosses indicate Christians. Numbers in parentheses show names repeated elsewhere in the genealogical tree.

Ardeatine Way, belonging to this family, there were found monuments of the Christian Flavii, and among other things, a fragment bearing a pagan formula: "Ex indulgentia Flaviae Domitillae."

There were also found inscriptions with the name of the Flavii, which de Rossi has published; near the basilica of Sts. Nereus and Achilleus is the tomb of St. Petronilla where the following inscription of one Flavius Sabinus was found:

ΦΛ · ΣΑΒΕΙΝΟΣ ΚΑΙ ΤΙΤΙΑΝΗ ΑΔΕΛΦΟΙ

Perhaps the bonds of family relationship united him to Flavia Petronilla, the so-called daughter of St. Peter, who was really a member of the *gens Aurelia,* and for that reason was laid to rest in their cemetery.[28]

Among the persons who confessed the faith under Domitian, Dion Cassius names Acilius Glabrio, who was consul in 91 at the same time as Trajan. Acilius Glabrio was condemned to fight a bear or a lion in the amphitheatre; he emerged victorius from this combat, only to be beheaded by order of the emperor. The motive for his execution had already been inferred, but there could no longer be any doubt about it after the discovery of a vast subterranean vault in the cemetery of Priscilla, containing numerous inscriptions in Latin and Greek which speak of the "Acilii Glabriones." One of these lines points unmistakably to Christianity. This vault, at first an independent structure, was later joined to the great cemetery on the Salarian Way in the fourth century, and even became a sort of confessional of the basilica of St. Sylvester, an indication that it was a place of venerated tombs.[29] The Acilius Glabrio spoken of by Dion Cassius was possibly the founder of the cemetery of Priscilla, and it may be an index demonstrating the family relationship of Pudens himself.[30]

Domitian caused those Christians who had been arrested in Jerusalem to be brought to Rome for questioning. He was convinced after this that Christianity could not harm his power, and immediately suspended the persecution.[13]

Shortly afterward Domitian was mortally wounded by a freedman called Stephen. Aubé has gone so far as to accuse the Christians of having been responsible for this assassination, out of revenge.[32] The accusation is entirely gratuitous. Suetonius[33] gives the names of the culpable persons, even telling us the sentiment which animated them: recounting how Stephen and the Empress Domitia herself, having read their own names on the list of the proscribed drawn up by the emperor, committed the crime to save themselves.

## Chapter III

## THE PERSECUTIONS OF THE SECOND CENTURY

### 1. The Persecution of Trajan

FROM a ruler such as Trajan one would have expected a greater show of justice toward the Christians than that displayed by Nero or Domitian. As a matter of fact, he did not molest them during the early period of his reign; but when Pliny the Younger, while governor of Bithynia, asked him (111 A.D.) how he was to act toward the Christians, who were very numerous in that province, Trajan answered by writing this singular rescript:

"Conquirendi non sunt; si deferantur et arguantur, puniendi sunt; ita tamen ut qui negaverit se Christianum esse idque re ipsa manifestum fecerit, id est, supplicando diis nostris, quamvis suspectus in praeteritum fuerit, veniam ex poenitentia impetret. Sine auctore vero propositi libelli, nullo crimine locum habere debent: nam et pessimi exempli, nec nostri saeculi est."[1]

This rescript is the first official example we possess of the proscription of Christianity, and it presupposes a special law or the application of a general law. Some think, as has been said, that Nero had already prohibited the existence of the Christians as a community, by promulgating for the first time that principle which was to be frequently invoked during the time of Tertullian: "Non licet esse vos."[2] However this may have been, the letter of Trajan constituted the ordinary and official method of judging the Christians until its final abrogation by the Edict of Milan, in 313. The persecutions, thus legalized, became regular happenings, and depended largely on the dispositions of the governors of the provinces. Thus it is that we see the fearful persecutions in France, in Spain and in Africa, while in Rome the Christians were being left in peace. Again, there were occasions when the Christians in Rome were persecuted and the faithful of the provinces remained unmolested. This terrible authority was possessed from the time of Trajan by the *Curatores civitatis*, who represented the emperor in every city and soon took the place of the municipal authority.

The martyrdom of St. Clement and St. Ignatius of Antioch is ascribed to the persecution of Trajan. The Acts of the martyrdom of St. Clement recount that he was condemned "ad metalla,"[3] taken to the Crimea, killed, thrown into the Black Sea with an anchor about his neck, and later buried on a small island close by. It is certain that there was an early Christian community in the Chersonese. Even though the *Passio* of St. Clement may be legendary, the existence and antiquity of such a community has been confirmed by the discovery of tombs, Christian inscriptions and also a basilica. And finally it is proper to state that on ancient coins of the kings of the Bosphorus, a century before the time of Constantine, we find engraved a representation of the cross.

At any rate we know that the tomb of St. Clement was not originally in Rome; the *Book of the Popes* tells us expressly that he was buried "in Graecias." His body was taken to Rome in the ninth century by St. Cyril and St. Methodius and deposited in a church where there had already been evidence of devotion to the saint, probably because it had been built in a place frequented by him.

In fact, under the ancient basilica of St. Clement, very close to a temple of Mithras, there was found a house of the first century which may be called the sanctuary of that particular locality. The transference of the body of St. Clement by

Sts. Cyril and Methodius is attested by a painting which may still be seen in the subterranean basilica.

St. Ignatius was taken from Antioch to Rome to be exposed to the wild animals in the Flavian amphitheatre. A portion of his epistle to the Romans indicates his sentiments on the eve of his martyrdom:

"Obsecro vos, ne intempestivam mihi benevolentiam exhibeatis. Sinite me ferarum cibum esse, per quas Deum consequi licet. Frumentum sum Dei, et per ferarum dentes molar, ut purus panis Christi inveniar. Feris potius blandimini, ut mihi sepulcrum fiant, nihilque mei corporis relinquant; ne, postquam obdormiero, gravis alicui fiam. Tunc vere Christi discipulus ero, cum neque corpus meum mundus videbit. Christum pro me supplicate, ut per haec instrumenta hostia inveniar."[4]

The Christians hid his body for some time, later taking it to Antioch and burying it in a local cemetery, "extra portam Daphniticam," where it remained in veneration by the faithful.

It is difficult to determine which persecutions were general after that of Trajan. One might really regard as general that of Hadrian (120-124), Marcus Aurelius (164-176), Septimius Severus (202-211), Maximian (235-237), Decius (249-251), Valerian (257-260), Claudius and Aurelian (269-275) and Diocletian (286-305). There were Christians put to death under other emperors but in such cases one treats of isolated martyrs.

## 2.  The Persecution of Hadrian

Hadrian (117-138) was an excellent administrator. For fourteen years he went from province to province throughout the Empire making many improvements, instituting reforms and building monuments. Yet although he was personally a tolerant ruler, the persecution continued unabated during his reign. Unfortunately we possess only legendary documents of this period.

Hadrian often had opportunities to deal with Christians in his correspondence with the governors of the provinces.[5] The most important of these documents is the letter written to L. Minucius Fundanus, the proconsul of Asia in 124 or 125. Its authenticity has been doubted, but without reason; St. Justin himself, who was a contemporary, speaks of it.[6] In this letter, the emperor tells the governor that it is permissible to persecute the Christians only when they have been accused of serious infractions of the law of the land, and that no attention should be given to the constant vulgar calumnies lodged against them. Quadratus, Aristides,[7] and later St. Justin, who were the first apologetes, took advantage of this letter, and others like it sent to the various governors, by beginning to speak in defense of Christianity against the brutal accusations of the pagans.[8]

### 3. The Persecution of Marcus Aurelius

Under Antoninus Pius, successor of Hadrian, there was no general persecution, though there continued to be occasional isolated martyrs, among whom was numbered St. Polycarp of Smyrna. The letter of the Church of Smyrna, which bears witness to a persecution of a local nature and to the death of its bishop, is an authentic document written in the same year as the martyrdom (155). There is mention in it of the anniversary which was to be celebrated, and of the veneration which already surrounded the tomb of the martyr.[9] During the same epoch, that is, toward the middle of the second century, appeared the *Apologies* of St. Justin.[10] There were two of these: one which he himself personally presented to Antoninus Pius and his sons Marcus Aurelius and Lucius Verus; the other addressed to Marcus Aurelius ten years later.[11]

With the reign of Marcus Aurelius there began a period of intense reform within the Empire, especially in religious matters. Syncretism became manifest everywhere: the various Oriental religions — of Egypt, of Persia, in a word, all the strange and exotic cults — spread throughout the Empire. Christianity profited by this spirit of tolerance and began to develop and expand as it had never done before. Everywhere there was evidence of the good influence of Christianity; and Christian principles began to make themselves felt in their opposition to certain general and long-established pagan customs. For example, the Christian custom of burying the dead developed, as against the pagan usage of cremation. Little by little cremation of bodies gave way to the Christian method of interment; niches for holding the urns containing the ashes of the dead soon disappeared, and in their stead appeared sarcophagi. Even Christian attitudes and thoughts began to exercise a certain influence over the enemies of the Christian faith, and the emperor seems to have come under its power as his writings show.

Marcus Aurelius, the philosopher, honest, pious, upright, should have favored the Christians; instead, his philosophical prejudices, superstitions and beliefs, and the public misfortunes (such as wars, pestilences and floods) which sorely afflicted the Empire, turned him into one of their cruelest persecutors.

The most terrible war of this period was that waged by Rome against the Marcomanni. When the emperor returned victorious to Rome, the Senate dedicated to him a magnificent column which still excites the admiration of all who behold it. (Centuries later, it was called the "Column of Antonine." However, an ancient inscription, which may still be seen in the Vatican, designates it as the "Column of Marcus"; the inscription of Sixtus V contains a historical error in attributing it to Antoninus Pius.) On the bas-relief of this column are represented the principal episodes of the expedition against the Marcomanni, including the one concerning the *Legio Fulminatrix,* the Thundering Legion, the most renowned of all the military divisions. The Roman army was hard pressed through lack of water; the Christian soldiers of the *Legio XII militenensis* began to pray, and a heavy shower answered their supplications. Dion Cassius reports the fact but ascribes it to an Egyptian magician or wizard. Baronius and Father Rocca relate the occurrence as a miracle and give it as their opinion that the bas-relief representing the soldiers in the act of catching the water in their shields is a symbolical figure of rain. Others, however, have denied this relation and see in this account rather a religious legend created by a false interpretation of the bas-relief. But the fact is independent of the monument. Appollinaris of Hieropolis,[12] Tertullian[13] and Dion Cassius speak of it; Marcus Aurelius himself, in a letter to the Senate, mentions this rainfall, and announces the success of the Roman army.[14] The Twelfth Legion did not receive its appellation of "Thundering Legion" from this happening, because it is known to have had that designation beforehand. Perhaps the emperor mentioned the fact to show that the legion had by this circumstance received honorable confirmation of its right to the title.

The persecution of Marcus Aurelius was long and cruel. In its first phase, toward the year 164, is recorded the martyrdom of St. Felicitas and her seven sons. The Acts which recount the fact form part of the collection of Ruinart; de Rossi[15] and Doulcet consider them authentic, Tillemont judges them to be very ancient, and other authors, as Fuehrer,[16] believe that they are only of the sixth century. But whatever may be the value of these Acts, the particulars of the *Passio* of St. Felicitas have always been incontestably established by the weighty authority of inscriptions, both liturgical and archeological. These Acts speak of two emperors, of whom only one was present, and of the prefect Publius. Publius Salvius Julianus was prefect of Rome in the year 162, and precisely at that time Marcus Aurelius resided in Rome, while his colleague was in the Orient.

The seven brothers were martyred before the eyes of their mother, and on this point St. Peter Chrysologus writes a very moving and magnificent discourse: "Discurrebat laetior inter confossa cadavera quam inter cunabula cara filiorum, quia internis oculis tot cernebat bravia quot vulnera, quot tormenta tot praemia, quot victimas tot coronas."[17] They were later buried in groups which the Philocalian Calendar gives thus: Felix and Philip in the cemetery of Priscilla; Martial, Vitalis and Alexander "in coemeterio Jordanorum," on the same Salarian Way; St. Januarius, the eldest son, together with their mother, in the cemetery of Maximus on the Salarian Way.

De Rossi assigned the martyrdom of St. Cecilia to the reign of Marcus Aurelius; but it is more probable that it occurred later. The opinions of the critics vary considerably on this point.[18]

The Scillitan martyrs[19] in Africa belong either to the end of the reign of Marcus Aurelius or the beginning of the reign of Commodus (180), as the latter continued the persecution which, especially in Africa, raged most fiercely and cruelly. In Rome there was another martyr: the Senator Appollonius, who had read an apology on Christianity on the floor of the Senate. He was surely interred near the city; but his tomb is unknown, as is the text of his apology.

After having persecuted the Christians for a time, Commodus began to treat them favorably. The *Philosophumena*[20] tells us that the Empress Marcia, his consort, was either a Christian or under instructions prior to becoming one, and to her good offices we must ascribe this change in Commodus.

It seems strange that the good emperors, such as Trajan, Hadrian and Marcus Aurelius, should have persecuted the Christians relentlessly, while those like Commodus, Heliogabalus and Gallienus, who were really cruel at heart, were their defenders. But this anomaly may be explained. We must remember that the former, entirely occupied with the preservation of Roman power, sought to protect and preserve it jealously from innovations, which in their opinion would harm or weaken it; while the latter, slaves to their passions, cared little for the Empire and less about religious questions of any sort.

The Christians had twenty years of peace, and during these years the new religion again filled the confines of the Empire and penetrated everywhere. Tertullian did not fear to say in his *Apologia*[21] that the Christians had left to the pagans almost nothing but their idols and their temples, and that if the Christians were to have retired from the society of their fellow-men, the pagans would have found themselves practically in solitude. In fact, during the third century greater deference was shown the Christians than ever before. They were in possession of their churches and their cemeteries, not only by private title but as a society; and it may be, as de Rossi supposes, that they availed themselves of the institution of the *Collegia funeraticia,* or that they enjoyed a tolerance equivalent to a legal authorization. It is certain that, under Gallienus, then under Maxentius, and finally after the Edict of Milan, it was to the churches and not to individuals that the confiscated cemeteries were restored.

## Chapter IV

## THE PERSECUTIONS OF THE THIRD CENTURY

### 1. The Persecution of Septimius Severus

MANY persons took advantage of the liberty enjoyed by the Christians under Commodus to visit the various churches, especially at Rome, either to be strengthened in the faith or to confirm the faith of the brethren.[1] To cite the best known of those who came to Rome, we may mention Florinus, Blastus, St. Irenaeus, disciple of St. Polycarp, and Abercius, Bishop of Hieropolis in Phrygia.

The imperial power continued favorably disposed toward the Christians until the beginning of the reign of Septimius Severus, who governed the Empire from 198 to 211. Tertullian writes of him in this strain: "Clarissimas feminas et clarissimos viros Severus sciens huius sectae esse, non modo non laesit, verum et testimonio exornavit, et populo furenti in nos palam restitit."[2] The good-will of the emperor lasted until a military expedition was sent to the Orient, where the scene of operations centered in Arabia and Mesopotamia. (The various episodes are represented on the great Arch of Septimius Severus in the Forum.) The persecution seems to have begun anew just at that epoch; Spartianus records that the emperor, while traversing Palestine, promulgated a number of edicts against the Jews and Christians: "In itinere Palaestinis plurima iura fundavit: Iudaeos fieri sub gravi poena vetuit: idem etiam de Christianis sanxit."[3] This edict was probably issued in 202. Aubé maintains that it refers only to the Jews and Christians of Palestine.

and that elsewhere both Jews and Christians enjoyed the same equal rights and liberty; but this opinion is untenable. It is certain that during this same period Septimius Severus was favorable to the Jews, who scarcely had any reason to fear, and that he was hostile to the Christians, whose spread continued to be a cause of great worry to the government. In fact, he and his son Caracalla allowed the Jews to hold almost any of the high offices and positions of trust in the government: "Iis qui Judaicam superstitionem sequantur Divi Severus et Antoninus honores adipisci permiserunt."[4] On the other hand, the better to strike at the Christians, Septimius Severus gave out a number of laws against organizations, making distinctions between those that were licit and those that were not adjudged to be so: "Prohibuit qui illicitum collegium coire dicuntur."

The funeral societies were permitted and their members, after securing a certain amount of money, could insure a tomb or a grave. Many ancient inscriptions indicate the existence of such organizations and their names: Aesculapius, Antinous, Sergia Paulina, etc. According to the opinion of de Rossi, the Christian community could still possess their own tombs because of this legal authority enjoyed by the burial organizations; in fact, Tertullian speaks of a monthly allowance which all the faithful had to pay for the upkeep of the cemeteries,[5] and the *Philosophumena* tells us that the deacon Callistus had the administration of moneys of the Church, having been chosen by Pope Zephyrin as the custodian of that cemetery which was later on to bear his name.[6]

All these facts hint at a special organization which even at this early period is characteristic of the Christian community, an organization which was certainly the object of the rescripts of Septimius Severus. But the emperor did not limit himself to these measures of a prohibitive and vexatious nature; Tertullian,[7] Eusebius,[8] Clement of Alexandria[9] and Orosius[10] all speak of a true and widespread persecution. It appears to have been provoked by an incident involving a Christian soldier, who refused to accept a wreath offered to him by one of his superior officers. The pagans seized the occasion to accuse the Christians of being enemies of the fatherland. At Carthage, a gladiator carried around a design consisting of an ass's head with the inscription, "The God of the Christians."[11] This caricature was repeated on the Palatine on that part of the palace contemporaneous with Septimius Severus, as a crude drawing showing a crucifix with the head of an ass; close by is a man who prays, with the inscription: "Alexamenos adores his God."[12] This caricature is preserved today in the National Museum at Terme.

Whatever may have been the pretext for the persecution, the real motive was surely the fact of the ever-increasing number of Christians. The persecution lasted until the death of Septimius Severus (211), and may even have continued for a short time under Caracalla. It was general, even though we do not possess records of it throughout the various regions of the Empire. In Rome, for instance, there is scarcely a mention of it, although it goes without saying that there also it had its quota of martyrs.

With respect to Africa, the records are more certain. Egypt witnessed the martyrdom of St. Potamiena. Tertullian indicates the date of the persecution at Carthage by naming the prefect under whom it took place: "Doleamus necesse est quod nulla civitas impune latura sit sanguinis nostri effusionem, sicut et sub Hilariano praeside, cum de areis sepulturarum nostrarum acclamassent: Areae non sint!"[13] The word *areae* had a special significance in Africa. Although it was rather easy in Rome to excavate subterranean cemeteries, it was necessary in other localities to build them in the open; for that reason they were called *horti, hortuli* and in Africa *areae*. An inscription from Caesarea in Mauritania records that a certain Evelpius, "Cultor Verbi," donated an "area" to the Church, to the "Ecclesia fratrum."

The Acts of St. Perpetua relative to this persecution constitute a very important document because of their authenticity and also because they concern the martyr herself. These Acts were published in the collection of Ruinart, and, in part, several other times. At first it was thought that we possessed only a Latin version of a Greek text, but it has been proved that the original was written in Latin.[14] According to the Acts, there was a great number of martyrs: "multos fratres martyres."

The account given of the theatre, and of the presence of the governor, points to the fact that the martyrdom of St. Perpetua occurred in Carthage itself. The arrest, the trial and questionings, the taking of her son, still carried at the breast, the plea of her pagan father that she yield and deny the faith, the imprisonment, the moments of doubt and discouragement and the mystical visions which reinforced her and prepared her for the conflict, are all minutely described. It is only on the eve of her martyrdom that she interrupts her narrative, or better, brings it to an end by writing in all simplicity: "Let him who shall behold the conflict continue my narrative." Two of her visions bear a special importance for us. In the first she saw one of her brothers, who had died young, striving to approach a fountain to slake his thirst, but in vain. Thinking that this might indicate that he was in a place of suffering, she prayed for him, and shortly afterward beheld him, surrounded by light, drinking at the fountain. Her expression, "Vidi Dinocraten . . . refrigerantem," is analogous to the expression "in refrigerio" of the inscriptions; that is, it is an allusion to the dogma of Purgatory. Even on the eve of her martyrdom, it seemed to the saint that she was in a garden in the midst of which stood a shepherd who called her and offered her milk. She took it and drank, while those who stood around said, "Amen!" This gives us an explanation of those pictures in the catacombs which represent the Good Shepherd with a pitcher of milk, a symbol of the Eucharist. The vision changes in the twinkling of an eye, and she sees herself in the amphitheatre. An Ethiopian comes toward her to slay her, but the saint, assisted by two youths of great strength, fights off and vanquishes the enemy. Finally the director of the games embraces and kisses her on the forehead saying: "Daughter, peace be with thee" — "Filia, pax tecum."

These symbolical concepts of the gladiator and athlete are often found on the primitive monuments of the Christians. In fact, they are often found united with the symbol of the Good Shepherd.

Accepting the testimony of St. Gregory of Tours,[15] we know that St. Irenaeus of Lyons was a victim of this conflict, which also destroyed a large number of martyrs in Asia Minor, especially in Antioch. It was probably in this persecution also that the celebrated St. Cecilia was put to death.

In 211 began the reign of Caracalla. The persecution continued, though with less cruelty and terror. With Heliogabalus, there was ushered in a period of peace. This tyrant had planned to found a new religion, of which Rome was to be the center, and he himself the high priest; perhaps he tolerated the Christians because of this, or more correctly because he was of Oriental birth, and favored Christianity as being of the same origin.

Alexander Severus also manifested feelings of toleration toward the Christians. It is said, though it cannot be proved conclusively, that his mother Mammea was herself a Christian. It is certain, however, as his biographer shows, that he made many concessions to the Church. Over the door of his palace, which he had thrown open to the public to render them justice, he had inscribed in large letters the following sentence, which breathes of the Bible: "Quod tibi fieri non vis, alteri ne

feceris."[16] To the Jews he left their privileges, to the Christians
their liberty: "Judaeis privilegia reservavit, Christianos esse
passus est."[17] It seems that he even got the idea of erecting
a temple to Jesus Christ.[18] An incident which occurred in
Transtevere provided the occasion for manifesting his sentiments. An oratory built close to the place where St. Mary's
in Transtevere now stands, had been taken from the Christians
shortly before he ascended the throne. It had been transformed
into a *taberna emeritoria,* destined to serve the veterans, perhaps
the *vigiles* who lived in the barracks close by, opposite the
modern church of St. Chrysogonus. The Christians had recourse to him in seeking to repossess the location, and he
listened to their requests and satisfied their desires by decree-
ing that it was better to consecrate a place to God than to
abandon it to drinkers of wine.[19] There is no trace of persecution during his reign, although there occurred scattered martyrdoms here and there, due to the hatred of some local governor.
Such is the death of Pope Callistus in Rome: an isolated fact
without juridical character. The aged pontiff was surprised by
the populace in a moment of overexcitement, and thrown into
a well. Through prudence, his body was deposited in the nearest cemetery, that of Calepodius on the Aurelian Way (this
cemetery has also at times been called the cemetery of Callistus), instead of being taken to the great papal cemetery on the
Appian Way. Urban, who succeeded Callistus, governed the
Church in the most complete tranquillity, and after his death
was buried in the cemetery on the Appian Way.

## 2.   The Persecution of Maximinus

The election of Maximinus was the signal for the outbreak
of a new persecution which, though it lasted but two years, was
cruel beyond measure. Maximinus elected to do exactly the
opposite of his predecessors; and because Alexander Severus
favored the Christians, he persecuted them. Pope Pontian was
condemned *ad metalla,* and taken to Sardinia, where he died.[20]
The obscure expression found in the Philocalian lists, "in insula

discinctus est," signifies that Pontian had abdicated, finding it impossible to govern the Church in captivity (235). He is the first example of a pope abdicating the Papacy; the only other instance was the case of Celestine V. Pontian's successor was Pope Anterus who, however, was actually put to death within a year, before Pontian himself. Anterus was probably martyred in January, 235. His inscription, discovered in the crypt of the popes in the cemetery of Callistus, carries only the title of bishop — ΑΝΘΕΡΩϹ ΕΠΙ — but it is broken, and perhaps the missing part contained the record of his martyrdom.

Gordian (238-243) succeeded Maximinus, to be succeeded by Philip, who was unworthy of being a Christian,[21] if the tradition is true that he rose to power by assassinating his predecessor, and later took part in all the pagan ceremonies, solemnly celebrating the millennium of Rome's founding. Eusebius[22] relates that, wishing to celebrate the feast of Easter in Antioch, Philip was forbidden by the bishop, whereupon he decided to do penance. During his reign and the pontificate of Fabian, the body of Pontian was solemnly transported to Rome and deposited in the cemetery of Callistus, where this inscription was recently discovered bearing the primitive sepulchral legend: ΠΟΝΤΙΑΝΟϹ ΕΠΙ · Μ[αρτυρ]. There is also a beautiful remembrance of it in an engraving before the papal crypt:

ΕΝ ΘΕΩ ΜΕΤΑ ΠΑΝΤΩΝ [ἁγίων Ἐπισκόπων] ΠΟΝΤΙΑΝΕ
ΖΗϹΗϹ

### 3.   The Persecution of Decius[23]

Decius reigned from 249 to 251. Aurelius Victor[24] and Vopiscus,[25] one of the authors of the *Historia Augusta,* are loud in their praises of Decius, proclaiming him a great emperor, austere, courageous and possessed of a scrupulous morality. It was perhaps his strong conviction of the greatness of Rome and her traditions that induced him to persecute the Christians, to execrate the memory of Philip, and actually to delete his name from the inscriptions.

In the first years of the reign of Decius, the Goths invaded Dacia, which had been conquered by Trajan. This afforded the opportunity, as in many instances of calamity in the past, of blaming the Christians for the public misfortune. The persecution of the Christians was begun anew and carried on cruelly, ably and in a coldly calculated manner. Pope Fabian was one of the first victims (January, 250); and Decius clearly stated that he would much prefer a competitor to the throne to the rivalry of the Bishop of Rome. The Church of Rome recounted, in one of its letters to the other Churches, the martyrdom of its head. We do not possess the text of this precious document: but do have the answer of St. Cyprian. The deposition of St. Fabian occurred on January 20, according to the ancient Liberian catalogue: "Fabiani in Calixti, Sebastiani in catacumbas." However, the two martyrs do not belong to the same period of persecution. The inscription of St. Fabian still exists in the chapel of the popes: ΦΑΒΙΑΝΟϹ ΕΠΙ ΜΡ ("martyr"). The last word is later than the remainder of the inscription and was perhaps made during the time of peace, as was that of Pontian.

After the death of Fabian the Roman Church remained without a head for more than a year. This period is known for its great number of martyrs. A few of the most illustrious were Calocerus and Partenius, the slaves of the consul Emilianus and tutors of his daughter Anatolia, whose history is so much like that of Sts. Nereus and Achilleus, domestics of St. Domitilla. The Acts record their death in 250, "Daciano et Grato conss." The Liberian Calendar, on the other hand, gives the date as 304, "Diocletiano IX et Maximiano VIII conss." According to de Rossi, this second date must be referred to a translation of the relics of the two martyrs to the cemetery of Callistus.[26] Their names are engraved on the wall of a chapel in which they were probably buried.

In brief, the persecution was general in Italy, Sicily, Spain and France; among the martyrs of France we should mention Saturninus, Bishop of Toulouse. This period also saw an unusual number of Christian apostates, lay, priestly and episcopal. St. Cyprian[27] says that Basilides, Bishop of León, sacrificed to the idols, and that Martial, Bishop of Mérida, was on friendly terms with the pagans and had his son buried in a grave belonging to one of their funeral guilds. The horror which this fact inspired in the Christians demonstrates how they shrank from even the possibility of mixing their graves with those of the pagans.

In Africa, and at Carthage in particular, the apostasies were more frequent. These weak Christians committed their betrayal in various fashions. Some, called *sacrificarii,* immolated victims on the altars of the idols; others, known as *thuriferarii,* offered incense; still others, spoken of as *libellatici,* were content to procure a declaration to the effect that they had offered sacrifice, whereas they had not done so in actual fact. Among that infinite mass of Coptic, Greek and Latin papyri recently recovered in Egypt, there has been discovered a fragment of one of these *libelli,* which Krebs published in 1893.[28] This papyrus, written in Greek, cites an instance in which Diogenes Aurelius, son of Satibus, makes an appeal to the commission on sacrifices of the small town of Alexandronesos, to obtain a certificate stating that he had taken part in the sacrifice to the idols and eaten the flesh of the victims. The local marks indicate June 6, 250, as the date of this important document, which explains the expressions, *libellum accipere, libellum tradere.*

In Egypt, whither the persecution next takes us, it was carried on with special fury and intensity. The center of persecution was Alexandria, a city full of a strange conglomeration of Greek, Roman and above all Egyptian superstitions. At the time of Decius these last-named enjoyed a vigorous revival, perhaps in opposition to the Christians; it is noteworthy that the name of Decius is the last imperial name which appears on the hieroglyphic inscriptions. The Christians fled in large numbers, and it was during this period that the monk St. Paul instituted the eremitic life in the desert. In 251, as the Goths were constantly advancing, Decius himself took the field against them, and after giving proofs of great valor, died on the field of battle. Under his successor Gallus, who associated himself with Volusianus, the persecution continued without abatement.

In June, 251, St. Cornelius was elected pope. A member or freedman of the *gens Cornelia,* he was the first pope to bear the name of an ancient and distinguished Roman family, for there is much doubt concerning the family connections of St. Clement and the Flavii Clementes. The election of St. Cornelius was disturbed by the schism of the partisans of Novatian, who presently broke away from the Church entirely and formed a community apart. This sect possessed various cemeteries in Rome, and its sectaries did not hesitate to steal the relics of the martyrs, as in the case of the body of Silanus, the youngest son of St. Felicitas, in order to have these cemeteries consecrated or blessed. St. Cornelius had a brief pontificate, dying during the persecution of Gallus at Centumcellae (Civitavecchia), in 252. He was honored as a martyr because of his cruel sufferings and was buried in the cemetery of Callistus, not in the chapel of the popes, but in another tomb, perhaps one belonging to his own family. His inscription which, in contrast to those of the other popes, is in Latin, may be seen in the cemetery of Callistus. It bears the glorious title of "Martyr."

It was a fragment of the inscription, discovered close to the Appian Way, which led de Rossi to suppose that it indicated the location of the cemetery of Callistus, and thus provided the occasion for the remarkable excavations which resulted in so many wonderful discoveries.

## 4.  The Persecution of Valerian

During the first years of the reign of Valerian, the Church recovered her tranquillity. With the authorization of the emperor, the pope returned from exile and remained in Rome until his death in the year 254. His funeral inscription was found in a broken condition in the cemetery of Callistus, where he was buried. He was also considered a martyr because of his sufferings and imprisonment, though it does not appear that his death was violent.

The persecution soon became even more rigorous. Valerian promulgated two edicts, one in 257, the other in the following year, as the Acts of St. Cyprian attest;[29] with the publication of

these edicts, the cemeteries of the Christians were confiscated
and they were prohibited from frequenting them. Notwithstanding this order, the Christians never entirely ceased to reunite
in the cemeteries. Those who attended one such meeting were
surprised by the soldiers of Valerian, and were buried alive in
the cemetery of Thraso, on the tombs of Sts. Chrysanthus and
Daria.

A celebrated episode of this persecution is the martyrdom
of St. Sixtus II, which came to be erroneously ascribed to
Stephen I, on the basis of manuscripts later than the *Liber pontificalis*. However, the true account has been reëstablished. St.
Cyprian[30] clearly speaks of the slaying of St. Sixtus in the cemetery itself, "in coemeterio," that is, in the papal cemetery of
Callistus on the Appian Way. One part of this cemetery,
in fact, was called *ad Sanctum Sixtum,* and the invocations
which the pilgrims scratched on the walls can still be seen:
"Sancte Suste," "Suste Sancte!" On the other hand, there is no
record of St. Stephen.[31] Sixtus was surprised by the soldiers
during the celebration of the Mysteries with his deacons. The
aged pope was taken to Rome, condemned, and again carried
back to the Appian Way where he was martyred. St. Lawrence,
the first of his deacons and his assistant, was, as is well known,
burned alive three days later.

These two splendid examples of the martyrs were followed
by another: that of Tarcisius, who was stoned to death like the
first martyr, St. Stephen, to whom St. Damasus compares him,[32]
because he would not yield the Sacred Species to the pagans.
His remains, which were preserved in the so-called crypt of Sts.
Sixtus and Cecilia in the cemetery of St. Callistus until the
eighth century, were then taken to the church of St. Sylvester
*in Capite.*

The fourth but not less celebrated martyr was Hippolytus.[33]
Of the three saints of this name, one was a priest and doctor
of Rome, the second Bishop of Porto, the third a soldier. It was
the first, according to de Rossi, who died under Valerian and
was interred on the Tiburtine Way in a crypt of which we have
a description in the verses of Prudentius;[34] his statue (now in

the Lateran) was found not far from this place, bearing an engraved list of his works. This celebrated crypt was rediscovered
by Marucchi and his assistants in 1881. From an inscription[35]
which Damasus dedicated to him, preserved in manuscript
at Leningrad, we know that St. Hippolytus was for a time
a follower of Novatian, though he later abjured his error.
Damasus, however, confesses that the history of St. Hippolytus
was not well known: "Haec audita refert Damasus, probat omnia Christus."[36]

Any number of names could be added, names of glorious
heroes of the faith who shed their blood during this barbarous
persecution, as for example, Sts. Protus and Hyacinth. Marchi
found the original inscription referring to St. Hyacinth; his
tomb, forgotten again after having once been brought to light,
was rediscovered recently in the cemetery of St. Hermes. Then
there is St. Pancratius, whose martyrdom was placed by more
than one author as having occurred during the persecution of
Diocletian. Finally, there are Sts. Abdon and Sennen, Persians,
who came to Rome not only to escape the persecution which
raged fiercely in their native land, but also to visit the tomb of
the apostles. Bosio came upon the crypt containing their relics
in the cemetery of Pontian.

Not less tried than the Church of Rome was that of Africa,
which lost its illustrious St. Cyprian, Bishop of Carthage. The
Acts of this martyr were composed from an extract of the verbal
process of the trial made by the deacon Pontius, an eyewitness
of the affair. The Christians of Carthage had a great procession
in honor of the remains of the martyr: "cum cereis et scolacibus
. . . cum voto et triumpho magno."[37] This shows that in spite
of the persecution, the bodies of the Christians were carried
openly to their cemeteries. Nevertheless, the cemeteries in that
country were also confiscated, because St. Cyprian's body was
laid to rest in a private cemetery: "in area Macrobii Candidi-
ani." The expression "cum voto" is an allusion to the funeral
rites; we find it in numerous inscriptions, as for instance, in
that of a virgin: "Ianuaria in pace votis deposita."

The memory of St. Cyprian has ever been great. At Rome
much devotion was shown to him, especially in the cemetery

of Callistus, where reposed the popes with whom he had had close relations. In the sixth century his picture was placed next to the image of St. Cornelius, giving pilgrims the impression that the bodies of both saints were in the same tomb.

In 260 Valerian was taken prisoner by Sapor, king of Persia. Gallienus succeeded him. He was a cruel and coarse emperor, and it was during his reign that there flourished the celebrated thirty tyrants. The Empire was subdivided into several governmental units, of which one of the most important was that of Gaul, with Treves as its capital. However, Gallienus, like Commodus, and perhaps through the influence of his wife, Salonina, who was also a follower of the true faith,[38] was favorable to the Christians. Eusebius[39] cites the edict in which he declared the persecution suspended and the cemeteries restored. It was at this time that Pope Dionysius, elected one year after the death of Sixtus II, instituted a new organization of the titles and cemeteries, which is spoken of in the *Liber pontificalis*: "Hic presbyteris ecclesias divisit et cimiteria constituit."

## 5. The Persecution of Claudius and Aurelian

Claudius II, the Goth, who succeeded Gallienus, was as valorous as Decius; he was imbued with that firm conviction of the greatness of Rome which made so many of the pagan emperors enemies of Christianity. The persecution he waged against the Church lasted about a year and a half, that is, from 269 to 270. Pagi[40] and Aubé[41] have denied the occurrence of this persecution, and Ruinart passes over the period in silence. Allard,[42] however, admits it, and for valid reasons. The Acts and Martyrologies bear witness to it; and it is evident also from the Acts of the Greek martyrs signalized by de Rossi[43] that this persecution began several years after Valerian, that is, in the year 269. The pretext for it was the war of the Goths; perhaps it was the Senate itself that began the persecution after the departure of the emperor in 269. The martyrs were numerous in Rome, in Ostia, in Porto: among those of Rome being the illustrious priest, St. Valentine, whose tomb Marucchi and his assistants discovered on the Flaminian Way. Some authors, confusing Claudius the Goth with Claudius I, have made the martyrs of this persecution the "Protomartyrs of Italy," and have placed them in close relation to the apostles. This is evidently false, because there was no persecution before that of Nero, as we have shown.

The persecution of Claudius was limited to Italy. In the Orient the Christians enjoyed the greatest possible liberty under the protection of Zenobia, queen of Palmyra, protectress of the unworthy Bishop Paul of Samosata. Claudius II died fighting the Goths, and his successor Aurelian ordered the persecution of which Eusebius,[44] St. Jerome,[45] St. Augustine,[46] and the author of De mortibus persecutorum speak. At the end of it he himself died: "Inter initia furoris sui exstinctus est."[47]

At the beginning of his reign Aurelian appeared to favor the Christians. When he conquered Zenobia, the inhabitants of Antioch asked him to expel Paul of Samosata, who, deposed because of his scandalous conduct, had refused to leave the episcopal residence, depending for protection on the queen. Aurelian listened to them and acquiesced in their demands, declaring that the episcopal residence was the property of that bishop who was in agreement with the others of Italy and Rome.[48] But once in Rome, he had the colossal Temple of the Sun built, whose dimensions are known from the Villa Colonna on the Quirinal; sought to revive paganism; and became the persecutor of Christianity. One of the first martyrs was St. Agapitus of Palestrina, whose Acts, although legendary, yet furnish us with various chronological data; as, for instance, the name of the prefect Flavius of Antioch, who was prefect in 269-270 and again in 272,[49] and consul in 273. The emperor was killed by his own soldiers in the war against the barbarians, toward the end of the persecution (275), and the Christians enjoyed a period of peace which lasted until the time of Diocletian.

With Aurelian the decadence of the Empire began. The barbarians continued to advance; it had become necessary to cede to them a portion of Dacia, of which there remained only

a *Dacia fictitia,* which was also called *Aureliana.* The barbarians soon reached the banks of the Danube. The fear of
seeing them enter Rome induced the Romans to surround the
city with new walls. They enclose the city even to this day, and
remain one of the most remarkable monuments of the decadence of the Empire of the Romans.

After Aurelian there reigned in quick succession: Tacitus
(276), Probus (276-282), who completed the circumvallation
of the city of Rome, Carus (282-283), Carinus and Numerianus
(283-284), and finally Diocletian (284-305), whose reign was
a period of true political revolution.

## Chapter V

## THE PERSECUTION OF DIOCLETIAN

DIOCLETIAN did not wish to shoulder the burden of
ruling the Empire alone; for that reason, he chose as his
associate Maximian Herculeus, conferring on him the title of
Augustus; and created two Caesars, Maximian Galerius and
Constantius Chlorus. Furthermore, he modified the division
and the government of the provinces, establishing dioceses and
prefectures. Finally, under him, Oriental usages and customs
were introduced to a very great extent in the Empire and at the
imperial court.

After having first favored the Christians, Diocletian became
the most terrible of all the persecutors of Christianity. Concerning this long, bloody and cruel persecution we shall relate
only the principal facts as handed down to us in Eusebius'
history,[1] the *De mortibus persecutorum,*[2] attributed to Lactantius, the numerous Acts of the martyrs, the hagiographies
and the Martyrologies. The picture may be divided into two
parts: first, the military persecution; secondly, the general persecution.

The first, which occurred in 290, was caused by the im-
prudent zeal, or better, the fanaticism, of some soldiers who,
following the teachings of Tertullian,[3] held that it was incom-

patible for a Christian to accept the honors conferred by the civil power. The government, provoked by this show of peculiar disposition, made it obligatory for the soldiers to take an oath of fealty by subscribing to a formula which could not be accepted by the Christians. Refusal to take this oath was punished with rigor as rebellion against military discipline. The most celebrated soldiers who were martyred at this time belonged to the Theban Legion, which was decimated twice in the provinces of Gaul by order of Maximian. Other martyrs were the saints called the *Quattuor Coronati,* interred in the cemetery which bears their name on the Labican Way;[4] and the four soldiers of the *Legio II Parthica* martyred at Albano and buried in the local cemetery.[5] But above all shines St. Sebastian, tribune of the Praetorian Cohort, who was attached in an especial manner to the person of the emperor. It is believed that he suffered death by being shot with arrows in the stadium of the Palatine — "in hippodromo," which expression refers to the fact that, at the time of this occurrence, the stadium had been transformed into a hippodrome. It is also believed that he was martyred a short distance from the place where now stands the actual church of St. Sebastian *in Palatio.*

During this first period, the martyrs were isolated. The general body of Christians seemed to increase in numbers, they were allowed to possess churches and cemeteries, and in the Orient, they even built churches in public. The military persecution was soon over and there ensued a period of peace. But in 303 Galerius went to Nicomedia expressly to convince the emperor of the necessity of destroying the Christians. Diocletian would not hear of it at first,[6] but later gave his consent and signed the edict of persecution. The two years from 303 to 305 were two bloody years, in which the number of martyrs was incalculable. Even though the Acts have oftentimes exaggerated these facts, and legendary documents have attributed to Diocletian things that happened at other periods, it is still certain that this persecution was the most savage of all.

As at the time of Valerian, the goods of the Christians were confiscated; for the first time, moreover, the archives of

the Church were destroyed.[7]  Many Acts of the martyrs speak
of this confiscation, and the *Liber pontificalis,* in the biography
of St. Sylvester, says of the cemetery of Cyriaca that it was occupied during this seizure, "tempore persecutionis." Material
traces of violence and destruction appear everywhere, even in
the cemetery of Callistus; it was at this period that the tomb of
the popes was filled with earth and abandoned, and St. Marcellinus and his successor St. Marcellus were buried in the cemetery of Priscilla.  The numerous lacunae which the Acts of the
martyrs, calendars and Martyrologies present concerning this
epoch are explainable by the destruction of the archives; this
is confirmed by the testimony of the *Breviculus collationis cum
Donatistis,*[8] a document preserved in the works of St. Augustine.
The schism of the Donatists arose precisely because of this loss
of the records of the Church.  Those commissioned to guard the
Christian archives at times handed over the Acts of the martyrs
or one or the other of the liturgical books; and the bishops,
priests or deacons who acted thus were held by Donatists to
have forfeited priestly orders.  The *Breviculus* contains, with
the record of a verbal process of the reunions held in Carthage
in reference to this altercation, a sample of an inventory of the
liturgical objects, the books and writings confiscated by the
persecutors.

No means were left untried in an effort to induce the
Christians to offer sacrifice to the gods or to the idols; public
places, squares, even the stores and business houses were
adorned with the statues of these deities, to whom it was
necessary to consecrate every act of one's public life by means
of sacrifice. Thus we have what came to be called *dies thurificationis,* just as at first there had been *dies traditionis* for hand-
ing over the sacred books. An inscription of this period has been
found at Mastai which records minutely these days of violence:
"in diebus thurificationis."[9]

The Christians, for the most part, were condemned *ad
metalla,* or *ad opera publica:* that is, to those pits in the earth
from which were obtained the materials used for building huge
monuments, or to cutting the columns used in constructing

many of the edifices so much admired at Rome. The baths of Diocletian were constructed at this time, and it is probable that Christians took part in their erection, especially in the arduous task of cutting and dressing the marble. Some Acts speak of the soldiers who supervised the Christians working in the mines.[10]

Chief among the confessors who labored on the construction of the baths were St. Saturninus, St. Cyriacus and Sts. Largus and Smaragdus.

In 305 Diocletian and Maximian abdicated, the first at Nicomedia, the second at Milan. Galerius and Constantius Chlorus became Augusti, and chose as Caesars Flavius Severus and Maximinus Daza. Galerius continued the persecution, but later on, when stricken by the malady of which he shortly died, published an edict of toleration. It is even said that he recommended himself to the prayers of the faithful (311). Maximinus, on the other hand, now that he ruled alone, organized a veritable revolt of public opinion against the Christians. It was at his instigation, as Eusebius recounts,[11] that some cities of the Empire besought the expulsion of the Christians. In an inscription discovered in Asia Minor and published by Mommsen, there is preserved for us the Greek text of a request of this kind which the citizens of Aricanda sent to the emperor. The letter is preceded by a Latin fragment of the rescript which had been promulgated.[12] The translation of the letter follows:

"To the saviours of the whole human race, to the divine Augusti, the Caesars Galerius Valerius Maximianus, and Flavius Valerius Constantine, and Valerius Licinianus Licinius; the earnest request and prayer of the faithful people of Lycia and Pamphilia. The gods of your fathers having shown you, O illustrious princes, that they protect those who defend religion, we believe it opportune for your eternal felicity, O sovereign masters, superior to all things, to have recourse to your immortal and royal power and demand of it that the Christians, who have been rebellious for so long a time, even to our own day, be destroyed and made to give up at once their mad ideas of taking away the honors owed to the gods. This immense boon to your subjects will be effected only if your immortal and divine power shall desire to take care to put a stop to the malicious work of these atheists, enemies of our religion; if you shall command them to devote themselves to the practice of the religion of your fathers for the good of your incorruptible and immortal Rule."

This inscription, perhaps of the year 311, was ensculptured after the coming of peace. It may be compared to a letter of the same tenor addressed to Maximian from the city of Tyre, in Phoenicia, a letter which Eusebius cites in his *History,* and which he says he saw cast in bronze in the forum of Tyre, joined with the imperial reply.

But during this persecution, which lasted, in spite of the edict of Galerius, until 312, the Christians had their cemeteries, their titles, and at Nicomedia, and perhaps at Rome also, even public churches. An inscription of the cemetery of Callistus records that the deacon Severus, with the consent of Pope Marcellinus, that is, at the time of Diocletian, had ordered a small room with a window excavated there, which proves evidently that the Christians also possessed the area overlying the catacombs. After the edict of 303, only the public cemeteries were confiscated, and if that of Cyriaca was seized, it indicated that it had been donated to the Church, and thereby had become the property of the Christian community.

It was for this reason that the papal cemetery of Callistus was confiscated and that Pope Marcellinus was therefore buried in the cemetery of Priscilla.

St. Marcellinus, just mentioned (304), was accused of having sacrificed to idols, but the legend arises undoubtedly from an apocryphal *Passio,* and the account is entirely false. It speaks of a council of bishops which was supposed to have been held in Sinuessa, an impossible thing during times of persecution. However, if Marcellinus was not guilty of apostasy, his responsibility for giving over the holy books to the pagans, and perhaps for some other acts of weakness, is not obviated or lessened.[13]

After his death the See of Rome remained vacant for some time; it was during this period that St. Peter, the exorcist, and

St. Marcellinus, priest, suffered martyrdom. St. Damasus gives us the particulars of both these martyrdoms, which he had gathered from the executioner himself. Their bodies, hidden through hatred of the Christians, were found again by the matron Lucilla and transported by her to the cemetery on the Labican Way, where some years ago the burial crypt containing their remains was again discovered. It must have been in this manner that the bodies of Sts. Castulus, Eutychius and Candida were hidden. St. Candida was converted by Peter and Marcellinus, arrested when she was leaving the cemetery and thrown by a watchman into the cemetery of Pontian. The body of St. Castulus was cast by soldiers into a pit on the Labican Way which later became a cemetery, as was also the body of St. Eutychius, which was found again after a long search by St. Damasus. To this period belong likewise the martyrs Simplicius and Faustinus and their sister Beatrice, buried on the property of Generosa. St. Soter was also among these. The family of St. Soter possessed more than one monument along the Appian Way and their cemetery was reunited with that of Callistus after the persecution. To St. Soter was also dedicated a small basilica not far from that of Sts. Sixtus and Cecilia. St. Ambrose, who was of the same family, speaks of her as a relative. Other celebrated martyrs of this persecution in Rome were Sts. Felix and Adauctus, whose tomb was also recently found again in the cemetery of Commodilla close to the Ostian Way.[14]

The election of Marcellus (308) happened during a period of relative peace, when Maxentius, who was favorable enough to the Christians, had restored numerous cemeteries to them. There were nevertheless some martyrs, and even the pontiff was persecuted. An unknown heretic, who had already apostatized, argued that even those who denied the faith in the persecution should be admitted to communion. This was the cause of an agitation for which Pope Marcellus was held to be responsible; he was accordingly sent into exile, where he died. This is the reason why he was honored as a martyr and his body transported to Rome, where it was laid to rest in the cemetery of Priscilla close to that of St. Marcellinus, whose deacon he had been.

This agitation and others instigated by trouble-makers, rigorists, etc., concerning the power of the Church to remit sins, continued until the time of the pontificate of Eusebius. St. Damasus clearly states this fact in a metrical inscription which he placed on his tomb and which was found in the cemetery of Callistus.[15] Eusebius was the glorious victim of the persecution which was begun by Diocletian, and which continued spasmodically even after this. From Sicily, where he died, his body was carried to Rome when the cemetery of Callistus was restored to the Christians.

Thus we come to the final page of this tragic history of blood, which lasted almost three centuries. We may ask ourselves how many there were who confessed the faith. Often the total has been exaggerated; but numerous other authors have attempted to diminish it beyond reason.[16] If one were to consider only the names mentioned in surviving documents which are indisputably authentic, their number would be comparatively small. But they do not of course represent the actual truth; the authors could not know all and recount all that happened. If the total number is unknown, still one must come to the conclusion, after reading the written documents, and seeing the testimony of the various monuments themselves, that a great multitude of Christians died amidst various torments. (Certain bodies which, until lately, were thought to be those of unknown martyrs, because they had been found in the catacombs with the countersign of a glass ampoule, have been shown not to be so. This sign has been proved to have no significance; and the supposed martyrs, held in veneration from the sixteenth century on, are not generally to be considered as such.)

Le Blant, in one of his most interesting studies on the sentences meted out to the martyrs,[17] makes the following comments:

"To those who had been punished by the authorities, there remained only one avenue of escape, to make an appeal against the condemnation: and it must redound to the courage of the martyrs if no recourse of this kind was ever made against the sentence imposed upon them . . . The martyr, conducted before a judge, did not try to sway him nor did he assume a sad expression of face which the accused sometimes affected to attempt to soften the hearts of the judges; but the martyr kept that smile and serenity, almost jubilant, up to the last moment, as becoming one who was about to enter into his glory. Not one text speaks of martyrs who had recourse to the sovereign, even if only to obtain a less frightful manner of death. There is only one instance where the word *appeal* fell from the lips of a martyr. If we are to believe Prudentius, who often reproduces the conclusions of the original writings from which he took his inscriptions, it must have been St. Romanus[18] who uttered it; but it was not to a human power that the faithful soul turned for recourse, but rather to Christ Who saw him and judged him, as He saw and judged his executioners."

## Chapter VI

## THE PEACE OF THE CHURCH

AT THE beginning of the fourth century, a sudden and profound change occurred in the relations between the Church and the Roman Empire. This change was to have the most happy consequences for the world at large. Two of the reigning emperors, Maxentius and Constantine, declared war against each other. The particulars of this conflict are well known to all: in October of 312 Maxentius was slain and his army routed, and Constantine, victorious and a Christian, entered triumphantly into Rome. An extraordinary happening had brought about the conversion of the emperor. Eusebius[1] had received the particulars of it from the emperor himself.

One day Constantine had seen in the heavens a luminous cross with the words: Ἐν τούτῳ νίκα; he had also beheld Christ the Redeemer, Who presented to him the model of the standard which he was to give to his soldiers. This standard, the *Labarum,* had the form of a cross and bore the monogram of Christ.[2] There are numerous reproductions which correspond to this description in general, but differ from it

slightly in particulars. A picture of it, for example, may be seen
on the coins minted during the reign of Constantine;[3] on two
sarcophagi of the Lateran Museum; and at times even on the
monuments of the catacombs. Thus at St. Agnes' there was
found a crown of stone with the monogram and inscription:
IN HOC SIGNO SIRICI (*vivas*). An allusion to the celebrated
vision can also be seen in the mosaics which adorn the basilica
of St. Constantia on the Nomentan Way, a mausoleum of the
family of Constantine. These mosaics represent the heavens
studded with stars surrounding the resplendent monogram of
Christ.

The battle which resulted in Rome's falling into the hands
of Constantine was fought near the gates of the city, at the
place called *Ad Saxa Rubra,* where the villa of Livia lay, on
October 28, 312. Numerous monuments record this auspicious
and epoch-making occurrence. On the Triumphal Way there
was built an arch with the materials taken from one of the
arches of Trajan; the sculpture finished at the time of Constantine clearly shows a representation of the celebrated battle
at the Milvian Bridge. One of the bas-reliefs portrays the
emperor addressing the people in the Forum; at the base one
recognizes the monuments of the Forum and Capitol. On each
of the two parts is engraved an immense inscription with the
words "instinctu Divinitatis," which are an allusion to the Christian beliefs of Constantine. Venuti[4] and Nibby[5] have represented, without any plausible reason, that the inscription may
have been modified by the substitution of the words "instinctu
Divinitatis" for others — "Diis faventibus" or "nutu Iovis
Optimi Maximi." When, in 1863, by order of Napoleon III, it
was possible to make exact measurements and investigations of
the arch, it was established that the inscription had not under-
gone any modification.[6] In 315, the date of the dedication of
this arch, Constantine had certainly shown himself a Christian.
In order to avoid offending the Senate, a general and vague
expression was selected, which was, however, sufficient to de-
clare him a Christian. In fact, the Christians were called
"cultores Dei," that is, worshippers of only one God.

A short distance from the Forum there was an immense statue of Constantine with the labarum, to which an inscription also made reference. Eusebius,[7] in his *De vita Constantini,* describes both the statue and the inscription. The statue is perhaps the one which is now to be seen in the vestibule of St. John Lateran. Another should adorn the apse of the basilica of Constantine; to it may belong, according to Petersen,[8] the colossal head which is on the Capitol in the courtyard of the palace of the Conservators.

The triumph of Constantine, in contrast to ancient triumphs, does not appear to have been celebrated with ceremonies of a superstitious or idolatrous character. It must be held as wholly without justification, therefore, that Professor Wagner, of Munich, in his beautiful restoration of the triumph of Constantine, otherwise so exact from the point of view of topography, has represented the emperor as ascending the Capitoline Hill to assist at a sacrifice at the altar of Jupiter.

Later Constantine went to Milan with his colleague Licinius; at Milan he published the edict which finally recognized the legal existence of the Church (May, 313). This edict ordered that the places of reunion and the cemeteries taken from the Church be restored: "Non ea loca tantum, ad quae convenire consueverunt (Christiani), sed alia etiam . . . ad jus corporis eorum, id est ecclesiarum, non hominum singulorum pertinentia."[9] Constantine added to this enormous donations, among which one might mention the Lateran, made to Pope Miltiades. This palace, the property of Plautius Lateranus, had been confiscated by Nero and had become meanwhile a sort of imperial villa. A wall of the house of the Laterani was utilized by Aurelian for the new circumvallation of Rome. When the apse of the basilica was repaired in 1877, the foundations of the ancient villa, and in particular the lead pipes with the words LATERANI, DOMVS LATERANORVM were uncovered. Constantine had received it as a gift from his wife Fausta, daughter of Maximian. The Lateran became the seat of the popes until the transference of the Holy See to Avignon. In the month of October, 313, Pope Miltiades held a council "in domo Faustae in Laterano."

Over and above the basilica of St. Saviour on the Lateran, Constantine constructed those of St. Peter, St. Paul, St. Lawrence, St. Agnes and Sts. Peter and Marcellinus; numerous others ascribed to him are of a later period. In the same manner must the legend of the donation of Rome to the pope be relegated to the company of unfounded stories. Constantine, according to this story, turned Rome over to the pope and then retired to Byzantium in order to allow the pontiff greater liberty.

We must not believe that Constantine prohibited paganism. He was officially bound to look after its interests because it was the recognized state religion. He permitted the practice of paganism to exist along with Christianity, retaining also the title of *Pontifex Maximus,* and his successors imitated him in this, up to Gratian (382 or 383), the first emperor to refuse this dignity. Constantine, however, did not take part in any act of idolatry. When the small town of Spello, in Umbria, requested permission to build a temple in honor of the emperor and his family, "templum gentis Flaviae," he gave his consent, but with this proviso: "Aedem Flaviae hoc est nostrae gentis ut desideratis magnifico opere perfici volumus, ea tamen observatione praescripta: ne aedis nostro nomine dedicata cuiusquam contagiosae superstitionis fraudibus polluatur."[10]

After the death of Licinius (324), Constantine showed himself more openly as a Christian. He was only a catechumen at the time, and in consequence, could not be admitted to all the liturgical functions; and in this manner he took part in the council of Nicaea in 325. He was baptized, according to Eusebius, in 337 in a city close to Nicomedia, shortly before his death. A legend dating from the fifth century speaks of his baptism in the Lateran Basilica in Rome, by Pope Sylvester who, according to this same legend, had taken refuge in Soracte. This story records a sickness and a miraculous cure of Constantine; but without doubt, all this refers to the fact that he had erected a baptistery at the Lateran where he had received the catechumenate; this structure is called the *Baptisterium Constantini* or even the *Baptismum Constantini.* The baptism of

Constantine was a fact of such great importance that it cannot be imagined that Eusebius would have invented the particulars; especially in view of the fact that all the bishops present at the Council of Nicaea could have verified with their own eyes whether the emperor was still a catechumen or had already received baptism.

Constantine certainly was guilty of some serious mistakes, the most blameworthy of which was the execution of Crispus, his own son. But taking everything into consideration, he deserved public gratitude for the good he did as a legislator, and for the liberty of conscience he conceded everyone. He suppressed execution by crucifixion and mitigated the horrors of slavery, banning the barbarous custom of branding slaves with a hot iron.[11]

It was at this time that the custom of placing an inscribed band around their necks arose; at times these bands bore Christian symbols.[12]

Even the mode of living among Christians saw great modifications. After the building of the basilicas, the liturgy was transformed and amplified. A noteworthy monument of this is found in the *Constitutiones Apostolicae,* which are certainly of this epoch. Cemeteries were built in the open, a thing which had been rare until this time, and their number increased noticeably. In place of primitive symbolism, Christian art began to employ historical decorations: images of the Saviour, the Virgin, the apostles. Christian sculpture began and sarcophagi multiplied. The Lateran Museum possesses a rich collection of these. Inscriptions developed, which supply us with the greater part of our historical information regarding the period. The style of these was detrimental to the primitive simplicity so evident in inscriptions before this period; metrical inscriptions are often encountered, while others show an isolated monogram, or bear the consular date.

Following Constantine, under the pontificate of Liberius, a great schism broke out over the Arian question. Constans, a friend of the Arians, exiled the pontiff. Liberius was accused of having attached his signature to an Arian formula. Not to

enter into the historical arguments which can be invoked in
favor of his orthodoxy,[13] a long inscription in the ancient
basilica of St. Sylvester on the Salarian Way praises him as a
defender of the Nicene faith: "Sacrilegis Nicaena fides electa
triumphat."[14] Moreover, certain inscriptions record the pontificate of Liberius, "sedente papa Liberio," and contrary to
usage, express the veneration of the Christians for this pope.
It is perhaps an indication of a protest against the usurper Felix
and a refutation of the calumnies against Liberius.

## Chapter VII

### THE CHURCH
### UNDER THE SUCCESSORS OF CONSTANTINE

### 1.  The Persecution of Julian the Apostate

THE BRIEF persecution of Julian the Apostate lasted from
362 to 363.  Julian was elected emperor after the death
of Constans, and remained on the throne from 361 to 363.  He
manifested his dislike for his predecessor by showing his hatred
for the Christians, from whom he was estranged perhaps by
the controversy and the scandals of the Arians. Ammianus Marcellinus[1] and other pagan writers who speak of Julian are all
in accord in declaring that his one ambition was to reëstablish
the cult of paganism.  However, they make no mention of any
persecution during his two years of rule.  This silence has induced many modern critics to deny that there was a persecution.
Boissier,[2] among others, extends himself in the attempt to prove
that Julian was never a persecutor.  But there is too much
strong proof to the contrary to be found in histories and in
Christian authors, such as St. Gregory Nazianzen,[3] who was a
friend of Julian in his youth, St. John Chrysostom,[4] Rufinus,[5]
Theodoret,[6] Socrates,[7] Sozomen,[8] St. Augustine[9] and others.
Other proofs are furnished by the Acts of the martyrs which,
although they may not be either contemporaneous or absolutely authentic, have nevertheless been substantiated by
archeological discoveries.

The persecution of Julian raged furiously throughout the Orient. At first he had resided in the Occident, especially at Lutetia Parisiorum (Paris), where one may still find, close to the Museum of Cluny, some of the foundations of the baths built by him. But once having ascended the throne, his habitual abode was in the Orient. St. Gregory Nazianzen, St. John Chrysostom, Socrates and Sozomen tell us of martyrs in Asia Minor, Phrygia and Palestine. The emperor wished to revive the Oriental cults, such as that of Mithras or Cybele, by purifying them and raising them to the level of Christianity. The cult of Cybele was modeled after that of the Christians; its priests had a sort of baptism and confirmation, an analogy which has led many critics into the error of attributing to that cult numerous Christian monuments. Julian was very superstitious. From the writings of Ammianus Marcellinus we know that he offered many sacrifices before setting out on any expedition;[10] and what had been said of Marcus Aurelius was repeated in his case: "The white bullock fears the victories of the emperor."

The Occident also had its martyrs. This was especially true of Rome. The Acts, generally interpolated, always mention Julian, although he was in the Orient. Perhaps this confusion occurred because of the name of another Julian, an uncle of the emperor, who really remained in Rome for some time. The most outstanding martyrs recorded in the hagiographic monuments of Rome are St. Gallican, St. Bibiana, St. John, priest, and Sts. John and Paul.[11]

## 2. The Final Triumph of Christianity

Julian the Apostate died in June, 363, and was succeeded by the Christian princes Jovian, Valentinian I, Gratian, Valentinian II and Theodosius. Under Valentinian I the Church was governed by St. Damasus (366-384). At the beginning of his pontificate, a schism arose. The rigoristic faction which believed Damasus had been a friend of Felix, the adversary of Liberius, elected Pope Ursinus; Damasus invoked the martyrs, and to their intervention he ascribed the ending of the schism. To show his gratitude for this great favor, he erected many monuments in their honor.

The Edict of Milan had not prohibited idolatry, which continued to exist especially in Rome, though Byzantium, the new Rome, was a city entirely Christian. But with the progress of Christianity, paganism was forced to reduce its sanctuaries, until finally it had only the temples of Vesta and Jupiter Capitolinus in the city. The temple of Vesta was the last to disappear; the fireplace in honor of the goddess represented the core or center of the Empire.

In 382, Gratian refused the public support previously given to the temples of the idols. Some private individuals continued to provide for their maintenance, however, until the time of the rule of Valentinian I and Valentinian II. The latter was slain by the barbarian Arbogastus, and in his place was chosen (392) Eugene,[12] a Christian general but weak, who was induced to take the pagans under his special protection. Theodosius instigated a political and religious revolt against him; his standard was the labarum, while Eugene gave his army the insignia of Hercules and entrusted to Jove the safe transit of his soldiers over the treacherous passages of the Alps. The decisive battle was fought in 394 at Aquileia; Theodosius emerged victorious and thus remained the sole ruler of the Roman world. His victory marked the definite triumph of Christianity. Historians generally fix the date of this occurrence as September 6, 394. It could not have happened much later, because Theodosius, who died in January, 395, still had time to go to Rome and complete a number of other tasks. Equally, it could not have been much earlier, because his victory was not yet known at Rome by the middle of September of the year in which it occurred. In fact, an inscription of this period has been found in the cemetery of Priscilla, which speaks of the consulate of Nicomachus Flavianus. We know from other sources that Nicomachus Flavianus was expelled, and thus ceased to be the legitimate consul, after the victory of Theodosius. The honorary tablet which had been dedicated to him in the Forum of Trajan was removed after his expulsion.[13]

Nicomachus Flavianus is known for his pagan fanaticism. In 1867, Delisle discovered a satirical poem in the National Library in Paris, which, like the *Contra Symmachum* of Prudentius, is a violent invective against pagan worship and its last sponsors and propagators. From this document, replete with allusions to contemporary facts, we know that Flavianus, after having made himself the leader of the party favoring Eugene, attempted a solemn restoration of pagan worship. The anonymous poet traces an odious picture of this consul: he represents him with all his vices and superstitions, reproves him for having pinned his hopes and his salvation on Jupiter Latinus, and declares that there is nothing more this deity can do for paganism. The author of the poem is evidently a contemporary, because he speaks of recent facts, of the construction of the temple of Flora (395), and of the widowhood of the wife of Flavianus, to whom he gives this advice:

"Desine, iam quaeso, talem deflere maritum,
De Iove qui Latio voluit sperare salutem."[14]

After the victory of Theodosius, Christianity became the official religion of the Empire. Up to this point, even when it had been legitimate and protected, the cult of paganism had continued to be its rival; this cult was now prohibited, and it was declared unlawful even for individuals to continue its support through financial aid. Idolatry was still able to hold out for some time, especially in Rome; but in the fifth century it no longer existed in the cities. Its persistence in the country districts and outlying towns is indicated by the fact that paganism derives its name from *pagus,* a country district, and *pagani,* country people.

Some have claimed that, immediately after the battle of Aquileia, the Christians destroyed the pagan monuments, and that their fanaticism was responsible for the destruction of the records of antiquity. This calumny does not stand up under the scrutiny of impartial criticism. The Christian emperors of the fourth century, even the most fervent, always had great respect for these monuments.[15] We know from Symmachus[16] that Constans, after coming to Rome, had admired the temples of the gods and left the pagan edifices intact: "Cum alias religiones sequeretur, has servavit Imperio." The Theodosian Code, produced about the middle of the fifth century, recommends their preservation as artistic and historical monuments. Zosimus[17] narrates that Serena, the wife of Stilicho, while visiting the temple of Cybele on the Palatine, took a string of precious stones and gold from the statue of that pagan divinity — an incident which shows beyond doubt that the temple was still standing. Numerous statues disappeared, but these were hidden by the pagans themselves. Under Sixtus IV a statue of Hercules, buried in this manner, was unearthed in the Boarian Forum, and stands in the Capitoline Museum. In the same way can be explained the finding of the celebrated Hercules of Mastai, which was dug up near the ruins of the theatre of Pompey.

If any outbursts of violence occurred, these must be ascribed solely to popular anger. A rough design in the cemetery of Pamphilus, on the Old Salarian Way, represents some persons lifting their hands toward a statue, and one of these individuals is shown pulling the statue down with a cord. But these particular acts cannot be said to be based upon any legal measures. On the contrary, numerous inscriptions made by the magistrates, and especially by the prefects of Rome, speak of the restoration of the temples, of statues replaced in their original positions following any accident, earthquakes, etc. All museums have inscriptions of this character.[18] Moreover, when the time came that certain pagan edifices were consecrated for Christian worship, great care was taken to preserve the ornaments which did not directly offend against the beliefs of Christians. Thus, the basilica of Junius Bassus on the Esquiline, dedicated first to St. Andrew and later to St. Anthony, still bore traces of the original decorations in the sixteenth century.[19]

In conclusion, Christianity in triumphing did not destroy but merely transformed and absorbed pagan civilization. The destruction of many of these monuments of pagan antiquity belongs to a much later period, namely to the Middle Ages and the Renaissance.[20]

# Part Three

## PRELIMINARY IDEAS ON THE ANCIENT CHRISTIAN CEMETERIES

### WITH SPECIAL REFERENCE TO THE CHRISTIAN CEMETERIES OF ROME

### INTRODUCTORY REMARKS

FROM the very inception of Christianity, the Christians desired to have places of burial for their own exclusive use. These places were the cemeteries. The Christians never adopted the custom of cremation; hence niches for the reception of funeral urns are always pagan.

The word *cemetery* ( ϰοιμητήριον, meaning dormitory) evidently takes its origin from a belief in the dogma of the Resurrection. Christians looked upon death, especially the death of the just, as a sleep or repose. They took this term from the Jews, just as they adopted the term ἐν εἰρήνῃ, "in peace," from them. Generally the name "cemetery" was applied to a group of tombs; only rarely was it given to an isolated tomb.

In our days the subterranean Christian cemeteries are for the most part indicated by the name of *catacombs,* even in archeological writings. This term originally meant only a particular place, especially a small place, as for example, the subterranean chamber close to St. Sebastian's, "locus ad catacumbas," "in loco qui dicitur ad catacumbas." Later this term was extended so as to include other Christian cemeteries.

*Catacomb* is taken from the Greek word ϰύμϐος, meaning a place which is concave and deep: such was the locality near St. Sebastian's, as recent excavations have demonstrated.

73

There are many who still imagine that the subterranean cemeteries were dug as places for coming together, for refuge or for habitual abode; but this is a grave error. The first Christians came together within the city limits, in the churches in the homes of private individuals, while the cemeteries served only as burial grounds, or as places for the celebration of liturgical functions on the anniversaries of the deceased — especially of the martyrs. If at times they were used as places of refuge by the Christians, this was only by way of exception and for a short time.

In Rome, for example, numerous churches have subterranean galleries, erroneously called catacombs. Properly speaking, there were no catacombs in the city itself, because the law of the Twelve Tables did not permit burial of this kind. The tombs found within the walls of Servius Tullius are archaic; those between the walls of Servius Tullius and Aurelian are even older. The true catacombs were all excavated outside the walls of Aurelian, and almost all of them are to be found between the first and third milestones. Their extension is remarkable, but it would be entirely fantastic to suppose that they reach to Ostia, Albano, Tivoli, etc., and that they were all connected by roads or tunnels, which some even imagine passed under the Tiber.

PAGAN COLUMBARIUM.

In reality, they were originally independent, even when they were built close to each other, like the cemetery of Callistus and that of St. Sebastian. Generally, the ancient galleries did not cross the consular highways; those that were dug under these roads belong almost entirely to the period of peace. Moreover, it should be noted that not all the tombs of the Roman Campagna are Christian cemeteries, any more than all Christian cemeteries are underground.

The early inhabitants of Latium were accustomed to cremate their dead; very ancient examples of crematory tombs were found recently in the archaic necropolis of the Roman Forum. The laws of the Twelve Tables take note of both methods of burial, cremation and interment; but the custom of cremation prevailed except in certain families, as for instance, the Scipios. During the period of the Antonines the swing was again back to interment; that is why sarcophagi are not earlier than this epoch. This change in custom may be attributed partly to the influence of Christianity or to the Oriental religions, such as the cults of Isis, Mithras, etc.

Along the consular highways pagan subterranean burial vaults are to be found which greatly resemble the Christian cemeteries, even to the possession of *loculi*. This explains why a cemetery of the worshippers of Jupiter Sabatius on the Appian Way was mistaken for a Christian cemetery. Even the ancient Jewish cemeteries, found along the Appian, Portuan and Nomentan Ways, resemble Christian cemeteries.

On the other hand, from the very beginning there were Christian cemeteries built above ground. There are many

examples of broken columns which must have been used in such open-air cemeteries, as for example that of the ἰχθὺς ζώντων found on the Vatican and preserved in the National Museum. The celebrated inscription of Abercius of Hieropolis was also used in such a cemetery. Thus we see how the Christians were able to secure the legal existence of their tombs even during times of persecution.

However, the major part of the ancient cemeteries of the Christians were subterranean. For one thing, the Christians wished to imitate the tombs of Palestine in general and that of the Redeemer in particular; although, as has been noted, the Oriental tombs were permanently closed,[2] while Christians, continually betaking themselves to the tombs of their dead to pray, had access to all their burying grounds. Moreover, the Christians preferred to build their tombs underground for reasons of prudence. While the inscriptions in the open are more or less veiled, we find those underground written very clearly and freely, as "Vivas in Christo" and others like it.

Did the Christians habitually use the sand-pits for burial? This opinion, held by almost everyone, even in our own day, is based largely upon the records which state that the martyrs were deposited "in arenario." Marchi deserves the credit for being the first to contradict this idea.[3] In the Roman Campagna, three varieties of tuff (tuffa) are to be found: a lithoid tuff which is a true building stone, used for many of the ancient pagan edifices of Rome and still employed in construction work; pozzalana, also called friable tuff, which forms an excellent cement for hydraulic purposes; and a granular tuff which is of no practical value. Hence we know that if the immense galleries found in the latter had been made for any other purpose than that of burial, their construction would have involved an enormous waste of labor and time. Moreover, actual ancient excavation pits have a form entirely different from that of the cemeteries; the galleries of the pits are short and wide, with inclined walls, while those of the cemeteries are long, narrow and cut vertically. Monuments have been found which confirm this conclusion, as that of Diogenes, of the cemetery of Domitilla. There was a great distinction between sand-pits and cemeteries. A number of paintings show excavators intent on preparing a place for burial in the tuff. The texts which mention "arenarium" or "crypta arenaria" do not present any great difficulty. The cemeteries bear a certain resemblance to the sand-pits; often they communicated with the sand-pits, which facilitated the extraction of earth and even permitted the persecuted

Christians to enter the cemeteries more easily. In fine, to give a definite meaning to the word, it is necessary to note that if *arenarium* denotes a sand-pit, *crypta arenaria* has rather the meaning of cemetery.

Therefore, only by way of exception did the Christians, as occasionally in certain regions of subterranean Rome, utilize the galleries of the sand-pits for burial purposes.

This third section of our volume will treat of the origin, the legality and the Christian character of the cemeteries. It will also deal with the tombs of the martyrs and those of a historical nature. It will mention the funeral rites and customs, the general form of the cemeteries, and finally, those cemeteries and monuments situated above ground.

## Chapter I

## ORIGIN AND LEGALITY OF THE CHRISTIAN CEMETERIES[1]

### 1. Foundation and History from Their Beginning to the Time of Their Abandonment

THE CHRISTIANS always showed great respect for their dead and the tombs containing their remains. In the Acts of the Apostles, it is said that the faithful took care of the body of St. Stephen: "curaverunt Stephanum."[2] The epistle of the Church of Smyrna relating to the martyrdom of St. Polycarp records the celebration of sacred rites at his tomb.[3] From this sentiment arose a vivid feeling of horror at the thought of the superstitious rites of pagan burial, and of the custom of cremation, which appeared to the Christians to be an outrage upon the body and to betoken a lack of faith in its final resurrection. It was for this reason that they built their own cemeteries. Like the Jews, the Christians had taken this custom from the Egyptians, who customarily buried their dead in subterranean vaults. Thus through the Christians this usage passed from the Orient to Rome. The Roman Campagna, with its flat, undulating terrain and the peculiar nature of its subsoil, lent itself admirably to such excavations.

In giving an outline of the history of the cemeteries, it is important to distinguish different periods. The cemeteries were originally tombs of families, privately owned and controlled. The Roman law declared the tomb a *locus sacer* (sacred place), and a *locus religiosus* (religious place), and as such it fell under the jurisdiction of the pontiffs, who alone possessed the right to permit the moving of bodies or the carrying out of any important modifications in connection with the graves. The tomb was considered sacred property and therefore inviolable. As such it did not fall under the laws governing succession or inheritance as other goods. "Hoc monumentum haeredem non sequitur" (H. M. H. N. S.), may often be read on the sepulchral monuments; again, such expressions are encountered as: "Hoc monumento dolus malus abesto," or "Hoc monumento dolus malus et jurisconsultus abesto." The tomb was destined for the use of the family only or any of its clients: "Sibi suisque, libertis libertabusque posterisque eorum." Its external area was marked off by means of broken columns or broken walls, and was called "area maceria clausa"; its limits were often indicated on the inscribed slabs: "in fronte pedes N., in agro pedes N." At times these may have been very extensive, and this would be noted on the inscriptions by indicating that it included a garden, a well, houses, which would then constitute a funerary dominion, with accommodations for giving banquets on the occasion of anniversaries. Similar information has been supplied to us by the testaments or wills of persons in which it would be stated that the owners of the tombs had ordained that certain ceremonies were to be carried out to perpetuate their memory. An ancient will, in the possession of the library of Basle, gives a list of the movable goods which were to adorn the rooms of the tombs.

This legislation and these burial customs favored the destined development of the Christian cemeteries, as it were, into places for liturgical reunions. In fact, during the first and second centuries, numerous cemeteries of this kind were established; they were, however, private cemeteries to which their rich proprietors admitted the bodies of those of the faith who were poorer. It may be believed that, from the beginning, cemeteries were built in connection with those places which served for reunions, as in the certain case of cemeteries of the fourth century when they were definitely established as titles.

It is not a difficult task to distinguish what still remains of the cemeteries dating from the first period. In Rome the oldest was the cemetery of Priscilla on the Salarian Way, which had its origin during the apostolic age. Numerous inscriptions in red attest to the fact that it is one of great antiquity. One of its primitive centers (nuclei) was the subterranean vault of the family of Manius Acilius Glabrio, who died in 94 or 95 of our era; this contains inscriptions in Greek and Latin of many of his descendants.

The crypts of Lucina, on the Appian Way, are situated under a monument which appears to be pagan. De Rossi supposed that the owners of the *area* must have been still pagans when they built this monument, and that, after their conversion to Christianity, the subterranean cemetery was established.

In the cemetery of Praetextatus, near the same road, it is equally easy to distinguish a nucleus of the earliest period in the *Spelunca magna,* the Great Cave, renowned for being the place where, among others, was buried the eldest of the sons of St. Felicitas (second century).

A third private cemetery stood on the Ardeatine Way and was originally the tomb of the family of Flavius Clemens, cousin of Domitian and of the two Flaviae Domitillae. The name of the Flavii has been rediscovered in numerous inscriptions of this cemetery.

During the third century, when the number of Christians had become very great, it was found necessary to have common cemeteries. The Church then made use of the privileges conferred by the law concerning associations. This second period, extending from the third century to the year 313, will be treated

in a special chapter later on. During this period, the cemeteries
were enlarged; often it may be noticed, even today, which part
formed the primitive nucleus, and which were the later additions, as de Rossi has shown in the case of the cemetery of
Callistus. Many of the cemeteries ceased to carry the names of
the original proprietors, taking instead the name of a pope who
had carried on some improvement, or of a martyr who came to
be venerated there. The private cemeteries, however, continued

THE *SPELUNCA MAGNA.*

to exist as before, even during the persecutions of Valerian and
Diocletian, when the common cemeteries were confiscated.

In the third period, extending from the reign of Constantine to Alaric (313-410), the immense subterranean necropolis

became still more extensive. Also, it began to be looked upon as a sanctuary. This occurred especially through the noble efforts of Pope Damasus, who sought to find and adorn the tombs of the martyrs. The Edict of Milan (313) proclaimed the legal existence of the Church as a society with the right to possess property, and with this recognition, open-air cemeteries could be freely built. Up to the time of the fifth century, nevertheless, some galleries continued to be excavated; these can be recognized by their paintings and inscriptions, and by the isolated monogram, which is generally encountered for the first time in periods of peace.

The most important period of work in the cemeteries of the Christians of Rome occurred during the pontificate of Damasus (366-384). Damasus embellished the crypts of the martyrs and composed numerous metrical inscriptions in their honor, the principal examples of which will be indicated in the chapter to be devoted to these cemeteries.

The Christians earnestly desired to be laid to rest beside the martyrs,[4] and these privileged places were difficult to obtain, "quod multi cupiunt et rari accipiunt." Very often small chapels were hollowed out near or behind the tombs of the martyrs: *retro sanctos*. To satisfy this devotion, even the paintings of a previous epoch were not spared. During this period, the gravediggers acquired great power; they disposed of the locations under the authority of the Church. A number of inscriptions are records of true contracts of sale, with the name of the excavator and the price of the tomb indicated: "Emit a fossore N., et solvit pretium," and so forth. Often the names of the witnesses to the sale are given: "Emptum locum a fossore N. praesentia fossoris N." It can also be shown that the price of a plot varied with the position or location of the tomb.

Basilicas came to be built over the cemeteries in Rome. These communicated with the subterranean tombs by means of lighted stairways. Toward the beginning of the fifth century, underground tombs became rare; in fact, there are instances found of galleries which were abandoned when only half completed. This change is in keeping with the definite triumph of

Christianity in 394, after the publication of the laws of
Theodosius.

The fourth period extends from the beginning of the fifth
century to the time when these underground cemeteries were
abandoned. De Rossi supposes that the consular inscriptions
of the subterranean cemeteries do not go beyond the year of
the capture of Rome by Alaric in 410, and that the burial monu-

*ARCOSOLIUM* IN THE CEMETERY OF CALLISTUS.

ments may, with few exceptions, be considered to antedate the
fifth century. This norm, which must be taken in a broad sense,
is important in correcting chronological errors regarding inscriptions and Christian paintings, particularly those dealing with
dogmatic topics, which some Protestant writers ascribe to the

late Middle Ages. It is indeed true that there are cemeteries having paintings dating later than the fifth century, but these are easily distinguished from those which are undeniably of the same period as the tombs. The symbolical paintings or those of a dogmatic nature are exclusively sepulchral, and therefore cannot but be of the first four centuries; the more recent paintings do not generally adorn any but the tombs of the martyrs, and are for that reason mainly decorative in character. Nevertheless it is important to bear in mind that, even during the sixth century some underground burials were made and adorned with paintings, though this occurred only in historical places held in veneration.[5]

If the cemeteries ceased to be ordinary places of burial in the fifth century, they continued to be places of devotion. The pious visitors have left in many places the record of their passage — their names, and perhaps an invocation or a prayer scratched into the mortar. These writings, called *graffiti* (*graffito*), are to be found in all the cemeteries, often furnishing the investigator with priceless bits of information. One finds such expressions as this: EIC MNEIAN EXETE, "In mente habete," etc. One of them, found in the cemetery of Priscilla, proved to be of great value, for it contains the date 375, and speaks of the Holy Sacrifice of the Mass having been offered on the tomb.

///I IDVS FEBR
///CONSS GRATIANI III ET EQVITI
///FLORENTINVS FORTVNATVS ET *Fe*
LIX AD CALICE BENIMVS

Many of these graffiti contain the names of the martyrs venerated in the individual cemeteries.

At the entrance of the chapel of the popes at St. Callistus', many graffiti can be seen traced in the walls; numbers may also be found in the crypt of Sts. Peter and Marcellinus and in that of the cemetery of Commodilla. Inscriptions of this kind cannot be confused in any way with the great inscriptions found in the cemeteries nor with those traced in the fresh mortar of the *loculi*.[6]

During the sixth century, at the time of the siege of the
Goths (537-538), the cemeteries were greatly damaged; they
were later restored under Pope Vigilius.

In 553 the army of Narses overcame the Goths in the
decisive battle of Vesuvius, and the whole of Italy fell under
the Byzantine domination. But in 568 the Lombards established
themselves in the north of Italy and began to make incursions
and commit depredations which at times took them to the very
gates of Rome, and resulted in great damage to the Christian
monuments. Pope Pelagius makes allusion to these troubled
times in his inscription composed for the basilica of St. Lawrence, which had been newly restored: "Gladios hostiles inter
et iras. . . ."

The marauding expeditions of the Lombards continued
under Gregory the Great, successor of Pope Pelagius. The
homilies of this pope give us a vivid description of these difficult times: "Ubique mors, ubique luctus, ubique desolatio, undique percutimur, undique amaritudinibus replemur."[7] But he
finally succeeded in obtaining their conversion during the reign
of Theodolinda and Agilulf. The priest John, sent by Theodolinda to Rome to ask for relics, carried back to her vials of
holy oils, and an Itinerary, which are still preserved at Monza.
Along with these, he also gave the queen mementoes of the
Holy Sepulchre, which she had requested. On these vials there
is a representation of the cross; but the Saviour, instead of having His hands and feet nailed, is shown with extended arms as
an *Orans* (a person in the act of prayer).

St. Gregory the Great has justly been called "ultimus
Romanorum," the last of the Romans.[8] The following century
was an epoch of ignorance and decadence. Roman art disappeared; the few monuments left from the seventh century
clearly show Byzantine influence. The sarcophagi and the inscriptions are very coarse. There are no consular dates, because
Justinian had abolished the consuls; at the beginning of 541,
mention is made — and it is repeated seventeen times — of the
*post consulatum* of Basilius, the last private person invested
with this dignity. In the seventh century, local dates begin to

appear, along with the names of the popes or the barbarian kings.

About the year 635, Pope Honorius I caused to be made the beautiful mosaic of St. Agnes. During his pontificate the translation of the martyrs began, though it was rare. He himself took numerous bodies from their original resting places, but only to place them in a superior location: this is perhaps what he did at St. Callistus' with respect to the bodies of St. Tarcisius and St. Zephyrin. From this period on, the Itineraries distinguish the martyrs *deorsum* from those reposing *in basilica sursum*. The sarcophagus of St. Pancratius underwent some change, its position being altered so as to bring it in alignment with the apse: "Corpus martyris quod ex obliquo aulae jacebat, altari insignibus ornato metallis loco proprio collocavit."[9] At this time the body of St. Valentine was also moved "in basilica magna quam Honorius reparavit."[10]

The seventh century is an epoch of great pilgrimages and the redaction of Itineraries. The author of one of these important documents, the *Notitia ecclesiarum urbis Romae,* certainly visited Rome during the pontificate of Honorius.[11]

Some years after the schism of the Monothelites, a persecution arose against the Catholics. The heretics, supported by the government of Byzantium, forced Pope Martin I into exile; he later died a martyr's death. The Emperor Constans II came to Rome and sacked it in 663, taking with him to Sicily, where he had his court, the gold and silver of the churches and other edifices, and the dome and gold-plated bronze ornaments of the Pantheon and the temple of Jupiter Capitolinus.

Under the pontificate of Sergius I (687-701), a great concourse of pilgrims came to Rome; numerous persons of importance, even sovereigns, visited the Eternal City. Caedwalla, king of the Saxons, already converted to Christianity, came to be baptized; he died a short time later and was buried in the atrium of the Vatican basilica; Bede has preserved the text of the inscription placed on his tomb.[12]

The Papacy already exercised great influence in the West, and numerous barbarian princes and rulers paid homage to the

Roman pontiff for their countries. But the city of Rome itself was in a miserable state. The *Liber pontificalis* and other documents attest to the fact that the population of the city had diminished considerably.

Having once become the rulers of Rome, the popes gave a new impulse to the city. They built churches, monasteries, etc., and the population began to increase. To consecrate the churches, it was decided to remove the relics of the martyrs, so that the faithful might more conveniently venerate them. It is known with certainty that, during the fifth, sixth and seventh centuries, the remains of the martyrs had not been disturbed in their subterranean cemeteries, and that there was only one tomb of Sts. John and Paul within the city proper: "In urbe Roma beatorum martyrum corpora Ioannis et Pauli tantum quiescunt," the Itineraries tell us;[13] and St. Leo I, or the author of the liturgy attributed to him, has these words: "Ut non solum passionibus martyrum gloriosis urbis istius ambitum coronares, sed etiam in ipsis visceribus civitatis sancti Ioannis et Pauli victricia membra reconderes."[14] It is true that we have a record of a translation made to the Pantheon under Boniface IV; but in reality this does not deal with a translation of bodies, but only of sacred mementoes, *memoriae, patrocinia sanctorum, pignora, sanctuaria,* all of which had touched the relics or the tombs of the saints.[15] It may be held that, with respect to such a translation, there is some mistake and its occurrence should be referred to a later period.

The first known translations were those of the bodies of Sts. Primus and Felician, from the suburban cemetery of Nomentum, about the year 648, and of St. Beatrice and St. Faustinus from the cemetery *ad sextum Philippi,* in the year 682. Pope Paul I, in 757, transported a large number of relics, among which was the body of St. Tarcisius, to consecrate the churches built by him, especially the basilica of St. Sylvester *in Capite* constructed on property belonging to his family. In the vestibule of this church is still to be seen the *Notitia nataliciorum sanctorum Martyrum;* it is a catalogue, redacted in a previous period, of the principal martyrs of whom this church possessed relics and who were honored in an especial manner there.

The most illustrious pope of the eighth century was Adrian I, who did not wish to take the bodies of the martyrs from the catacombs, and therefore made a last effort to preserve the cemeteries. He restored them to something of their pristine beauty, and sought to keep alive the custom of repairing to them to celebrate the anniversaries of the martyrs. The list of his works to the end of his life has been preserved for us in the *Book of the Popes*. The work of Adrian was continued by his successor, Leo III, but it was of no avail. The Roman people had already lost the habit of frequenting the subterranean cemeteries.

For this reason, Paschal I, about the year 817, felt himself constrained to resume the practice, begun by Paul I, of removing the bodies of the martyrs from their original resting places in the catacombs.

Even the most important chapels were almost entirely in ruins. The Roman Campagna had become a desert, unhealthy, uninhabitable, in spite of all the attempts of Popes Zacharias, Adrian I and Leo III to save both the culture and the habitations of the region by founding the *domus cultae*.[16] It became evident that it was impossible to allow the relics to remain in uninhabited places. They belonged, properly, in churches; and moreover, the abuse of selling relics had begun to make its appearance. History has preserved the names of several of those who engaged in this unholy traffic. One of the most noted was the deacon Deusdona, who seems to have had the cemetery of Sts. Peter and Marcellinus under his administration and who profited by selling in Germany the bodies of the martyrs of this cemetery. Such commercial transactions in relics were carried on especially in the countries beyond the Alps; in all the French towns there was manifest a great desire to possess relics of the Roman saints, especially of St. Sebastian, St. Alexander, St. Agnes, St. Cecilia, St. Cornelius, St. Peter, St. Paul, St. Tarcisius, etc.[17]

Pope Paschal decided to move into the city the bodies of the popes deposited in the cemetery of Callistus. He failed at first to find the body of St. Cecilia, and thereupon believed it had been stolen by the Lombards. However, the saint herself subsequently revealed to him where to search for her sepulchre, and he found it exactly on the spot the vision had indicated.[18] The church of St. Praxedes received the relics of many martyrs, whose names are engraved on marble tablets; and the confessional then constructed as a remembrance, and placed in the galleries of the catacombs, has served as a model for the confessionals of other churches. This great translation occurred on July 20 in the year 817.[19]

Later, Leo IV explored the cemetery of Priscilla, where he found the bodies of Aquila and Prisca and probably those of Pudens, Praxedes and Pudentiana also. By the second half of the ninth century, the Roman catacombs had been despoiled of all their riches. They were not, however, entirely abandoned; they were still frequented, Mass was celebrated there on occasions, and Pope Nicholas I actually restored many of them.[20] Until the tenth century, probably, religious functions were still held in the catacombs under the supervision of the patriarch of the Lateran.

The only cemeteries which remained in veneration were those of St. Sebastian, St. Lawrence, St. Pancratius and St. Valentine; the others were abandoned and forgotten so completely that not even their entrances remained a matter of knowledge. Those of St. Peter and St. Paul had been absorbed by the basilicas. Close to the four aforementioned cemeteries there were monasteries, whose religious had come to act as guardians of these sanctuaries.

It did not take long for great confusion concerning the ancient cemeteries to arise. The popular imagination ascribed to St. Sebastian every record of the cemeteries on the Appian Way and the Ardeatine Way; to St. Lawrence, all those of the cemeteries along the Tiburtine Way; to St. Pancratius all those along the Aurelian Way.

The cemetery of St. Valentine was very much frequented.
A document of the eleventh century, preserved in the chronicle
of St. Michael's *ad Mosam,* tells us of a visit made by a pilgrim
who came to St. Valentine's to request relics. The cemetery was
called "coemeterium ubi semper ardent lampades."[21]

## 2.  The Corporative Property of the Christian Churches[22]

Having given an exposition of the history of the cemeteries
to the time of their abandonment, we will develop in more
detail one point of special importance. It concerns the property
of the Church in the centuries of persecution.

By the beginning of the third century, the cemeteries were
already quite extensive. With the increase in the number of
Christians, it was natural that the galleries of the cemeteries
should also develop.

It is certain that during the third century, certain cemeteries
were no longer in the possession of private individuals, but
were owned by the Church herself. There are proofs of this,
not only in the edict of 313, but also in the fact of the wholesale
confiscations perpetrated under Valerian in 258 and Diocletian
in 303, which were followed by restitutions under Gallienus
and Maxentius.

The Edict of Milan gave to the Christians the churches
which belonged to them, "ad ius corporis eorum pertinentia."[23]

The edict of the Emperor Maximinus Daza, published in
the same year (313) and recorded by Eusebius,[24] gives analogous orders to the governors of the provinces. Even during the
periods of persecution, Gallienus had made a similar restitu-
tion; Eusebius[25] places this in 259, or immediately after the
persecution of Valerian (258). The *Book of the Popes* bears
witness to the same fact in the biography of Pope Dionysius:
"Hic presbyteris ecclesias divisit, et coemeteria, et parochias,
dioeceses restituit." Gallienus, continues Eusebius, wrote to
numerous bishops giving them permission to repossess their
cemeteries: τὰ τῶν καλουμένον κοιμητηρίων χωρία. Aurelian com-
pelled Paul of Samosata to restore to the legitimate bishop of

Antioch all the goods which he had usurped. In fact, he understood the property rights of the Christians so well, that in a discourse addressed to the senators, reported by Vopiscus, he reproves them for not having consulted the Sibylline Books, "quasi in Christianorum ecclesia, non in templo deorum omnium tractaretis."[26] Exactly the same is read in the life of Alexander Severus, written by Lampridius: "Dicebatque grave esse, cum id [the publication of the names] Christiani et Iudaei facerent in praedicandis sacerdotibus qui ordinandi sunt: non fieri in provinciarum rectoribus, quibus fortunae hominum committerentur."[27] Finally, we know from the *Philosophumena* that Pope Zephyrinus, at the beginning of the third century, placed his deacon Callistus over the administration of the cemetery on the Appian Way: Εἰς τὸ κοιμητήριον κατέστησεν.

With what right could the Church possess property in her own name? It is not true to say that she possessed it as a religious society, because Christianity was always looked upon and treated as a *religio illicita,* an illegal religion. There have been two hypotheses to explain the facts,[28] one of them proposed by de Rossi, the other by Duchesne.

According to de Rossi, the Church possessed property as a funerary association, and as such was well known and generally recognized.

From the times of the Republic, there had existed in Rome funerary societies, composed especially of artisans of the various trades or guilds, such as metal workers, carpenters, cooks, etc., whose aim it was to prepare for themselves a common tomb. Such an organization was, generally speaking, a mutual aid society, as is borne out by the numerous inscriptions which attest to the existence of these funerary societies and indicate their possession of property.[29]

Until the end of the second century, these funerary organizations were permitted to exist only within the city; in the outlying districts they might have served as a pretext for political societies. Septimius Severus permitted them, under certain conditions, to organize in all the towns of the Empire, as we can see from the Digest.[30] From this point, the organizations spread everywhere. They bore distinct names, such as that of their founder or of a patron divinity — for instance, "Collegium quod est in domo Sergiae Paulinae"; "Collegium eorum qui una epula vesci solent."[31] Many of these associations were organized to take care of the poor who were unable to provide a family tomb, but who were bound to contribute a monthly payment — "Permittitur tenuioribus stipem menstruam conferre," as we read in the Digest itself.

All these dispositions accord perfectly with what we know of the customs of the Christians of the third century. This provision of the Digest can be made to agree with what Tertullian has to say: "Modicam unusquisque stipem menstruam die vel cum velit et si modo velit et si modo possit, apponit."[32] From the time when the Church first appears to possess property until the time of the publication of the edict of Septimius Severus, there is a complete record. From an inscription of Lanuvium (Civita-Lavinia), placed in the sepulchral room of the society of Aesculapius in the second century, we can easily understand how the constitution of such organizations could have concealed the funeral rites of the Christians.[33] After having indicated the date (136) and the place of reunion which was the headquarters of the association, this inscription begins by giving in its preamble, the Roman law permitting such societies: "Qui stipem menstruam conferre volent . . . in collegium coëant unde defuncti sepeliantur"; then it quotes the *lex collegii,* fixing the amount each is to be taxed or the quota allotted to each member: "HS C N(ummum et) V(ini) boni amphoram; item in menses sing(ulos) a(sses) V "; it continues by specifying the penal clauses: "Item placuit ut quisquis mensib. contin(uis) . . . non pariaverit, et ei humanitus acciderit, eius ratio funeris non habebitur"; the same constitution, however, assures to members in good standing the anniversary rites; it determines the "ordo coenarum: VIII id. mar. natali Caesenni . . . patris. V kal. dec. nat. Ant (inoi). Idib. aug. natali Dianae et collegii"; it even contains a note of a banquet: "Vini boni amphoras singulas, et panes as(sium) qui numerus collegi fuerit, et sar-

das (nu)mero quattuor, strationem caldam cum ministerio";
it confers privileges on those who had been invested with various duties in the organization and punishes those who,have
disturbed the order indicated.[34]

In the same manner, the Christians had their rendezvous
and their agapes,[35] which formed an integral part of their
liturgical functions.

De Rossi also strengthens his hypothesis by quoting an
inscription discovered in Algiers, close to the city of Cherchel,
the ancient Caesarea of Mauritania, at present preserved in the
Museum of Algiers.[36] This inscription runs as follows:

AREAM AT SEPVLCRA CVLTOR VERBI CONTVLIT
ET CELLAM STRVXIT SVIS CVNCTIS SVMPTIBVS
ECLESIAE SANCTAE HANC RELIQVIT MEMORIAM
SALVETE FRATRES PVRO CORDE ET SIMPLICI
EVELPIVS VOS SATOS SANCTO SPIRITV

ECLESIA FRATRVM HVNC RESTITVIT TITVLVM. M. A. I. SEVERIANI C. V
EX ING. ASTERI.

A Christian, Evelpius, "cultor Verbi," founded a place of
burial, "aream ad sepulcra," and constructed a "cella" on this
funerary dominion. The property was later left to the Church,
and when the inscription was destroyed, the community restored
it. The "Ecclesia fratrum" might have been the name of the
Christian society of Africa; on the other hand, it might have
been called the "Collegium Cultorum Verbi."[37]

Finally, the Philocalian catalogue seems to indicate that the
names of the popes, who were the heads of the community of
Christians, were officially known to the Roman authorities.
This catalogue, which mentions the depositions of the popes
from the year 254 to 354, and the two tables containing a list
of the burials of the bishops and martyrs which is found an-
nexed to the document itself, appear to have had the same
origin as the parallel list of the prefects of Rome; they must
have been extracted under Liberius from the archives of the
city. We know that the funerary societies, in order to be legally
recognized, must have furnished the name of their supervisor,
who in all Christian communities was naturally the bishop. It

was this title that Pope Zephyrin gave to his deacon Callistus when he officially proposed him for the administrator of the cemetery along the Appian Way, as the *Philosophumena* plainly tells us. Hence, de Rossi concludes that the archives had a list of the names of the bishops of Rome as heads of the "Ecclesia fratrum," or presidents of the funerary organizations of the Christian community.

For a more general argument, it is difficult to suppose that the Church was recognized throughout the entire Empire as a unique society. It is easier to believe that the Christian community formed a particular society, or perhaps even several societies, without the authorities' knowing anything at all about the bonds that united each of them to the others. At any rate, this new method of possessing property did not interfere with the existence of private cemeteries to which, during times of persecution, the bodies of some of the martyrs could be transferred for concealment, as happened, for example, when the bodies of the Apostles Peter and Paul were moved to the Appian Way.

This is the solution proposed by John Baptist de Rossi and adopted by the greater number of historians and archeologists.

Duchesne, however, does not find it sufficiently proved from the facts at hand;[38] in fact, it seems to him to be quite unlikely. To him, the collective property of the Christian cemeteries is rather connected with the tolerance which the Christian enjoyed during the reign of Commodus. Given (what he does not actually concede) that the registers of the prefects may have been consulted to fill in the data concerning the consuls at the time of the depositions of the popes, it would follow that the prefecture would have known of the existence of the Christian society and its heads; however, it does not follow that it would be recognized as an authorized funerary association, "because it would have been necessary for the churches to accept a *legal fiction* in order to receive official transformation into funerary associations. Moreover, it would have involved: (1) that the churches themselves were agreeable, a fact which is neither attested nor easily reconciled with the known horror of both Tertullian[39] and Cyprian[40] for this sort of association; (2) that the police authority had agreed to ignore its existence. This point presents especial difficulty. A funerary organization was a society composed of a small number of persons; a church in a large city like Rome, Alexandria, Antioch or Carthage must have counted, in the third century, thirty, forty or even fifty thousand members. Who can imagine Pope Fabian, St. Cyprian or St. Dionysius of Alexandria going to the prefecture to proclaim himself head of an organization of *Cultores Verbi*, composed of 50,000 persons, associated for the purpose of procuring a convenient burying place? ... It seems more natural to believe that if, after the death of Marcus Aurelius, the Christian communities enjoyed a long period of peace, if they again succeeded in possessing immovable goods, which were evident and considerable, such was the case because they were tolerated or even recognized without any legal fiction, as churches, as religious societies. . . .The records do not give us either any testimony or suspicion of *legal fictions,* funerary associations or anything of the kind."[41]

Over and above these two hypotheses, other explanations might be suggested. The Church might be looked upon as having possessed property under the names of private individuals, who would have been considered the legal owners in the eyes of the civil power. This would somewhat resemble conditions occasionally found in our own day in certain localities where, after the confiscation of their common goods, some religious communities, also not recognized legally, can possess property under the name of a simple private person. If the Church had desired to make use of this means in the third century, the Roman authorities would not have been able to prevent it.

It may be admitted that the civil authority knew that such places or such landed properties belonged to the Christians, but recognized them as belonging to private individuals in order to save its face and preserve the forms of legality.

It is likely that the Christians, according to places, times and circumstances, had recourse to all the expedients which were of avail to protect their belongings and secure their cemeteries. Thus they may have possessed some of these under the aegis of the pagan undertaking guilds, while others were held under the protection of whatever particular association, or under the name of whatever particular intermediate individual, best suited the exigencies of the case. Whatever explanation one adopts to cover the situation, there still remains the incontestable fact of the collective property of the Christian cemeteries.

Toward the middle of the third century, the cemeteries of the Church of Rome were placed under the titles of the city;[42] every cemetery depended on the title nearest to its location, as the inscriptions bearing the names of these titles themselves show very positively.

Thus the cemetery of Domitilla was joined to the title of Fasciola, today known as Sts. Nereus and Achilleus; in fact, its inscriptions mention some members of the clergy "of Fasciola"; the cemeteries of the Nomentan Way were placed under the title of Vestina, now known as St. Vitalis, and those of the Tiburtine Way under the title of Praxedes and St. Clement; those of the Labican Way (Sts. Peter and Marcellinus) were called Dominicum, or of the title of St. Eusebius.

The cemetery of Callistus depended directly on the pope, and an inscription records that his authorization was necessary to complete or undertake any work performed there. The cemetery of Priscilla depended on the *titulus Pastoris* (St. Pudentiana). This may have been the title of the Bishop of Rome; it was probably the seat of the ecclesiastical administration before the foundation of the cemetery of Callistus. The organization of these titles was certainly prior to the period of peace, but it underwent all sorts of modifications in the following periods. After the Edict of Milan, the Church could freely possess its cemeteries and its places of reunion.

## Chapter II

### GENERAL ASPECT OF THE CATACOMBS; FUNERAL RITES[1]

#### 1.  Terms Used in Connection with the Early Christian Cemeteries[2]

THE TERMS adopted to indicate the different parts of the cemeteries are partly traditional and partly conventional.[3]

The cemeteries consist of a network of intersecting galleries.  To each of these galleries it was customary to give the name of *ambulacrum* (corridor), a word used in the technical language of the Romans.  But an inscription of the cemetery of Priscilla, which as yet has not been well studied, gives us to understand that the early Christians used the term *cryptae* when speaking of these galleries.[4]

In the walls of these galleries, the tombs or *loci* are hollowed out.  They are simple cavities of dimensions to receive one, two or even three bodies.  They are built symmetrically and in alignment with the general direction of the galleries.  Ordinarily, several *loci* or niches were placed or built one above the other, the number depending on the height of the wall. The opening of one of these *loci* has the form of a rectangle; a groove dug around the margins of the vaults permitted them to be closed by the insertion of a slab of marble or brick.  The term *locus* is found often in the inscriptions; but the diminutive *loculus* has prevailed in the language of the archeologist. *Loculi* are not only found along the galleries, but even in the burial vaults (*cubicula*) and the stairways.  The highest are usually the oldest, because the level of the excavation was lowered, little by little and with a measured plan in mind, as need dictated.  This was observed as far back as 1864 by Michael Stephen de Rossi in his work entitled *Analisi geologica ed architettonica della Roma sotterranea.*

From the beginning, the form of the Christian cemeteries was different from that of the pagan *columbaria* (so called because they looked very much like dove-cotes), the niches of which contained urns with the ashes of the cremated bodies.

A tomb of more pretentious character than the others and much in use was known, from its form or structure, as the *arcosolium*.[5] Such a tomb consisted of an arched niche in the wall beneath which a grave was dug for one or more bodies, to be closed later by a marble slab laid flat over the opening. The word *arcosolium* is often met with in the inscriptions, for example, in the celebrated epitaph of the deacon Severus in the catacomb of St. Callistus: "Cubiculum duplex cum arcisoliis et luminare" — "a double burial vault with arched tombs and

GEOLOGICAL AND ARCHITECTONIC SECTION
THROUGH A PART OF THE CEMETERY OF CALLISTUS.

an airshaft." The term *arcosolium, arcisolium, arcusolium* is composed of the words *arcus,* that is, the arch formed by the upper part of the tomb, and *solium,* which refers more properly to the huge marble bathing receptacles or bathtubs used by the pagans, which had the form of a square trunk.

NORTH

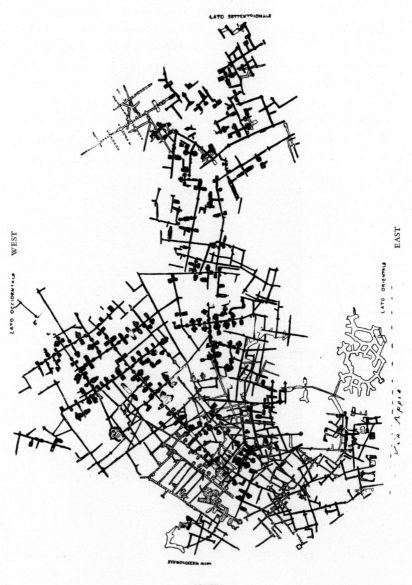

SOUTH

GENERAL LAY-OUT OF THE CEMETERY OF CALLISTUS.

These arched tombs do not go back to any great antiquity. It seems that the early Christians at first made use of large niches in which were placed the sarcophagi, of either marble or terra cotta. The entrance of the cemetery of Domitilla contains a *loculus* decorated with stucco representing a sarcophagus; but this is an exceptional arrangement, just as the tomb which may be seen a short distance from it is an exception to the rule. It is built to represent a room without any doors, but which could be entered by an opening closed by means of a

A BURIAL VAULT (*CUBICULUM*) AND A CORRIDOR (*AMBULACRUM*)
IN THE CEMETERY OF STS. MARCELLINUS AND PETER.

stone. This is without doubt a tomb made in imitation of the tomb of the Redeemer. The adjoining wall of the *arcosolium*

was known as the *parieticulum* ("little wall"), as one may read
in the following inscription published by Marchi:[6]

DOMVS. ETERNALIS. AVR. CELSI. ET. AVR.
ILARITATIS COMPARI. MEES (*sic*)
FECIMVS NOBIS ET NOSTRIS ET
AMICIS ARCOSOLIOS (*sic*)
CVM PARIETICVLO SVO IN PACEM

More ancient than the *arcosolium* is the primitive form of
tomb: a square, boxlike excavation or *solium,* surmounted not
by an arched vault, but by a plain vault. This corresponds to
that form of tomb which de Rossi calls a "table tomb," encountered in Rome in the cemeteries of Callistus, Domitilla
and Priscilla.

CORRIDOR (*AMBULACRUM*) IN THE CEMETERY OF PRISCILLA.

Small rooms called *cubicula* opened off every side of the
galleries. These were the tombs of families such as those whose
inscriptions may still be seen in the cemetery of Domitilla — M.
ANTONIVS . RESTVTVS . FECIT . HIPOGEV . SIBI . ET
SVIS; or in the cemetery of Callistus — BITVS SIBI ET SVIS;
or in a cemetery on the Latin Way — CVBICVLVM CON-
TALI. Or they were tombs set aside for the members of an

association, because even in the cemeteries there have been found traces of funerary associations which grew up in the bosom of the Church. The plural names, *Eutychii, Pelagii,* etc., found in certain inscriptions point to associations of such a nature. The chapels (of a private character, as their restricted size indicates) had doors, as may be seen from the holes in the posts which once supported door hinges.

UNDERGROUND GALLERIES IN THE CEMETERY OF PRISCILLA.

Other chapels, of a more pretentious character, which contained at times the tombs of martyrs, are distinguished by archeologists by the name *cryptae* or crypts. The Acts of the martyrs and the Martyrologies often employ this term, which in the plural indicates a general subterranean excavation, and in the singular a gallery. Some of these chapels were set aside for liturgical purposes or ceremonies and were thus actually underground churches. In the cemetery of Callistus there are numerous examples of such. The so-called chapel of Miltiades really served as a place of reunion, and the remains of a bench which ran around the whole chapel may still be seen; the chapel facing this one must have been reserved for women. In the same manner, in a liturgical crypt of the Greater Cemetery of

St. Agnes, can be recognized the sanctuary, the *presbyterium,* the bishop's throne and the triumphal arch. These subterranean churches of the catacombs have very diverse forms; some of them are square, others are rectangular, others polygonal. A circular one, very important, which de Rossi called the chapel of Soter, is to be found in the region of Callistus. These chapels often contain paintings, architectural decorations, columns, capitals, friezes, architraves, etc.

ARCHED TOMB (*ARCOSOLIUM*)
IN THE CEMETERY OF CALLISTUS.

Even before the peace of the Church there were places of reunion in the cemeteries. We have the testimony of the Acts of the martyrs to this effect; but to this proof we can add the testimony of a beautiful and very ancient inscription of the cemetery of Priscilla in which the faithful are invited to pray in the cemetery: "Vos precor, O fratres, orare huc quando venitis" — "I beseech you, brethren, to pray when you come here."

It is also undeniable that, even in the smaller chapels, the anniversaries of the deceased were religiously kept. Tertullian[7] and the author of a commentary attributed to Origen[8] give us proof of this fact. St. Augustine expressly tells us that the Holy Sacrifice of the Mass was offered near the sepulchre,[9] as was the case at the funeral of his mother: "Cum offerretur sacrificium pretii nostri, jam juxta sepulcrum posito cadavere prius quam deponetur"[10] — "As is offered the Sacrifice of our Redemption close to the sepulchre after the body has been placed in it before its interment." It may be believed that this domestic liturgy of the smaller chapels of the cemeteries may have given rise to the low Mass. In the sanctuaries where reposed the bodies of the martyrs, the liturgy was celebrated with greater solemnity. During the period of peace, the solemn liturgy was reserved for the major basilicas. This solemn celebration was known as the *Missa publica,* while that of lesser solemnity was maintained in the crypts and was called the *Missa ad corpus.*

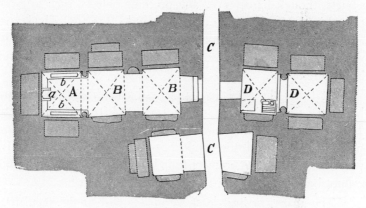

LITURGICAL CRYPT
IN THE GREATER CEMETERY OF ST. AGNES.

## 2.  Funeral Customs

In the study of ancient cemeteries, we still find some vestiges of the funeral rites of the early Christians and a confirmation of what St. Augustine[11] and Prudentius[12] tell us.

The body, enveloped in a sheet, was deposited in a *locus,* in an *arcosolium* or in a sarcophagus. Next, spices and flowers were scattered over the bier. Bosio, Marchi and de Rossi affirm that they could still perceive the odor of the spices when they opened certain sarcophagi. Even the flowers are often depicted on the *arcosolia* or engraved on the stones.

At times, fragments of glass are found at the foot of tombs which generally belong to those cemeteries built after the period of peace. Many of these tombs are inscribed with isolated monograms, or even with the names of the consuls. Very often these fragments were nothing more than portions of the cups used in the agapes (love-feasts), placed in such localities as a sign of honor or as a mark to identify a portion of a sepulchre. It may even be supposed that these vials were also employed to disinfect the galleries and purify the air which had become vitiated by the emanations arising from decomposing bodies.

Again we find, close to the body, various objects: rings, signets, though hardly ever any precious objects, such as were placed in the tombs of the Egyptians and Etruscans. The lamps fixed to the base of the tombs were lighted to mark the anniversaries, or for other reasons. Often traces of smoke may still be distinguished.

At times the Christians practised embalming, in remembrance of the burial of our Redeemer and in conformity with Jewish usage. But they performed this operation in a very imperfect manner, with the result that the bodies were but poorly preserved; the few mummies found in the catacombs certainly cannot be compared with the Egyptian mummies.

The agape, or love-feast, formed a part of the sepulchral rite and was celebrated near the cemetery, but outside the underground precincts. In the cemetery of Domitilla there can be seen a place which had been put to this use. It is an arched room or hall which precedes the main entrance of the tombs of the Flavii; one can still see the supports of a bench cut into the wall and a well close by. The three-apsed room of the cemetery of Callistus, probably destroyed during the persecution of Diocletian, and later transformed into an oratory with important sepulchres, must have been originally set aside for these feasts of the Christians. The funeral banquets were certainly more solemn on the occasion of the anniversaries of the martyrs: "Agapes nostrae pauperes pascunt," says St. Augustine,[13] thereby attesting that this custom still persisted in his day.

Moreover, there were banquets given in homage to the deceased and in honor of the martyrs: it was to these that the name *refrigerium* was applied. Recent excavations carried on close to and under the basilica of St. Sebastian have done much to clarify this point, which was little understood. These will be treated in their proper place.

The removal of the bodies was carried out with a certain solemnity. At Carthage, the body of St. Cyprian was transferred "cum voto et triumpho magno."[14]

After the deposition of a body in a *locus* or tomb, the opening to it was closed by means of bricks or slabs of marble. The inscriptions or epitaphs often contained the date of the deposition, a notice which was very helpful in determining the anniversary celebration: *Depositio*, Κατάθεσις. Then followed the name of the month, often the day of the week, and more rarely, the consular date.

### 3.  The Tombs of the Martyrs

When the body laid to rest in a tomb was that of a martyr, the tomb was always marked with some special sign. How can we now recognize these tombs? The one and only certain sign is the solemn title of *martyr,* as can be seen in the epitaphs of Popes Fabian and Pontian, in that of St. Cornelius in the cemetery of Callistus, and at St. Hermes' concerning the martyr Hyacinth: "Depositus Hyacinthus martyr." This title could also be abbreviated to the letter "M." Thus, in the cemetery of Priscilla, a tomb carries the inscription: VERIC | M | VNDVS. Placed in such a position, the letter M cannot be the initial of the given name; it indicates, most probably, the tomb of a martyr who is entirely unknown.

On the tombs of the known martyrs there have never been found formulas of prayers for the repose of the soul, as for example, "Refrigeret," "Pax tecum," etc., otherwise so frequent on the tombs of the ordinary faithful; for these would have been useless and needless in the case of a martyr. Another absolutely certain sign is furnished by the ampoules or vials,

when these actually contain blood. Prudentius notes the habit
which the early Christians had of recovering the blood of the

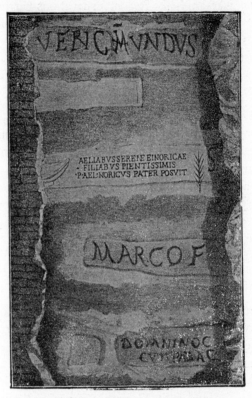

WALL WITH INTACT SEPULCHRES
IN THE CEMETERY OF PRISCILLA.

martyrs, "spongia pressa rapit"; but he does not mention the
custom of placing it in the sepulchres, although he says that
it was kept at home as a precious relic: "ut domi reservent
posteris."[15] St. Gaudentius of Brescia, in speaking of Sts. Gervase and Protase, says that he has proof of their martyrdom:
"Tenemus sanguinem, qui testis est passionis."[16] It appears,
however, that at times the blood of the martyrs was placed
either in the sepulchre or near it; in fact, an African inscription
to this effect might be cited, dating from the time of Diocletian,
in which is recorded the "depositio cruoris sanctorum
martyrum."

But to prove whether the contents of the vases whose fragments are often found in the sepulchres, was actually blood, it is
necessary to have recourse to a chemical analysis. Only on this

RESTORATION OF THE PAPAL CRYPT
IN THE CEMETERY OF CALLISTUS.

condition may the vial be taken as a criterion demanded by the
Congregation of Rites to establish the presence of the body of a
martyr. Great care must be exercised before admitting that the
vials (*phialae*) which are so often met with in the burial vaults
of the cemeteries, may be taken as signs of martyrdom. They
are not generally considered to be incontrovertible proof. It is
impossible to believe that the vials which are found broken or
attached to the outside walls of the tombs contained blood;
furthermore, it is usual to find them on sepulchres dating from
the period of peace, an epoch in which there were no martyrs.
Too many have fallen into error when speaking or writing on

this point, especially during the period beginning with the seventeenth century and ending with the founding of the Commission on Sacred Archeology by Pius IX, in 1851. One of the first duties undertaken by this commission was to forbid the removal of bodies from tombs which furnished the above-mentioned doubtful criteria, since it could not be proved that such bodies were those of martyrs.[17]

Other signs are on the whole false and inadmissible, notwithstanding the fact that they once were considered certain. Thus, for example, it was formerly believed that the palm could be taken as an indication of martyrdom; but the palm, as an emblem, is also found on pagan monuments in allusion to martial victories, to commemorate the triumph of a chariot-driver in the circus, or of a gladiator in the amphitheatre. For the Christians it might have signified merely their victory over the world and their passions. In the same category belongs the monogram ☧. Many took this to be a sign of martyrdom, and erroneously translated it as meaning "Pax Christi" ("the peace of Christ"), or even "Passus pro Christo" ("Suffered for Christ"); in reality it is an abbreviation of the name of Christ, ΧΡΙΣΤΟΣ. It is indeed true that the monogram was rarely used before Constantine; it was only after the declaration of religious peace that it came into common use.

Hence we do not possess any other signs for the tombs of unknown martyrs but the title, or the vase which shows *indubitable evidences of blood*. De Rossi laid down certain rules for determining the tombs of the historical martyrs, which are now used to establish their identity. It is known that, in connection with these tombs, there were subsequently constructed numerous oratories and basilicas. Even if these monuments fell into ruin, there remained certain traces of their existence near the venerated crypts. Such evidences as the stairways leading to these places, built by Damasus and other popes, always leave behind some vestige of their former existence. These were the principal indications which guided de Rossi in his researches.

Inscriptions and paintings which came after the period of subterranean burial are, for the same reason, secure criteria.

The pilgrims desired to come as close to the bodies of the martyrs as was permissible, and in the easiest possible manner, for which reason the course they followed was rather restricted. In the galleries through which such pilgrims passed, they at times wrote their names and the name of the local martyr himself, followed by invocations such as: "In mente habeas in orationibus tuis," "In mente habete," etc. ("Remember us in your prayers," "Keep us in mind"). Even the priests who had celebrated Mass in the chapel often left their names and their domicile or title. It is necessary to distinguish between these writings scratched on the walls by the pilgrims and the inscriptions which were traced on the vaults on the day of burial. Generally only the first have any historical or topographical importance.

These crypts are those which we call *historical crypts,* such as, for example, the celebrated crypts of the popes of the third century in the cemetery of Callistus. (See page 107.)

Paintings also furnish us with valuable indications. Those found on the arched vaults (*arcosolia*) and in the private chapels generally belong before the fifth century, a period in which, little by little, the custom of subterranean interment ceased, the tombs of the martyrs continuing, meanwhile, to be venerated and decorated. For this reason, a cemetery containing a sepulchre which evidently does not belong to one of the ordinary faithful, and showing paintings dating later than the fifth century, must be judged to be a venerated spot. Thus in the chapel of St. Cecilia we may see Byzantine paintings of the seventh century, in which, along with an image of the Saviour, the saint is pictured dressed in the habiliments of a Byzantine empress. To this same category belong the paintings on the crypt of St. Cornelius which date from the sixth century. In the cemetery of Pontian, the images of the Saviour, of Sts. Abdon and Sennen and of Sts. Pigmenius and Milix, also manifest characteristics of sixth-century Byzantine art. In the cemetery of St. Valentine, some traces of paintings of Byzantine character were sufficient to enable the excavators to rediscover the chapel of the martyr who had given his name to the whole cemetery.

The same thing happened in January, 1904, when the discovery of beautiful Byzantine paintings enabled the excavators to identify the subterranean basilica of Sts. Felix and Adauctus in the cemetery of Domitilla near the Ostian Way.

## Chapter III

### CEMETERIES AND MONUMENTS IN THE OPEN

THE OLDER archeologists did not know of the cemeteries in the open. The first one to reveal their existence was Settele; in his dissertations published in the *Acts of the Roman Academy of Archeology,* he made known those of St. Con-

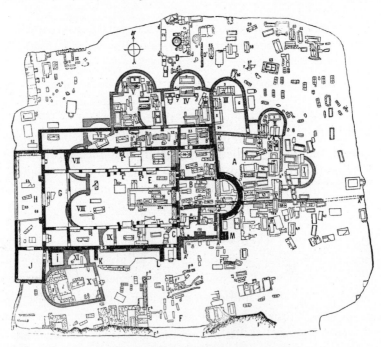

SALONA (DALMATIA).
EXAMPLE OF A VAST OPEN-AIR CEMETERY.

stantia and St. Valentine. Settele himself did not know that there were any others.

To these original researches, Marchi added information

concerning the cemetery of St. Cyriaca. De Rossi has shown that open-air cemeteries are rather numerous. Many chapters of de Rossi's monumental work, *Roma sotterranea,* are devoted to their description.[1] Still others were discovered outside of Rome: at Ostia, Porto, Palestrina in Italy, at Julia Concordia in Friuli,[2] at Salona in Dalmatia,[3] and at Vienne in France.[4]

In these cemeteries, the sepulchres and the sarcophagi were deposited in a basilica, as may be seen at Maurisanac, north of Salona, at Syrmium (ancient Pannonia), at Julia Concordia, etc. An inscription discovered in 1864, among the ruins of such a basilica dedicated to St. Agapitus in Palestrina, makes allusion to *metae,* funerary pillars which surround a tomb, or perhaps the very open-air cemetery itself:

> Haec domus PlacidIANORVM . NVNCVPABITVR
> Martyris introitus EccleSIAEQVE . ATRIA . SANCTI
> Iustitiae sedes fidei domuS AVLA . PVDORIS.
> Vix puer ingRESSVS . LETABILI TVMVLO . METAS etc.[5]

The *area*[6] was surrounded by walls or delimited by pillars, as in the case of pagan cemeteries. The extension of these *areae* was often indicated in the inscriptions themselves.

The tombs were ordinarily rather poor. While in the underground cemeteries the vaults are dug in the vertical wall, the cemeteries in the open have structures which look like walled wells with horizontal closures, where as many as ten bodies were placed one above the other. These tombs are spoken of as *formae,* the word ordinarily used for designating canals and aqueducts. This term comes down to us from an inscription published by Boldetti. It was found in the pavement of St. Mary's in Transtevere.

> ANNIBONIVS FECIT SIBI ET SVIS
> LOCVM HOMINIBVS N VIII INTRO FORMAS
> EC TON EMON PANTON TVTO EMON

The expression "intro formas" was interpreted by Marchi as "infra formas," as if the tomb were placed between two aqueducts. But the inscription certainly reads "intro formas." Only by way of exception were *formae* built in the underground cemeteries. The stone or slab used to cover the *formae* was generally much more massive and heavier than the ones used to cover the subterranean *loculi;* hence the origin of these stones may be recognized from their dimensions. Even the inscriptions make a distinction: those of the fifth century belong rather to the cemeteries in the open. Numerous slabs of this kind indicate the capacity of the tomb by using such words as *biscandens, triscandens,* whereas in the catacombs the terms used were *bisomus, trisomus.* Oftentimes one encounters formulae carrying a malediction against profaners: "Cum Juda partem habeat" — "May he have a part with Judas," etc. Of course, it was much easier to profane these monuments than tombs placed below the surface. The walls often seem to imitate the form and style of arched vaults (*arcosolia*) and underground galleries.

The open-air cemeteries contained a great number of sarcophagi, disposed as a rule along the walls of the basilicas or the walls which formed the boundaries of the cemeteries. They were protected by roofs called *teglata.* In an inscription still preserved we read: LOCVS EMPTVS SVB TEGLATA IN BASILICA BALBINES[7] — "The place purchased under the roof in the Basilica of the Balbines." The more expensive sarcophagi were surmounted by small roofs upheld by pilasters, called *teguria, ciboria.* Marble grates (trellises) closed off the space reserved for the tomb; such grates were known as *transennae* or even *clatra* or *hermulae,* especially when they had small pillars surmounted by busts. A painting in the cemetery of Cyriaca represents a tomb of this kind with its grates (*transennae*) and its *hermulae* (small posts which bear busts); to show that the monuments had been set aside for a specific purpose, the artist drew the pictures of grazing cattle on the walls. (See cut on following page.)

As may be seen at Salona, there were within the area of the cemetery a great number of *cellae memoriae,*[8] mausoleums in memory of the deceased, some with one apse, called *cella absidata* or simply *cella,* others with three or more apses, known as *cella trichora, hexachora,* etc. Some mausoleums were of

great size, like that of St. Helena on the Labican Way, the one
dedicated to St. Constantia, etc. Close to the locality where this
last is situated can be distinguished the walls which originally
made up a part of the suburban imperial palace, and which subsequently were transformed into walls for the cemetery.

The cemeteries in the open were without doubt sacked by
the Goths under Vitiges in the year 537. The devastations
spoken of in the *Book of the Popes* were especially perpetrated
on these monuments, in the midst of which, as Procopius tells
us, the barbarians had pitched their camp. Some years afterward, that is, under the pontificate of John III (560-573), there
was inaugurated a radical change in the administration of the
cemeteries. After having been allocated or joined to some title,

*ARCOSOLIUM* IN THE CEMETERY OF CYRIACA.
Fourth century.

as had been the case up to this time, they passed under the
direct jurisdiction of the pontifical palace. It was during this
epoch that cemeteries began to be built in the city proper. A
cemetery was either established or increased in size on the Esquiline, close to St. Bibiana's, *ad ursum pileatum,* distinct from
one of the same name on the Portuan Way. Soon it became

the custom for every parish to have its own cemetery, constructed on the model of the early cemeteries. Naturally, the
great basilicas always remained the centers of interment.[9]

## Chapter IV

## DOCUMENTS RELATING TO THE TOPOGRAPHY OF THE ANCIENT CEMETERIES OF ROME

THE MOST ancient document in which are registered the
feasts of the martyrs celebrated in the Christian cemeteries
of Rome is the so-called *Feriale* or *Day-Book,* which is in fact
a calendar compiled about the year 354.[1] In it are indicated
the more solemn feasts which were celebrated in Rome at the
time of Constantine. Of this list, all but two, the feasts of
Christmas and St. Peter's Chair, indicate the times of the liturgical reunions which were held in the cemeteries to commemorate
the anniversaries of the martyrs. The text of this priceless
document follows:

### Depositio Martyrum

VIII  kal. ianu. — Natus Christus in Bethlehem Iudeae.
XIII  kal. febr. — Fabiani in Callisti et Sebastiani in catacumbas.[2]
XII   kal. febr. — Agnetis in Nomentana.
VIII  kal. mart. — Natale Petri de Cathedra.[3]
Non. mart. — Perpetuae et Felicitatis Africae.
XIIII kal. iun. — Partheni et Caloceri in Callisti Diocletiano VIIII et Maximiano
       VIII conss. [a. 304].
III   kal. iul. — Petri in catacumbas et Pauli Ostense, Tusco et Basso conss.
       [a. 258].
VI    idus iul. — Felicis et Philippi in Priscillae et in Iordanorum Martialis
       Vitalis Alexandri et in Maximi Silani (hunc Silanum martyrem Novati
       furati sunt) et in Praetextati Ianuari.
III   kal. aug. — Abdon et Sennen in Pontiani quod est ad Ursum pileatum.
VIII  idus aug. — Xysti in Callisti et in Praetestati Agapiti et Felicissimi.
VI    idus aug. — Secundi Carpophori Victorini et Severiani, Albano — Ostense
       VII Ballistaria — Cyriaci Largi Crescentiani Memmiae Iulianae et
       Smaragdi.
IV    idus aug. — Laurenti in Tiburtina.
Idus aug. — Ipoliti in Tiburtina et Pontiani in Callisti.

XI    kal. sept. — Timotei Ostense.
V     kal. sept. — Hermetis in Basillae Salaria Vetere.
Non. sept. — Aconti in Ponti et Nonni et Herculani et Taurini.
V     idus sept. — Gorgoni in Lavicana.
III   idus sept. — Proti et Iacinti in Basillae.
XVIII kal. octob. — Cypriani Africae — Romae celebratur in Callisti.
X     kal. octob. — Basillae Salaria Vetere Diocletiano VIIII et Maximiano VIII
      conss. [a. 304].
Pr.   idus octob. — Callisti in via Aurelia milliario III.
V     idus nov. — Clementi Semproniani Claudi Nicostrati in Comitatum.
III   kal. dec. — Saturnini in Trasonis.
Idus dec. — Ariston in portum.

Then follows the list of the ancient cemeteries of Rome.
The oldest of these was added to the *Notitia regionum Urbis
Romae* (*Notes on the Localities of the City of Rome*), which is
of the fourth century, and to the primitive catalogue which may
be ascribed to the fifth century. The later portion is of the
Middle Ages and was united to the *Book of Wonders* (*Mira-
bilia*). For the text of this catalogue, see below, the last column
in the synoptic guide of the Itineraries of the cemeteries.[4]

PRIMITIVE CATALOGUE OF THE PRINCIPAL CEMETERIES OF ROME (taken from the
*Notitia regionum Urbis Romae,* IV century. Codex Vat. Lat. 3851; DE ROSSI,
*Roma sotterr.,* 1, p. 131).

Cimiterium Priscillae ad Sanctum Silvestrum via Salaria — Cimiterium Iordanorum ad Sanctum Alexandrum via Salaria — Cimiterium Praetextati ad
Sanctum Ianuarium via Appia — Cimiterium Domitillae Nerei et Achillei
ad Sanctam Petronillam via Ardeatina — Cimiterium Catacumbas ad Sanctum
Sebastianum via Appia — Cimiterium Calixti ad Sanctum Sixtum via Appia
— Cimiterium ad duas lauros ad Sanctum Petrum et Marcellinum via Labicana — Cimiterium Balbinae ad Sanctum Marcum et Marcellianum via
Ardeatina — Cimiterium ad Sanctam Columbam ad caput S. Ioannis in
clivum Cucumeris — Cimiterium ad insalatos ad Sanctum Felicem via
Portuensi — Cimiterium Pontiani ad Ursum pileatum Abdon et Sennen via
Portuensi — Cimiterium Bassillae ad Sanctum Hermen via Salaria — Cimi-
terium Basillei ad Sanctum Marcum via Ardeatina — Cimiterium Com-
modillae ad Sanctum Felicem et Adauctum via Ostiensi — Cimiterium Cale-
podii ad Sanctum Calixtum via Aurelia — Cimiterium Trasonis ad Sanctum
Saturninum via Salaria.

This catalogue lists sixteen cemeteries, though the cemeteries of subterranean Rome were certainly more. This list seems
to indicate only those of major importance.[5]

Following these we have the Itineraries of the seventh
century, which may be considered documents of the greatest

importance for the topography of the Roman catacombs. Although they were composed at a late period, they still preserve for us valuable information on the grouping of the catacombs and the tombs of the martyrs. Over and above this, they enable us not only to establish the topography but also to reconstruct the history of the ancient cemeteries, to make a classification of them in chronological order, to distinguish in each catacomb the more ancient regions from those of a more recent date. Thus, for example, we can appreciate the antiquity of the cemetery of Priscilla, because we know from the Itineraries that it was there that Pudentiana and Praxedes, daughters of Pudens, were interred. In the seventh century, the catacombs were still in good condition, and were even visited. For this reason the authors of these Itineraries were able to observe and note many particulars which would be impossible for us to recognize at this late date.

In the Itineraries, the names of the cemeteries are not indicated, but only the group of martyrs buried in them; the names of the cemeteries themselves are taken from the *Feriale*, the Catalogue, and from other correlative documents. Finally, these Itineraries were really guides which were meant to serve the devout visitors to the sanctuaries of the martyrs, and they may have been composed in Rome by one or more authors who well understood the topography of the catacombs.[6]

The first of these Itineraries known to archeologists is one of the more recent. Inserted in a document of the twelfth century, the *Gesta regum Anglorum* (*Deeds of the English Kings*), it bears the name of the chronicler, William of Malmesbury. It was probably compiled for the use of the crusaders, but based on an Itinerary much more ancient; this would explain why it cites the names of all the catacombs which in the twelfth century were for the most part already forgotten. With startling exactness, this guide mentions all the gates of Rome and the highways that leave it. It also gives a very correct idea of the position of each cemetery.[7] This was the only Itinerary known to Anthony Bosio; it appears, however, that he became acquainted with it rather late and, for that reason, may not have been able to make much use of it.

A second Itinerary, discovered in the library of the monastery at Einsiedeln, was published by Mabillon,[8] and is known under the name of the *Itinerary of Einsiedeln* or the *Anonymous Guide of Mabillon*. The author was an unknown pilgrim of the time of Charlemagne. He had evidently made a personal visit to Rome, and copied numerous inscriptions, both Christian and pagan; he describes the principal monuments and even some of the Roman ceremonies. Another Itinerary, *De locis ss. Martyrum quae sunt foris civitatis Romae* (*Concerning the Tombs of the Holy Martyrs Which Lie outside the City of Rome*), was discovered about the middle of the eighteenth century in a manuscript of the library of Wuerzburg, and published by Eckart. It is a much completer guide than the Itinerary of Einsiedeln.[9]

We have a source of very great value in the double Itinerary found by the religious of St. Emmeram in the manuscripts of Salzburg, and published in 1777 as an appendix to the works of Alcuin (incidentally, these Itineraries have no relation to Alcuin).[10] The first is entitled *Notitia ecclesiarum urbis Romae* — *Notes on the Churches of the City of Rome;* the second, very much the same as the Itinerary of Wuerzburg, *De locis scis Martyrum quae sunt foris civitatem Romae*. Both of these are redactions of the same original work, and they have the exact topographical order. The authors evidently obtained their information at first hand, for they indicate the very number of steps that must be climbed to ascend or descend to certain places, they show where the tombs of the martyrs actually lie, and in the description of the tombs of the popes, they note that St. Eusebius was "in altero loco," "in another tomb." Even their errors, which are identical, prove that they were eyewitnesses. Their reason for saying that the body of St. Cyprian was buried in the cemetery of Callistus was that they saw the image of the African martyr depicted close to that of St. Cornelius. If one of these pilgrims gives to the sister of

Damasus the name of Martha, while in reality her name was Irene, it happened because he read an inscription on the Ardeatine Way in which the poet-pope speaks of "Martha soror," and did not comprehend that this was simply an allusion to the sister of Lazarus. The author of the *Notitia ecclesiarum urbis Romae* began his visits in the city itself: "Primum in urbe Roma beatorum martyrum corpora Joannis et Pauli tantum quiescunt in basilica magna et valde formosa" — "First in the city of Rome where the bodies of the blessed martyrs John and Paul alone rest in the great and very beautiful basilica." This was the only church in the city which contained the bodies of martyrs at that time. He continued his journey to St. Valentine "ad aquilonem" — "to the north" — then going "ad orientem" — "to the east"; and thus he visited the two Salarian Ways, and finally the Nomentan, Tiburtine, Labican and Latin Ways. He speaks of tarrying at great length along the Appian Way, from which he went to the Ardeatine and Ostian Ways, visited Transtevere after crossing the Tiber, and finally arrived at the tomb of St. Peter, the goal of his journey.

The other Itinerary (*Liber de locis* — *Book of Tombs*) inverts this order of visiting the cemeteries, for it commences at St. Peter's and ends at St. Valentine's. This difference in direction helps to check the exactness of the information given.

The manuscripts of the two Itineraries of Salzburg, published more than a century ago, were subsequently forgotten. John Baptist de Rossi brought them to light again when he discovered them in the library of Vienna (Ms. 795), making of them a more accurate edition than had been published by the monks of St. Emmeram. They play a part in the synoptic tables of the Itineraries published by de Rossi in the first volume of his *Roma sotterranea*.[11]

Besides the two Itineraries of Salzburg, de Rossi's monumental work contains the Itineraries of Malmesbury and Einsiedeln; a fragment of a catalogue transcribed in the fifteenth century,[12] the catalogue of the so-called *Papyrus of Monza;* an important extract, topographically, of the biography of Pope

Adrian I, from the *Book of the Popes;* and finally, an elenchus of the cemeteries taken from the *De mirabilibus novae et veteris Urbis Romae* (*Concerning the Wonders of the Old and New City of Rome*), a species of rough guide made about the

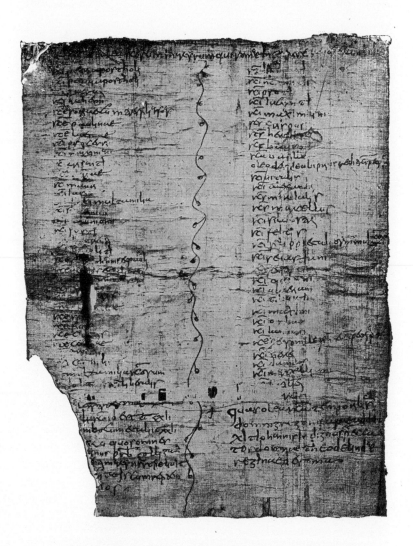

PAPYRUS OF MONZA CONTAINING INFORMATION
ON THE OILS GATHERED IN THE CATACOMBS OF ROME
NEAR THE TOMBS OF THE MARTYRS.

eleventh century, containing many ridiculous legendary accounts, along with exact information.

A truly precious document, having a great topographical
value, is the *Papyrus of Monza,* that is, the *Catalogue of Oils,*
listing the oils which a certain John, of the court of Queen

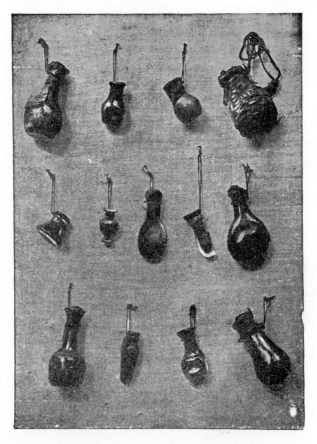

VIALS OF THE OILS IN THE TREASURY
OF THE CATHEDRAL OF MONZA.

(From a photograph taken by Bar. R. Kanzler).

Theodolinda in the time of Pope St. Gregory (590-604),
took from the burning lamps in the crypts of the martyrs. Not
being able to obtain any relics of the saints, because they were
not distributed in those early days, he carried these remem-

brances of the Roman catacombs from Rome to the pious princess in Monza.[13]

The original Catalogue (*Notitia oleorum*) is written on a sheet of paper preserved in the cathedral of Monza, where there are also kept a number of labels of papyrus (*pittacia*), which must have been tied to the vials containing the oils. The names of the saints, written on the labels, are arranged in topographical groups; but these groups were later transcribed in the *Notitia* of the same John with no attention to the topographical order of the groups in the various Ways nor to the succession of the Ways themselves.[14]

The Catalogue begins in this manner: "Notitia de olea ss. Martyrum qui Romae in corpore requiescunt, id est . . . " — "Notes concerning the oils of the Blessed Martyrs whose bodies repose in Rome, that is . . ." the names of the saints follow. At the end there is this annotation: "Quas olea sancta temporibus domni Gregorii papae adduxit Johannis indignus et peccator dñe Theodelindae reginae de Roma [sic]"—"Which holy oils John, an unworthy servant and sinner, brought to Lady Theodolinda, queen, from Rome during the times of our Lord Pope Gregory."

The information contained in this papyrus must be supplemented by that of the *notula,* the catalogue of the labels of papyrus attached to the vials; and by an accurate study of these documents, important conclusions may be arrived at. It was supposed, for example (the information given by this catalogue not having been carefully examined) that the memorial of the first Chair of St. Peter was to be found in a cemetery on the Nomentan Way; but it has been shown by weighty arguments that, instead of this, the memorial indicated in the papyrus ("Sedes ubi prius sedit sanctus Petrus" — "the Chair where St. Peter first sat") must refer to the group on the New Salarian Way.[15]

The great importance of these documents having been indicated, it is believed that it will be very helpful to complete this general information by reproducing in their entirety all

those precious topographical texts relating to the monuments
of the suburban cemeteries which have already been published
by de Rossi in the first volume of his *Roma sotterranea*.[16]

The reader, in studying these Itineraries, may be able to
form a sufficiently exact idea concerning the disposition of the
ancient Christian cemeteries in the suburban region of Rome,
and of the sepulchres of the principal martyrs venerated in each
one of these underground sanctuaries. Such has been the hope
in inserting these synoptic tables in the present *Manual*.

NOTE: The synoptic tables of the Itineraries in the section which follows give us a brief description of
the more important cemeteries (catacombs). A
pilgrimage of these begins at the Vatican cemetery because of the great importance of the tomb
of the Apostle Peter. From this point, it continues
to the next catacomb on the Aurelian Way, then
on to the Portuan Way, etc., until finally it ends
with the Flaminian Way. The tables given here,
however, follow the reverse order, beginning with
the Flaminian Way and thence passing to the
Salarian Way, etc.; they have been reproduced
exactly as given in Volume I of de Rossi's *Roma
sotterranea*.

## SYNOPTIC TABLES OF THE ITINERARIES

| I | II | III | IV | V |
|---|---|---|---|---|
| INDICES OLEORUM QUAE COLLEGIT IOANNES ABBAS | ITINERARIUM EX UNICO CODICE SALISBURGENSI | EPITOME LIBRI *DE LOCIS SANCTORUM MARTYRUM* E CODICIBUS SALISBURGENSI PURO, WIRCEBURGENSI PURO ET SALISBURGENSI INTERPOLATO | *NOTITIA PORTARUM, VIARUM, ECCLESIARUM* CIRCA URBEM ROMAM E WILLELMO MALMESBURIENSI | INDEX COEMETERIORUM E LIBRO *MIRABILIUM URBIS ROMAE* |
| INDEX OLEORUM<br>Scorum Io-hannis et Pauli.<br><br>PITTACIUM AMPULLAE<br>Scs Ys... Ion, scs Iohannis et scs Iohannis et Pauli. Paulus. | Primum in Urbe Roma beatorum martyrum corpora Iohannis et Pauli tamen (1) quiescunt in basilica magna et valde formosa.<br><br>(1) *Fortasse* tantum. | Basilica, quae appellatur Iohannis et Pauli, ubi ipsi ambo in uno tumulo iacent.<br><br>Basilica s. Bonifacii martyris, ubi ipse dormit. | Intra Urbem in monte Coelio sunt martyres Ioannes et Paulus in sua domo quae facta est ecclesia post eorum martyrium, et Crespinus et Crespinianus et s. Benedicta. In eodem monte est ecclesia s. Stephani protomartyris, et ibi reconditi sunt martyres Primus et Felicianus; in monte Aventino s. Bonifatius et in monte Nola s. Taciana pausant. | Coemeterium ad Ursum pileatum ad s. Bibianam. |

INTRA URBEM

| | I | II | III | IV |
|---|---|---|---|---|
| | INDEX Coemeteriorum (mutilus) *e Notitia Regionum Urbis Romae* | INDICES OLEORUM quae collegit Ioannes Abbas | ITINERARIUM ex unico Codice Salisburgensi | EPITOME libri *de locis sanctorum Martyrum* e Codicibus Salisburgensi puro, Wirceburgensi puro et Salisburgensi interpolat |
| **VIA FLAMINIA** | | | Deinde intrabis per urbem ad aquilonem, donec pervenies ad portam flamineam, u- bi s. Valentinus martyr quiescit via flaminea in basilica magna, quam Honorius reparavit, et alii martyres in aqui- lone plaga sub terra. | K. Inde prope [*i. e. pro pe ecclesiam S. Ioannis a clivum Cucumeris*] iuxta v am Flamineam apparet e clesia mirifice ornata Valentini martyris, ubi ips corpore iacet et multi sar cti ibidem sunt sepulti [*in terpolator ex Itinerario a didit* in aquilonali plaga.] |

<table>
<tr><td rowspan="2">VIA SALARIA VETUS ET CLIVUS CUCUMERIS</td><td>Coemeterium ad septem columbas ad caput s. Ioannis in clivum cucumeris.<br><br>Coemeterium Basillae ad s. Hermen via Salaria.</td><td>PITTACIA AMPULLARUM<br><br>*Sca Felicitas cum...* scs *Bonifati*us scs Hermis scs *Protus...* scs Crispus scs *Hercula- nus...*<br>—<br>...scs *Systus,* scs Liberalis... scs Blastro et multa milia s... alii CXXII et alii sci XLV...</td><td>INDEX OLEORUM<br><br>Sce Felicitatis cum septem filios suos Sci Bonifati Sci Hermitis Sci Proti Sci Iacynti Sci Maximiliani Scs Crispus Scs Herculanus Scs Bauso Sca Basilla<br>—<br>Sci Io*han*nis Sci Li*ber*alis Sce Lucinae *Sci* Blastro et multorum sco- rum, *sed et* alii sci id est CCLXII *in un- um* locum et alii CXXII *et alii* sci XLVI quos omnes Iu- stinus prb col- liga *sci Lan- renti* martyris sepelivit.</td><td>Deinde vadis ad ori- entem donec venias ad ecclesiam Iohannis martyris via Salinaria, ibi requiescit Diogenus martyr et in altero cu- biculo Bonifacianus, et Fistus martyr sub ter- ra, sub terra Blastus martyr: deinde Iohan- nis martyr, postea Lon- guinus martyr. Dein- de vadis ad australem via Salinaria donec venies ad s. Ermetem, ibi primum pausat[in] ba[silica? Bas]ilissa virgo et martyr, in altera et martyr Ma- ximus et s. Ermes martyr longe sub ter- ra. Et in altera spe- lunca Protus martyr et Iacintus, deinde Victor martyr. Postea eadem via pervenies ad s. Pampulum martyrem XXIIII gradibus sub terra.</td><td>K. Inde haud proc [*i. e. ab ecclesia S. M chaelis mill. VII*] in oc dente iuxta viam eande [*i. e. Salariam*: vox ea dem *est ab interpolator* in cryptis sub terra LXX gradibus s. Pamphilus s. Candidus, sanctusq Cyrinus cum multis ma tyribus iacet. K. Et in in occidentem tenden bus apparet basilica s. B mes ubi ipse martyr iac [longe in terra: *haec i terpol. ex Itinerario*]. I sunt s. Crispus et s. He culanus et s. Maximili nus et s. Basilessa et Iacintus [K. In alte spelunca s. Iacinctus *terp. ex Itin.*] et s. Prot [s. Victor *interp. ex Itin* et s. Leopardus cum mul martiribus sepulti. K. In non longe est in occider ecclesia s. Iohannis ma tyris, ubi caput eius in a loco sub altare ponitur, alio corpus: ibi s. D genes et s. Fistus [*co Wirc.* Sistus] et s. L eratus, et s. Blastus et Maurus et s. Longi mater Iohannis sunt sepu [et alii mille CCXX martyres, *singulari ma additum*].</td></tr>
<tr></tr>
</table>

| V<br><br>NOTITIA PORTARUM,<br>*viarum, ecclesiarum*<br>circa<br>Urbem Romam<br>e Willelmo Malmesburiensi | VI<br><br>TOPOGRAPHIA<br><br>Einsiedelnensis | VII<br>EXCERPTA TOPOGRAPHICA<br>e<br>Vita Hadriani I | VIII<br>INDEX<br>Coemeteriorum<br>e libro<br>*Mirabilium*<br>*Urbis Romae* |
|---|---|---|---|
| Secunda porta Flaminea, quae modo appellatur s. Valentini, et Flaminea via et um ad pontem Molbium pervenit vocatur via Ravennana quia ad Ravennam ducit. Ibi n primo miliario foris s. Valentinus in sua ecclesia requiescit. | In via Flaminea foris murum in dextera s. Valentini, in sinistra Tiberis. | | |
| Tertia porta Porticiana *lege* Pinciana] et via eodem modo appellata, sed cum pervenit ad Salariam nomen perit; et ibi prope in eo loco qui icitur cucumeris requiescunt artyres Festus, Iohannes, Liberalis, Diogenes, Blastus, ucina et in uno sepulcro CLX [*al.* CCXXXX] et in tero XXX. Quarta porta et a Salaria, quae modo s. Silestri dicitur. Ibi iuxta viam Hermes requiescit et s. Vaella et Protus et Iacinctus, aximilianus, Herculanus, rispus, et in altero loco rope requiescunt sancti marres Pamphilus et Quirinus XX gradibus in imo terrae. | *Topographia*<br><br>In via Pinciana extra civitatem in [sinistra] s. Basilisse, s. Proti et Iacinthi, s. Hermetis; in dextera s. Pamphili, s. Ioannis caput.<br><br>—<br><br>*Fragmenta*<br><br>In via Pincia Pamphilus, Basilissa, Protus, Iacinthus, Hermes. Ubi dominus coecum illuminavit, arcus, murus. | § 79. Basilicam coemeterii ss. martyrum Hermetis, Proti et Hyacinthi atque Basillae mirae magnitudinis innovavit. Coemeterium vero s. Felicitatis etc. [*vide hic in Salaria nova*]. | Coemeterium s. Hermetis et Domitillae [*Petrus Mallius addit*: est foris portam Pincianam, ubi est ecclesia s. Hermetis martyris].<br><br>Coemeterium s. Marcelli via Salaria vetere [*e libro Benedicti canonici*]. |

VIA SALARIA NOVA

| I | II | III | IV |
|---|---|---|---|
| INDEX Coemeteriorum (mutilus) *e Notitia Regionum Urbis Romae* | INDICES OLEORUM quae collegit Ioannes Abbas | ITINERARIUM ex unico Codice Salisburgensi | EPITOME libri *de locis sanctorum Martyrum* e Codicibus Salisburgensi puro, Wirceburgensi puro et Salisburgensi interpolat |

| I | II | III | IV |
|---|---|---|---|
| Coemeterium Priscillae ad s. Silvestrum via Salaria.<br><br>Coemeterium Iordanorum ad s. Alexandrum via Salaria.<br><br>Coemeterium Thrasonis ad s. Saturninum via Salaria. | PITTACIA AMPULLARUM<br><br>*Sedes u b i* prius sedit scs Petrus *ex oleo scs Vitalis scs Alexander,* scs Martialis scs Marcellus *sci* Silvestri sci Felicis sci Filippi et alior- *um multo*rum scorum.<br><br>—<br><br>*Scs* Grisantis scsqu Darias scs Maurus *scs* Iason et alii sci multa milia *sci* Saturnini et scs ...a[u]pinio.<br><br>—<br><br>*..Sca Felicitas cum... scs Boni- fati*us scs Her- mis etc. [*vide Salariam vete- rem*]. | INDEX OLEORUM<br>Oleo de sede ubi prius sedit scs Petrus<br>Sci Vitalis<br>Sci Alexandri<br>Sci Martialis<br>Scs Marcellus<br>Sci Silvestri<br>Sci Felicis<br>Sci Filippi et aliorum mult. scor.<br><br>—<br><br>Sci Grisanti<br>Sce Dariae<br>Sci Maur<br>Sci Iason et alii sci mul- ta milia<br>Sci *Satur*nini<br>Sci Ti*pi*nionis<br><br>—<br><br>Sce Felicita- tis cum septem filios suos.<br>Sci Bonifati<br>S c i Hermetis etc. [*vide Sa- lariam vet.*]. | Deinde venies ad s. Felicitatem altera via, quae similiter Sa- laria dicitur, ibi illa pausat in ecclesia sur- sum et Bonifacius pp et martyr in altero loco et filii [*lege* filius] eius sub terra deor- sum. Deinde eadem via pervenies ad ec- clesiam s. Saturnini papae et martyris: in altera ecclesia Daria virgo et martyr pau- sat et Crisanti mar- tyr. Postea pervenies eadem via ad spe- luncam ubi s. Hilaria martyr: deinde eadem via ad s. Alexandrum martyrem, ibi pausant Theodolus et Eventus et longe in interi- ore spelunca Alexander martyr requiescit. Po- stea ascendens eadem via ad s. Silvestri ec- clesiam ibi multitudo sanctorum p a u s a t: primum Silvester san- ctus papa et confessor et ad pedes eius s. Syricus papa et in dex- tera parte Celestinus papa et Marcellus epis- copus; Philippus et Felix martyres et mul- titudo sanctorum sub altare maiore et in s p e l u n c a Crescencius martir, et in altera s. Prisca martyr et Fimitis pausat in cubiculo quando exeas et in al- tera s. Potenciana martyr et Praxidis. | K. Iuxta viam Salaria ecclesia est s. Felicitat ubi ipsa iacet corpore, i et Sillanus filius eius un de VII est sepultus et Bo ifacius [papa *interp. e Itin.*] cum multis sanct ibi dormiunt. K. Iux eandem viam s. Saturn nus [papa *interp. ex Itin* cum multis martyrib dormit [*alia manus ada dit* in alia quoque ecc sia s. Chrisantus et Dar virgo et LXII martyres propeque ibi s. Alexand et s. Vitalis sanctusq Martialis, qui sunt tres septem filiis Felicitat cum multis martyrib iacent [ibi in interiore sp lunca s. Theodolus Eventus *interp. ex Itin.* Ibi et VII virgines id s. Saturnina et s. Hilar s. Dominanda, s. Sero s. Paulina, s. Dona s. Rogantina requiescur K. Iuxta eandem via Salariam s. Silvester quiescit [ad pedes eius Siricius papa *interp.* *Itin.*] et alii quampluri id est s. Caelestinus, Potentiana, s. Praxedis, Marcellus [eps *interp. Itin.*], s. Crescentianus, Maurus, s. Marcellinus, Prisca [sancta Fimitis *terp. ex Itin.*], s. Paulu s. Felicis unus de septe s. Philippus unus de s tem, s. Semetrius, et una sepultura CCCLX [*al.* CCCLXV] [sub alta maiore *interp. ex Itin* Per eandem quoque vi venitur ad ecclesiam Michaelis septimo millia ab Urbe. |

| V<br><br>NOTITIA PORTARUM,<br>*viarum, ecclesiarum*<br>circa<br>Urbem Romam<br>e Willelmó Malmesburiensi | VI<br><br>TOPOGRAPHIA<br><br>Einsiedelnensis | VII<br><br>EXCERPTA TOPOGRAPHICA<br>e<br>Vita Hadriani I | VIII<br><br>INDEX<br>Coemeteriorum<br>e libro<br>*Mirabilium*<br>*Urbis Romae* |
|---|---|---|---|
| Deinde [*vide Salariam ve-erem*] basilica s. Felicitatis, bi requiescit illa et Silanus ılius eius et non longe Bo-ifatius martyr. Ibidem in al-era ecclesia sunt Crisantus et Daria et Saturninus et Maurus t Iason et mater eorum Hil-ria et alii innumerabiles. Et ı altera basilica s. Alexander, 'italis, Martialis filii s. Felici-ıtis. Et sanctae VII virgines aturnina, Hilarina, Dominan-a, Rogantina, Serotina, Pau-na, Donata. Deinde basilica , Silvestri ubi iacet marmo-e tumulo coopertus et mar-res Caelestinus, Philippus et 'elix et ibidem martyres CCLXV in uno sepulcro re-uiescunt, et prope Paulus et rescentianus, Prisca et Se-etrius, Praxedis, Potentiana ausant. | In via Salaria extra civitatem in [sinistra] s. Sa-turnini: in dextera s. Felicitatis cum septem filiis. | § 79. Coemeterium s. Fe-licitatis via Salaria una cum ecclesiis s. Silvani martyris et s. Bonifacii confessoris atque pontificis uno cohaerentes so-lo mirae restauravit magnitu-dinis. Sed et basilicam s. Sa-turnini in praedicta via Sa-laria positam una cum coem. ss. Chrysanthi et Dariae re-novavit atque coemeterium s. Hilariae innovavit. § 80. Im-mo et coem. Iordanorum, videlicet ss. Alexandri et Vi-talis et Martialis martyrum, seu ss. septem Virginum a novo restauravit. Pariter in eadem via Salaria coem. s. Sil-vestri confessoris atque pon-tificis aliorumque sanctorum multorum in ruinis positum renovavit. | Coemeterium Pri-scillae ad pontem salarium.<br><br>Coemeterium ad clivum cucumeris.<br><br>Coemeterium Thrasonis ad s. Saturninum.<br><br>Coemeterium s. Felicitatis.<br><br>[*Coem. ad cli-vum cucumeris hic falso positum; per-tinet ad Salariam veterem*]. |

| I | II | III | IV |
|---|---|---|---|
| INDEX Coemeteriorum (mutilus) *e Notitia Regionum Urbis Romae* | INDICES OLEORUM quae collegit Ioannes Abbas | ITINERARIUM ex unico Codice Salisburgensi | EPITOME libri *de locis sanctorum Martyrum* e Codicibus Salisburgensi puro, Wirceburgensi puro et Salisburgensi interpola[t] |
| **VIA NOMENTANA** *pittacium periit* | INDEX OLEORUM Sce Agnetis et aliarum multarum martyrum. Sci Y....tion [*incertum est, utrum hoc nomen spectet ad viam Nomentanam*]. | Et postea vadis ad orientem quousque pervenies ad s. Emerentianam martyrem quae pausat in ecclesia sursum et duo martyres in spelunca deorsum Victor et Alexander. Deinde via Numentana ad ecclesiam s. Agnae quae formosa est, in qua sola pausat et ipsam episcopus Honorius miro opere reparavit. | K. Iuxta viam Nume[n]tanam est s. Nicomed[es] et iuxta eandem viam b[a]silica s. Agnes mirae pu[l]chritudinis ubi ipsa co[r]pore iacet, propeque i[bi] soror eius Emerentian[a] in alia tamen basili[ca] dormit. Ibi quoque [in] singulari ecclesia Consta[n]tia Constantini filia [re]quiescit; sanctusque Ale[x]ander, s. Felicis, s. P[ri]pia, s. Victor et alii mu[lti] ibi dormiunt. |
| **VIA TIBURTINA** *pittacium periit* | INDEX OLEORUM Sci Systi Sci Laurenti Sci Yyppoliti | Postea illam viam demittis et pervenies ad s. Ypolytum martyrem qui requiescit sub terra in cubiculo, et Concordia mulier eius martyr ante fores, altero cubiculo s. Triphonia regina et martyr, et Cyrilla filia eius et martyr, quas meditus [*lege* Messius; *antiqua manus in margine scripsit* Claudius] Decius interfecit uxorem et filiam, et s. Genisius martyr. Postea pervenies ad ecclesiam s. Laurentii, ibi sunt magnae basilicae duae in quarum quis speciosiorem et pausat, et est parvum cubiculum extra ecclesiam in hoc occidentur [*haec corrupta sunt*]. Ibi pausat s. Abundius et Herenius martyr via Tiburtina; et ibi est ille lapis quem tollent digito multi homines | K. Iuxta viam Tibu[rti]nam [prope murum ci[v]tatis ecclesia est s. ][I]nuarii episcopi et ma[r]tyris, eademque vi[a] ecclesia est s. Agap[e] multum honorabilis m[ar]tyrum corporibus. K. prope eandem viam [ec]clesia est s. Lauren[tii] maior in qua corpus e[ius] primum fuerat humatu[m] et ibi basilica nova mi[rae] pulchritudinis, ubi i[pse] modo requiescit. Ibi q[uo]que sub eodem alt[ari] Abundus est depositus foris in portico lapis [super] qui aliquando in co[llo] eiusdem Abundi pen[de]bat in puteum missi: Hereneus, Iulianus, [Pri]mitivus, Tacteus, Ner[eus] seus, Eugenius, Iustin[us] Crescentianus, Roma[nus] sunt sepulti, et s. [...] |

| V<br><br>*NOTITIA PORTARUM,*<br>*viarum, ecclesiarum*<br>circa<br>Urbem Romam<br>e Willelmo Malmesburiensi | VI<br><br>TOPOGRAPHIA<br><br>Einsiedelnensis | VII<br><br>EXCERPTA TOPOGRAPHICA<br>e<br>Vita Hadriani I | VIII<br><br>INDEX<br>Coemeteriorum<br>e libro<br>*Mirabilium*<br>*Urbis Romae* |
|---|---|---|---|
| Quinta porta Numentana. bi s. Nicomedes presbyter t martyr, itemque via eodem nodo dicitur. Iuxta viam s. agnetis et ecclesia et corpus, 1 altera ecclesia s. Emerentiana et martyres Alexander, 'elix, Papias. In septimo 1illiario eiusdem viae s. papa Alexander cum Eventio et 'heodulo pausant. | In via Numentana foris murum in sinistra s. Agnes, in dextra s. Nicomedis. | § 85. Ecclesiam beatae Agnetis martyris seu basilicam beatae Emerentianae, pariter et ecclesiam beati Nicomedis, sitam foris portam Numentanam..., quae a priscis marcuerant temporibus, a novo renovavit. | Coemeterium sanctae Agnetis.<br><br>Coemeterium fontis sancti Petri. |
| Sexta porta et via Tiburti-a, quae modo dicitur s. Laurentii, iuxta hanc viam iacet Laurentius in sua ecclesia : Habundius martyr. Et ibi rope in altera ecclesia pau-ant hi martyres Ciriaca, Romanus, Iustinus, Crescentian-s, et ibi non longe Ipolitus el basilica s. Ippolyti, ubi ise cum familia sua pausat, l est XVIII [*al.* XXVIII]. t ibi requiescunt beata Tri-honia uxor Decii et filia eius irilla et Concordia nutrix us. Et in altera parte viae lius est ecclesia [*al.* basilica] gapiti martyris. | In via Tiburtina foris murum in sinistra s. Ypoliti, in dextra s. Laurentii. | § 75. Basilicam s. Laurentii martyris, ubi sanctum corpus eius quiescit, adnexam basilicae maiori, quam dudum isdem praesul construxerat, ultro citroque a novo restauravit. Immo et ecclesiam s. Stephani iuxta eam sitam, ubi corpus s. Leonis episcopi et martyris quiescit, similiter undique renovavit una cum coemeterio beatae Cyriacae seu adscensum eius. § 85. Coemeterium beati Hyppolyti martyris iuxta s. Laurentium... a novo renovavit. | Coemeterium in agro Verano ad s. Laurentium. |

| I | II | III | IV |
|---|---|---|---|
| INDEX<br>Coemeteriorum<br>(mutilus)<br>*e Notitia<br>Regionum<br>Urbis Romae* | INDICES OLEORUM<br><br>quae collegit Ioannes Abbas | ITINERARIUM<br><br>ex unico<br><br>Codice Salisburgensi | EPITOME<br>libri *de locis<br>sanctorum Martyrum*<br>e Codicibus<br>Salisburgensi puro,<br>Wirceburgensi puro<br>et Salisburgensi interpola⸱ |
| *Sequitur* VIA TIBURTINA | | | nescientes quid fa-ciunt. Et in altera ec-clesia sursum multi martyres p a u s a n t. Prima est Cyriaca sancta vidua et mar-tyr, et in altero loco s. Iustinus, et iuxta e u m s. Crescentius martyr et multitudo sanctorum, longe in spelunca deorsum s. Romanus martyr. Pos-tea ascendes ad ec-clesiam s. Agapiti mar-tyris et diaconi s. Syx-ti papae. | riaca, s. Simferosa et Iu⸱ tina cum multis martyr⸱ ribus sunt sepulti. K. I de in boream sursum monte basilica s. Hipp⸱ lyti est, ubi ipse cum ⸱ milia sua tota XVIII ma⸱ tyres iacet. Carcer ibi ⸱ in quo fuit Laurentius. ⸱ est Triphonia uxor De⸱ Caesaris et Cyrilla fil⸱ eius: inter utrasque Co⸱ cordia et s. Geneseus, multi martyres ibi sunt. |
| VIA LABICANA | Coemeterium ad duas lauros ad ss. Petrum et Marcellinum via Labicana. | | Ad Helenam v i a Campana multi mar-tyres pausant. In aqui-lone parte ecclesia Helenae primus Tibur-tius martyr. Postea intrabis in speluncam ibi pausant ss. mar-tyres Petrus presbyter et Marcellinus martyr. Postea in interiore an-tro Gorgonius martyr, et multi alii, et in uno loco in interiore spe-lunca XL martyres, et in altero XXX mar-tyres, et in tertio IIII coronatos et s. Helena in sua rotunda. | K. Iuxta viam vero I vicanam ecclesia est Helenae ubi ipsa corp⸱ iacet. Ibi sancti isti d⸱ miunt, Petrus, Marcel⸱ nus, Tiburtius, ss. XX milites, Gorgonius, G nuinus, Maximus, IV C ronati id est Claudi⸱ Nicostratus, Simpronian⸱ Castorius, Simplicius: et in cryptis sub terra numera martyrum mul⸱ tudo sepulta iacent [ Iuxta viam vero Praene⸱ nam iuxta aquaeduct⸱ ecclesia est s. Straton⸱ episcopi et martyris, et Castoli, quorum corp⸱ longe sub terra sunt sep⸱ ta. [*Haec verba alia ma⸱ addita*]. |

| V<br>*NOTITIA PORTARUM,*<br>*viarum, ecclesiarum*<br>circa<br>Urbem Romam<br>e Willelmo Malmesburiensi | VI<br><br>TOPOGRAPHIA<br><br>Einsiedelnensis | VII<br>EXCERPTA TOPOGRAPHICA<br>e<br>Vita Hadriani I | VIII<br>INDEX<br>Coemeteriorum<br>e libro<br>*Mirabilium*<br>*Urbis Romae* |
|---|---|---|---|
| Septima porta modo Maior citur, olim Sirucrana [*al.* racusana, *lege* Sessoriana] :ebatur et via Lavicana dici-, quae ad beatam Helenam .dit. Ibi sunt prope Petrus, arcellinus, Tiburtius, Gemi-s, Gorgonius, et quadraginta lites et alii innumerabiles, non longe sancti quatuor onati. | In via Prenestina foris murum in d e x t e r a forma Claudiana, in si-nistra s. Helena, s. Marcellinus et Pe-trus. | § 50. Coemeterium beato-rum Petri et Marcellini via Lavicana iuxta basilicam bea-tae Helenae renovavit et tec-tum eius, id est s. Tiburtii et eorumdem sanctorum Petri et Marcellini noviter fecit, et gradus eius, qui descendunt ad eorum sacratissima corpora, noviter fecit, quoniam nullus erat iam descensus ad ipsa sancta corpora. | Coemeterium in-ter duas lauros ad s. Helenam. |

| I | II | III | IV |
|---|---|---|---|
| INDEX<br>Coemeteriorum<br>(mutilus)<br>e *Notitia*<br>*Regionum*<br>*Urbis Romae* | INDICES OLEORUM<br><br>quae collegit Ioannes Abbas | ITINERARIUM<br><br>ex unico<br><br>Codice Salisburgensi | EPITOME<br>libri *de locis*<br>*sanctorum Martyrum*<br>e Codicibus<br>Salisburgensi puro,<br>Wirceburgensi puro<br>et Salisburgensi interpol |

**VIA LATINA**

| | | | |
|---|---|---|---|
| | | Deinde pervenies ad s. Gordianum martyrem, cuius corpus requiescit sub altare magno in ecclesia s. Epimachi, et Quintus et Quartus martyres iuxta ecclesia[m] in cubiculo pausant, et longe in antro Trofimus martyr. Deinde pervenies eadem via ad speluncam, hic requiescit... (1) eadem via s. Eugenia virgo et martyr in cubiculo ecclesiae pausat, et in altero loco Emisseus martyr.<br><br>(1) *Hic aliqua desiderantur.* | K. Iuxta viam vero tinam ecclesia est s. Go ani, ubi ipse cum fra Epimacho in una sepultu I b i quoque Quartus Quintus: ibi Sulpitius Servilianus et s. Sophia Trophimus cum m u l t martyribus sepulti dor unt. K. Et. iuxta eanc viam Tertuliani est bas ca, ubi ipse c u m mu martyribus iacet. Eccl quoque s. Eugeniae iu eam viam est, ubi ipsa c matre sua in uno tum iacet: ibi s. Stephanus p cum toto clero suo num XXVIII martyres: ibi Nemeseus, s. Olimphius Simpronius, s. Theodo s. Superius, s. Obloteris Tiburticanus martyres s sepulti [et eadem via clesia est s. Stephani pr martyris *additum alia nu*]. |

**VIA APPIA**

| | | | |
|---|---|---|---|
| Coemeterium Praetextati ad s. Ianuarium via Appia.<br><br>Coemeterium Catacumbas ad s. Sebastianum via Appia.<br><br>Coemeterium Calisti ad. s. Xystum via Appia. | PITTACIA AMPULLARUM<br>...*Sca Sapien*-tia, sca Spes, sca Fides, sca *Cari-tas*, *sca* Caecilia scs T a r s i c u s, *scs Cornelius et* multa milia sanctorum.<br><br>*Sci Sebastian*i scs Eutycius, scs Q u i r i n u s, *scs Valerian*us, scs Tiburtius, scs Maxim*us*, *scs* Urban*u*s, *scs* Ia-nuarius. | INDEX OLEORUM<br>Sce *Soth*eris<br>Sce *Sapi*entae<br>Sce Spei<br>Sce Fides<br>Sce *Carit*atis<br>Sce *Cec*iliae<br>Sci Tarsicii<br>Sci Cornilii<br>et multa milia sanctorum.<br><br>Sci Sevastiani<br>Sci Eutycii<br>Sci Quirini<br>Sci Valeriani<br>Sci Tiburti<br>Sci Maximi<br>Sci Orbani<br>Sci Ianuari | Postea pervenies via Appia ad s. Sebastianum martyrem, cuius corpus iacet in inferiore loco, et ibi sunt sepulcra apostolorum Petri et Pauli, in quibus XL annorum requiescebant. Et in occidentali parte ecclesiae per gradus descendis ubi s. Cyrinus p a p a et martyr pausat. Et eadem via ad aquilonem a d ss. martyres Tiburtium et Valerianum e t Maximum. Ibi [intrabis in | K. Iuxta viam App in orientali parte civi ecclesia est s. Suteris tyris, ubi ipsa cum m martyribus i a c e t, et i eandem viam ecclesia e Syxti papae ubi ipse mit. Ibi quoque et Cae virgo pausat, et ibi s. sicius et s. Geferinus uno tumulo iacet, et il Eusebius et s. Coloceru s. Parthenius per se sin iacent et DCCC mar ibidem requiescunt. K de haud procul in co terio Calisti Corneliu |

| V<br>*NOTITIA PORTARUM,*<br>*viarum, ecclesiarum*<br>circa<br>Urbem Romam<br>Willelmo Malmesburiensi | VI<br><br>TOPOGRAPHIA<br><br>Einsiedelnensis | VII<br>EXCERPTA TOPOGRAPHICA<br>e<br>Vita Hadriani I | VIII<br>INDEX<br>Coemeteriorum<br>e libro<br>*Mirabilium*<br>*Urbis Romae* |
|---|---|---|---|
| Octava porta s. Ioannis quae ad antiquos Asseranica [*al.* senarica, *lege* Asinaria] dicatur. Nona porta Metrosa *ge* Metrovia] dicitur et con istis ambabus via Latina et. Decima porta et via Laa dicitur. Iuxta eam requient in una ecclesia martyres rdianus et Epimacus, Sulpis, Servilianus, Quintus, artus, Sophia, Tryphenus, et prope in alio loco Tertullis et non longe ecclesia beaEugeniae, in qua iacet et udia mater eius, et Stephas papa cum clero suo numeXIX et Nemesius diaconus. | In via Latina extra civitatem in sinistra oratorium s. Mariae, s. Gordiani: in dextera s. Ianuarii, oratorium s. Sixti, s. Eugenia, ad s. Theodorum [*vide viam Appiam*]. | § 78. Basilicam s. Eugeniae tam intus quamque foris a novo restauravit. Simili modo et basilicam s. Gordiani atque Epimachi, s e u coemeterium eiusdem ecclesiae, Simplicii et Serviliani, atque Quarti et Quinti martyrum, et beatae Sophiae una cum coemeterio s. Tertullini foris portam Latinam a novo in integrum renovavit. | Coemeterium Gordiani foris portam Latinam. |
| Undecima porta et via diciAppia. Ibi requiescunt s. bastianus et Quirinus, olim ibi requieverunt stolorum corpora. Et lo propius Romam sunt tyres Ianuarius, Urbanus, on, Quirinus, Agapitus, Fesimus. Et in altera ecclesia rtius, Valerianus, Maxi, nec longe ecclesia s. Caee martyris; et ibi recondint Stephanus, Sixtus, Zefus, Eusebius, Melchiades, cellus Eutichianus, DionyAntheros, Pontianus, Lupapa, Optatus, Iulianus, | *Fragmentum I*<br><br>In via Appia Soter, Xistus, Urbanus, Marcellianus et Marcus, Ianuarius, et ecclesia ubi decollatus est Xistus, Sebastianus. [*Vide viam Ardeatinam*].<br><br>*Fragmentum II*<br><br>Inde [*id est a ss. Marco et Marcelliano*] ad s. Soterum, inde ad s. | § 76. Ecclesiam apostolorum foris portam Appiam milliario tertio in loco, qui appellatur Catacumbas, ubi corpus beati Sebastiani martyris cum aliis quiescit, in ruinis praeventam a novo restauravit. § 78. Ecclesiam beati Tiburtii et Valeriani atque Maximi, seu basilicam s. Zenonis una cum coemeterio ss. Urbani pontificis, Felicissimi et Agapiti atque Ianuarii et Cyrini martyrum foris portam Appiam uno cohaerentes loco, quae ex priscis marcuerant temporibus, a novo restauravit. | Coemeterium Calisti iuxta catacumbas.<br><br>Coemeterium Praetextati inter portam Appiam...... ad s. Apollinarem. |

| I | II | III | IV |
|---|---|---|---|
| INDEX Coemeteriorum (mutilus) e Notitia Regionum Urbis Romae | INDICES OLEORUM quae collegit Ioannes Abbas | ITINERARIUM ex unico Codice Salisburgensi | EPITOME libri de locis sanctorum Martyrum e Codicibus Salisburgensi puro, Wirceburgensi puro et Salisburgensi interpol. |

*Sequitur* VIA APPIA

| | | III | IV |
|---|---|---|---|
| | | speluncam magnam et ibi *addita in margine*] i n v e n i e s s. Urbanum episcopum et confessorem, et in altero loco Felicissimum et Agapitum martyres et diaconos Syxti, et in tertio loco Cyrinum martyrem, et in quarto Ianuarium martyrem. Et in tertia ecclesia rursum [*lege* sursum] s. Synon martyr quiescit. Eadem via ad s. Caeciliam, ibi innumerabilis multitudo martyrum. Primus Syxtus papa et martyr. Dionisius papa et martyr, Iulianus papa et martyr, Flavianus martyr, s. Caecilia virgo et martyr, LXXX martyres ibi requiescunt deorsum. Geferinus papa et confessor sursum quiescit. Eusebius papa et martyr longe in antro requiescit. Cornelius papa et martyr longe in antro altero requiescit. Postea pervenies ad s. virginem Soterem e t martyrem [eadem via venis ad ecclesiam parvam ubi decollatus est s. Xystus cum diaconibus suis: *addita in margine*], cuius corpus iacet ad aquilonem. | Cyprianus in ecclesia d miunt. [Et in altera s lunca s. Calocerus dia nus: *alia manu additu* K. Iuxta eandem v quoque ecclesia est mu rum sanctorum, id est uarii, qui fuit de sep filiis Felicitatis maior n Urbani, Agapiti, Felic mi, Cyrini, Zenonis, fra Valentini, Tiburtii, Va ani [et Maximi: *addi* *alia manu*], et multi r tyres ibi requiescunt. K iuxta eandem viam eccl est s. Sebastiani mart ubi ipse dormit ubi sun pulturae apostolorum quibus XL annos qui runt. Ibi quoque et C nus martyr est sepultu |

| V<br><br>NOTITIA PORTARUM,<br>*viarum, ecclesiarum*<br>circa<br>Urbem Romam<br>Willelmo Malmesburiensi | VI<br><br>TOPOGRAPHIA<br><br>Einsiedelnensis | VII<br><br>EXCERPTA TOPOGRAPHICA<br>e<br>Vita Hadriani I | VIII<br><br>INDEX<br>Coemeteriorum<br>e libro<br>*Mirabilium*<br>*Urbis Romae* |
|---|---|---|---|
| ilocerus, Parthenius, Tarsiti-, Policamus, [*al.* Politanus] artyres. Ibidem ecclesia s. ornelii et corpus. Et in al- a ecclesia sancta Sotheris, et n longe pausant martyres ppolitus, Adrianus, Eusebi-, Maria, Martha, Paulina, ileria, Marcellus; et prope pa Marcus in sua ecclesia. | Sixtum: ibi et s. Flavianus et Anthe- ros et Miltiades; inde ad s. Corneli- um; inde ad s. Se- bastianum. Inde re- vertendo per viam Appiam ad ecclesi- am ubi s. Systus cum suis diaconibus decollatus est.<br><br>*Topographia*<br>[*vide viam*<br>*Latinam*]<br><br>In e a d e m via [*Appia*] extra civi- tatem in sinistra ad s. Ianuarium, ubi Syxtus martyrizatus est, s. Eugenia, ad s. Theodorum. In dextera s. Petronel- la Nerei et Achil- lei, Marci et Mar- celliani, ad s. So- terum, s. Cornelii, Xisti, Faviani, An- theros, et Militia- dis, ad s. Sebasti- anum [*vide viam*<br>*Ardeatinam*]. | | |

| I | II | | III | IV |
|---|---|---|---|---|
| **INDEX** Coemeteriorum (mutilus) *e Notitia Regionum Urbis Romae* | **INDICES OLEORUM** quae collegit Ioannes Abbas | | **ITINERARIUM** ex unico Codice Salisburgensi | **EPITOME** libri *de locis sanctorum Martyrum* e Codicibus Salisburgensi puro, Wirceburgensi puro et Salisburgensi interpola |

### VIA ARDEATINA

| | | | | |
|---|---|---|---|---|
| Coemeterium Domitillae Nerei et Achillei ad s. Petronillam via Ardeatina. | PITTACIUM AMPULLAE <br><br> Sca Petronilla, scs Nereus, scs Acilleus, scs Damasus, s c s Marcellinus, scs Marcus. | INDEX OLEORUM <br><br> Sce Petronillae filiae sci Petri Apostoli. Sci Nerei Sci Damasi Sci Marcelliani *Sci Acillei* *Sci Marci* | Et dimittis viam Appiam et pervenies ad s. Marcum papam et martyrem, postea ad s. Damasum papam et martyrem via Ardeatina, et ibi in altera ecclesia invenies duos diaconos et martyres Marcum et Marcellianum fratres germanos cuius corpus quiescit sursum s u b magno altare. Deinde descendis per gradus ad ss. martyres Nereum et Achilleum. | K. Iuxta viam Ardea nam ecclesia est s. Petr ellae; ibi quoque s. Ner et s. Achilleus sunt et ir Petronella sepulti. K. prope eandem viam s. I masus papa depositus est soror eius Martha. Et alia basilica non lor Marcus e t Marcellia sunt honorati, et adhuc alia ecclesia alius Mar cum Marcellino in hon habetur. |
| Coemeterium Balbinae ad s. Marcum [et Marcellianum *haec delenda*] via Ardeatina. | | | | |
| Coemeterium Basilei ad s. Marcum [*adde* et Marcellianum] via Ardeatina. | | | | |

### VIA OSTIENSIS

| | | | | |
|---|---|---|---|---|
| Coemeterium Commodillae ad s. Felicem et Adauctum via Ostiensi. | *pittacium deest* | INDEX OLEORUM <br><br> Sci Pauli Apostholi. | Et sic vadis ad occidentem et invenies s. Felicem episcopum et martyrem, et descendis per gradus ad corpus eius, et sic vadis ad s. Paulum via Ostensi, et in australi parte cerne ecclesiam s. Teclae supra montem positam, i n q u a corpus eius quiescit in spelunca in aquilone parte. | K. In parte australi c tatis iuxta viam Osten Paulus apostolus corp pausat et Timotheus epi pus et martyr, de quo minit liber Silvestri, ibi dormit et a n t e fron eiusdem basilicae orator est Stephani martyris. pis ibi, quo lapidatus Stephanus, super altare positus. <br><br> K. Inde haud procu meridiem monasterium aquae Salviae, ubi cap Anastasii est et locus decollatus est Paulus. P quoque basilicae Pauli clesia s. Teclae est, ipsa corpore iacet. |

| V<br>*NOTITIA PORTARUM,*<br>*viarum, ecclesiarum*<br>circa<br>Urbem Romam<br>e Willelmo Malmesburiensi | VI<br><br>TOPOGRAPHIA<br><br>Einsiedelnensis | VII<br><br>EXCERPTA TOPOGRAPHICA<br>e<br>Vita Hadriani I | VIII<br>INDEX<br>Coemeteriorum<br>e libro<br>*Mirabilium*<br>*Urbis Romae* |
|---|---|---|---|
| Inter viam Appiam et Osti-nsem est via Ardeatina, ubi unt Marcus et Marcellianus, t ibi iacet Damasus papa in ua ecclesia. Et non longe s. etronilla et Nereus et Achil-eus et alii plures. | *Fragmentum I*<br>In via Appia<br>Soter, Xistus, Ur-banus, Marcellianus et Marcus, Ianua-rius etc.<br>[*Horum nominum ordo perturbatus: vi-de fragmentum II et viam Appiam*].<br><br>*Fragmentum II*<br>Deinde [*id est a s. Paulo apostolo et a ss. Felice, Adaucto et Emerita*] ad s. Petronellam et Ne-reum et Achilleum. Inde ad s. Marcum et Marcellianum. In-de ad s. Sotherum *etc.* [*vide viam Ap-piam*].<br><br>*Topographia*<br>In via Appia, in dextera, s. Petron-ella Nerei et Achil-lei, Marci et Mar-celliani, ad s. So-terum *etc.*<br>[*vide viam Ap-piam*]. |  | Coemeterium Bal-binae via Ardea-tina.<br><br>Coemeterium Ior-danorum, Nerei et Achillei via Ardea-tina.<br>[*Utrumque coem. e libro Benedicti canonici: sed vox* Iordanorum *huc per errorem translata*]. |
| Duodecima porta et via Osti-sis [*al.* Ostensa] dicitur, mo- porta s. Pauli vocatur, quia xta eam requiescit in ecclesia a. Ibidemque Timotheus mar-r, et non longe in ecclesia s. eclae sunt martyres Felix et dauctus et Nemesius. In aqua lvia est caput Anastasii mar-ris. | Inde [*id est a monte Aventino et balneo Mercurii*] ad portam Ostensis; in-de per porticum u-que ad ecclesiam Mennae, et de Men-na usque ad s. Paulum apostolum. Inde ad s. Felicem et Adauctum et Emeritam. |  | Coemeterium s. Cy-riaci via Ostiensi [*Petrus Mallius ad-dit ubi est ecclesia s. Cyriaci*].<br><br>Coemeterium In-nocentium ad s. Pau-lum [*e libro Bene-dicti canonici*]. |

| I<br>INDEX<br>Coemeteriorum<br>(mutilus)<br>*e Notitia<br>Regionum<br>Urbis Romae* | II<br>INDICES OLEORUM<br>quae collegit Ioannes Abbas | III<br>ITINERARIUM<br>ex unico<br>Codice Salisburgensi | IV<br>EPITOME<br>libri *de locis<br>sanctorum Martyrum*<br>e Codicibus<br>Salisburgensi puro,<br>Wirceburgensi puro<br>et Salisburgensi interpola[ |
|---|---|---|---|
| *Sequitur* VIA OSTIENSIS | | | K. Et non longe inde [<br>clesia s. Felicis est, ubi i[<br>dormit, cum quo, quan[<br>ad coelum migravit, pari[<br>properabat Adauctus,<br>ambo requiescunt in u[<br>loco. Ibi quoque et Non[<br>seus martyr cum plurin[<br>iacet. |
| **VIA PORTUENSIS**<br><br>Coemeterium<br>ad<br>insalsatos<br>[*al.* ad<br>insalatos]<br>ad<br>s. Felicem<br>via Portuensi.<br><br>Coemeterium<br>Pontiani<br>ad<br>ursum pileatum,<br>Abdon<br>et Sennen<br>via Portuensi. | | In occidentali parte<br>Tiberis ecclesia est be-<br>ati Felicis martiris, in<br>qua corpus eius quies-<br>cit, et Alexandri mar-<br>tyris [et s. Sabinae mar-<br>tyris. Deinde etiam in<br>aquilone parte ecclesi-<br>ae s. Pauli paret ec-<br>clesia s. Aristi et s.<br>Christinae et s. Victo-<br>rae ubi ipsi pausant].<br>Deinde descendis<br>ad aquilonem et in-<br>venies ecclesiam s.Can-<br>didae virginis et mar-<br>tyris, cuius corpus ibi<br>quiescit. Descendis in<br>antrum et invenies ibi<br>innumerabilem multitu-<br>dinem martyrum; Pu-<br>menius martyr ibi quies-<br>cit, et Milix martyr in<br>altero loco, et omnis<br>illa spelunca impleta<br>est ossibus martyrum.<br>Tunc ascendis et per-<br>venies ad s. Anastasium | K. Iuxta viam vero P[<br>tuensem, quae et ipsa [<br>occidentali parte civita[<br>est, s. Abdon et s. Senn[<br>scsque Milex et s. Vinc[<br>tius, s. Polion, s. Iulius,<br>Pymeon, s. Felix, s. S[<br>plicius, s. Faustinus,<br>Beatricis dormiunt. |

| V<br>*NOTITIA PORTARUM,*<br>*viarum, ecclesiarum*<br>circa<br>Urbem Romam<br>e Willelmo Malmesburiensi | VI<br><br>TOPOGRAPHIA<br><br>Einsiedelnensis | VII<br><br>EXCERPTA TOPOGRAPHICA<br>e<br>Vita Hadriani I | VIII<br>INDEX<br>Coemeteriorum<br>e libro<br>*Mirabilium*<br>*Urbis Romae* |
|---|---|---|---|
| Tertiadecima porta Portu-sis dicitur et via. Ibi prope ecclesia sunt martyres Fe-x, Alexander, Abdon et Sen-es, Symeon, Anastasius, Poli-, Vincentius, Milex, Candi- et Innocentia. | In via Portensi extra civitatem in dextra Abdo et Sennes. | § 80. Ecclesiam s. Felicis po-sitam foris portam Portuensem a novo restauravit. Simulque et basilicam ss. Abdon et Sennen atque beatae Candidae una cum ceteris sanctorum coemeteriis in idipsum pariter renovavit. | Coemeterium Ursi ad Portensam.<br><br>Coemeterium s. Fe-licis via Portuensi. |

| I | II | III | IV |
|---|---|---|---|
| **INDEX** Coemeteriorum (mutilus) *e Notitia Regionum Urbis Romae* | **INDICES OLEORUM** quae collegit Ioannes Abbas | **ITINERARIUM** ex unico Codice Salisburgensi | **EPITOME** libri *de locis sanctorum Martyrum* e Codicibus Salisburgensi puro, Wirceburgensi puro et Salisburgensi interpola |

*Sequitur* VIA PORTUENSIS

| | | | papam et martyrem, et in alio Polion martyr quiescit. Deinde intrabis in ecclesiam magnam: ibi sancti martyres Abdo et Sennes quiescunt. Deinde exeas et intrabis ubi s. Innocentius papa et martyr quiescit. | |

VIA AURELIA

| Coemeterium Calepodii ad s. Calixtum via Aurelia. | PITTACIUM AMPULLAE *Sci Pancr*ati sci Artemi, sca Sofia cum tres filias *suas,* sca Paulina, sca Lucina, sci Processi sci *Mar-tinia*ni. | INDEX OLEORUM Sci *Pancr*ati Sci Arthemi Sce Sofiae cum tres filias suas Sce Paulinae Sce Lucinae Sci Processi Sci Martiniani | Deinde ambulas ad s. Pancratium, cuius corpus quiescit in formosa ecclesia via Aurelia, quam s. Honorius papa magna ex parte reaedificavit, et in illa ecclesia intrabis longe sub terra et invenies Ardhimium martyrem; et in altero loco s. Paulinum martyrem, et in altero antro s. Sobiam martyrem et duae filiae eius Agapite et Pistis martyres, et ascendis sursum et pervenies ad ecclesiam; ibi quiescunt s. Processus et Martinianus sub terra, et s. Lucina virgo et martyr in superiori. Deinde pervenies eadem via ad sanctos pontifices et martyres duos Felices. Postea eadem via pervenies ad ecclesiam; ibi invenies s. Calistum papam et martyrem, et in altero [loco] in superiori domo s. Iulius papa et martyr. | K. Inde haud procul sinistra manu iuxta via Aureliam s. Processus, Martianus, s. Pancratius, Paulinus, s. Arthemius, Felix, s. Calistus, s. Cal pus cum multis sepulti cent. |

| V<br>*NOTITIA PORTARUM,*<br>*viarum, ecclesiarum*<br>circa<br>Urbem Romam<br>e Willelmo Malmesburiensi | VI<br>TOPOGRAPHIA<br>Einsiedelnensis | VII<br>EXCERPTA TOPOGRAPHICA<br>e<br>Vita Hadriani I | VIII<br>INDEX<br>Coemeteriorum<br>e libro<br>*Mirabilium*<br>*Urbis Romae* |
|---|---|---|---|
| Quartadecima porta et via ꞁurelia, quae modo porta s. 'ancrati martyris dicitur, quod ıxta eam requiescit in sua ec‑꠸esia, et alii martyres Pau‑nus, Arthemius, s. Sapientia ꞁm tribus filiabus Fide, Spe, ꞁharitate. In altera ecclesia rocessus et Martinianus, et in ꞓrtia Felices duo, et in quarta ꞁ Calixtus et Calepodius, et in ꞁuinta s. Basilides duodecimo ꞁiliaro. | *Fragmentum*<br>Inter Aurelia et Portuensis Processus et Martinianus et Panchratius, Abdo et Sennes.<br><br>*Topographia*<br>In via Aurelia extra civitatem [*in sinistra*] S. Pan‑cratii, in dextera Processi et Martini‑ani. | § 73. Basilicam beati Pan‑cratii martyris nimia vetustate dirutam atque ruinis praeven‑tam in integrum a novo nimio decore una cum monasterio s. Victoris ibidem sito restauravit. | Coemeterium Ca‑lepodii ad s. Pan‑cratium.<br><br>Coemeterium s. Agathae ad giru‑lum.<br><br>Coemeterium Iulii via Aurelia [*ex Be‑nedicto canonico*]. |

| I | II | III | IV |
|---|---|---|---|
| INDEX<br>Coemeteriorum<br>(mutilus)<br>*e Notitia<br>Regionum<br>Urbis Romae* | INDICES OLEORUM<br><br>quae collegit Ioannes Abbas | ITINERARIUM<br><br>ex unico<br><br>Codice Salisburgensi | EPITOME<br>libri *de locis<br>sanctorum Martyrum*<br>e Codicibus<br>Salisburgensi puro,<br>Wirceburgensi puro<br>et Salisburgensi interpolat |
| | *pittacium deest* INDEX OLEORUM<br>Sci Petri Apostholi. | Et sic intrabis via Vaticana donec pervenies ad basilicam beati Petri, quam Constantinus imperator totius orbis condidit, eminentem super omnes ecclesias et formosam, in cuius occidentali plaga beatum corpus eius quiescit. | Primum Petrus in pa te occidentali civitatis iux viam Corneliam ad miliar um primum in corpor requiescit, et pontifical ordo, excepto numero pau co, in eodem loco in tum bis propriis requiescit. I quoque iuxta eandem via sedes est apostolorum mensa et recubitus eoru de marmore facta usqu hodie apparet. Mensa qu que, modo altare, qua Petrus manibus suis fec ibidem est. K. Iuxta ea dem quoque viam s. Ru na, s. Secunda, s. Mari s. Marius, s. Ambacu, Audafax et alii quam plu mi sancti iacent. |

VIA CORNELIA

| V<br>*NOTITIA PORTARUM,*<br>*viarum, ecclesiarum*<br>circa<br>Urbem Romam<br>e Willelmo Malmesburiensi | VI<br>TOPOGRAPHIA<br>Einsiedelnensis | VII<br>EXCERPTA TOPOGRAPHICA<br>e<br>Vita Hadriani I | VIII<br>INDEX<br>Coemeteriorum<br>e libro<br>*Mirabilium*<br>*Urbis Romae* |
|---|---|---|---|
| Prima porta Cornelia quae modo porta s. Petri, et via Cornelia. Iuxta eam ecclesia beati Petri sita est, in qua corpus eius iacet, auro et lapidibus parata. Etenim nullus hominum scit numerum sanctorum martyrum qui in eadem ecclesia pausant. In eadem via ecclesia altera in qua requiescunt sanctae virgines Rufina et Secunda. In tertia ecclesia sunt Marius et Martha et Audifax et Abacuc filii eorum. | | | |

## Chapter V

## A BRIEF ACCOUNT OF THE ANCIENT CHRISTIAN CEMETERIES OF ROME[1]

### 1.  The Vatican Cemetery[2]

IN THIS section, a very brief description of the Christian cemeteries of Rome will be given. Following the topographical order, it will begin with the Vatican and continue on to the Aurelian Way, etc., which is the order adopted by Bosio in his *Subterranean Rome,* and indicated in the Itinerary of the tombs. Some knowledge of the inscriptions composed by Damasus for each of these cemeteries is indispensable. Their texts will be given, therefore, in dealing with each of the cemeteries. Through these inscriptions we are able to acquire important knowledge regarding the various monuments.

The Vatican cemetery, in all likelihood, owes its origin to the Roman protomartyrs of the persecution of Nero.

The first victims of the persecution begun by this emperor after the burning of Rome, in the year 64, were certainly martyred in the imperial gardens situated near the Circus of Nero.[3] They were the first fruits of the Roman Church, and from this epoch, as stated above, the origin of the Vatican cemetery probably dates. At that time there was already in existence in the vicinity of the imperial villa an actual necropolis, separated from the Circus by means of the Cornelian Way, as is proved by numerous pagan burial inscriptions dating from these early times, which have been unearthed in this locality. Along with these inscriptions, many remains of pagan cemeteries for the reception of cinerary urns have been found.

The tomb of the Apostle Peter was the most renowned monument of this cemetery, since he was buried here immediately after his martyrdom. The holy apostle's actual coming to Rome, the authenticity of his martyrdom and his burial on the Vatican, have been demonstrated elsewhere.[4] Pope Anaclete erected an oratory (*memoria*) over the tomb of St.

Peter.[5] The *Book of the Popes* speaks of this oratory, but does not say that Anaclete buried St. Peter, as some have recently supposed. The area of this cemetery must have been restricted, because when the foundations of the basilica were laid, the remains of pagan cemeteries were found a short distance from the papal altar. The tomb of the apostle was probably a small room built partly below and partly above ground. Access to it could be had from the Cornelian Way, on which stood the small oratory which Pope Anaclete had raised in the apostle's memory.[6] It was here that the first popes were interred, but nothing now remains of their tombs; they were destroyed in the process of reconstructing the two successive basilicas.[7]

The tombs of the Apostles Peter and Paul are indicated respectively in the cemeteries on the Vatican and on the Ostian Way, by Caius, a priest of the beginning of the third century.[8]

The Emperor Constantine enclosed the sarcophagus which contained the body of the apostle, within a covering of bronze, surmounting it with a cross of gold with an inscription recorded in the *Book of the Popes* in the life of Pope Sylvester. The same emperor also built a magnificent basilica over the tomb of the apostle, of which we can still reconstruct the form and the principal ornaments. The inscriptions adorning the body of the apse and the triumphal arch have been preserved for us, the first by the codex of Einsiedeln, the second by other books or lists of inscriptions.

After the erection of the basilica, the open-air cemetery increased in size; the Vatican soon became covered with chapels, sepulchres and mausoleums. Pope Damasus carried out important works here, and built a baptistery, after preventing the waters from flooding the sepulchres: a condition which had done great damage up to that time.

An imperial mausoleum was also erected during the time of Honorius. It was circular in form, later becoming the church of St. Petronilla. It stood close to the place occupied by the sacristy.

Among the more important monuments of the Vatican cemetery might be mentioned the sepulchres of Junius Bassus and Anicius Petronius Probus. Junius Bassus died while prefect of the city, shortly after he had received baptism, in 359. His sarcophagus may still be seen in the Vatican grottoes, completely adorned with bas-reliefs of a symbolic nature, and with scenes taken from the Old and New Testaments.[9]

The sarcophagus of Anicius Petronius Probus and his wife Anicia Proba is preserved in the modern chapel of the Pietà, along with a copy of the original inscription; the inscription itself is at present in the nearby Petrine Museum, which contains a remarkable collection of pieces from the old and the new basilica. Over and above these, there was the mausoleum of the imperial family at the place where the sacristy now stands. The tomb of St. Gregory the Great belongs to the sixth century and that of Caedwalla, king of the Saxons, dates from the seventh. During the second half of the eighth century, Paul I converted the mausoleum of the imperial family of Honorius into the chapel of St. Petronilla, whose body was taken there from the Ardeatine Way.

During the ninth century, the basilica was profaned by the Saracens.[10] As stated before, the sarcophagus of St. Peter, visible up to this time, was perhaps hidden in those perilous days, because from that period on, we no longer find any reference to it.

Of the ancient Constantinian basilica, preserved until the sixteenth century, we possess several descriptions and delineations made by writers of that century and the previous one. From a manuscript of Eton College, near Windsor, we have a design which represents the state of the basilica toward the beginning of the twelfth century.[11]

In early times there were numerous inscriptions in this cemetery; at present only thirty of these are preserved in the Vatican Crypts.[12] In this subterranean cemetery, we distinguish the New Crypts, which surround the tomb of St. Peter, and the Old Crypts, which are farther away; they extend to the chapel of the Sacrament and still show traces of the ancient pavement.

The central part of the New Crypts consists of the crypt of St. Peter, erected by Clement VIII behind the chancel of the

Confessional. In the other galleries and chapels, several burial inscriptions are preserved which date from the fourth, fifth and sixth centuries, and come down to us from the time when the cemetery surrounded the basilica. The Old Crypts also contain, among other important monuments of the Middle Ages and the Renaissance, some valuable ancient epitaphs.[13]

An example of one of the inscriptions composed by Pope Damasus, still preserved for us in a corridor of the New Crypts, will be of interest:

CINGEBANT LATICES MONTEM TENEROQVE MEATV
CORPORA MVLTORVM CINERES ATQVE OSSA RIGABANT
NON TVLIT HOC DAMASVS COMMVNI LEGE SEPVLTOS
POST REQVIEM TRISTES ITERVM PERSOLVERE POENAS
PROTINVS AGGRESSVS MAGNVM SVPERARE LABOREM
AGGERIS IMMENSI DEIECIT CVLMINA MONTIS
INTIMA SOLLICITE SCRVTATVS VISCERA TERRAE
SICCAVIT TOTVM QVIDQVID MADEFECERAT HVMOR
INVENIT FONTEM PRAEBET QVI DONA SALVTIS
HAEC CVRAVIT MERCVRIVS LEVITA FIDELIS

The inscription records the labor of drying up the cemetery of the Vatican, ordered by Pope Damasus, as was the baptistery which was built where a spring of water was encountered during the work of repair.

## 2.   The Cemeteries of the Aurelian Way[14]

### a. CEMETERY OF OCTAVILLA OR OF ST. PANCRATIUS[15]

This cemetery anciently bore the name of Octavilla. It was there that St. Pancratius, a youthful martyr, perhaps of the time of Diocletian, was buried. He was a native of Phrygia, but the details of his life are very obscure. He was beheaded on the Aurelian Way, and a matron by the name of Octavilla gathered the remains and placed them in a private cemetery which she possessed on the same Aurelian Way, "in praedio suo" — "on her own property" — as the text says. This cemetery was clearly distinguished from the adjoining one of Calepodius in the most ancient documents, but it was confused with it later on.

A basilica was erected over the tomb of the martyr, perhaps at the very beginning of the peace of the Church. This was restored about the fifth century by Pope Symmachus.[16] During the seventh century, Honorius I (630) rebuilt it and changed the position of the sarcophagus, which at the time of the construction of the basilica had been left in its original place, "ex obliquo aulae," as an inscription handed down to us by the Itinerary of Einsiedeln attests.[17]

Because the body of this martyr was never transferred to the city, this locality always remained a place of great veneration. This explains why, in the Middle Ages, all the other Christian traditions of the Aurelian Way were centered here.

Today scarcely anything remains of the ancient basilica, which was entirely renovated in modern times. The relics of St. Pancratius were profaned and scattered during the French Revolution. This cemetery, as well as the basilica, was attached to the title of St. Chrysogonus.

Today the cemetery may be entered by a stairway of modern construction situated behind the church. It is not extensive, and is of little importance at present; but nevertheless it deserves to be explored and completely unearthed. It is hoped that the Committee organized for this purpose may carry out its plans.

### b. CEMETERY OF STS. PROCESSUS AND MARTINIANUS[18]

Sts. Processus and Martinianus, according to the story of their lives, were the prison-keepers of Sts. Peter and Paul. By the same account, they were martyred shortly after the apostles by being beheaded on the Aurelian Way; they were buried close by, by the matron Lucina.

It is supposed that the cemetery of Sts. Processus and Martinianus extends between the Panfili villa and the Pellegrini vineyard, but principally under the villa. The various galleries of the subterranean vaults lying beneath these two properties must communicate with one another, as their respective courses seem to show. From general indications, the center of the cemetery may perhaps be at the second entrance to the villa. This, in fact, was once an important burial region, since there are numerous galleries cut at regular distances, still having many sepulchres which have not been opened. There are ancient supports built to reënforce the walls, and there are also traces of an ancient stairway.

The accessible galleries lying under the vineyard are completely devastated, although the tombs, which are very spacious, can be seen to be of great antiquity.

On the sepulchre of the martyrs Processus and Martinianus, there was erected during the fourth century a basilica, where St. Gregory the Great delivered one of his homilies;[19] and the *Book of the Popes* gives a record of the work done here by Pope Gregory III in 732. Paschal I moved the bodies of these martyrs to the Vatican, where there was later built an oratory in their honor. This was succeeded by the modern altar, situated in the body of the transverse nave, to the right of the new basilica. During the Middle Ages, the cemetery and the basilica bore the name of St. Agatha, a fact recorded in the *Book of the Popes*.[20] In the *Libro dei censi,* the *Book of the Census,* by Cencius Camerarius, it is called "Coemeterium B. Agathae ad girulum" — "the cemetery of Blessed Agatha at the mill."

### c. CEMETERY OF THE TWO FELIXES[21]

The reason for the title of this cemetery has not as yet been explained. One of the "two Felixes" appears to have been Pope Felix II, whose life is involved in mystery. Some believe that the other was Pope Felix I, a martyr of the third century; in fact, several compilations of the *Book of the Popes* record that Felix "built a basilica on the Aurelian Way, where he lies buried" ("fecit basilicam via Aurelia, ubi sepultus est"). On the other hand, the Catalogue of Sixtus III, preserved in the manuscripts of Klosterneuburg and Göttweig, names Felix I as among those popes who were buried in the papal crypt on the Appian Way. The same fact is brought out in the Liberian Catalogue. Hence this martyr may possibly have been another of the same name.

Bosio believed that a certain "domnus Felix" ("Lord Felix") mentioned in an inscription on the pavement of the church of St. Cecilia in Transtevere, designated Pope Felix I.[22] However, the epithet *domnus* was applied to every martyr.

The exact location of the cemetery of the two Felixes has not been established as yet.

### d. THE CEMETERY OF CALEPODIUS[23]

The cemetery of Calepodius is located in the Lamperini vineyard, facing the hospice of St. Pius V, at about the third mile of the Aurelian Way. It is recorded in the Acts of St. Callistus that this pontiff ordered the body of the priest Calepodius, who had been thrown into the Tiber, to be buried in the abovementioned cemetery. Calepodius was martyred under Alexander Severus. When Callistus, following a popular uprising, was thrown into a well near the place now occupied by the church of St. Mary in Transtevere, he was interred in the cemetery of Calepodius which was near by. This was done out of caution, it being deemed dangerous to take his body to the papal crypts on the Appian Way. Callistus was martyred in the year 222. In the fourth century, Julius I was also buried there. He had built a basilica in honor of St. Callistus in this cemetery,[24] of which remnants may still be seen in the small house in the Lamperini vineyard. The ancient workmanship of the apse gives this relic importance, and makes it worthy of being taken from its present profane use to serve some better purpose. The entrance of the cemetery is found a short distance from this apse; it is in a very dilapidated condition and its galleries are cluttered with rubbish. Perhaps the present canteen marks the spot which was once the center of a historical region; there are indications of an airshaft, such as one sees in the great crypts of the martyrs, as well as the beginning of a vast gallery which runs in the direction of the ruins of the basilica.

The body of St. Callistus was removed in the ninth century to the basilica of St. Mary in Transtevere, where it is at present venerated.

## 3. The Cemeteries of the Portuan Way[25]

### a. THE CEMETERY OF PONTIAN[26]

This cemetery has nothing to do with Pope Pontian, but derives its name from an unknown Christian who lived during the third century. It was by the merest accident that Bosio, in 1618, discovered the tombs of the martyrs of this cemetery. He came into it not by the ancient entrance but through another opening.

The Itineraries record a large number of martyrs interred in these catacombs, but the most celebrated are St. Abdon and St. Sennen, who suffered martyrdom under Valerian in the year 257 or 258, according to the Roman Martyrology. Beside them were buried two other martyrs, perhaps their companions, Milix and Vincent.

At the beginning of the fourth century, another group of tombs was formed, those of Sts. Pollio, Candida and Pigmenius, spoken of by the Acts of Sts. Peter and Marcellinus. After the peace of the Church, two oratories were erected in this place, one in honor of Sts. Abdon and Sennen, the other to St. Candida. The first was the more magnificent and must have been connected with the underground galleries.

During the fifth century, two popes were interred in one of these oratories. The Itineraries speak of these two, Anastasius I (402) and Innocent I (417), as martyrs, but this is an error. The various centers of historical interest are reached by means of a magnificent stairway, which was discovered by Bosio. These subterranean places are adorned with paintings in Byzantine style, still very well preserved. There is also an ancient baptistery,[27] with a painting representing the crowning of the martyrs Abdon and Sennen.

### b. THE CEMETERY OF ST. FELIX[28]

The cemetery of St. Felix must have been of great importance, because it gave its name to the Portuan gate and a part of the Way; but it has not been found. Without doubt it must have been a short distance from that of Pontian, and was

probably situated on the right side of the road because there is
a stream of water on the left.

This cemetery was also called *ad insalsatos*: a name
which probably arose from a corruption of the term *ad infula-
tos,* which refers perhaps to the Persian tiara (*infula*) with
which the Persian martyrs Sts. Abdon and Sennen were represented in some ancient paintings near by.[29]

### c. THE CEMETERY OF GENEROSA[30]

Generosa was the owner of a cemetery where the martyrs
Simplicius, Faustinus and Beatrice were buried. The name of
the cemetery was determined by an inscription on the sarcophagus enclosing the remains of the three martyrs, when
they were moved to the church of St. Bibiana.[31]

Faustinus and Simplicius were martyred and their bodies
cast into the Tiber during the great persecution of Diocletian,
probably on July 29, 303. Their sister Beatrice, assisted by the
priests Crispus and John, gathered their remains and interred
them in a cemetery which was situated at the sixth mile of the
Portuan Way, beneath the property of a certain Philip, *ad sextum Philippi.* Toward the end of the seventh century (683)
Pope Leo II removed their relics to St. Bibiana's. It was at this
time that the inscription of the sarcophagus came to light.

Nothing more was known of this monument until the
middle of the nineteenth century, when a series of remarkable
discoveries was made here (1858-1864), close to the wood-
lands belonging to the Arvali brothers. The outlines of the
temple of the goddess Dia were uncovered at this time; and
situated a short distance from the foundations of the pagan
temple, the excavations also brought to light a small edifice
built during the time of Pope Damasus. It was immediately
recognized as the basilica of the martyrs, though there is nothing left but the apse and a part of the walls.

Next to this basilica (which is small, as was the cemetery
itself), the most important monument is the crypt of the martyrs. It is of irregular form, and there is an admirable painting
behind the apse, not earlier than the sixth century, in which

are pictured five figures: the Saviour in the middle; to the right, Sts. Simplicius and "Viatrice"; to the left, St. Faustinianus or Faustinus and St. Rufinianus. The painting represents the *Coronatio martyrum,* "the coronation of the martyrs."

The cemetery was frequented until the seventh century. There was also a cemetery in the open, as was the custom in most cases. This was abandoned in the seventh century, as is recorded in the Itineraries. The bodies of the martyrs are at present to be found at St. Bibiana's and St. Mary Major's.[32]

### 4.  The Cemeteries of the Ostian Way[33]

#### a. THE TOMB OF ST. PAUL[34]

According to the apocryphal Acts and Martyrologies, the body of St. Paul was buried on the Ostian Way, in the property of a Christian matron by the name of Lucina. These testimonies, which are considerably later than the time of the peace of Constantine, are confirmed by documents of much greater antiquity. The body of the apostle, buried on the property of Lucina, remained there until it was removed to the hiding place on the Appian Way, along with the body of St. Peter. The bodies were later returned to their respective tombs.[35]

According to the *Book of the Popes,* Constantine also built a basilica over the tomb of St. Paul in the year 324 or 325. The inscription, which can still be seen on the sarcophagus facing the center of the papal altar, has been judged by some archeologists as belonging to the epoch of Constantine. It reads thus: PAVLO . APOSTOLO . MART.

The Constantinian basilica was not a large one. It had an entrance on the Ostian Way where the actual apse of the edifice now stands. In 386, Valentinian II built a new one, of which the modern building is a reproduction as regards grandeur, form and orientation. We know the text of the letter written by the emperor on this occasion to the prefect of Rome, Sallustius.[36] The work done by Valentinian was continued by Theodosius and completed later by Honorius, as is attested by the poetic inscription on the triumphal arch.

Galla Placida, sister of the Emperor Honorius, who died a Christian in 450 A.D., carried on the work of decorating and embellishing the basilica under the auspices of Leo I. The other inscription which encircles the arch refers to her.

The cemetery of Lucina, where St. Paul was interred, was greatly damaged by the erection of the basilica,[37] because it was originally a cemetery in the open. The Ostian Way ran between the little hill and the apse of the actual basilica. The triangle which it formed with the street running transversely behind the papal altar, delimited the area of the tomb of St. Paul. Valentinian II must have destroyed the transverse street to build the new basilica, which was much more extensive than that of Constantine.[38]

## b. THE CEMETERY OF COMMODILLA[39]

Ancient documents indicate that the tombs of Sts. Felix and Adauctus, who were martyred during the persecution of Diocletian, were to be found in this cemetery. The tombs of the two virgins, Digna and Emerita,[40] were also here. This cemetery was rediscovered by Boldetti in 1720, but remained almost inaccessible until the time of the recent excavations of the Commission, in 1904.[41]

The basilica of St. Felix and St. Adauctus, found in that year, was built, as the Acts tell us, during the time of peace: "tempore pacis edificata est basilica."[42] It is of irregular form, with a large niche in the middle and two lateral apses; the walls were decorated with paintings of the sixth century, probably under Pope John I (523-526), who "renovated the cemetery of Sts. Felix and Adauctus," as the Book of the Popes informs us. Near the entrance of the basilica may be seen a fresco representing the Saviour giving the keys to St. Peter, on whose left is St. Paul; St. Felix and St. Stephen are depicted on the right, on the left there is another saint and then St. Emerita.

A little further ahead there is another painting of the sixth century over the tomb of a woman by the name of Turtura. In the center of the picture there is an effigy of the Virgin Mary seated with the Divine Child; to the right of the throne is

St. Felix, to the left St. Adauctus in the act of protecting Turtura. On the pilaster, between the altar and the tomb, another
painting represents St. Luke.[43]

The tomb of the two martyrs Felix and Adauctus lies in
the large niche, where the saints are represented at least twice,
and where they lay "in uno loco," as one of the Itineraries
informs us.

On the left of the apse of the basilica there is an opening
to a burial gallery, excavated toward the end of the fourth
century. This may be considered a true *retro sanctos*, or hiding
place "behind the saints"; it is notable because it offers a rare
example of almost perfect preservation of galleries walled up
by the early Christians. It was reopened only in 1904.

During the progress of the excavations, many inscriptions
were discovered. The most important of them is the one in-
forming us that the work of embellishment begun by Damasus
was later completed by his successor Siricius (335-394).[44]

The inscription commemorative of the martyrs Felix and
Adauctus follows:

O SEMEL ATQVE ITERVM VERO DE NOMINE FELIX
QVI INTEMERATA FIDE CONTEMPTO PRINCIPE MVNDI
CONFESSVS CHRISTVM COELESTIA REGNA PETISTI
O VERE PRETIOSA FIDES COGNOSCITE FRATRES
QVA AD COELVM VICTOR PARITER PROPERAVIT ADAVCTVS
PRESBYTER HIS VERVS DAMASO RECTORE IVBENTE
COMPOSVIT TVMVLVM SANCTORVM LIMINA ADORNANS

## c. The Tomb of St. Timothy[45]

Timothy, mentioned in the Martyrology on August 22,
was a priest who came from Antioch to Rome during the reign
of Diocletian. He suffered martyrdom and was buried by a
matron of the name of Theona near the body of St. Paul: "ut
Paulo apostolo," say his Acts, "ut quondam Timotheus ad-
haereret."

In 1872, excavations were made to the left of the Ostian
Way facing the apse of the basilica of St. Paul, but the results
were not such as had been hoped for. Midway on a stairway

whose walls contained inscriptions of Greek and Latin names, an *arcosolium* was discovered, which unfortunately lacked all inscriptions or paintings. De Rossi believed, however, that he was able to identify this vault as the tomb of St. Timothy.[46]

### d. The Cemetery of St. Thecla[47]

This cemetery lies under the vineyard of the Serafini, shortly beyond the bridge of St. Paul. Boldetti called it the "cemetery at the little bridge of St. Paul"; or again, "the anonymous cemetery." Armellini recognized it as the cemetery of St. Thecla. We know nothing of the life of this saint. She was probably buried near the tomb of St. Paul because she had the same name as the apostle's well-known follower. The historical crypt has the appearance of an irregular basilica, being nothing more than a large room with pilasters; vaults were hewn in the walls. The niches, which correspond to the apse, still give evidence of former paintings. The tomb of the saint was probably situated here. The galleries are unusually wide and in some of the vaults as many as five tiers of graves can still be seen.

### 5.   The Cemetery of the Ardeatine Way[48]

### The Cemetery of Domitilla[49]

This is the largest of all the cemeteries of subterranean Rome. Bosio thought it formed a part of the cemetery of Callistus, but de Rossi, who was instrumental in determining the ancient topography of this important burial zone, recognized its true identity by means of two inscriptions which gave the name of Flavia Domitilla.

The cemetery of Domitilla was originally the tiny domestic tomb of the Flavii who were Christians, relatives of the Flavian emperors. It later became an immense public cemetery of the Church.

Three regions may be distinguished in this cemetery: the first, of the first and second centuries, has in addition certain centers of a later date, namely, the basilica of Sts. Nereus and Achilleus, with the tomb of Veneranda (fourth century), where there is a painting representing the deceased being introduced to heaven by St. Petronilla; the second is the section of the Flavii, which lies at the end of the large stairway; the third is the region of Ampliatus.

The basilica of Sts. Nereus and Achilleus (discovered in 1874) was erected in 390 or 395 over the original tombs of the martyrs. It has three naves and almost all the ancient columns, but only the foundations of the *scola cantorum* remain. The bishop's throne was situated in a niche in the apse, facing which must have been the altar built over the tomb of the saints. To it must have belonged the marble fragments of the grating, the column with the inscription "martirio di Sant' Achilleo," and a fragment of the cornice with outlines of the name of the same martyr. Many fragments of paintings and numerous inscriptions are attached to the walls. These are not only of a Christian character; many are pagan. Among these, several carry the title of Fasciola, to which this basilica was attached.

The underground chapel of the Flavii,[50] discovered in 1865, had its entrance on the public highway. The walls and their structure indicate great antiquity. To the right there is a room with a bench around the sides (for the agapes), and two cubicles, one of which shows pagan paintings representing genii and flowers; to the left there is another room with a well.

The gallery which begins at the entrance runs to an underground chapel of special form, which never from the beginning possessed graves, but only two large niches on the right side and two on the left. This very ancient chapel, which was certainly Christian, as is borne out by several ancient paintings and inscriptions still in place, would be the most important chapel of the catacombs if it had not been so badly damaged by continual visits from 1714 to the end of the century. The names of many of these visitors, some of them of historical importance, are found there.

Another notable and ancient region is that near the basilica of the Flavii Aurelii, where among other tombs was one of the aforementioned "Flavius Sabinus and Titiana, brother and sister."[51]

The upper level is noteworthy for the cubicle of Ampliatus,[52] with decorative paintings, commonly called Pompeian, of the second century. An inscription in marble with the name AMPLIATI is still in position in the arched vault. The person bearing this name has already been discussed in another section of this volume and his relations to St. Paul indicated.[53]

A region close to this, dating from the third and fourth centuries, also called "of the Madonna," contains numerous paintings, the most important of which is that of the Blessed Virgin, depicted between two *loculi;* the Virgin is veiled and seated, holding on her knees the Infant Jesus; at each side are the Magian Kings, four in all.

One section of this region is called "of the apostles," because it contains a fresco depicting the Saviour in the midst of the apostles. The walls are covered with numerous scenes which have been explained by Wilpert as portraying a grain market with its warehouses, boats on the Tiber, and workmen loading and unloading them. De Rossi supposes that this portion of the cemetery belonged to an association or corporation of bakers. The third section also contains other paintings and inscriptions of the fourth century, the most outstanding of which is that of the gravedigger Diogenes.

On the right wall of the basilica one may still read the reproduction of the inscription which Pope Damasus placed on the tomb of the martyrs Nereus and Achilleus:

MILITIAE NOMEN DEDERANT SAEVVMQVE GEREBANT
OFFICIVM PARITER SPECTANTES IVSSA TYRANNI
PRAECEPTIS PVLSANTE METV SERVIRE PARATI
MIRA FIDES RERVM SVBITO POSVERE FVROREM
CONVERSI FVGIVNT DVCIS IMPIA CASTRA RELINQVVNT
PROIICIVNT CLYPEOS PHALERAS TELAQVE CRVENTA
CONFESSI GAVDENT CHRISTI PORTARE TRIVMPHOS
CREDITE PER DAMASVM POSSIT QVID GLORIA CHRISTI

This inscription completes the notices given by the Acts. By it we are informed that the two saints were soldiers who had participated in persecuting the Christians, were later converted and died the death of martyrs.

## 6.  The Cemeteries of the Appian Way[54]

### a. THE CEMETERY OF CALLISTUS[55]

This remarkable cemetery probably had its origin in the second century, but received its present name at the beginning of the third, from Callistus, deacon of Zephyrin, who appointed him administrator of the cemetery, as the *Philosophumena* bears witness. Callistus, having become pope, enlarged the necropolis, which in the third century became the official place of interment of the popes.

The oldest part of the cemetery is considered to be that part which de Rossi called "the crypts of Lucina." Here are found inscriptions dating from the second century, and two cubicles with paintings in the Pompeian style, also from the beginning of the second century; in the first cubicle may be seen the baptism of the Saviour, in the second, the symbolical images of the dove, lambs with a bowl of milk, and fish. Pope St. Cornelius was later buried in this section.

Besides the crypts of Lucina, de Rossi distinguishes four other parts: (1) the cemetery properly called "of Callistus," with the crypts of the popes, of St. Cecilia and St. Eusebius, and the galleries of the Sacraments; (2) that part which he erroneously called "the cemetery of St. Soter," and which had its own stairway; (3) a large section dating from the fourth century, lying toward the north, called "the region of Liberius," because in it are to be found some inscriptions from the times of Pope Liberius; (4) a region even more to the north, still in large measure unexplored, which originally must have been a separate cemetery corresponding to that of Marcus and Balbina. According to recent studies and discoveries, the tombs of Damasus and Sts. Marcus and Marcellianus[56] ought to be between the cemetery of Callistus and that of Domitilla. However, it is certain, from whatever angle the matter is viewed, that the two tombs pointed out by some guides as belonging to Damasus and Sts. Marcus and Marcellianus are not theirs. That recently ascribed to Pope Damasus cannot be his, since it antedates his pontificate and since, moreover, he was interred in a basilica built above ground and not in a subterranean vault. The imprint of the inscription relating to the mother of Damasus found there, comes from another place. Over and above these, there are several sand pits close to the crypts of Lucina, behind the crypt of St. Cecilia and toward the center of the cemetery near the section of Liberius, where the memorial of those Greek martyrs said to be buried in sand pits of Hippolytus ought to be found.

In the crypt of the popes, only five of the fifteen inscriptions have been found, namely, those of Pontian, Anterus, Fabian, Lucius and Eutychian. The inscription ascribed to Pope Urban by de Rossi is doubtful.

In the fourth century, Damasus adorned the venerable crypt, placing two celebrated metrical inscriptions there. One records all the more outstanding memorials of the cemetery of Callistus, and is still to be seen in the crypt. (See following page.) The other is the inscription dedicated to Pope Sixtus II, describing the scene of his martyrdom, and indicating the zeal and eager rivalry with which the Christians met death:

TEMPORE QVO GLADIVS SECVIT PIA VISCERA MATRIS
HIC POSITVS RECTOR COELESTIA IVSSA DOCEBAM
ADVENIVNT SVBITO RAPIVNT QVI FORTE SEDENTEM
MILITIBVS MISSIS POPVLI TVNC COLLA DEDERE
MOX VBI COGNOVIT SENIOR QVIS TOLLERE VELLET
PALMAM SEQVE SVVMQVE CAPVT PRIOR OBTVLIT IPSE
IMPATIENS FERITAS POSSET NE LAEDERE QVEMQVAM
OSTENDIT CHRISTVS REDDIT QVI PRAEMIA VITAE
PASTORIS MERITVM NVMERVM GREGIS IPSE TVETVR

Pope Damasus also placed the following inscription on the tomb of Tarsicius in the cemetery of Callistus. It is of great importance, as bearing on the dogma of the Eucharist:

PAR MERITVM QVICVMQVE LEGIS COGNOSCE DVORVM
QVIS DAMASVS RECTOR TITVLOS POST PRAEMIA REDDIT
IVDAICVS POPVLVS STEPHANVM MELIORA MONENTEM
PERCVLERAT SAXIS TVLERAT QVI EX HOSTE TROPAEVM
MARTYRIVM PRIMVS RAPVIT LEVITA FIDELIS
TARSICIVM SANCTVM CHRISTI SACRAMENTA GERENTEM
CVM MALE SANA MANVS PETERET VVLGARE PROFANIS
IPSE ANIMAM POTIVS VOLVIT DIMITTERE CAESVS
PRODERE QVAM CANIBVS RABIDIS COELESTIA MEMBRA

INSCRIPTION OF POPE DAMASUS IN THE CEMETERY OF CALLISTUS.

(Type of Damasian characters).

In the crypt adjoining that of the popes, the renowned martyr St. Cecilia[57] was interred toward the beginning of the third century. Her crypt was decorated many times, as can be seen from traces of paintings dating from the fifth, the seventh, and perhaps even the ninth century. The relics of the saint were removed from this place in the year 821 by Pope Paschal I and carried to the church erected over the place of her martyrdom in the Transtevere. The crypt, following this, was abandoned and not found again until 1854.

A short distance from the crypt of the popes, there is a very important gallery from which the five so-called "chambers of the Sacraments" open off. The most important of these are the first, second and fifth, containing priceless frescoes from the beginning of the third century which represent in a symbolical manner the Sacraments of Baptism, Penance and the Holy Eucharist.[58]

Another historical center of great importance is the crypt of Pope Eusebius, who died in exile in Sicily in the year 310, during the reign of Maxentius. A copy of the Damasian epitaph found there reveals an episode in the history of the Roman Church hitherto unknown, namely, the schism instigated by a certain Heraclius concerning the question of the *lapsi,* the lapsed, i.e., Christians who had denied their faith in periods of stress and then wished to be admitted to the Church again·

### DAMASVS EPISCOPVS FECIT

HERACLIVS VETVIT LAPSOS PECCATA DOLERE
EVSEBIVS MISEROS DOCVIT SVA CRIMINA FLERE
SCINDITVR IN PARTES POPVLVS GLISCENTE FVRORE
SEDITIO CAEDES BELLVM DISCORDIA LITES
EXTEMPLO PARITER PVLSI FERITATE TYRANNI
INTEGRA CVM RECTOR SERVARET FOEDERA PACIS
PERTVLIT EXILIVM DOMINO SVB IVDICE LAETVS
LITORE TRINACRIO MVNDVM VITAMQVE RELIQVIT

### EVSEBIO EPISCOPO ET MARTYRI

At the right and left of the text, in two vertical lines, the writer put his own name and an expression of affection for

Pope Damasus: FVRIVS DIONYSIVS FILOCALVS SCRIBSIT—DAMASI
SVI PAPAE CVLTOR ATQVE AMATOR.

Facing the crypt of Eusebius there is another in which is
preserved an inscription referring to Pope Caius.

A little further on toward the Ardeatine Way, Damasus
has constructed his own tomb, close to the tombs of his mother
and his sister Irene, who had consecrated herself to God although not yet twenty years of age.

The epitaph composed by Damasus for his own tomb was
often copied by the early pilgrims.  It contains a solemn profession of faith in the dogma of the Resurrection:

QVI GRADIENS PELAGI FLVCTVS COMPRESSIT AMAROS
VIVERE QVI PRAESTAT MORIENTIA SEMINA TERRAE
SOLVERE QVI POTVIT LAZARO SVA VINCVLA MORTIS
POST TENEBRAS FRATREM POST TERTIA LVMINA SOLIS
AD SVPEROS ITERVM MARTHAE DONARE SORORI
POST CINERES DAMASVM FACIET QVIA SVRGERE CREDO

Another inscription which is very beautiful and replete
with affection was composed by Damasus and placed on the
tomb of his sister Irene:

HOC TVMVLO SACRATA DEO NVNC MEMBRA QVIESCVNT
HIC SOROR EST DAMASI NOMEN SI QVAERIS IRENE
VOVERAT HAEC SESE CHRISTO CVM VITA MANERET
VIRGINIS VT MERITVM SANCTVS PVDOR IPSE PROBARET
BIS DENAS HIEMES NECDVM COMPLEVERAT AETAS
EGREGIOS MORES VITAE PRAECESSERAT AETAS
PROPOSITVM MENTIS PIETAS VENERANDA PVELLAE
MAGNIFICOS FRVCTVS DEDERAT MELIORIBVS ANNIS
TE GERMANA SOROR NOSTRI NVNC TESTIS AMORIS
CVM FVGERET MVNDVM DEDERAT MIHI PIGNVS
     HONESTVM
QVAM SIBI CVM RAPERET MELIOR TVNC REGIA COELI
NON TIMVI MORTEM COELOS QVOD LIBERA ADIRET
SED DOLVI FATEOR CONSORTIA PERDERE VITAE
NVNC VENIENTE DEO NOSTRI REMINISCERE VIRGO
VT TVA PER DOMINVM PRAESTET MIHI FACVLA LVMEN

During the excavations carried on in 1903 beneath the
modern monastery of the Trappists, an imprint of the inscription composed by Damasus for his mother Laurentia was
discovered:

HIC . DAMASI . MATER . POSVIT . LAVR*entia membra*
QVAE . FVIT . IN . TERRIS . CENTVM . MINVS *octo per annos*
SEXAGINTA . DEO . VIXIT . POST . FOE*dera sancta*
PROGENIE . QVARTA . VIDIT . QVAE *laeta nepotes*

b. THE CEMETERY OF ST. SEBASTIAN *ad Catacumbas*[59]

The cemetery of St. Sebastian was the first one to receive the name Cemetery *ad Catacumbas,* a term which was later applied to all the other cemeteries. The most important memorial of a historical nature connected with it is the temporary deposition of the remains of the holy Apostles Peter and Paul "in loco qui dicitur Catacumbas" — "in the place called the Catacombs."

This fact is recorded in the well-known inscription of Pope Damasus:[60]

HIC HABITASSE PRIVS SANCTOS COGNOSCERE DEBES
NOMINA QVISQVE PETRI PARITER PAVLIQVE REQVIRIS
DISCIPVLOS ORIENS MISIT QVOD SPONTE FATEMVR
SANGVINIS OB MERITVM CHRISTVM QVI PER ASTRA SECVTI
AETHERIOS PETIERE SINVS REGNAQVE PIORVM
ROMA SVOS POTIVS MERVIT DEFENDERE CIVES
HAEC DAMASVS VESTRAS REFERAT NOVA SYDERA LAVDES

In this inscription, Damasus refers to the ancient tradition of the burial of the bodies of the two apostles in the catacombs on the Appian Way. This appears to have occurred when some Orientals wished to take their bodies to the Orient. The bodies, however, remained in Rome, and were later removed to their ancient tombs; hence Damasus says that Rome deserved to keep the relics of those who had become its citizens.

The provisional apostolic tomb on the Appian Way always remained an object of great veneration. For this reason, a small cemetery was begun there, and later a basilica was built which, to the end of the eighth century, was called "the basilica of the Apostles." It is this that certain codices of the *Book of the Popes* ascribe to Damasus. It was only in the ninth century that the structure became known as the basilica of St. Sebastian.

In the process of excavating, begun in this locality in 1915, resumed after an interruption in 1919 and then continued to

1921, very valuable inscriptions and invocations directed to the Apostles Peter and Paul were found. A subterranean hiding place of great depth was also discovered. This must have been the place where the memory of the deposition of the remains of the apostles was held in reverence.[61]

The excavations carried on in our own days have brought to light not only a *Memoria Apostolica,* an Apostolic Oratory, but also noteworthy sarcophagi with various figures on them, in which the lives of the apostles are frequently represented. Moreover, the entire level of the ancient basilica erected in the fourth century over the oratory of the apostles, has been uncovered. Along with these discoveries, numerous mausoleums constructed in close proximity to the oratory and antedating the building of the basilica were also unearthed.

St. Sebastian, tribune of the first cohort of the Praetorian Guards, suffered martyrdom during the first period of the persecution of Diocletian, probably in the year 290, after having been pierced with arrows and beaten with lashes. His body was thrown into a sewer, recovered by the matron Lucina and carried to the Appian Way "close to the footsteps of the Apostles" ("apud vestigia Apostolorum"), as the records of his martyrdom tell us. Besides St. Sebastian, there were buried in this cemetery Quirinus, Bishop of Siscia, whose body was removed thither toward the end of the fourth century, and Eutychius, to whom Damasus dedicated a beautiful poem which is preserved in its entirety on one of the walls of the basilica:

EVTYCHIVS MARTYR CRVDELIA IVSSA TYRANNI
CARNIFICVMQVE VIAS PARITER TVNC MILLE NOCENDI
VINCERE QVOD POTVIT MONSTRAVIT GLORIA CHRISTI
CARCERIS INLVVIEM SEQVITVR NOVA POENA PER ARTVS
TESTARVM FRAGMENTA PARANT NE SOMNVS ADIRET
BIS SENI TRANSIERE DIES ALIMENTA NEGANTVR
MITTITVR IN BARATHRVM SANCTVS LAVAT OMNIA
    SANGVIS
VVLNERA QVAE INTVLERAT MORTIS METVENDA POTESTAS
NOCTE SOPORIFERA TVRBANT INSOMNIA MENTEM
OSTENDIT LATEBRA INSONTIS QVAE MEMBRA TENERET
QVAERITVR INVENTVS COLITVR FOVET OMNIA PRAESTAT
EXPRESSIT DAMASVS MERITVM VENERARE SEPVLCRVM

The known parts of this cemetery, with the exception of a few galleries of the earliest portion, belong to the fourth century, but it is in a state of ruin because it is the one cemetery which has always remained accessible. In bygone centuries, in fact, this locality was the center of subterranean Rome. To this place all the traditions of the Appian Way were ascribed, especially those which properly belong to the cemetery of Callistus.

It is the merit of de Rossi that he restored the true topography of these cemeteries on the Appian Way with every certainty, by making use especially of the information which is contained in the *Feriale* of the fourth century, as well as that in the Itineraries.[62]

### c. THE CEMETERY OF PRAETEXTATUS[63]

This cemetery received its name from its owner, perhaps a relative of the Cecilii. In fact, St. Cecilia buried her husband Valerian here, as well as Tiburtius and Maximus. The cemetery already existed in the second half of the second century, as is evident from the fact that St. Januarius, first-born of St. Felicitas, who suffered martyrdom under Marcus Aurelius (162), was buried here. In 1857, his crypt was discovered in the Great Cavern, adorned with paintings of a classical style and a dedicatory inscription by Pope Damasus:

BEATISSIMO . MARTYRI
IANVARIO
DAMASVS . EPISCOP .
FECIT

Quirinus, the tribune who was martyred under Hadrian, was also interred in this part of the cemetery. Later on, the martyrs Felicissimus and Agapitus were buried here. They were deacons of Sixtus II (258), whose record was discovered by Armellini in a graffito in 1874.[64] A common tomb of magnificent dimensions is ascribed to these martyrs. It is supposed to be located in the aforementioned Great Cavern, a short distance from that of St. Januarius.[65]

This tomb was also adorned by a metrical inscription during the pontificate of Pope Damasus:

ASPICE ET HIC TVMVLVS RETINET COELESTIA MEMBRA
SANCTORVM SVBITO RAPVIT QVOS REGIA COELI
HI CRVCIS INVICTAE COMITES PARITERQVE MINISTRI
RECTORIS SANCTI MERITVMQVE FIDEMQVE SECVTI
AETHERIAS PETIERE DOMOS REGNAQVE PIORVM
VNICA IN HIS GAVDET ROMANAE GLORIA PLEBIS
QVOD DVCE TVNC XYSTO CHRISTI MERVERE TRIVMPHOS

FELICISSIMO ET AGAPITO DAMASVS

This Damasian inscription, which had been known only from a book containing selections of epitaphs, came to light in its original magnificent form a few years ago (1927). During the demolition of the church of St. Nicholas of the Caesarini, a large slab of marble used for paving the church was found. Upon inspection, it was seen to have the original Damasian inscription on the side turned to the ground. It is now preserved in the museum of the cemetery of Praetextatus.

In 1850, a burial chapel with very valuable paintings was discovered in another section of the cemetery, at the foot of the original stairway. These paintings date from the second century and contain one scene which was thought to represent Christ being crowned with thorns. Marucchi inclines to the belief that it shows Christ on the banks of the Jordan. This crypt, which is improperly called the crypt "of the Passion," ought to be known as the crypt "of Urania," because an ancient inscription relating to Urania was found here.

In our own day, important works of excavation have been completed by the Pontifical Commission of Christian Archeology in the cemetery of Praetextatus. As one may surmise from the above account, the cemetery possessed oratories and *mem-*

*oriae;* and even before these, a sumptuous villa belonging to the teacher of the Emperor Marcus Aurelius, Herod Atticus, whose family certainly had some connection with this Christian cemetery, as may be inferred from several inscriptions.

In the completion of this work, there came to light a great number of pieces of sarcophagi, which in part occupied the most important crypts of the cemetery and especially the so-called Great Cavern. This material has been analyzed, organized and systematized into five almost complete and very valuable sarcophagi, one of which may well have been the tomb of the Emperor Balbinus.

With the restoration of pagan sarcophagi, numerous fragments of Christian paintings were discovered, which, gathered together in a small museum built in the cemetery, offer the student an easy method of recognizing Christian sculpture of the second half of the third century.

## 7. The Cemeteries of the Latin Way[66]

The cemeteries of the Latin Way and the Aurelian Way are the only ones of all subterranean Rome which have never been regularly explored. According to the Itineraries, we may group the Christian cemeteries found on the Latin Way into three sections, following their topographical order:

### a. THE CEMETERY WITH THE CHURCH OF ST. GORDIAN

"ubi ipse com fratre Epimacho in una sepultura [iacet]" ("where he lies with his brother in a common tomb"), near a group consisting of Sts. Quartus, Quintus and others.

### b. THE BASILICA OF TERTULLINUS

### c. THE CHURCH OF ST. EUGENIA WITH THE CEMETERY OF APRONIAN

Two underground vaults were discovered which probably belonged to the heretical Gnostics. One was the property of a certain Trebius Justus.[67]  Another Gnostic cemetery was found recently close to the small Manzoni Road.[68]

## 8.  The Cemeteries of the Labican Way[69]

### a. THE CEMETERY OF ST. CASTULUS[70]

According to the Acts, Castulus, a valet of the Emperor Diocletian, had a wife by the name of Irene of whom the Acts of St. Sebastian speak.

Castulus, denounced as a Christian, was condemned to be thrown alive into a pit along the Labican Way, located not far from the city where he was later interred.  Fabretti discovered the cemetery in the year 1672.  In 1864, during the building of the railroad, several galleries of this cemetery were encountered, but it was necessary to wall up the entrance, situated near the aqueduct of Felix.[71]

### b. THE CEMETERY OF STS. MARCELLINUS AND PETER[72]

In this cemetery, the Itineraries record various groups of martyrs, principally of the time of Diocletian.

Sts. Marcellinus and Peter, the one a priest, the other an exorcist, were martyred on the Cornelian Way, at a place then called *Sylva Candida* ("White Forest").  St. Damasus gave the particulars of their supreme sacrifice at the hands of the executioner in a poem dedicated to their memory:

MARCELLINE TVOS PARITER PETRE NOSSE TRIVMPHOS
PERCVSSOR RETVLIT DAMASO MIHI CVM PVER ESSEM
HAEC SIBI CARNIFICEM RABIDVM MANDATA DEDISSE
SENTIBVS IN MEDIIS VESTRA VT TVNC COLLA SECARET
NE TVMVLVM VESTRVM QVISQVAM COGNOSCERE POSSET
VOS ALACRES VESTRIS MANIBVS MVNDASSE SEPVLCRA
CANDIDVLO OCCVLTE POSTQVAM IACVISTIS IN ANTRO
POSTEA COMMONITAM VESTRA PIETATE LVCILLAM
HIC PLACVISSE MAGIS SANCTISSIMA CONDERE MEMBRA

The bodies of Sts. Marcellinus and Peter were buried close to the martyr Tiburtius, son of Chromatius, prefect of Rome.

We have no evidence of the tomb of St. Gorgonius; we do not know anything more of him than is contained in the text of an inscription written in his honor by St. Damasus:

MARTYRIS HIC TVMVLVS MAGNO SVB VERTICE MONTIS
GORGONIVM RETINET SERVAT QVI ALTARIA CHRISTI
HIC QVICMQVE VENIT SANCTORVM LIMINA QVAERAT
INVENIET VICINA IN SEDE HABITARE BEATOS
AD COELVM PARITER PIETAS QVOS VEXIT EVNTES

We know very little of the Four Crowned Martyrs (*Quattuor Coronati*). It may be said that their history constitutes one of the most difficult problems of hagiography.

This locality also contained the tomb of Helena, the mother of Constantine, who later constructed a basilica at this place in honor of Sts. Marcellinus and Peter. The bodies of these martyrs remained in the subterranean crypts until the year 826, when they were removed and carried first to France and then to Germany, where they are still venerated.

In the course of his explorations, Bosio again found the cemetery, investigated it and described a room which he believed was the historical crypt of the martyrs. But later, in 1896, when important excavations were made there, the true crypt was discovered.[73]

This cemetery contains many paintings; some of them, of exceptional importance, will be mentioned in treating of ancient Christian art. The most noteworthy are scenes of the agapes (fourth century); one painting represents the marriage feast at Cana and the image of the Blessed Virgin who offers the Child Jesus to the adoration of the Magi (third century).

## 9.   The Cemeteries of the Tiburtine Way[74]

### a. THE CEMETERY OF CYRIACA OR OF ST. LAWRENCE[75]

This cemetery was so named after a Christian widow, Cyriaca, but it owes all its importance to the fact that the great St. Lawrence was buried there in 258.[76] The cemetery occupied the area which was later taken over by the basilica under the present hillock, and the building of a modern cemetery has greatly damaged the subterranean monuments. Among the paintings still preserved, we should mention those which adorn the tomb of a Christian virgin of the fourth century with the rare representation of the parable of the Wise and Foolish Virgins, the denial of St. Peter, the miracle of the manna, etc.

The Damasian inscription, now lost, which once adorned the tomb of the martyrs, was (by way of exception) in distichs:

VERBERA CARNIFICIS FLAMMAS TORMENTA CATENAS
VINCERE LAVRENTI SOLA FIDES POTVIT
HAEC DAMASVS CVMVLAT SVPPLEX ALTARIA DONIS
MARTYRIS EGREGIVM SVSPICIENS MERITVM

The Emperor Constantine erected over the body of this great martyr a basilica designated as *ad corpus,* that is, built on the same level as the crypt; but as this was not large enough to take care of the visiting multitudes, Pope Sixtus III (432) constructed the new basilica, called *basilica major,* "the Greater Basilica."

In the original *basilica ad corpus,* there were buried in the fifth century Popes Zosimus (418), Sixtus III (440), and Hilary (467). One of their niches is at present occupied by the tomb of Pope Pius IX. This basilica, containing the original tomb of the martyr St. Lawrence, was entirely rebuilt by Pope Pelagius II in the sixth century; the *basilica major* was completely restored by Pope Honorius III at the beginning of the thirteenth century.

## b. THE CEMETERY OF ST. HIPPOLYTUS[77]

This cemetery lies on the left side of the Tiburtine Way. The history of St. Hippolytus is very obscure, and excavations made up to the present time have not uncovered monuments which might solve the many moot points concerning him.[78] No more light is shed on the whole question by a perusal of the Damasian inscription placed on the tomb of the martyr:

HYPPOLYTVS FERTVR PREMERENT CVM IVSSA TYRANNI
PRESBYTER IN SCISMA SEMPER MANSISSE NOVATI
TEMPORE QVO GLADIVS SECVIT PIA VISCERA MATRIS
DEVOTVS CHRISTO PETERET CVM REGNA PIORVM
QVAESISSET POPVLVS VBINAM PROCEDERE POSSET
CATHOLICAM DIXISSE FIDEM SEQVERENTVR VT OMNES
SIC NOSTER MERVIT CONFESSVS MARTYR VT ESSET
HAEC AVDITA REFERT DAMASVS PROBAT OMNIA CHRISTVS

This merely indicates that he was a schismatic priest, who
later returned to the Church and suffered martyrdom for the
faith.

Excavations made in 1882-1883 brought to light a small
underground basilica dedicated to St. Hippolytus,[79] composed
of a double vestibule, an oblong nave, and a sanctuary with an
apse. The basilica was devastated by the Goths and for that
reason restored by Pope Vigilius in the year 538. There are
many galleries in evidence behind the apse and numerous others
on the side, but they are almost entirely in ruins.

The small subterranean basilica contains a fine collection
of local inscriptions.

A short distance from here, there was discovered in the
sixteenth century a beautiful statue of St. Hippolytus which is
preserved in the Lateran Museum. (See Part V, Chapter VIII,
"Early Christian Sculpture," section 2, "Statues.")

## c. THE CEMETERY OF ST. AGAPITUS(?)

A group of burial galleries was encountered in 1926 while
work was being done in the region to the left of the Tiburtine
Way. Some of these were in ruins, others were explored and
examined, but their deplorable condition obliged the Commission of Sacred Archeology to abandon them. While the
work continued, according to the Regulatory Plan, a cave-in
occurred in January, 1929, in the region where the excavation
had been made in 1926, and following this incident, the presence of new galleries opened up a completely fresh field of
investigation. An entirely unknown burial region was found,

its greater part preserved intact, with inscriptions still in place, gilded glass, various articles of furniture, and money or coins.

Excavations following the discovery led many to suppose that this group of burial galleries formed part of a very extensive cemetery of the Tiburtine Way, having nothing in common with those of Hippolytus and Cyriaca. Ancient Itineraries assign to the Tiburtine Way, besides the two aforementioned cemeteries, a basilica in honor of St. Agapitus, the location of which has not yet been definitely determined. It may be that this new cemetery is the one over which the basilica was later erected; it seems almost certain that it is the cemetery so beautifully reproduced by Fornari (see *Rivista di Archeologia Cristiana,* sixth year, p. 183). At any rate, it cannot be included as a part either of the cemetery of Cyriaca or that of Hippolytus.

## 10. The Cemeteries of the Nomentan Way[80]

### a. THE CEMETERY OF ST. NICOMEDES[81]

The cemetery of St. Nicomedes is of great importance because it was situated very close to the walls of the city of Rome. Its origin may perhaps go back to the Apostolic Age.

According to the Acts, Nicomedes was condemned to be executed by means of leaden thongs, *plumbatis caesus,* and then cast into the Tiber, during the time of Domitian. A follower recovered the body of the martyr and laid it to rest close to the city "in the garden of Justus close to the walls" ("in horto Justi prope muros").

In 1863, a small cemetery beneath the villa of the Patrizi was found. De Rossi identified it as that of Nicomedes. This cemetery was completely explored during the process of excavating, in 1901-1902, and was found to be very small. The first level communicates with a sand pit, the second contains a splendid gallery showing evidence of very ancient construction; at the foot of the stairway there is a cubicle with three arched vaults, in one of which some inscriptions are scratched on the walls.

The identification made by de Rossi of this cemetery is
not certain. In the course of the work done in 1913 under the
great railway depot, traces of a Christian cemetery much larger
than the first were met with, and it is very probable that this
latter is the true cemetery of Nicomedes.

## b. THE CEMETERY OF ST. AGNES[82]

Few and vague are the notices we have concerning this
illustrious martyr. Her legend reads that Agnes, having refused
a proposal of marriage on the part of the son of the prefect,
was sentenced to a house of ill-fame, where, however, she was
preserved from every violence. Later she was thrown into a
flaming furnace but remained there unharmed. Then Aspasius,
the prefect, ordered her to be executed by the sword. Her body
was buried by her relatives on the Nomentan Way, on some
property belonging to them: "in praediolo suo." These facts
have been gathered from her Acts, which are not prior to the
fifth century, a work of St. Ambrose, a hymn of Prudentius,
and an inscription of Pope Damasus which is at present preserved at the foot of the stairway leading to the basilica:

FAMA REFERT SANCTOS DVDVM RETVLISSE PARENTES
AGNEN CVM LVGVBRES CANTVS TVBA CONCREPVISSET
NVTRICIS GREMIVM SVBITO LIQVISSE PVELLAM
SPONTE TRVCIS CALCASSE MINAS RABIEMQVE TVRANNI
VRERE CVM FLAMMIS VOLVISSET NOBILE CORPVS
VIRIBVS IMMENSVM PARVIS SVPERASSE TIMOREM
NVDAQVE PROFVSVM CRINEM PER MEMBRA DEDISSE
NE DOMINI TEMPLVM FACIES PERITVRA VIDERET
O VENERANDA MIHI SANCTVM DECVS ALMA PVDORIS
VT DAMASI PRECIBVS FAVEAS PRECOR INCLYTA MARTYR

The martyrdom of St. Agnes is held to have occurred
during the persecution of Valerian, or (according to others) in
the preceding persecution of Decius. It does not seem possible
that it happened so late as the persecution of Diocletian.[83]

The cemetery existed, without doubt, before the deposition
of St. Agnes, but after she was buried there, it underwent great

development; the result was a cemetery of three levels in which one may distinguish three different regions:

1.   To the left of the basilica, the primitive network which antedates the third century;

2.   A region of the third century between the basilica, the Nomentan Way and St. Constantia's;

3.   Two groups of galleries of the fourth century, one under the Nomentan Way, the other communicating with the cemetery of St. Constantia.

The basilica of St. Agnes was built over the very tomb of the saint, at the level of the most ancient part of the cemetery. The actual basilica is the one reconstructed by Pope Symmachus; the original was erected by Constantine.

## c. The Greater Cemetery of St. Agnes on the Nomentan Way, Improperly Called by Some "The Ostrian Cemetery"[84]

This cemetery has its entrance some distance from the basilica of St. Agnes beneath the Leopardi villa. The older archeologists called it the cemetery of St. Agnes — even de Rossi, who only at a later date came to believe that this might be the Ostrian cemetery where there existed an oratory in commemoration of the Sacrament of Baptism administered by St. Peter, and of his original Chair (See). But later studies and recent discoveries have convinced archeologists that this designation (Ostrian) is inexact, and that the oratories of the early apostolic preaching in Rome should rather be looked for in the cemetery of Priscilla on the Salarian Way.[85]

Among the monuments, a species of small subterranean basilica is outstanding. It is hewn entirely out of the tuff, with presbytery, episcopal chair, seats for the clergy, niches for liturgical use, two columns and a triumphal arch. This double crypt certainly served as a rendezvous in early times, and also as a place for liturgical purposes. It is a veritable underground church, and was in use perhaps during the times of the persecution. In a crypt beside it, it was once believed to be possible to read the name of St. Peter depicted in red in the apse of the basilica, but it was later recognized that this reading arose from a false impression. The same may be said of a fantastic notion which held that the chair cut into the tuff was the chair of St. Peter. This chair and others like it in the same cemetery were used for liturgical purposes. Similar structures have also been found in other cemeteries. In this crypt, one recognizes without the slightest doubt the tomb of the foster-sister of St. Agnes, the martyr Emerentiana. The martyrs Victor and Alexander were also buried in the crypt. There is a goodly number of paintings in this cemetery, but the most important is the one which adorns an arched vault in a room of the fourth century. It represents the Blessed Virgin, richly dressed, in the act of prayer; facing her is the Infant Jesus. On the right and left side of the painting is the monogram of Constantine turned to the center of the *arcosolium* to indicate that the Infant is really Christ.

### d. The Cemetery of St. Alexander[86]

This cemetery was found in 1855, at the tenth kilometer of the Nomentan Way.

According to the *Book of the Popes,* Pope Alexander I, of whom a commemorative inscription was found here, was buried in this cemetery. Some modern critics suppose, how-ever, that the Alexander entombed here was a local martyr from Ficulea or Nomentum; this question is not yet definitely settled. On the other hand, it must be admitted that the tradition regarding the pope is very ancient.

The magnificent basilica was constructed during the fourth century. Important remains of it are still visible, and there also may be seen the tomb of the martyr and some parts of the original altar. The cemetery is of rough work and not very extensive; the chambers are small, and the graves badly closed. It was a country cemetery.[87]

## 11.  The Cemeteries of the New Salarian Way[88]

### a. THE CEMETERY OF ST. FELICITAS[89]

This was also called the cemetery of Maximus, after its founder, of whom, however, nothing is known. St. Felicitas was laid to rest here along with her youngest son, Silanus. Their tombs were discovered following the excavations of 1885.[90] In fact, a small underground basilica was discovered in which was preserved a Byzantine painting representing the figure (bust) of the Saviour, and beneath Him the figures of St. Felicitas and her sons, with some of the letters of their names still visible. The walls of the basilica contain various inscriptions, many of which show the consular date. The cemetery is divided into two levels, both in a ruinous state. The second level shows remains of a small baptistery.

The entrance to this cemetery is at present to be found on the Simetan Way.

### b. THE CEMETERY OF THRASO[91]

Thraso was a rich Roman citizen who buried many martyrs on his property on the Salarian Way. Among them was Saturninus, to whom Damasus dedicated an epitaph.[92] The entrance to a large underground chapel which may correspond to the cemetery of Thraso, is to be found on the villa formerly belonging to the Odescalchi, now the property of the Sisters of the Visitation. This is situated to the left of the road, but almost all the galleries of this underground monument await excavation.

### c. THE CEMETERY OF THE JORDANI[93]

This cemetery, situated under the Massimo and Savoy villas, is the deepest of subterranean Rome. At least five levels may be recognized. Groups of its galleries are separated, besides, by an immense sand-pit, in a part of which Chrysanthus and his wife Daria were probably buried in the time of Valerian. Their Acts speak of certain Christians who were gathered

together to pray at their tomb and were buried alive beneath a
heap of stones in this very place.  This cemetery was one of
the most renowned of sanctuaries, a fact recorded by St.
Gregory of Tours.  The Itineraries make mention of a group
of seventy soldiers buried here, and another of seventy-two
martyrs.  In this locality were also interred three sons of St.
Felicitas, Alexander, Vitalis and Martial.

During the course of the excavations carried on in 1872,
many inscriptions were found and important frescoes were uncovered.[94]  A portion of one inscription seems to belong to the
martyr St. Alexander.  A very beautiful section of this cemetery
was discovered in 1578, beneath the Sanchez vineyard, later
belonging to the della Rovere.  A little further away, paintings
and inscriptions were encountered, which were subsequently
destroyed.  The accidental discovery of this region gave rise
to the phrase "Subterranean Rome."  It was rediscovered in
1921 in the course of reconstructive works then in progress.
In our own day, the paintings and inscriptions of this cemetery
have been amply reproduced by Prof. E. Iosi in the *Rivista di
Archeologia cristiana,* eighth and ninth years.

### d. THE CEMETERY OF PRISCILLA[95]

This is the most renowned and the oldest of the Christian
cemeteries of Rome.  It takes its name from Priscilla, the mother
of the Pudens who, according to one tradition, gave hospitality
to St. Peter in his home on the Viminal, where today stands
the church of St. Pudentiana.  In this cemetery were buried
Aquila and Prisca, disciples of St. Paul; Pudentiana and Praxedes, with their father Pudens; Felix and Philip, sons of St.
Felicitas; the martyr Crescention, and Popes Marcellinus and
Marcellus.  Following the peace of the Church, a basilica was
erected, which was recently brought to light, and has once more
become an object of veneration.  In it were venerated the bodies
of Sts. Felix and Philip, and it was here that the pilgrims also
saw the tombs of Popes Marcellus, Sylvester, Siricius and Celestine.  Pope Liberius and Vigilius were also entombed here.  A
special study of the whole cemetery undertaken by the

author, induced him to conclude that it must have been in this, and not in any other cemetery on the Nomentan Way, that there was preserved a record of the first preaching of St. Peter in Rome.

The reference to the group of martyrs interred in the cemetery of Priscilla and in the adjoining one of the Jordani, found in the catalogue of Monza (sixth century), contains the expression: "sedes ubi prius sedit s. Petrus" — that is "the first residence of St. Peter."

Among the most important discoveries in the cemetery is the chapel of the gravediggers, called the "Grecian chapel" because of two inscriptions found on one of the walls. This is a veritable church, divided into two parts by an arch and entirely adorned with paintings showing scenes taken from the Old and New Testaments; the most valuable fresco lies over the apse and was discovered by Wilpert,[96] who published an account of it under the title of *Fractio Panis* — the *Breaking of Bread.* The contiguous region is dug out of an ancient sand-pit, and through fear of the whole structure yielding or caving in, the walls were reënforced with pillars which here and there hid graves. In the most ancient section are some tombs of the second century, still intact, with many inscriptions which, instead of being cut in marble, are painted in red on plaques. A chapel contains an admirable picture of the Virgin, the oldest extant example of such a painting in the catacombs, for it goes back to the beginning of the second century. In another chamber, of the third century, a scene depicting the consecration of a virgin is found, showing a bishop seated on a chair typical of the iconographic tradition of St. Peter.

During the excavations of 1888-1889,[97] a large underground chapel of the Acilii Glabriones was discovered; traces of paintings in the adjacent galleries, as well as the marbles found there, prove that it was richly decorated. The names of the proprietors are given, along with proofs of their faith in the Christianity which they professed. These are still to be seen in several inscriptions engraved on the sarcophagi. Until recently it was held that one of the two rooms covered with marble must have contained the tomb of the consul Acilius Glabrio, whose execution was ordered by Domitian.[98] But it is more probable that the tomb of Pope Marcellinus lay in this room, placed near the tomb of the martyr Crescention.[99]

Even the magnificent baptistery found here, which may reasonably be connected with the upper basilica of St. Sylvester situated near by, concurs in establishing an extraordinary record relative to the local tradition of the first work of evangelization of St. Peter and the administration of Baptism by him.

In the vicinity of the Grecian chapel, a splendid nympheum, transformed into a burial crypt, was discovered. This very singular monument may be brought into relation with the phrase "ad nymphas s. Petri." There is, then, every proof that this is the one cemetery which may be called the *coemeterium Ostrianum* (because there was a reservoir nearby from which water could be drawn — *haustorium* ).

In the second level, rich in important inscriptions, one can recognize a magnificent cemetery in itself, containing its own stairways and its own sections; a cemetery of great importance, which has not as yet been sufficiently explored and studied.

The Damasian inscription in honor of the martyrs Felix and Philip contains in its first part an exposition of the symbol of faith employed in Baptism:

QVI NATVM PASSVMQVE DEVM REPETISSE PATERNAS
SEDES ATQVE ITERVM VENTVRVM EX AETHERE CREDIT
IVDICET VT VIVOS REDIENS PARITERQVE SEPVLTOS
MARTYRIBVS SANCTIS PATEAT QVOD REGIA COELI
RESPICIT INTERIVS SEQVITVR SI PRAEMIA CHRISTI
CVLTORES DOMINI FELIX PARITERQVE PHILIPPVS
HINC VIRTVTE PARES CONTEMPTO PRINCIPE MVNDI
AETERNAM PETIERE DOMVM REGNAQVE PIORVM
SANGVINE QVOD PROPRIO CHRISTI MERVERE CORONAS
HIS DAMASVS SVPPLEX VOLVIT SVA REDDERE VOTA

Another interesting inscription by Pope Damasus, which records the sanguinary disturbances provoked by the *lapsi,* is placed on the tomb of Pope Marcellus (309). We may read it in the collection of inscriptions:

VERIDICVS RECTOR LAPSOS QVIA CRIMINA FLERE
PRAEDIXIT MISERIS FVIT OMNIBVS HOSTIS AMARVS
HINC FVROR HINC ODIVM SEQVITVR DISCORDIA LITES
SAEDITIO CAEDES SOLVVNTVR FOEDERA PACIS
CRIMEN OB ALTERIVS CHRISTVM QVI IN PACE NEGAVIT
FINIBVS EXPVLSVS PATRIAE EST FERITATE TYRANNI
HAEC BREVITER DAMASVS VOLVIT COMPERTA REFERRE
MARCELLI VT POPVLVS MERITVM COGNOSCERE POSSET

## 12.  The Cemeteries of the Old Salarian Way[100]

### a. THE CEMETERY OF ST. PAMPHILUS[101]

This cemetery takes its name from a martyr whose history
is unknown, and of whom a record was found only in 1865. De
Rossi, after having traversed several galleries in a sad state of
ruin, came to a chamber where a number of Biblical scenes were
roughly made in charcoal. There is also a unique scene
representing a figure endeavoring to pull a statue from its
pedestal by means of a rope. De Rossi interpreted this scene
and showed its importance, for he recognized in it an allusion
to the abolition of paganism under Theodosius.[102]

Shortly after this the chamber was filled in, and later (in
1919) was found anew. Finally, in March, 1920, while a
foundation was being dug for a factory on the Paisiello Way,
the principal part of this cemetery was discovered, with many
galleries and tombs still intact, along with the historical crypt
with an altar and graffiti.[103]

In this crypt one may see two chairs hewn in the tuff next
to an arched vault, exactly like those found in the Greater
Cemetery of St. Agnes; a fact which proves that these chairs
were used for liturgical or ritualistic purposes only.[104]

### b. THE CEMETERY OF BASILLA OR ST. HERMES[105]

The oldest tomb in this cemetery was that of Hermes,
attributed to the time of Hadrian. Later the martyr Basilla
was buried here in the third century. Bosio saw here a great
subterranean basilica which is the largest of such underground
churches known. It was probably built within a preëxisting
edifice, and at the time of peace was extended over the tomb of

the martyr Hermes. It was here that his name was found inscribed in marble in Damasian characters.

A number of other martyrs of the time of Valerian were interred in this cemetery, for example, Protus, Hyacinth and Basilla, whose tomb was held in great veneration, and supplied the name for the entire necropolis. Up to the year 1845, it was believed that the bodies of the two martyrs Protus and Hyacinth were removed to the city during the ninth century; but in 1845, the tomb of Hyacinth was discovered in this cemetery, still untouched and with its original inscription. The work of excavation, suspended after this discovery was made by Marchi, was resumed in 1894. At that time the stairway built at the time of Damasus was found, and several important inscriptions were brought to light.

Of the following inscriptions, the first, recently discovered near the tomb of Sts. Protus and Hyacinth, records that the stairway was built at the time of Pope Damasus:

ASPICE DESCENSVM CERNES MIRABILE FACTVM
SANCTORVM MONVMENTA VIDES PATEFACTA SEPVLCRIS
MARTYRIS HIC PROTI TVMVLVS IACET ATQVE
    HYACINTHI
QVEM CVM IAMDVDVM TEGERET MONS TERRA CALIGO
HOC THEODORVS OPVS CONSTRVXIT PRESBYTER INSTANS
VT DOMINI PLEBEM OPERA MAIORA TENERET


The second was found near the tomb of both martyrs:

EXTREMO TVMVLVS LATVIT SVB AGGERE MONTIS
HVNC DAMASVS MONSTRAT SERVAT QVOD MEMBRA
    PIORVM
TE PROTVM RETINET MELIOR SIBI REGIA COELI
SANGVINE PVRPVREO SEQVERIS HYACINTHE PROBATVS
GERMANI FRATRES ANIMI INGENTIBVS AMBO
HIC VICTOR MERVIT PALMAM PRIOR ILLE CORONAM


Among the paintings of this cemetery an interesting example may be cited in which there is a figure of one deceased being presented to Christ by the two local martyrs, a scene once explained by Bosio as illustrating a sacred ordination. There is also a noteworthy chamber in this cemetery containing a painting which represents the Saviour and the Twelve Apostles, all seated on chairs.

### c. THE CEMETERY *in Clivo cucumeris*[106]

This cemetery which is also known as the cemetery *ad septem columbas,* "at the seven doves," remains entirely unexplored and unknown on the Pincian Way beneath the so-called Meadows of the Acid Waters. Numerous martyrs were interred here whose history is unknown; only their names may be gathered from the Itineraries: John a priest, Liberalis, Diogenes, Boniface, Longinus and Blastus. From an ancient inscription we know that the martyr Liberalis had been consul: "Factus de consule martyr."

## 13.   The Cemetery of the Flaminian Way

### THE CEMETERY OF ST. VALENTINE[107]

St. Valentine, a priest of the Roman Church, died a martyr during the reign of Claudius the Goth (268-270), and was interred at the first mile of the Flaminian Way.

Bosio saw and described the crypt containing the tomb of the martyr without, however, recognizing it. After his time it was barbarously transformed into a canteen, and thus it remained until the year 1877, when Marucchi was able to recognize in the Tanlongo vineyard the level of the cemetery described by Bosio, and to find again the Byzantine paintings seen by him, which prove that the crypt over the entrance of the cemetery was the burial crypt of the martyr St. Valentine. After the burial of St. Valentine, the small underground chapel began to be enlarged, and several new corridors were cut out close to his tomb. The historical crypt was adorned and painted many times. The most important paintings are those of the Blessed Virgin with the Child Jesus, and one of the Crucifixion, unique up to that time in the Roman catacombs (seventh century).

Near the crypt a basilica was built by Pope Julius I (341-352), around which an immense open-air cemetery sprang up, and spread out to the base of the Parioli mountains. The excavations carried out in 1888 brought to light some remains of this basilica, which are still visible, as well as an epigraphical collection of inscriptions which are very important — especially those of a consular nature. Several years ago some fragments of an inscription dedicated by Pope Damasus to the martyr St. Valentine were found. This is perhaps the outstanding and most elegant example of Damasian epigraphy. All these inscriptions are preserved in their proper place in the cemetery.

The basilica had three naves, with several columns of ordinary Doric and others of Corinthian; between the middle nave and the apse there is a corridor, in the center of which a square niche appears exactly under the outlines of the altar. Pope Honorius, in all probability, transported the body of the martyr from the crypt to the grave under this altar of the basilica, where it remained until the twelfth century, when it was then moved to St. Praxedes'.

## Chapter VI

### THE SUBURBICARIAN CEMETERIES

#### (CEMETERIES PERTAINING TO THE SMALL TOWNS AND HAMLETS IN THE IMMEDIATE ENVIRONS OF ROME) [1]

ON THE CORNELIAN WAY. — In the locality known as the White Forest, at the tenth mile, is to be found the cemetery of Sts. Rufina and Secunda;[2] at the twelfth mile is the cemetery of Sts. Maris, Martha, Audifax and Abachum.

ON THE TRIUMPHAL WAY. — A nameless cemetery at the fourth mile.[3]

ON THE AURELIAN WAY. — The cemetery of Basilides at the ninth mile.[4]

ON THE PORTUAN WAY. — The cemeteries of Porto, like those of Ostia, were not subterranean. In 1822, Nibby[5] discovered a cemetery in which many inscriptions were found, now preserved in the episcopal palace of Porto[6] and in the Christian Museum of the Lateran.

ON THE OSTIAN WAY. — At the seventh mile, the oratory of Sts. Cyriacus, Largus and Smaragdus.[7] There were also open-air cemeteries at Ostia, though none of them has been found; the only proof we have of their existence is from the testimony of the inscriptions.[8]

ON THE ARDEATINE WAY. — At the fourth mile there is a nameless cemetery, known today as the "Nunziatella," from a nearby chapel.[9] At the seventh mile the cemetery of St. Philicola should be situated.[10]

ON THE APPIAN WAY. — At the tenth mile, Boldetti[11] discovered a small underground Christian chapel of the ancient town of Bovillae. Near Albano there is to be found the cemetery of St. Senator, with important paintings;[12] traces of cemeteries have been found at Nemi,[13] Anzio,[14] and Velletri.[15]

ON THE LATIN WAY. — Near the fifth mile, a nameless cemetery is known to exist;[16] at ancient Tusculum not a single hypogeum has been discovered although we have many references which point to their existence.[17] At the thirtieth mile of the Latin Way, where it joins the Labican Way, there was a cemetery of St. Hilary *ad bivium,* "at the cross-roads."[18]

ON THE LABICAN WAY. — Boldetti discovered the cemetery of St. Zoticus at the tenth mile. This cemetery was described by Stevenson.[19]

ON THE PRAENESTINE WAY. — Near ancient Gabi, now destroyed, is the cemetery of St. Primitive and other martyrs.[20] At the twenty-fifth mile stands the oratory of the martyr St. Agapitus, who was interred near the city of Praeneste.[21]

ON THE TIBURTINE WAY. — At the ninth mile, Stevenson recognized the oratory of St. Symphorosa and her seven sons.[22]

ON THE NOMENTAN WAY. — Consult page 176 for references concerning St. Alexander. At the fourteenth mile lies the cemetery of Primus and Felicianus *ad arcus Nomentanos,* "at the Nomentan arches"; at the sixteenth mile is situated the cemetery of St. Restitutus.[23]

On the Salarian Way. — The cemetery of St. Antimus at the twenty-third mile;[24] and at the twenty-fifth, the cemetery of Sts. Tiburtius, Hyacinth and Alexander; at about the thirtieth mile is the cemetery of St. Jetulius, near the hamlet of Gavis, not to be confused with its homonym on the Praenestine Way.[25]

On the Flaminian Way. — At the twentieth mile, the cemetery *ad Vigesimum* near Capena;[26] at the twenty-seventh mile, near Rignano, the records point to the cemetery of St. Theodora, where the martyrs Abundius, Abundantius, Marcian and John were buried.[27]

On the Cassian Way. — At the twenty-sixth mile there was a cemetery of St. Alexander, a bishop, which was called *ad Baccanas* from its location.[28]

Heretics are known to have been quite numerous in Rome from the second century on. It is certain that they had their own cemeteries, which were distinct from those of the Catholic Church. Up to the present, only three groups of tombs of Christian heretics have been recognized in Rome. Two of these were discovered a few years ago on the Latin Way; a third, of major importance, and adorned with very valuable paintings of the third century, was discovered recently on Manzoni Road, within the actual limits of the city. This last and one of the first two seem to belong to the Valentinian heretics.[29]

## Chapter VII

### THE PRINCIPAL CEMETERIES
### OF THE REMAINDER OF ITALY[1]

ANCONA. — Indications and evidences of a Christian cemetery were obtained through the discovery of inscriptions and from a Christian burial chamber.[2]

AQUILA. — Catacombs of St. Victorine in Amiterno, near Aquila.[3]

AQUILEIA. — A Christian cemetery above ground. Many and important inscriptions are to be found in the local museum.

AREZZO. — A Christian cemetery.[4]

ASCOLI. — The cemetery of St. Emidius.[5]

ATRIPALDA (near Avellino). — A cemetery where the martyrs Hypolistus, Sabinus, Crescentius and Romulus were buried.[6]

AVELLINO. — The cemetery of St. Almatia or of the Annunciation.[7]

BAIA. — The cemetery of St. Sosius, deacon, companion in martyrdom of St. Januarius.[8]

BASSANO. — A Christian cemetery near St. Eutytius, beneath the ruins of the basilica of St. Mary *de luco*.[9]

BAZZANO. — Near St. Victorine, about two miles from Aquila, is a Christian cemetery.[10]

BIEDA (the ancient Blera). — The cemetery of Sts. Sentia and Vincent.[11]

BOLOGNA. — A cemetery.[12]

BOLSENA. — The cemetery of St. Christina.[13]

BRACCIANO. — The cemetery of St. Macarius.[14]

BRESCIA. — The cemetery of St. Latinus.[15]

CAGLIARI. — The Christian cemetery of Bonaria and of St. Antioch on an island of the same name, and the Christian cemetery of Bonorva.[16]

CAPUA. — The cemetery of St. Priscus.[17]

CASTELLAMMARE DI STABIA. — Cemetery of St. Catellus; grotto and necropolis of St. Blasius.[18]

CATANIA. — Christian cemeteries.[19]

CERVETERI (the ancient Caere). — A Christian cemetery.[20]

CHIUSI.—Catacombs of St. Mustiola and of St. Catherine.[21]

CIVITAVECCHIA (Centumcellae). — A Christian cemetery.[22]

CORNETO TARQUINIA. — Christian tombs.[23]

FALERI. — Cemetery of Sts. Gratilianus and Felicissima.[24]

FERENTILLO (near Spoleto). — A Christian cemetery.[25]

FERENTUM. — Cemetery of St. Eutytius.[26]

GIRGENTI. — Cemetery of Giambertone; grottoes of Frangipani.[27]

LENTINO. — A Christian cemetery.[28]

LUCCA. — A cemetery called the *Cella martyrum*.[29]

MARSALA. — A Christian hypogeum.[30]

MAZZARA (in Sicily). — A Christian hypogeum.[31]

MESSINA. — The catacomb of St. Placidus.[32]

MILAN. — Cemetery of Philip and Caius, where the martyrs Gervase, Protase, Nabor and Felix were interred; the cemetery of Paulinus *ad fontem;* the cemetery of Castritianus; the cemetery of St. Calimerus.[33]

NAPLES. — Cemetery of Sts. Agrippinus and Januarius, today known as the "cemetery of St. Januarius of the Poor"; the cemetery of St. Gaudiosus, called "la Sanità" or "Santa Maria della Sanità"; the cemetery of St. Ephebus or Eusebius, at present known as Old St. Ephrem; the cemetery of St. Severus.[34]

NARNI. — The *area* or cemetery of the Christians.[35]

NEPI. — The cemetery of Sts. Tolomeus and Romanus.[36]

OTRICOLI. — The cemetery of St. Medicus.[37]

PADUA. — The cemetery of the Holy Martyrs.[38]

PALERMO. — The cemetery of St. Mary *de Cripta* or *de Grutta;* the cemetery near the Ossuna gate; the cemetery near the church of St. Michael; the cemetery near the gate of Mazara; the crypt of the Blessed Pauls.[39]

PAVIA. — A Christian cemetery.[40]

PORTOGRUARO (the ancient Julia Concordia). — Necropolis of the Christians in the open.[41]

POZZUOLI. —Catacombs of St. Proculus.[42]

PIPERNO (the ancient Privernum). — The cemetery of Sts. Asterius, Julius and Montanian.[43]

RAGUSA. — A Christian cemetery.[44]

RAVENNA. — A Christian cemetery near St. Appollinaris *in Classe.*[45]

SELINUNTE. — A Christian cemetery.[46]

SESSA (the ancient Suessa Aurunca). — Catacombs.[47]

SYRACUSE. — Fuehrer and Orsi have found in Syracuse and its environs a number of very fine underground chapels and cemeteries. Mention may be made of the catacomb of St. John, the catacomb of Cassia and that of St. Mary of Jesus;

and of the underground chapels of Lentini, Valle del Molinello, Priolo, Canicatti, St. Alphanus, Pantalica, and many others.[48]

SORIANO (ancient Surrina). — The cemetery of St. Eutychius.[49]

SORRINA NUOVA. — A Christian cemetery.[50]

SPOLETO. — The cemetery of Sts. Gregorius and Abundantia; the cemetery of the Church of the Apostles; the cemetery of St. Vitalis and Tertius della Pieve, near Spoleto.[51]

SUBIACO. — The cemetery *ad aquas altas*.[52]

SUTRI. — The cemetery of St. Juvenal.[53]

THARROS (in Sardinia). — A Christian cemetery.[54]

TERNI. — The cemetery of St. Valentine; the *area Vindiciani* near Terni.[55]

TRASACCO (near Fucino). — The cemetery of St. Caesidius.[56]

TROPEA (in Calabria). — A Christian cemetery.[57]

VENOSA. — Christian catacombs.

VITERBO. — The cemetery of St. Salvator of Rovello, near Viterbo.[58]

VULCI. — The Christian cemetery discovered by Kellermann.[59]

## Chapter VIII

## ANCIENT CEMETERIES OUTSIDE OF ITALY[1]

## MALTA[2]

ON THE island of Malta there are still preserved numerous subterranean Christian cemeteries, similar as regards their structure and excavation to the cemeteries of Sicily. The principal ones are those of Abazio, of St. Agatha, of St. Cataldus, of St. Mary of the Grotto, of St. Mary of Virtue, of St. Paul and St. Venera.

## DALMATIA

MARUSINAC. — A cemetery.

POLA. — A cemetery.[3]

SALONA (Manastirine). — A cemetery with burial cells and basilica.[4]

SIRMIO.[5]

# FRANCE

ALIS-CAMPS.[6] — A cemetery.[7]

CLERMONT. — A cemetery.[8]

LYONS. — Subterranean cemetery of St. Irenaeus.[9]

MARSEILLES. — Crypt of St. Victor.

POITIERS. — Subterranean cemetery.[10]

UZES. — A small subterranean cemetery.[11]

VIENNE. — A cemetery.[12]

# GERMANY

COLOGNE. — Cemetery of St. Ursula.[13]

SALZBURG. — Cemetery of St. Maximian.

TREVES. — Cemetery of St. Eucharius, of St. Maximinus and of St. Paulinus.[14]

# GREECE

ATHENS. — Christian cemeteries.[15]

CHALCIDICE. — Subterranean cemetery.[16]

MELOS. — Subterranean cemetery.

# SPAIN

ARIONA (Alba Urgavonensis). — A cemetery.[17]

ELVIR. — A cemetery.[18]

SARAGOSSA. — A cemetery.[19]

SEVILLE. — A cemetery.[20]

# SWITZERLAND

AGAUNO. — A cemetery.[21]

# ASIA MINOR

*In Cilicia*:
ANAZARBUS. — Subterranean cemetery.[22]
*In Phrygia*:
EUMENIA. — A cemeterv.[23]
*In Lycaonia*:
ISAURIA. — Cemeteries.[24]
SELEUCIA. — Subterranean cemetery.[25]
*In Lycia*:
APHRODIAS. — A cemetery.[26]
*In Palestine*:
HAIFA. — Subterranean cemetery.[27]

# NORTH AFRICA[28]

CARTHAGE. — Cemetery where the tombs of St. Perpetua and companions were located.[29]

CHERCHEL (the ancient Caesarea of Mauritania). — The place where the celebrated inscription of the burial area by the name of "Ecclesia fratrum," "the Church of the Brethren," was found.[30]

CYRENE. — Subterranean cemetery.

CONSTANTINA (the ancient Corba). — Hypogeum of Praecilius.[31]

HADRUMETUM (the modern Sousse). — Subterranean cemetery.[32]

LAMBESIS. — A cemetery.[33]

LAMPTRAE (the ancient Leptis Minor Tripolis). — A cemetery.[34]

MADAURIA. — A cemetery.[35]

SULLECTUM (the modern Salakta). — Subterranean cemetery.[36]

TABARCA (the ancient Thrabaca). — A cemetery.[37]

TICZIRT. — Cemetery with burial cells.[38]

TIPASA. — Cemetery and tomb of St. Salsa.[39]

## EGYPT

AKHMIN (the ancient Panopolis).— Christian necropolis.[40]

ALEXANDRIA. — Subterranean cemetery of Karmouz; catacomb of Abou-el-Achem, of Agnew, of Moustapha, of the Rufini, of Qabbary. Over and above this, numerous underground chapels have been found.[41]

ANTINOE. — Christian necropolis.[42]

ARSINOE. — A cemetery.[43]

BAOUIT. — Christian necropolis.[44]

EL BAGAOUAT. — Christian necropolis.[45]

A cemetery near the great sanctuary of St. Menna in the desert of Lybia.[46]

# Part Four

## CHRISTIAN EPIGRAPHY

In ancient Christian cemeteries there were inscriptions, paintings and sculptures: the following sections treat, therefore, of Christian epigraphy and ancient Christian art.

## Chapter I

### GENERAL REMARKS
### CONCERNING ANCIENT CHRISTIAN INSCRIPTIONS

AS A GENERAL rule, pagan inscriptions are cut into the cinerary urns or pillars; Christian inscriptions, on the contrary, are almost always incised in marble slabs or plaques. Some of them are beautiful examples of paleography, but on the whole their character is obscure. Their meaning must be gathered from supplementary information obtained from the locality, their Christian allusions, and other inferential indications.

The inscriptions which record the *cursus honorum,* "grades of honor," are generally pagan, as are those which carry the abbreviations: V. Θ.; IN FR P. IN AGR P.; H. M. H. N. S.[1] The pagan inscriptions practically never give the time of death or burial. The Christians, on the other hand, because of their different concept of death, very often indicated these data in order to be able to celebrate the anniversaries of death, burial, etc., of the deceased.

Another probable indication of the pagan origin of inscriptions is the simultaneous presence of the three names:

*praenomen,* the given name; *gentilitium,* clan; and the *cogno-men* or family name. Christian inscriptions ordinarily omit the *praenomen* or given name. When they carry all three names, such inscriptions are generally very ancient.

Greek inscriptions are always older than Latin. Thus if a region yields a considerable number of Greek inscriptions, it can be supposed that such a locality is very old. Greek inscriptions disappear entirely during the fifth century.

Two expressions are particularly characteristic of Christian inscriptions — the formulae IN PACE and DEPOSITVS, as will be seen later.

Among the primitive examples of Roman inscriptions, de Rossi was able to determine two types of paleography. One, known as the Priscillian, is formed of inscriptions depicted in red on the slabs. Some examples, all taken from the cemetery of Priscilla, are given:

"Agapitus. May he rest in peace."

The other type, made up of fine lettering in classical style, is common to inscriptions engraved in marble.

Christian inscriptions are the more ancient the greater their simplicity. The oldest contain only the names, a word or two, or some aspiration, for example, PAX TECVM . IN DEO.

Cemetery of Callistus.
Showing the anchor, the oldest representation or symbol of the cross.

Cemetery of Priscilla.

Cemetery of Priscilla.

Cemetery of Priscilla.

Later on the inscriptions record the date of burial: DEP., D., DEPOS., DEPOSITVS, DEPOSITIO, ΚΑΤΑΘΕCΙC, KAT.; then the day of the month with the terms used in the Roman calendar, as the *calends*, the *nones*, the *ides*.

The earliest Christian inscriptions are triangular or round; later on, especially during the third and fourth centuries, the ivy leaf was employed (this was *Hedera distinguens*, classical ivy); some have erroneously explained it as symbolizing the heart.

After the fourth century, the character of primitive simplicity disappears and its place is taken by eulogistic formulas.

The phrase *in pace,* in peace, adopted from Jewish epigraphy, is found employed uninterruptedly in every age, and often refers even to the living. An example of this last use may be seen in the inscriptions on cups which formed part of the service of the agapes or feasts: VIVAS IN PACE DEI — "May you live in the peace of God." Generally, however, this phrase is reserved as a prayer for the repose of the deceased, as PAX TECVM; DORMIAS IN PACE — "Peace be with you" or "May you sleep in peace." Or again, other devices are used expressing the same underlying thought: DORMIS IN PACE, EN EIPHNH:

ΦΙΛΟΥΜΕΝΗ
ΕΝ ΕΙΡΗΝΗ ΣΟΥ
ΤΟ ΠΝΕΥΜΑ

"O Philomena, may your spirit be in peace."

Cemetery of St. Agnes. Later. Museum, IX, 28.

Oftentimes the purpose of these inscriptions is to show that the person died in the peace of the Catholic Church: DECESSIT IN PACE FIDEI CATHOLICAE. "He departed in the peace of the Catholic faith." This formula is often abbreviated thus: IN P.; IN PC.; EI (ἐν εἰρήνῃ); EN EIP.

Somewhat later, we find the phrases: HIC JACET . . . BONAE MEMORIAE — "Here lies . . . . of happy memory."

Very often a qualifying noun is added to the inscription: H. F. — "an honorable woman"; FAMVLA DEI, FAMVLA CHRISTI — "servant of God, servant of Christ"; V. H. — "an honorable man." The expression ANCILLA CHRISTI — "servant of Christ" — is older and has the same meaning as VIRGO DEI — "virgin of God." The phrases RECESSIT A SAECVLO, VIXIT IN HOC SAECVLO, IN HOC TVMVLO REQVIESCIT — "Departed this world," "He lived in this world," "He rests in this grave" — are all of the times of peace. In fact, all those which speak of the sale of a tomb or the purchasing of a burial place from a caretaker, such as LOCVS EMPTVS A FOSSORE, PRETIVM DATVM FOSSORI, etc. ("Grave purchased from the digger," "Price paid to the digger"), date from the last period of the catacombs.

EMPTVM LOCVM AB AR
TAEMISIVM VISOMVM
HOC EST ET PRAETIVM
DATVM FOSSORI HILA
RO ID EST FŌL Ñ⋈ð PRAE
SENTIASEVERI FOSSETLAVRENT

Cap. Museum and Later. Museum, X, 29.

Christian inscriptions of a metrical nature are, for the most part, later than Constantine. At times these inscriptions contain classical allusions, especially verses taken from Virgil. The following verse from the Aeneid is often found:

"Abstulit atra dies et funere mersit acerbo"[2]
("Cut off by a black day and buried in an untimely grave.")

Other metrical inscriptions composed in free verse, a variety of poetry begun in the third century by the Christian poet Commodianus,[3] are of this same category. The inscription of the deacon Severus at St. Callistus', and that of St. Agapitus in Palestrina,[4] are in free verse. This species of poetry continued in use during the fourth and fifth centuries.

In inscriptions of a later period, we notice deprecatory formulas or even maledictions against those who would attempt to violate the tomb:

MALE PEREAT INSEPVLTVS
JACEAT NON RESVRGAT
CVM JVDA PARTEM HABEAT
SI QVIS SEPVLCRVM HVNC
VIOLAVERIT.[5]

At times even the expression: ANATHEMA SIT . . . MARAN ATHA ("The Lord cometh"), is encountered.

The orthography of the inscriptions is one of the factors which permit the investigator to fix the date of the writing. Generally, the most ancient are the most correct. From the beginning of the fourth century on, errors often creep in; many letters are changed or are written according to the popular pronunciation: BIXIT (*vixit,* "lived"), BIBAS (*vivas,* "may you live"), VISOMVS (*bisomus,* "holding two bodies"), etc. There are also instances of the use of familiar terms — TATA for father, NVNNVS for grandfather (*avus*) — or of popular idioms which formed a part of the *sermo* or *lingua rustica,* the speech or language of the country people, as for example, TOTI TRES, "all three," etc.

Even the ideographic signs and symbols furnish precious guides to go by. Thus the dove with a twig or branchlet of the olive, or either used separately, are symbols of peace, employed as substitutes for the phrase IN PACE; the anchor, the concealed symbol of the cross, was much used during the first three centuries; the fish represents the Redeemer, Whom it accompanies or for Whom it substitutes the name in the acrostic ΙΧΘΥC. Often, however, this sign may signify simply one of the faithful.[6] Another symbol much used is that of the palm, expressing victory; to this is often added the laurel wreath or the athletic crown.

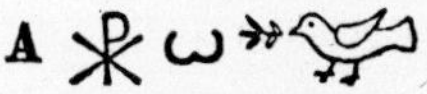


NICELLA VIRGO DEI QVAE VI
XIT ANNOS PM . XXXV . DE
POSITA . XV . KAL MAIAS BENE
MERENTI IN PACE

Later. Museum, XI, 1.

EXVPERANTIO PAT
ER SVVS FILIO DVLCI
SSIMO QVI BIXIT ANN
IS. VI. ET DIES. XXX.

Later. Museum, XIII, 1.

x M x AVR x AMMIANVS x FECIT x

SIBI x ET COIVGE SVE CORNE

LIAE TRVFERATI BENE CONBE

x NIEN  TIBVS

Cemetery of St. Hermes.
Later. Museum, XIV, 22.

Later. Museum,
XIV, 24.

The isolated dove or the dove in the act of flying represents the soul which wings its way to heaven; that is why this symbol often precedes the words IN PACE, in order to express or signify: *Anima tua, spiritus tuus in pace,* "May thy soul or thy spirit be in peace." At times, however, the dove follows the wording SPIRITVS TVVS. The vase is the symbol of the good acts of the Christian. It may even stand for the repose of the soul in paradise, and for the refreshment which is wished for the deceased. In such cases this design expresses the aspirations often repeated in the inscriptions: SPIRITVS TVVS IN REFRIGERIO; DEVS REFRIGERET SPIRITVM TVVM — "May your spirit be at rest"; "May God refresh your spirit."

MAXIMIANVS SATVRNINA DORMIT IN PACE

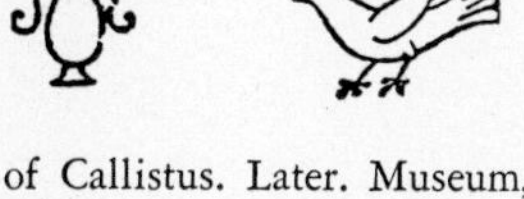

Cemetery of Callistus. Later. Museum, IX, 35.

Sometimes, though rarely, to convey the idea of the reward that the soul will receive, there will be cut in the marble of the tomb a measure of wheat, in allusion to the Scriptural phrase, "mensuram bonam et confertam," "a good measure and pressed down."[7]

Other symbols which are less frequent are the peacock, sign of immortality; and a ship sailing toward a lighthouse, symbol of the soul making for the haven of salvation. Or the ship may stand alone; it may even be found with the monogram of Christ in place of the lighthouse. Then the horse is sometimes found, in allusion to the words of St. Paul: "Cursum consummavi . . . Sic currite ut comprehendatis" — "I have run my course . . . So run that you may receive."[8]

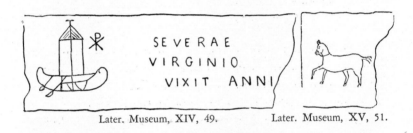

Later. Museum, XIV, 49.        Later. Museum, XV, 51.

Ship making for port.

Cemetery of the Jordani. Later. Museum, XVI, 63.

A very common and important symbol is that of the monogram of Christ which, in its most ancient form, is composed of the two letters I and X, which are the first letters of the two words Ἰησοῦς Χριστός; it is found thus in the second and third centuries:

TI⊗TAI

Cemetery of Praetextatus. Later. Museum, XIX, 7.

The monogram ☧, formed of the letters X, P (Χριστός) is known as the Constantinian monogram, in recollection of the labarum; not because it was not known to those who lived before that time, but because Constantine adopted it as a symbol for his standard.

Nevertheless, there has not been found a sure inscription with the isolated monogram predating Constantine. A piece of marble in the cemetery of St. Hermes carries this monogram with the consular date GAL. COS, a date which can be read to mean either (FAVSTO ET) GAL(LO) COS (298), or GAL(LICANO) COS; in the latter case it would belong to either the year 317 or 330, and therefore to the Constantinian epoch. In the most ancient texts, the monogram is not employed ordinarily as an isolated symbol, but only as an abbreviation (*compendium scripturae*). It is in this guise that it figures in a Greek inscription of Priscilla: COI ΔΟΞΑ ΕΝ ☧. (*Gloria tibi in Christo*).⁹

After Constantine, the monogram appears in various forms. That of the labarum ☧ persisted until the end of the fourth century, later becoming ☧ or ⳨; this last type took the name of "monogrammatic cross." Another form in use at all times is that of the so-called "crux gammata," swastika, or gammadion ⅃⌐; followed in turn by the monogram showing A and Ω ⳨. Finally, in the fifth century, we find the simple cross ✝, the symbol characteristic of the definitive triumph of Christianity. Keeping these general facts in mind, it must be admitted that at times, although rarely, the cross is found in inscriptions even during the first epochs of the Church.

 LVCILLA IN PACE

Cemetery of Cyriaca. Later. Museum, XIV, 30.

ROMAN 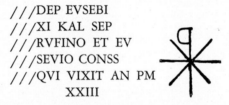 SABINVS

Cemetery of Callistus. Later. Museum, XIV, 37.

///DEP EVSEBI
///XI KAL SEP
///RVFINO ET EV
///SEVIO CONSS
///QVI VIXIT AN PM
XXIII

The year 347. Cemetery of Cyriaca. Later. Museum, IV, 21.

Cemetery of Cyriaca. Later. Museum, XI.

## Chapter II

### CONSULAR INSCRIPTIONS[1]

TO ARRIVE at an understanding of the age of an inscription, the only sure criterion is that of chronological signs or marks. And of these, the signs of the popes and bishops are the only ones which can be taken as entirely and truly Christian. They are found, however, only during the epoch of peace. Dating from the fourth century, we have three or four funerary inscriptions which carry these marks: SVB LIBerio papa; SVB DAMASO EPISCOPO.[2] Some others are to be found on monumental inscriptions:

> SALBO LEONE EPISCOPO
> SALVO SIRICIO EPISCOPO ECCLESIAE SANCTAE

The word *salvo* indicates that the pope was still living. At other times, however, the word *temporibus* is employed to express this idea:

> TEMPORIBVS SANCTI INNOCENTII EPISCOPI[3]

The metrical inscriptions do not have a fixed form; the one of the mosaic of St. Sabina's begins thus:

> "Culmen apostolicum cum Coelestinus haberet,
> Primus et in toto fulgeret Episcopus orbe."[4]

Even more rarely is any indication denoting the time appended to the names of the bishops of the provinces and of the cities of the Roman world. An inscription of Parenzo (sixth century) mentions the name of the local bishop: EVPHRASIVS ANTISTITES TEMPORIBVS SVIS ANNVM AGENS XI. There are very few analogous examples.

To fix the time, the Christians used the consular dates, for the most part, as did the pagans. However, the consular signs became frequent only subsequent to the third century. The reason for this fact is not to be sought in the peace the Church enjoyed after this time, because even during the second and third centuries there were periods of tranquillity; moreover, we have examples of consular dates from the time of Diocletian:

CATILIAE IN PACE FILIE
DVLCISSIME INGENVA
MATER . FECIT . D .
P . VIIII . K . IVL . DIO
CLETIANO III . ET MAXI
MIANO II

The year 287. Cemetery of Hippolytus. Later. Museum, IV, 5.

VIBIVS . FIMVS . R . VII . KAL . SEP .
DIC . IIII . ET . MAX . COS .

The year 290. Cemetery of Callistus.[5]

The reason is rather that the pagans themselves did not use these dates habitually in their burial inscriptions; the Christians merely followed the general custom. De Rossi gave the following as a unique consular inscription of the first century. It dates from the third consulate of Vespasian (the year 71):

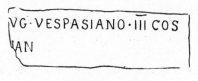

Later. Museum, IV, 1.

But Gatti maintains that this may be a fragment of a pagan consular inscription used by the Christians to close one of their graves.

At present, only two consular inscriptions are ascribed to the second century. These are scratched in mortar and, according to Boldetti, both come from the cemetery of Lucina on the Appian Way:

*an*N . XXX . SVRA ET SENEC . COSS

The year 107.

SERVILIA . ANNORVM XIII
PIS . ET . BOL . COSS

"During the consulate of Piso and Bolanus."[6]

The year 111.

The number of consular inscriptions increases during the third century, as has been said. The Lateran Museum has some dating from the years 238, 273, 279, 290, 298: and many others have been discovered during the latest excavations. Christian inscriptions with dates become very numerous during the fourth century. An example of the Constantinian era is given:

℞ ASELLVS ET LEA PRISCO PATRI BE///
✗ QVI BIXIT ANNIS LXIV MENSI///

⚶ IN SIGNO ✗ DIES XI XII

V. K. OCT. D BASSO ET ABLAVIO CONSS

The year 331. Cemetery of St. Agnes. Later. Museum, IV, 11.

It is necessary to make a distinction between the chronological signs found on inscriptions of the city of Rome and those of the provinces, because in Rome only the consuls are indicated, whereas in the provinces the names of the governors are often added. By way of exception, some few inscriptions found in Rome also carry the name of the emperor, as for example, a Greek inscription referring to an epoch in which the civil government had been upset, with the consequent interruption of the succession of consuls. This occurred in the year 307, under Maxentius, when inscriptions contain the phrase Ἐπὶ Μαξεντίω.

This type of Christian inscription does not reveal any partisanship; usurpers as well as the legitimate rulers, persecuting princes and sovereigns favorable to Christianity, are named without distinction. In fact, there are instances in which Christians even added the epitaph Divus to the name of the rulers, an adjective which in its original significance referred to the pagan religion or its practices. It was not used by the Christians until the time of Constantine, when we find the word has become synonymous with "of happy memory," "of holy memory." Thus we find Athalaric, a Christian prince, conferring such a title on his father Theodoric, also a Christian: "Theodorico divae memoriae" — "To Theodoric of happy memory."

Moreover, the chronological era in use in Rome was that dating from the founding of the city, *anno ab Urbe condita,* whereas in some provinces the chronological era or calendar began with the domination of the Romans, the so-called *aera provincialis,* "provincial era." The well-known inscription of Alexander, copied in part in that of Abercius, is dated according to the Phrygian era, which began with the reorganization of the province of Asia in 84 B.C.

In Egypt there was current a special calendar for the Christians; it was the so-called "era of the martyrs," which began in the year 283, during the reign of Diocletian.

The consuls were either *ordinary* or *supernumerary.* The first assumed their duties on the first of January and were supplanted by the latter in case of death or removal. Christian inscriptions and consular holidays carry only the names of the ordinary consuls; pagan inscriptions, on the other hand, often include even the names of the supernumerary consuls. This general practice is supposed to have ceased after Constantine, but the opinion is erroneous, because we find examples even in the fourth and fifth centuries. The cipher after the names of the consuls indicates the number of times they had received the title. The specification of the consular dignity is scarcely ever found written in full, but is abbreviated thus: COS. COSS. CONS. CONSS. (so and so being consuls).

IANVARA IN PACE DEPOSITA . XI . KAL SEPT
CL . ANTONIO ET FL . SYAGRIO CONSS.

The year 382. Cemetery of Cyriaca. Later. Museum, V, 26.

The consular inscriptions at times preserve for us a record of contemporary political happenings, such as revolutions, usurpations, etc. Thus in the year 307, following the seizure of power by Maxentius, there was a break in the consular order, and we encounter a new inscriptional formula for that period. It repeats the names of the consuls of the year 306, Constantius Chlorus and Maximian, after which we find the phrase POST SEXTVM CONSVLATVM, "after the sixth consulate," or simply POST SEXTVM, because both these rulers had had the consulate the same number of times:

Cemetery of Sts. Peter and Marcellinus. Later. Museum, IV, 9.

Again in the year 346, inscriptions do not cite the ordinary consuls, but use the words POST CONSVLATVM AMANTII ET ALBINI, because the names of the ruling consuls for 346 had not been promulgated. In 350, Maxentius made himself master of the Roman world and assumed the imperial dignity. Inscriptions of this period, in order not to use the name of the usurper, employ the phrase: POST CONSVLATVM LIMENII ET CATVLLINI.

Toward the end of the fourth century, the phrase: D (*Domino*) N (*Nostro*) COS, or if there were two: DD NN CONSS (*dominis nostris consulibus*), was used to designate sovereign consuls.

HIC POSITA EST ANIMA DVLCES
INNOCA SAPIENS ET PVLCRA NOMINE
QVIRIACE QVE VIXIT ANNOS. III. M. III. D.
     VIII.
DP. IN PACE. III. ID. IAN. CONSS. DN. TEVDOSIO
AVG. II ET MEROBAVDE. VC. III.

The year 388. From the Ostian Way. Later. Museum, V, 31.

During the year 395 the Empire was divided, and with this division of territory there came a consequent division of authority. There were consuls for the Orient as well as for the

Occident. In inscriptions of this epoch, from the Occident, there is very frequently mention of only one consul. Thus, for the year 399, the West did not recognize Eutropius, the favorite of Arcadius, who had chosen him consul. For that reason, only Theodore, chosen by Honorius, is named: FLAVIO MAGNO THEODORO COS. This formula is even amplified or repeated to fill in the space which would have been occupied by the other name. Even as late as 404, we find Honorius mentioned alone:

DEPOSITA CONSTANTIA. VI. K̄A
L. IVLIAS HONORIO AVG. VI
CONSVLE DIE DOMINI
CA QVAE VIXIT ANNOS PL
VS MINVS SEXAGINTA BE
NEMERENTI IN PACE

The year 404. Cemetery of St. Sebastian. Later. Museum, IV, 27.

However, there are cases in which both consuls are mentioned; but because the promulgation of the two names had not been made at the same time throughout the Roman world, the name of the known consul would be followed by some reference to the other, as seen on this inscription from Milan: ET EO QVI DE ORIENTE FVERIT NVNTIATVS.

QVI EST DEPOSITVS DIE . IIII . KAL///
OCTOBR . CONSVLATV D///
HONORII XII ET THEODOS///
VIII AVGVSTORVM

ET IVGALIS EIS SAVRA INL . F . SIM///
QVIESCIT QVI EST DEP . PRID . KL . MART///
FESTO VC CONS . ET QVI DE ORIENTE FV///
NVNTIATVS

The years 418 and 439.

Theodoric, after conquering Italy in 493, personally selected the consuls of the West; and to the end of the period of the Gothic War, in 535, the inscriptions record only one consul.

But after the coming of Belisarius to Italy, the name of the Eastern consul again appears on the inscriptions. The name of Belisarius himself is often cited:

✠HIC REQVIESCIT IN PACE IOHANNIS $\overline{V H}$
OLOGRAFVS PROPINE ISIDORI QVI VIX*it*
$\overline{ANN}$. PLVS $\overline{M}$. XLV. $\overline{DEP}$ ⚭ X. KALEN. IVNIA*s*
CONSVLATV VILISARI VC.

The year 535. Vatican Crypts.

During the reign of Justinian, public documents almost always carry the names of the emperors. The last individual to be vested with consular dignity was Basilius in the year 541, and following this, the date was fixed by means of the formula *post consulatum Basilii*. This dignity was assumed by the Byzantine emperors, though not without exception. The inscription of the column of Phoca indicated the year 608 by using the phrase mentioning the post-consulate of the emperor: POST CONSVLATVM PIETATIS EIVS ANNO V. This is one of the last instances of the mention of consuls.

At the beginning of the sixth century, the names of the barbarian kings make their appearance. Marks of the Christian era begin only during the eighth century, although they had been introduced during the sixth century by Dionysius Exiguus.

It should also be noted that there are several variants among the expressions ordinarily used up to this time. During the fourth century, for the formula N** COS, there is substituted another CONSVLATV N**, and the expression *post-consulatum* was shortened to P C. The name of the ruler was followed by AVG; and whenever there were several rulers, they were indicated by the letters AVGG DD NN or AVGGG DDD NNN. During the fifth century, this was written AA VV GG; in the sixth century, the adjective PP (*Perpetuus,* "Perpetual") was added to the title.

The *Consular Holidays* inform us of the agreement of the consular dates with the Roman era. Of the numerous documents of this nature, the first was the Capitoline Calendar, begun under Augustus in the year 724 of the founding of Rome, and discontinued after the year 12 of the Christian era. This was written in marble and affixed to the walls of the house of the pontifex maximus on the Sacred Way.

Among the later calendars and manuscripts, the most important are the Philocalian Calendar, which contains a list of the prefects of Rome and of the consuls from 254 to 354; the Calendar of the Paschal Canon, which arose in consequence of the debate on the celebration of Easter, naming the consuls from 312 to 412; the *Chronicle* of St. Athanasius; an extract of a Syrian translation of his letters (published by Cureton in 1848, and translated by Cardinal Mai); and the Catalogue of the Consular Calendar in Vatican manuscript 2077, which gives the consuls from 354 to 398 and the consuls of the West until the year 437, with a few lacunae.

The Calendar of St. Prosper of Aquitania goes to the year 455; that of Idatius, Bishop of Galicia, to 468;[7] the Consular Calendar of Verona runs from 439 to 486; the *Chronicle* of Cassiodorus, secretary of Theodoric, to the year 559. The Oriental calendars are not of much use in studying Roman inscriptions.[8]

To fix the date of a consular inscription, it is necessary to determine the names of the consuls mentioned and compare them with the list contained in the calendar known as the *Consular Holidays.*

In concluding our study of the chronological marks of the Christian inscriptions, we may summarize the following rules:

The oldest are the simplest and best written.

The most ancient formulas are: VIVAS IN DEO, PAX TECVM, PAX TIBI; the expressions DEPOSITVS, DEPOSITIO, come later; and HIC IACET, HIC POSITVS EST are from the end of the fourth century: the eulogistic phrases, MIRAE BONITATIS, INCOMPARABILI, etc., are from the end of the fourth and especially of the fifth century.

The inscriptions which are the most ancient record the *praenomen,* the *gentilitium* and the *cognomen,* according to classical usage. Later on, the *praenomen* was dropped; toward the end of the fourth century only the *cognomen* is cited. In many cases new names appear, which are of distinctly Christian origin, such as *Martyrius, Paschasius, Adeodatus, Evangelius, Iohannes, Beatus,* etc. At times such names express a sentiment of humility, as *Projecticius, Fimus, Stercorius,* etc.; these latter were already in use in the third century.

Such names as *Fides, Spes, Agape,* etc., which are found in the most ancient inscriptions, as for example, in the cemetery of Priscilla, were probably surnames in common, domestic or familiar usage.[9]

Almost all Christian burial inscriptions bear reference to the concepts of resurrection and a future life; some of them have also a special dogmatic importance and significance. These will be treated briefly in the following pages.

## Chapter III

## DOGMATIC INSCRIPTIONS

DOGMATIC inscriptions properly so called are fairly numerous, and are found in all the cemeteries. Many of them antedate the period of peace, and consequently they provide us with absolutely certain proofs of the primitive faith of the Church. Even the inscriptions of this nature dating from the fourth and fifth centuries are important because they represent an age which was close to the period of the persecutions. The following pages give some principal examples, arranged according to the most important points of dogma.

### 1. Belief in One God

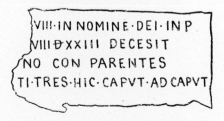

Cemetery of Cyriaca. Later. Museum, VIII, 2.

The expression "In nomine Dei" is the initial formula for every solemn Christian act. Hence the worship of Christ is the worship, par excellence, of the one true God, and the essential negation of polytheism.[1] It was for this reason that the Christians were called *Cultores Dei,* worshippers of God (not of gods).[2] Very frequent is the use of the phrase IN DEO, "in God."

"May you live in God."

Cemetery of Priscilla.

Boldetti cites an inscription which gives a beautiful testimony to the effect that, in common with all Christians, a certain dead man had believed in only one God:

IN . VNV . DEV . CREDIDIT.

### 2.   The Divinity of Christ

MARCO VENEME
RENTI . PERSICOMENI
CONPAR. IN PACE. IN NO
MINE ☧ QVIEES
CIT / / /ANN
VS QVINQVE

Later. Museum, VIII, 10.

It is evident that in this inscription the monogrammatic name of Jesus Christ (*in nomine Christi*) is substituted for that of God (*in nomine Dei*).

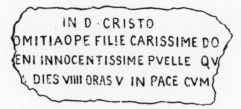

"In Christ God."

Cemetery of Cyriaca. Later. Museum, VIII, 3.

The museum of Venice possesses an inscription which came from the Roman catacombs, wherein the formula in ordinary use, IN PACE, is followed by the expression, IN. DO. MI. NO. TRO. D.C.T.: "In Domino nostro Deo Christo" — "In our Lord God Christ."

AEQVĪTIO . IN ☧ DEO . INNOFITO
BENE . MERENTI . QVI . VIXIT
AN . XXVI . M . V . D . IIII . DEC . III NON . AVG.

"In Christ God."

Cemetery of Cyriaca. Later. Museum, VIII, 4;
see plate on page 215.

REGINA VIBAS
IN DOMINO
ZESV

"In the Lord Jesus."
Later. Museum, IX, 17.

AVGVRINE IN
DO M̄ ET ☧

"In the great God and Jesus Christ."
Cemetery of Callistus.

The following expressions are also found in Greek:

ΕΝ ΘΕΩ ☧, ΕΝ ΘΕΩ ΚΥΡΙΩ ☧, ΕΝ ΘΕΩ ΧΡΙΣΤΩ, ΕΝ ΘΕΩ ΚΥΡΙΩ ΧΡΙΣΤΩ — "In God Christ," "In God, our Lord Christ."

"May the light be with you, O Ermaiscus.
May you live in our Lord Christ."

Later. Museum, VIII, 6.

ΤΗϹΕΜΝΟΤΑΤΗ ΚΑΙ ΓΛΥΚΥΤΗ
ϹΥΜΒΙω ΡΟΔΙΝΗ ΑΥΡ ΔΙΟϹΙΟδω
ΡΟϹ ΤΕΘΕΙΚΑΤ ΟΚΥΡΜΕΤΑϹΟΥ

"To the worthiest and sweetest wife, Rodina, placed by
Aurelius Diosiodorus. May the Lord be with you."

Cemetery of Priscilla.

These inscriptions are generally prior to the rule of Constantine; but their date cannot be determined with any great precision. A later inscription has the legend: D . M . ☧ . S ("Deo Magno Christo Sacrum" or "Deus Magnus Christus Salvator") which may mean either "Sacred to the great God

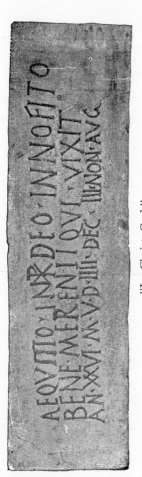

"In Christ God."
Cemetery of Cyriaca. Later. Museum, VIII, 4.

"Nourished by God Christ and the Martyrs."
Later. Museum, VIII, 14.

Christ," or "The Great God Christ the Saviour." In an inscription from the cemetery of Priscilla, which is not later than the third century, we read:

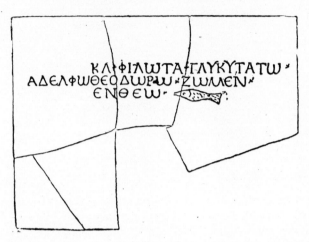

"Claudius Philota to his dearest brother Theodore. May we
live in God,"

followed by the sign of the fish which signifies: "Jesus Christ,
the Son of God, Saviour."

The word IXΘΥC ("fish") may also be considered a profession of faith in the Redemption, because this symbolic word,
like the figure of the fish, was for the faithful a translation of
the names and titles of the Saviour:

IHCOYC XPICTOC ΘΕΟΥ ΥΙΟC CΩTHP

"Jesus Christ, Son of God, Saviour."[3]

```
CECILIVS · MARITVS · CECILIAE
PLACIDIANAE · COIVGI · OPTIME
MEMORIAE · CVM · QVA · VIXI · ANNIS X ·
BENE : SE · NE · VLLA · QVERELLA      IXOYC
```

Cemetery of Priscilla. Later. Museum, VIII, 13.

Here the word IXΘΥC is evidently a symbol and does not
enter into the meaning of the text of the inscription. To this
same group of dogmatic inscriptions belong the very well
known inscriptions of Abercius and Pectorius, of which we
shall speak later.

### 3.  Belief in the Holy Ghost

CAR KΥRIACO
FIL· DVLCISSIMO
VIBAS N SPIRITO SAN

"May you live in the Holy Spirit."

Cemetery of Callistus.

At times the expression "Spiritus Sanctus," "Holy Spirit," is applied to the faithful: SPIRITVS TVVS BENE REQVIES-CAT — "May your spirit rest well"; or to the saints: INTER SPIRITA SANCTA, SPIRITA SANCTA IN MENTE HABE-TE, AD SPIRITA SANCTA — "Among the holy spirits," "remember the holy spirits," "to the holy spirits."

The following inscription of the National Museum of Rome reads: ΕΝ ΑΓΙΩ ΠΝΕΥΜΑΤΙ ΘΕΟΥ — "In the Holy Spirit of God." The text from which this is taken is as follows:

ΠΡΩΤΟΣ | ΕΝ ΑΓΙΩ | ΠΝΕΥΜΑ | ΤΙ · ΘΕΟΥ | ΕΝΘΑΔΕ | ΚΕΙΤΑΙ | ΦΙΡΜΙΛΛΑ | ΑΔΕΛΦΗ | ΜΝΗΜΗϹ | ΚΑΡΙΝ

"Protus lies here in the Holy Spirit.  Firmilla his sister erected this as a memorial."

Cemetery of St. Hermes.

### 4.  Belief in the Blessed Trinity

*Iu*CVNDIANVS *qui credidit*
*in* CRISTVM IESV*m vivit in*
*Patr*E . ET . FILIO . ET . IS*Piritu Sancto*

Cemetery of Domitilla.

An inscription found in the region of the tombs of the Acilii Glabriones, in the cemetery of Priscilla, provides us with a notable example of the doxology:

Ο · ΠΑΤΗΡ · ΤΩΝ · ΠΑΝΤΩΝ · ΟΥ**C** · ΕΠΟΙΗ**C**Ε**C** · Κ
ΠΑΡΕΛΑΒΗ**C** · ΕΙΡΗΝΗΝ · ΖΟΗΝ · Κ · ΜΑΡΚΕΛΛΟΝ
**C**ΟΙ · ΔΟΞΑ · ΕΝ ☧ ⚓

"O Father of all, Thou Who hast created them, receive
Irene, Zoe and Marcellus. Glory be to Thee in Christ."

The inscriptions relating to the Sacraments of Baptism
and Holy Eucharist will be given further on.

## 5.    The Veneration of the Saints

The veneration of the martyrs by the early Christians may
also be proved by inscriptions in which they are invoked, and
by the fact that the early Christians desired to be buried close
to their tombs. Some examples of this will be given.

In the inscriptions we often read formulas which run: AD
SANCTA MARTVRA, AT IPPOLITV, AT CRISCENTIO-
NEM, AD DOMNVM HIPPOLYTVM, AD DOMNVM
CORNELIVM, IN CALLISTI AD DOMNVM CAIVM, AD
DOMNVM VAL*entinum*, etc. ("At the place of the Holy
Martyrs," "Near Hippolytus," "Near Crescention," "Near St.
Hippolytus," "Near St. Cornelius," "In the cemetery of Callis-
tus," "Near the tomb of Caius," "Near St. Valentine," and
so on).

The titles *Domnus, Domna,* were given to the martyrs.

FILICISSIMVS . ET . LEOPAR*da emerunt*
BISOMVM . AT . CRISCENT*ionem martirem* INTROIT*u*

Burial vault placed near the tomb of the martyr Crescention
in the cemetery of Priscilla.

///SEVFROSINI ET DECENSIES QVE CESQVET
///VS OCTOB QVE VIXIT ANNo XXX ET III ET MENSE.
///LIAPA PARENTIBVS SVIS TABLAM POSVIT BE
///BUS IN P AD SANCTA MARTVRA

Cemetery of St. Agnes.

The Christians desired to be buried near the martyrs in
order to be under their holy protection, and be taken to heaven
by them. An inscription placed on the wall of the Constantinian basilica of St. Lawrence outside the Walls expresses this
concept of the intercession of the martyrs:

. . . . . . . . . . . . . . . . .

CVIQVE PRO VITAE SVAE TESTIMONIO SANCTI
MARTYRES APVT DEVM ET ☧ ERVNT ADVOCATI . . .

The same sentiment induced the living to recommend the
deceased to the martyrs, especially those of the same cemetery:

SOMNO HETERNALI
AVRELIVS . GEMELLVS . QVS BIXIT . AN///
CARISSIMO . BENAEMERENTI . FECIT IN PAC//
CONMANDO BASILLA INNOCENTIA GEMELLI

"I recommend to St. Basilla the innocent Gemellus."
Cemetery of Basilla. Later. Museum, VIII, 16.

MARTYRES. SANCTI
IN. MENTE. HAVITE
MARIA

"Remember Mary."
Aquileia.

DOMINA BASILLA COM
MANDAMVS TIBI CRES
CENTINVS ET MICINA
FILIA NOSTRA CRESCEN///
///QVE VIXIT MENS . X . ET DES//

Cemetery of Basilla. Later. Museum, VIII, 17.

The following inscriptions are also to be referred to the veneration of the saints:

PETRVS ET PANCARA BOTVM PO
SVENT MARTYRE FELICITATI
Cemetery of St. Felix.

CORPVS. SANCTIS. COMMEN
DAVI. IRENE TIBI CVM
SANCTIS QVINTIA VALE
IN PACE
Capua.

The expression, NVTRICATVS DEO CHRISTO MAR-TVRIBVS, which is met with in one inscription,[4] records a custom mentioned by Prudentius, and preserved for us in the devotions of the early Christians. This was the custom of consecrating babies to God and to the martyrs, especially St. Lawrence:

"Videmus illustres domos,
Sexu ex utroque nobiles
Offerre votis pignora
Clarissimorum liberum.
Vittatus olim Pontifex
Adscitur in signum crucis,
Aedemque, Laurenti, tuam
Vestalis intrat Claudia."[5]

The inscriptions oftentimes make mention of the feasts of the saints. A certain Pecorius records the octave of the feast of Sts. Processus and Martinianus, which falls on the ninth day of July:

PECORI DVLCIS ANIMA BENIT IN CIMITERO . VII .
IDVS IVL. D. POSTERA DIE MARTVRORV[6]

From the Aurelian Way, where the cemetery of Sts. Processus and Martinianus was located. Later. Museum, VIII, 25.

In an inscription at St. Sebastian's, we read: MARCELLI DIE *Natali* (January 16); an epitaph from the cemetery of Cyriaca has NATALE SA*ncti Laurent*I (August 10). A Greek inscription found at Syracuse informs us that the deceased woman was interred on the feast day of St. Lucy (December 13):

ЄΟΡΤΗ ΤΗϹ ΚΥΡΙΑϹ ΜΟΥ ΛΟΥΚΙΑϹ

Many are the inscriptions which may be referred to the doctrines of praying for the dead, and praying to the dead for the benefit of the living. This indicates the early Christians' belief in heavenly bliss on the one hand, and on the other, their adherence to the teaching of the Communion of Saints. A most beautiful example illustrating this is the following:

"Gentianus, a believer, who died in peace after living 21 years, 8 months and 16 days. In your prayers remember us, because we know that you are with ☧ [Christ]."

Later. Museum, VIII, 15.

This inscription is very important, because it not only records the practice of praying for the dead, but also indicates the theological reason for it.

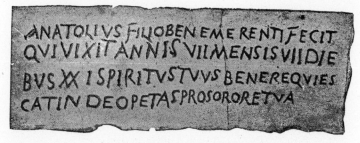

"Anatolius erected this monument to his well-deserving son, who lived 7 years, 7 months and 20 days. May your soul rest well in God. Intercede for your sister."

Later. Museum, VIII, 19.

A Greek inscription from the cemetery of Domitilla expresses, at one and the same time, a wish and a prayer:

ZHCAIC · EN · KΩ · KAI · EPΩTA · ΥΠEP · ΗΜΩΝ

"May you live in the Lord and pray for us."

The following is also important:

"Intercede for us with the saints."

Cemetery of Priscilla.

PAVLO FILIO MERENTI IN PA
CEM TE SVSCIPIAN OMNIVM INSPIRI
TA SANCTORVM QVI VIXIT ANNOS . II . DIES . N . I

"May the souls of all the saints receive thee."
From the Roman catacombs; at present in the Museo Del Bagno.

SABBATI DVLCIS
ANIMA PETE ET RO
GA PRO FRATRES ET
SODALES TVOS

"Pray for your brothers and your companions."
Cemetery of Sts. Gordian and Epimachus.
From Muratori, *Nov. Thes.,* p. 1934.

ATTICE SPIRITVS TVVS
IN BONO ORA PRO PAREN
TIBVS TVIS

"Pray for your parents."
Cemetery of Callistus. From Muratori, *Nov. Thes.,* p. 1833.

"Live in peace and pray for us."
Cemetery of Domitilla.

SOZON . BENEDICTVS
REDIDIT . AN . NOBE
BERVS . ✼ . ISPIRVM
IN . PACE . ET . PET . PRO NOBIS

"May the true Christ receive thy spirit in peace. Intercede for us."
Cemetery of the Jordani.

PETE PRO PARENTES TVOS
MATRONATA MATRONA
QVE VIXIT . AN . I . D . I . L . II

"Pray for your parents."
Later. Museum, VIII, 18.

In some inscriptions, an appeal is made to other believers to pray for the dead. Thus we read, in an inscription in the Lateran Museum, the plea that everyone reading the epitaph remember to pray for the deceased: VT QVISQVE DE FRATRIBVS LEGERIT ROGET DEVM VT SANCTO ET INNOCENTE SPIRITO AD DEVM SVSCIPIATVR. ("That every one of the brethren reading this, pray that God receive the holy and innocent soul.")

A prayer of this kind, directed to the faithful who took part in the liturgical reunions, is found in an important and very ancient inscription still preserved in the cemetery of Priscilla:

EVCHARIS . EST . MATER . PIVS . ET . PATER . EST *mihi* / / /
VOS . PRECOR . O . FRATRES . ORARE . HVC . QVANDO . VENI*tis*
ET . PRECIBVS . TOTIS . PATREM . NATVMQVE . ROGATIS
SIT . VESTRAE . MENTIS . AGAPES . CARAE . MEMINISSE
VT . DEVS . OMNIPOTENS . AGAPEN . IN . SAECVLA . SERVET

"I beseech you, brethren, when you come together to offer
prayers in common to the Father and Son, kindly
remember dear Agape, till God receives
her in heaven."

The expression "precibus totis" indicates, without doubt,
the common prayers offered by the faithful when they came
together in the cemetery.

"Vita eterna" ("eternal life," "repose" or "rest") and "refrigerio" ("refreshment") are ideas which find frequent expression in Christian inscriptions:

Cemetery of St. Agnes. Later. Museum, IX, 18.

The monogram reads: "May you live in Christ."

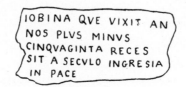

"She departed this life, and entered into peace."
Cemetery of Callistus.

Of great significance is the prayer for the refreshment of
the soul, an expression which was explained when treating of
the Acts of St. Perpetua.[7] The Church has preserved this idea
in her liturgy in the *memento* for the dead: "Ipsis, Domine, et
omnibus in Christo quiescentibus locum refrigerii, lucis et pacis
ut indulgeas deprecamur" — "To them, O Lord, and to all who
rest in Christ, we beseech Thee grant a place of refreshment,
light and peace."

"Bolosa, may God give you refreshment. She lived 30 years, and departed this life on the 13th day before the Kalends of October ☧."

Later. Museum, IX, 12.

*Val*ERIO VOLVSIANO
VTYCHETIS FILIO
OFORTVNATO QVI VIM
S PASSI SVNT
GIA PIENTISSIMIS
REFRIGERET NOSQ*ui*
*omnia po*TEST

"May He Who can do all things give us rest."
Museum of Marseilles.

MVRELIVS IA*nuarius* (?).....
CARE REFRIGER\*a*.......

"Dear, may you have peace."
Cemetery of Priscilla.

PRIVATA. DVLCIS
IN. REFRIGERIO
ET. IN. PACE

De Rossi, *Bullett.*, 1886, p. 129.

BONO INSPIRI
TO MARIANI
DEVS REFRIGE
RET

Philippeville, Africa. C. I. L. VIII, 819.

PARENTI /// *fi*LIO
BONOSO FE*ce*RVNT
BENE MERENTI IN
PACE ET IN REFRI
GERIV ///
QVI VIXIT . *Ann* . X

Cemetery of St. Hermes.

IANVARIA BENE REFRIGERA ET ROGA P
RO NOS

Cemetery of Callistus. Vase signifying refreshment, and lamp signifying light.

It is noteworthy that in this inscription there are two ideas of prayer, namely, prayer for the deceased, and prayer of the deceased for the living: "Bene refrigera — et roga pro nobis" —"Rest well, and pray for us."

VICTORIA REFRIGER*et*
ISSPIRITVS TVS IN BON*o*

Cemetery of Domitilla.

AGATEMERIS. SPI          EVGENI
RITVM. TVVM. INTER       SPIRITVVS
SANCTOS                  IN BONO

"That your spirit may be numbered among the saints."

Cemetery of Callistus.

M . E M

VTVLIVS CALLIGONVS
SEMPER IN D VIVAS
DVLCIS ANIMA

"May you always live in God, sweet soul."

Later. Museum, IX, 5.

AGAPE VIBES
IN AETERNVM

Later. Museum, IX, 30.

"Amerimnus erected this to the memory of Rufina, his dearest and
well-deserving wife. May God refresh your soul."

Later. Museum, IX, 13.

A beautiful inscription found at Rome, near St. Sabina's,
in 1891 and now in the Capitoline Museum, reads:

ATTICE
DORMI IN PACE
DE TVA INCOLVMITATE
SECVRVS ET PRO NOSTRIS
PECCATIS . PETE . SOLLICITVS

"Thou who art sure of thy salvation, pray unceasingly
for our sins."

The better to understand the value of this inscription it is
necessary to recall the ancient liturgical prayers, especially a
very important document published by Mone.[8] This treats of a
prayer composed during the periods of persecution, beseeching
God to give strength not only in times of trial but also in
times of peace: "Deus cuius tam immensa est bonitas quam
potestas, praesta . . . si quies adridat te colere, si tentatio ingruat
non negare . . . Sanctorum tuorum nos gloriosa merita ne in
poenam veniamus excusent; defunctorum fidelium animae quae
beatitudine gaudent, nobis opitulentur; quae consolatione in-
digent, Ecclesiae precibus absolvantur." ("God Who art not
only boundless goodness but also power, grant, we beseech
Thee, peace if it please Thee, temptation if it be Thy will. . . .

Grant that in view of the glorious merits of Thy saints, we do not fall into pain; may the souls of the faithful departed who are enjoying bliss assist us; may those who lack this consolation be forgiven by the prayers of the Church.")

At times, we find liturgical formulas even in inscriptions, especially those in Greek, whether of the Orient or of Rome: Μνήσθητι Κύριε, MEMENTO DOMINE ("Remember, O Lord," etc.). An example of this is:

ΔΗΜΗΤΡΙϹ · ΕΤ · ΛΕΟΝΤΙΑ ☧
ϹΕΙΡΙΚΕ ΦΕΙΛΙΕ · ΒΕΝΕΜΕΡΕΝ
ΤΙ ΜΝΗϹΘΗϹ · ΙΗϹΟΥϹ
Ο ΚΥΡΙΟϹ ΤΕΚΝΟΝ . . .

. . . "Lord Jesus, remember our daughter . . ."

Cemetery of Domitilla.

Again, at times there is a reference to the belief in the resurrection:

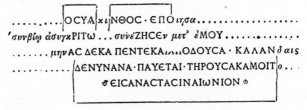

. . . . . . . . . |ΟϹΥΑ|*κ ι|*ΝΘΟϹ · ΕΠΟ*ιησα* . . . . . . . . . . . . . . . . .
*'συνβίῳ ἀσυγκ*ΡΙΤѠ . . . *συνέ*ΖΗϹΕ*ν μετ' ἐ*ΜΟΥ . . . . . . . . . . . . .
. . . . . . *μην*ΑϹ ΔΕΚΑ ΠΕΝΤΕΚΑ₍₎₎₎ΟΔΟΥϹΑ · ΚΑΛΑΝ*δαις*
. . . . . . . . . . |ΔΕΝΥΝΑΝΑ · ΠΑΥΕΤΑΙ · ΤΗΡΟΥϹΑΚΑΜΟΙΤ|*ο* . .
❦ ΕΙϹΑΝΑϹΤΑϹΙΝΑΙѠΝΙΟΝ ❧

Cemetery of Priscilla.

In the last line of the inscription we read: "Till the eternal resurrection."

## 6. Inscriptions Referring to the Sacraments of Baptism and Holy Eucharist

Some inscriptions also allude to the Sacraments, especially to Baptism and Confirmation, in these words: GRATIAM SANCTAM CONSECVTVS EST, FIDEM ACCEPIT; or simply PERCEPIT, ACCEPIT,[9] FIDELIS DE SAECVLO RECESSIT, POST SVSCEPTIONEM SVAM; or even to solemn Baptism: ALBAS SVAS OCTABAS PASCHAE AD SEPVLCRVM DEPOSVIT.

An inscription engraved on the tomb of a child records the title of "faithful," which proves that even at this time the practice of infant baptism was in force: QVI CVM SOLDV (*solide*) AMATVS FVISSET A MAIORE SVA ET VIDIT HVNC MORTI CONSTITVTVM ESSE PETIVIT DE AECLESIA VT FIDELIS DE SECVLO RECESSISSET. The following is an example showing that a baby was baptized at the point of death, which proves that Baptism administered to children was considered valid:

> TYCHE . DVLCIS
> VIXIT . ANNO . VNO
> MENSIBVS . X . DIEB . XV
> ACCEPIT . VIII . K ///
> REDDIDIT . DIE . SS

Cemetery of Priscilla.

That is to say, "He received the grace . . . and gave up his soul on the above-mentioned day." In an inscription of the year 279 we read: QVI. GRATIAM. ACCEPIT. D. N. (*Domini nostri*). In Greek, we find:

ΚΑΛΩϹ · ΗΞΙΩΜΕΝΟϹ ΤΗΝ · ΚΑΡΙΝ · ΤΟΥ · ΘΕΟΥ
"Who was made worthy of the grace of God."

Confirmation is expressed by the phrases: SIGNATVS. MVNERE. CHRISTI (Bolsena): "Signed with the gift of Christ"; CONSIGNATA . A . LIBERIO PAPA (Spoleto): "Signed by Pope Liberius."

The title or name of the catechumen is also found. We read, in a beautiful inscription from the Tiburtine Way, now preserved in the Museum of the German cemetery in Rome:

ΕΝΘΑΔΕ ΚΙΤΕ ΒΙΚΤΟΡ ΚΑΤΗ ΚΟΥΜΕΝΟϹ ΑΙΤΩΝ ΕΙΚΟΣΙ

ΠΑΡΘΕΝΟϹ Ο ΔΟΥΛΟϹ ΤΟΥ ΚΥΡΙΟΥ ΙΕϹΟΥ ☧

"Here lies Victor a catechumen, virgin, twenty years of age, servant of our Lord Jesus Christ."[10]

The Sacrament of Penance was not usually mentioned in the primitive inscriptions. Only the epitaph of a certain Adjutor can be listed — "Adjutor, qui post acceptam poenitentiam

migravit ad Dominum" — "Adjutor, who after receiving penance, departed to the Lord."

Inscriptions referring to the Sacraments, especially to the
Eucharist, will be found in Part V, "Ancient Christian Art,"
under the heading "Sacraments." They are those of Abercius
and Pectorius, the former of the second century, the latter of
the third, and bear witness to the faith of the first Christians in
the dogma of the Holy Eucharist.

Finally, several other inscriptions are given here representing symbols which were used as ideographic signs. The two
which follow show the anchor (the cross, and hope in the
cross). This is the oldest symbol.

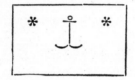

Cemetery of Priscilla.

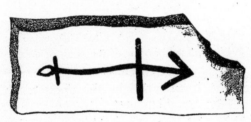

Cemetery of Priscilla.

The dove betokens the soul freed from its bodily shackles,
and the ship is the symbol of the course of human life.

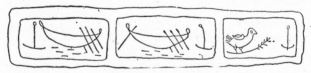

Cemetery of Priscilla.

The following is important because it shows the union of
the anchor (symbol of hope in the cross) and of the dove near
a tree (the blessed soul in the garden of heaven):

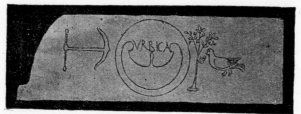

Cemetery of Callistus.

Oftentimes there will be scenes from the Old and New Testaments, showing Noe, Daniel, the Epiphany and the miracles of Christ.

THE EPIPHANY.
Later. Museum, XIV, 1.

THE RESURRECTION OF LAZARUS.
Later. Museum.

There are also pictures of the saints as intercessors for the dead:

ASELLV BENEMERE
NTI QVI VIXSIT ANNV
SEX MESIS OCTO DIES
XX ψ II

ST. PETER AND ST. PAUL AS INTERCESSORS.
Later. Museum, XIV, 42.

Other ideographic signs are: The Good Shepherd, an Orans (praying figure), a port with a lighthouse, a palm, a crown, the monogram in various forms, and lastly, the cross, which (with some exceptions) begins to make its appearance during the fifth century, as has already been said.

## Chapter IV

## INSCRIPTIONS REFERRING TO THE SACRED HIERARCHY

### 1.  The Popes

THE FIRST inscription of this class, from Africa, refers to the Church in the beautiful phrase, "Ecclesia Fratrum," "the Church of the Brethren," and records the donation to the Church of AREAM . AT . SEPVLCRA . CVLTOR . VERBI . CONDIDIT, etc. — "An *area* for graves, given by a believer in the Word," etc.

The most ancient inscriptions relating to bishops which we possess are those found in the crypt of the popes in the cemetery of Callistus. The oldest is that of Anterus or Anterotis (235):

"Anterus, Bishop."

The second is that of Pope Pontian (236), who abdicated the dignity of the Papacy while in exile and died after his successor Anterus:

"Pontian, Bishop and Martyr."

The third is that of Pope Fabian, martyred in 250:

"Fabian, Bishop and Martyr."

The title "martyr" on the inscription of Fabian and Pontian was probably added later to distinguish the tombs of those popes who had really suffered martyrdom from those who had not.

The inscription of St. Cornelius is found in another part of the cemetery, where there was probably a tomb of the *gens Cornelia.* This circumstance also explains why his inscription is in Latin and not in Greek, as were the others.

"Cornelius, Martyr and Bishop."
The year 252.

In the chapel of the popes follow the inscriptions of Pope Lucius (257) and Pope Eutychian (283), who was not a martyr. According to de Rossi, another fragment which is to be seen in the chapel of the popes might belong to the tomb of Pope Urban, though this is uncertain.

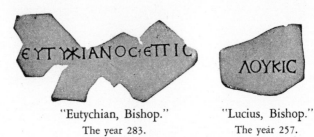

"Eutychian, Bishop."          "Lucius, Bishop."
The year 283.                 The year 257.

"Urban, Bishop."

In another chapel of the same cemetery, there is preserved an inscription of Pope Caius (296):

Γ[ΑΙΟ]Υ ☙ ΕΠΙ[ΣΚΟΠΟΥ]
ΚΑΘ ☙
[ΠΡΟ · Ι] ΚΑΛ · ΜΑΙΩ[Ν]

"The deposition of Caius, Bishop, the 22nd day of April."[1]

## 2. Bishops

In the Roman catacombs, the inscriptions belonging to bishops are very rare. Outside the city, however, there are memorials of local bishops, as, for example, in the cemetery of St. Alexander, on the Nomentan Way.

+ HIC . REQVIESCIT . IN . PACE . ADEODATVS . EPISC . QVI .
    Vixit
ANN | PL . M . LXVII . ET . SED . ANN . II . ET . M . VIIII
DEP . SVB . D . PRID . KAL . DECEMB.

In Rome we know of only one inscription of a bishop from Albano (cemetery of Domitilla) and an epitaph of a bishop by the name of Leo, who probably had his see a short distance from Rome.[3] Some inscriptions of bishops are also found in other places, but none of them is from the first three centuries.

## 3.  Priests and Inferior Ministers[4]

Numerous inscriptions record priests who must have been the titulars of various city districts, to which the administration of the cemeteries was attached:

LOCVS PRESBYTERI BASILI TITVLI SABINE

St. Paul's.

ΔΙΟΝΥCΙΟΥ
ΙΑΤΡΟΥ
ΠΡΕCΒΥΤΕΡΟΥ

"Tomb of Dionysius,
Priest and Physician."

Cemetery of Callistus.

LOCVS VALENTINI PRESB

Cemetery of St. Agnes.

LOCVS GERONTI . PRESB .
DEPOSITVS . IIII . KAL . IVL .
CONS . EPARCHI AVITI

The year 456.

LOCVS maximi
PRAESBYTERI

St. Agnes'.

PRAESBYTER HIC SITVS EST CELERINVS NOMINE DICTVS
CORPOREOS RVMPENS NEXVS QVI GAVDET IN ASTRIS
DEP . VII . KAL . IVN . FL . SYAGRIO ET EVCERIO

The year 381.  Cemetery of St. Agnes.

HIC qVIISCIT ROMANVS PBB
qVI SEDIT PBB . ANN XXVII MX
DEP . X KAL . AVG
CON . SEVERINI . VS CL

PAVLVS . PRESBYTER
St. Mary's in Transtevere.

"Who was priest," etc.
The year 461. Later. Museum, VII, 10.

AVR . TIT . PRISCAE . SORORI . BENEMERENTI . QVAE BIXIT

"Aurelius of the title of Prisca," etc.

Later. Museum, XIII, 16.

More uncommon is the title of deacon. On a fragment found near the basilica of St. Sebastian we read:

. . . DIACONI EPI / / /

"Deacon of the Bishop . . ."

De Rossi has published, in Volume I of *Subterranean Rome* (cemetery of Callistus), the inscription of Severus, a deacon of Pope Marcellinus. It is in free verse, as follows:

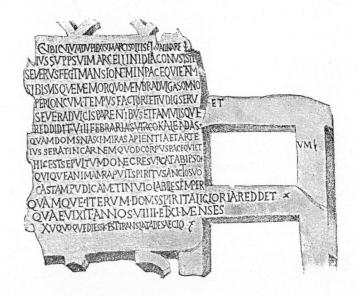

"Cubiculum duplex cum arcisoliis et luminare
iussu papae sui Marcellini diaconus iste
Severus fecit mansionem in pace quietam
sibi suisque memor quo membra dulcia somno
per longum tempus factori et iudici servet
Severa dulcis parentibus et famulisque
reddidit VIII februarias virgo kalendas
quam Dominus nasci mira sapientia et arte
iusserat in carnem quod corpus pace quietum

> hic est sepultum donec resurgat ab ipso
> quique animam rapuit spirito sancto suo
> castam pudicam et inviolabile semper
> quamque iterum dominus spiritali gloria reddet
> quae vixit annos VIIII et XI menses
> XV quoque dies sic est translata de saeclo."

This inscription tells us that Severus, deacon of Pope Marcellinus, had a double chamber with arches and a shaft made as a tomb for his family during the time of this pope (†304).

On the other hand, there are many inscriptions of inferior ministers, such as exorcists, acolytes, notaries, guardians, grave-diggers, etc. These are often mentioned in connection with the title of the district to which they belonged.

An inscription of a subdeacon of the fourth region of the cemetery of St. Agnes has also been found:

LOCVS IMPORTVNI SVBDIAC . REG . QVARTAE

Exorcist:

PRIMVS EXORCIST ///      PAVLVS EXORCISTA
FECIT                    DEP . MARTYRIES
Later. Museum, X, 18.      Cemetery of Callistus.

Lector:

MIRAE INNOCENTIAE . ADQ . EXIMIAE
BONITATIS . HIC . REQVIESCIT . LEOPARDVS
LECTOR . DE . PVDENTIANA . QVI . VIXIT
ANN . XXIV . DEP . VIIII . KAL . DEC .
RICOMEDE . ET CLEARCO . CON .

The year 384.

That is to say: "Lector of the title of Pudens."

V
FAVOR FAOR ⟸⟹ LECTOR
St. Agnes'.[5]

HIC POSITVS EST PETRVS IIII IDVS
MARTIAS QVI VIXIT ANNIS XVIIII
DEPINPACE PHILIPPO ET SALIA
    COS . DVO FRATRES
VENANTIVS LECTOR DE PALLACINE QVI VIXIT
A . XX . DEP . XII . KAL . SEP .

Basilica of St. Mark. The year 348.

The title of Pallacina is that of St. Mark.

CLAVDIVS . ATTICIA
NVS . LECTOR
ET CLAVDIA
FELICISSIMA
COIVX

Fabretti, *Inscr. domest.*, p. 557, No. XXVII.

CINNAMIVS OPAS LECTOR TITVLI FASCIOLAE
AMICVS PAVPERVM
QVI VIXIT ANN ψ XLVIV MENS ψ VII ψ
DVIIII DEPOSIT . IN PACE IX KAL . MART .
GRATIANO IIII ET MEROBAVDE CONSS.

St. Paul's. The year 377.

The title of Fasciola is that of Sts. Nereus and Achilleus.

Notary:

HIC . QVIESCIT . BRITTIVS
DALIA / / / /E NOTARI
/ / / /VS / / / /SV / / /
PRAECO / / / /SOMN / / /
PACIS . XII . KAL . IVNIAS
CONSVLATV . ONORI

Spoleto. The year is uncertain.

Acolyte:

IN PACE ABVNDANTIVS ACOL.
REG . QVART . TIT . VESTINE QVI VIXIT ANN . XXX .
DEP . IN . P . D . NAT . SCI MARCI MENSE OCT . IND . XII .

    This treats of the title of St. Vitalis, indicating the feast
of St. Mark, Pope, occurring in the month of October.

The following refer to the gravediggers who sold the tombs:

SERBVLVS EMIT BISOMV
A LEONTIV FOSSORE

Later. Museum, X, 24.

"He bought a tomb for two bodies."

CONSTANTIVS ET SOSANNA
SEVIVI LOCVM SIBI EMERVNT
PRAESENTIS A☧ω OMNIS FOS
SORES

Cemetery of Commodilla. Later. Museum, VI, 26.

"They bought a tomb in the presence of all the gravediggers."

## 4. Virgins, Widows and the Simple Faithful

The title of *virgin* indicates a person consecrated to God.

In the first centuries of the Church, holy virgins formed an aristocracy in the community of the faithful, and received, as is known, a special mention in the prayers and a particular place in the churches. Their burial inscriptions are numerous.

VICTORIA . BIRGO . DEI . QVAE . VI
XIT . ANNIS . XXVIII . IN PACE
III . IDVS . FEBR .

BICTORIA FIDELIS BIRGO
QVE VIXIT ANNIS XVII
MENSIS VIIII DIES V IN PACE
DE FVCTA V IDVS SEPTEMB

IANVARIE BIRGINI
BENEMERENTI IN
PACE BOTIS DEPOSITA

Vatican. Gal. Lap.

The word BOTIS (*votis*) in their epitaphs probably indicates solemn liturgical functions.[6]

Besides the deacons, the Church in the early ages also had deaconesses, who likewise went by the name of widows, χῆραι, *viduae,* and often were in fact virgins, *virgines canonicae.* They occupied themselves especially with works of charity, but they also had special liturgical duties to perform in the administration of Baptism and the celebration of the agapes.[7] The inscriptions make a special mention of their particular status:

OC . TA . VI . AE . MATR . ON . AE
VI . DV . AE . DE . I

"Widows of God."

St. Sabina's. Later. Museum, XI, 2.

DAFNE VIDVA Q . CVN VIX ///
ACLESIA NIHIL GRAVATIT A //

St. Mary's in Transtevere.

This widow Daphne is praised because she never lived at the expense of the Church: "Ecclesiam nihil gravavit" — "In nothing did she burden the Church."[8]

VRANIE . AVR . DOMNAE . MORTE
LEONTIVS . NEOFITVS . Q . V . AN . XXXIII . DP . XV . KAL
OCTOB . NICOMACHO . FLABIANO . CONSS .

The year 394. Cemetery of Priscilla.[9]

☧ PAVLINO NEOFITO
IN PACE QVI VIXIT ANOS VIII

Cemetery of Cyriaca. Later. Museum, XI, 17.

RFVI*llo neo*FITO D V . . .
VIXIT *an.* II *d. XI* QVINTILIANVS
PATER *filio dulciss*IMO IN PACE X̄P̄Ī

St. Agnes'.

SERONTIO PEREGRINO
BENEMERITO DVLCISSIMO
NVTRITORI VALENS QVI VIXIT
IN PACE ANNOS XXVII DECESSIT
III KAL . DECEN . DIE BENERIS
Cemetery of Cyriaca. Later. Museum, XI, 13.

## Chapter V

## INSCRIPTIONS REFERRING TO THE FAMILY AND TO CIVIL LIFE

### 1. The Family

LVCRETIOPAVLO INFANTIDVLCIS
SIMOQVTBIXITA NNOVNOMENS
HIDIESXVILVCRETIVSEVTYCHES
ETLVCRETIAMAXIMILLAPARENES

Cemetery of Priscilla.

LVCRETIO TIMOTHEO
QVI VIXIT ANN LXXVI
BENEMERENTI IN PACE
VXOR ET FILII

Later. Museum, XIII, 7.

ΖΩΡΑC ΚΑΙ ΜΑΡΚΕΛΛΟC
ΔΥΟ ΑΔΕΛΦΟΙ

"Zoe and Marcellus, brother and sister."
Later. Museum, XIX, 19.

DVLCISSIMO FRATRI
FORTVNATO N PACE
DP V . NO OCT
Later. Museum, XIII, 14.

DIONYSODORAE . FILIAE . DVLCISSIMAE
VICTORIA . MATER . FAVSTINVS . PATER
NICE . SOROR . VICTOR . FRATER
Greater Cemetery of St. Agnes. Later. Museum, XX, 16.

IVLIANICE QVE VICXIT ANNIS
XL IN PACE MECVM
Cemetery of Cyriaca. Later. Museum, XVII, 2.

FLORENTIA MERCVRIO COIVGI BENEMERINTI CVM QVEM
VIXIT ANNOS L . MENSES X . SEMPER CONCORDES
DEPOSITVS VI . IDVS IVNIAS .
Later. Museum, XIII, 8.

PVELLE VRBICE CON / / /
QVIA EIVS OBSEQV / / /
SEMPER . NOBISCON / / /
IN MATRIMONIO QVE VI / / /
P . M . XXX . DECESSIT DIE XIII KAL / / /
IN PACE ET IN NOMINE ☧ FILII EIVS
New St. Mary's. From a ms. of Bruzio.

BENEMERENTI CONIVS
NOMEN IZOPIRVS CVM
QVE VIX . ANN . VIIII DVLCIS
VALE
Cemetery of Cyriaca. Later. Museum, XVII, 8.

The word "matrimonium" ("matrimony") is very rare;
but the words "concubinatus," "concubina," which are frequent
in pagan inscriptions, are never met with. A bas-relief from
the Albani villa has the unusual representation of Christian
matrimony.[1]

Other inscriptions mention "alumni" ("children"), "nutritores" ("nurses"), etc.

CASSINO ALVMNO QVI
VIXIT ANNO I MENSIBVS II
PATRONI . ET . MATER
Later. Museum, XIII, 20.

DVLCISSIMAE FILIAE PVBLICE
MAXIMINVS PATER ET SYLLECT / / /
EVNOEA NVTRITORES
Later. Museum, XIII, 31.

SIMPLICI ALVMNO          ANNV ET M . VIII ET DI
SVO QVEM AMAVIT          ES XXIII VERNACLVS
TENERITER QVI VIXIT          BEBECE

Cemetery of St. Agnes. Later. Museum, XIII, 24.

The expression *alumnus* (θρεπτός) is properly Christian, even though at times it may appear on pagan inscriptions. The word was used of children adopted by strangers and nourished by nurses (*nutritores*); Christians often took care of and baptized abandoned children.[2]

ISPIRITO SANCTO BONO
FLORENTIO QVI VIXIT ANIS XIII
CORITVS MAGISTER QVI PLVS AMAVIT
QVAM SI FILIVM SVVM ET COIDEVS
MATER FILIO BENEMERENTI FECERVNT

Later. Museum, XVII, 3.

FRONIMVS . VICTORINO . ET
SEVERAE . AMICIS DIGNISSIMIS

From Ostia. Later. Museum, XXI, 1.

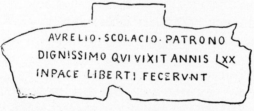

AVRELIO · SCOLACIO · PATRONO
DIGNISSIMO QVI VIXIT ANNIS LXX
INPACE LIBERTI FECERVNT

Cemetery of Callistus. Later. Museum, XIII, 19.

The epithet "libertus" ("freedman"), so often found in pagan inscriptions, is very rare in Christian epigraphy. When it is used of a Christian, it can be taken to indicate a slave made free at the moment of Baptism.

For a loftier reason, the word "servus" ("servant") is never found. The Christian is only a servant of God, a servant of Christ, though this phrase is especially used in inscriptions which are not very ancient. Lactantius wrote: "Apud nos inter servum et dominum interest nihil, quia pares nos esse credimus" — "There is no difference among us between a servant and his master, because we believe we are equal."[3]

An indication of social class is scarcely ever found; but we do meet, at times, inscriptions which point to the senatorial status by using the abbreviation VC ("vir clarissimus") or CF ("clarissima femina") — "a most illustrious man (or woman)." At times, even a position held by the deceased is indicated.

AELIVS SATVRNINVS
CASSIE FARETRIAE CLARISSIME
FEMINE COIVGI BENEME
RENTI DEPOSTIO TERTV NO
NAS FEBRARIAS

Cemetery of Callistus.

PETRONIAE . AVXENTIAE C . F
. . . . . . . . . . . . . . . . . . . . . . . . . . . . . . . . . . . . . . . . . . . . . . . . . . . . . . . . .
LIBERTI . FECERVNT BENEMERENTI . IN PACE

Cemetery of Callistus.

HIC QVIESCIT IN PACE LAVRENTIVS
SCRIBA SENATVS DEP . DIE . IIII . IDVVM . MART .
ADELFIO VC CONS.

The year 451. St. Mary's in Transtevere.

A burial inscription of Bolsena is dedicated to "Maecius Paternus, defender and patron of the city"; and in the last line there is found a beautiful expression, "Pax tibi cum sanctis" — "Peace be to you with the saints."

## 2. The Professions

Very numerous are the Christian inscriptions carrying the notice of the professions of the deceased. Their variety demonstrates forcibly that Christianity had penetrated within a short time into every class of Roman society.[4] We have records of soldiers, as for example, the Praetorian Guards attached to the imperial household, those employed in public offices, etc.

In this epitaph there is a noteworthy phrase, "singulari officina":

FL·CASTINO· SINGVLARI OFF· P·P·Q·VIX·AN· P·M·XXX
COLLEGAS KAR· POSVERVNT

Later. Museum, XII, 9.

The following is also notable:

PREPO
SITVS
MEDIAS       OFFICINA
TINORVM . DE MONETA .
                PRIMA

Ostia. Later. Museum, XII, 17.

The deceased to whom the preceding inscriptions relate were employed in the mint.

The following was a courier, or mailman:

> RVFVS TABELLA
> RVS DEPOSITVS IIII IDV
> DEC. 

Cemetery of St. Agnes. Later. Museum, XII, 18.

This commemorates a marble-worker:

> HIC POSITVS EST SILBANVS MARMORARIVS
> QVI . V . AN . XXX . ET FECIT CVM VXORE AN . III
> ET MENSIS III DEPOSITVS IIII KAL IVLIAS

Later. Museum, XII, 23.

This inscription mentions a fisherman:

> ////DVL . KAR .
> HONERATIAE . SANCTIPE///
> AMAV///. QVI . DECS .
> ANNORVM XVI
> FILIA . LEPORI . PISCATORIS
> SEXT . X . KAL . DEC . SATVR
> NINVS . AMATOR . FE///

Later. Museum, XII, 22.

Inscription of a sailor:

> IVLIVS CREDEN
> TIVS QVI NABIGA
> VIT . EX . BAGENSE
> REGIONE EST IN PACE

Cemetery of St. Hippolytus. Later. Museum, XIII, 32.

Of a gardener:

> PASCASIVS . ORTOLANVS///
> ///I IDS IVLIAS///

St. Agnes'.

During the excavations carried out in 1904, inscriptions mentioning a gardener ("pomerarius"), a keeper of elephants ("elephantarius"), and a leather-worker ("corarius") were discovered in the cemetery of Commodilla.

## Chapter VI

## INSCRIPTIONS WITH SPECIAL WORDING

DE ROSSI designated these as "Epitaphia dictionis singularis," and made a fine collection of them, now preserved in the Lateran Museum. A few examples of those of greater importance are given:

PATER FILIO SILBINIANO
BENEMERENTI IN PACE
QVI ABET DEPOSSIONE BRVMIS

"Buried in the winter."

Cemetery of Cyriaca. Later. Museum, XVII, 31.

LOCVS TRI
SOMVS VIC
TORIS IN CRV
TA DAMASI

"A tomb for three bodies in the underground vault beneath the basilica of Damasus."

Ardeatine Way.

SABINI BISO
MVM SE BIBVM
FECIT SIBI IN CYME
TERIVM BALBINAE
IN CRYPTA NOBA

"Tomb for two in the cemetery of Balbina in a new gallery."

Later. Museum, XVII, 20.

This is an example of a votive inscription:

SANCTIS . MARTVRIBVS
PAPRO . ET . MAVROLEONI
DOMNIS . VOTVM . REDD .    ☧
CAMASIVS QVI ET ASCLEPIVS . ET VICTORIN .
NAT . H̄ . DIE . XIII KAL . OCTOB .
PVERI . QVI . VOT . H̄ . VITALIS . MARANVS
ABVNDANTIVS . TELESFOR

On the reverse of the same marble slab, we find:

DOMNIS . SANCTIS
PAPRO . ET . MAVROLEONI
✗ MARTVRIBVS ✗
CAMASIVS QVI ET ASCLEPIAS ET VICTORINVS///
NATAL . HAB . D XIII KAL . OCTOB .
///ANE . VITALIS
///TI TELESPOS.

From the baths of Diocletian. Later. Museum, I, 7, 12.

This double inscription, in honor of Sts. Papias and Maurus, is without doubt an *ex voto* memorial dedicated by an artist and his children or pupils.

Others containing unusual phraseology are:

NATVS PVER NOMINE PASCASIVS
DIES . PASCALES PRID NON . APRIL
DIE IOBIS FLI CONSTANTINO
ET RVFO VV . CC CONSS QVI VIXIT
ANNORVM VI . PERCEPIT
XI KAL MAIAS . ET ALBAS SVAS
OCTABAS PASCAE AD SEPVLCRVM
DEPOSVIT D . IIII KAL MAI FL BASILIO
V C CONS

The years 457 and 463. Urbino.

Pascasius died eight days after his baptism, and laid his white baptismal dress on his tomb on the octave of Easter.

IACET DECORA
MERCVRINA QVAE
VIXIT ANNOS XX
OVIIT XIII . KAL . MA
IAS VIGELIA PASCE
CALIPO V . C . CONS .

The year 447. Lyons, France.

The woman mentioned in the above inscription died on the vigil of Easter.

PVER NATVS
DIVO IOVIANO AVG . ET
VARRONIANO COSS .
ORA NOCTIS IIII
VIXIT . IN VIII IDVS MADIAS
DIE SATVRNIS LVNA VICESIMA
SIGNO APIORNO NOMINE SIMPLICIVS

The year 364. Capitol. Museum.

The foregoing gives the day of the month, the day of the week, the phase of the moon, and the sign of the zodiac (Capricorn).

M . AELIVS . TIGRINVS
OB . REFRIGERIVM C / / /
DOMVM . AETERNAM
VIVVS . FVNDAVIT

Terni.

CAELIVS
HIC DORMIT
ET . DECRIA
QVANDO DEVS
BOLVERIT

From Ostia. Later. Museum, XXI, 8.

LOC
APHRODISAAES
CVM DEVS
PERMISERIT

From Ostia. Later. Museum, XXI, 5.

LAVRENTIA MELIS DVL
CIOR QVIESCE . IN PACE
"Sweeter than honey."

Cemetery of Cyriaca. Later. Museum,
XVII, 9.

IVSTE NOMEN
TVM IN AGAPE

Later. Museum, XVII, 4.

PANCRATI
BENEDICTE

Cemetery of Praetextatus.
Later. Museum, XXI, 28.

The following are notable for their singularity of design. The two names are found inscribed in monogram on a sarcophagus in the cemetery of Priscilla:

RVFILLA

RVSTICVS

It is also noteworthy that, outside of Rome, one encounters formulas and phrases very often repeated. At Ostia, HIC DORMIT; at Bolsena, PAX TIBI CVM SANCTIS (often abbreviated as C. S.); in northern Italy, CONTRA VOTVM POSVIT; in Germany, IN HOC TITVLO REQVIESCIT FE-

LICITER; TITVLVM POSVIT; in the second Belgian Province, FECIT DIES; at Vienne, in France: VIVIT IN PACE.

There are other special phrases, forms, etc., found in other localities.

## Some Formulas Employed in Greek Inscriptions

Greek inscriptions are generally older than Latin. They are found especially during the first two centuries, while from the third century on they are encountered in diminishing numbers. In burial inscriptions we often find the word designating "burial" — ΚΑΤΑΘΕϹΙϹ — and expressions like the following: ΕΝ ΕΙΡΗΝΗ, ΕΝΘΑΔΕ ΚΙΤΕ, ΕΝ ΕΙΡΗΝΗ ΚΟΙΜΗϹΙϹ, ΕΝ ΙΡΗΝΗ ΚΟΙΜΗϹΙϹ ϹΟΥ, ΑΥΤΟΥ, ΑΥΤΗϹ — "In peace," "Here lies," "In peace," "They sleep," "His (or her) sleep, repose," etc. The last expression is found especially in Jewish inscriptions.

The age of the deceased is indicated by the phrase ΕΖΗϹΕ ΕΤΗ — "lived so many years." The numbers, as is shown here, were indicated by the letters of the Greek alphabet:

$$A = 1, \ B = 2, \ \Gamma = 3, \ \Delta = 4, \ E = 5,$$
$$\varsigma = 6, \ Z = 7, \ H = 8, \ \Theta = 9, \ I = 10,$$
$$K = 20, \ \Lambda = 30, \ M = 40, \ \text{etc.}$$

The following are some examples of Greek epitaphs and inscriptions:

"Dear, remember me."
Cemetery of Priscilla.

ΤΩ · ΓΛΥΚΥΤΑΤΩ
ΥΙΩ ΚΥΡΙΑΚΩ
ΟΙ ΓΟΝΙϹ ΕΝ ΕΙΡΗΝΗ

"Our dearest son Cyriacus, his parents. May he rest in peace."
Gall. lap. Vat.

ΜΑΓΝΩ ·
ΥΙΩ · ΓΛΥΚΥΤΑΤΩ

"To Magnus, dearest son."

Cemetery of Priscilla.

ΟΝΗϹΙΜΟϹ · ΚΑΙ
ϹΕΜΝΗ ΓΟΝΕΙϹ
ΕΠΙΚΤΗΤΩ ΤΕ
ΥΙΩ ΓΛΥΚΥ
ΤΑΤΩ ΕΠΟΙΗ
ϹΑΝ

"Onesimus and Semne, his parents, erected this memorial
to their dearest son Epictetus."

Cemetery of Priscilla.

ΚΑΛΛΙϹΤΟϹ ΑΠΟ ΤΗϹ
ϹΙΚΕΛΙΑϹ ΕΝΘΑΔΑΙ
ΚΙΜΕ ΠΑΡΟΙΚΗϹΑϹ
ΕΤΕ ΤΕϹϹΕΡΑΚΟΝ
ΤΑ ΚΑΤΟΙΚΩ ΤΟΝ
ΕΩΝΑ

"Here rests Callistus of Sicily, who died at the age of 40.
He has eternal rest."

Greater Cemetery of St. Agnes.

ΕΠΙ ☧
ΚΤΗΤΟ
Ϲ · ΓΑ · ΙΑ
ΝΗ · ΤΗ · Χ
ΡΗϹΤΟ
ΤΑ · ΤΗ · Α
ΔΕΛΦΗ

"Epictetus, to his dearest sister, Gaiane."

Greater Cemetery of St. Agnes.

The expressions ΤΡΕΠΤΟϹ, ΤΡΕΨΑΜΕΝΟΣ, correspond to the words "child," "orphan."

ΠΕΤΡΟϹ · Ο · ⌀
ΘΡΕΠΤΟϹ
ΓΛ · Υ · Κ · Υ · Τ · Α ·
ΤΟϹ · ΕΝ ΤΕΩ

"To dearest Peter, child of God."

Gall. lap. Vat.

The phrase ΜΝΗΜΗϹ ΧΑΡΙΝ — "In memory of" etc. —
is also very commonly found.

ΙΟΥΓΤΕΙΝΗ ΓΥΜΒΙΩ ΑΕΙΜΝΗΓΤΩ
ΕΡΜΗΓ ΜΝΗΜΗΓ ΧΑΡΙΝ

"To my unforgettable wife, Justina. Placed in her memory
by Hermes."

Gall. lap. Vat.

The phrase ΟΥΔΕΙΓ ΑΘΑΝΑΤΟΓ (that is, "No one is
immortal") often met with on pagan monuments, is also encountered at times in Christian inscriptions. The two following
examples show this:

ΤΕΡΤΙ · ΑΔΕΛΦΕ
ΕΥΞΥΧΙ ΟΥΔΙΓ
ΑΘΑΝΑΤΟΓ

"O Tertius, my brother, be of good spirit, no one is immortal."

Cemetery of Priscilla.

ΘΑΡΓΙ ΑΓΚΙΜΕ
ΟΥΔΙΓ ΑΘΑ
ΝΑΤΟΓ

"Be of good soul, O Askimus, no one is immortal."

Gall. lap. Vat.

It should also be remembered that there are Latin inscriptions in Greek characters, or Greek epitaphs in Latin characters.
These anomalies may be explained by the fact that some marble-
workers were better able to cut Greek characters in the marble,
while others excelled in Latin.

## Chapter VII

## HISTORICAL INSCRIPTIONS

IN CHRISTIAN epigraphy, historical inscriptions form a
very important group. The most noteworthy are those
known as Damasian because they were composed by Pope Damasus. Many historical epitaphs were copied during the seventh and eighth centuries. These have come down to us in the
so-called *Epigraphical Sylloges,* or *Books of Inscriptions.*

## 1. Damasian Inscriptions[1]

Damasus was born at the beginning of the fourth century, about the year 305, during the persecution of Diocletian, since St. Jerome says that "he was almost eighty years old when he died under Theodosius," who in turn died in 384.[2] The *Book of the Popes,* Baronius, Ciaconus and Perez[3] call him a Spaniard. He was of Spanish or Portuguese extraction, but, as Tillemont and Merenda recognized, he was born in Rome. His father was one of the clergy connected with the archives of the Roman Church in the district near the theatre of Pompey. He held successively the offices of chancellor, lector, deacon and bishop, as Damasus says in an inscription left by him in the archives of the same church.

A few years ago Marucchi showed, with some plausibility, that the father of Damasus may have been a certain bishop, Leo, interred in the cemetery of St. Lawrence in the *Agro Verano.*[4]

"Hinc Pater, exceptor, lector, levita, sacerdos
Creverat hinc meritis quoniam melioribus actis," etc.[5]

We also know the name of the mother of Damasus. She was called Laurentia and died after Damasus had become pope.

Damasus held the same offices as his father, and seems to have belonged to the faction opposed to Pope Liberius. Hence, when he was elected to succeed Liberius, some of the latter's partisans elected an anti-pope by the name of Ursicinus. But Damasus was successful in overcoming all the discords which troubled the Church. He attributed this triumph to the protection of the martyrs, and in gratitude for the favor, he immediately set to work preserving, embellishing and restoring their tombs. He sought out those that had fallen into oblivion or were covered by ruins, enlarged the galleries, repaired shafts and opened up new ones, constructed stairways in the neighborhood of the historical crypts, and fulfilled his vow in every possible manner:

> "Pro reditu cleri Christo praestante triumphans
> Martyribus sanctis reddit sua vota sacerdos."[6]

But above all, Damasus was the poet of the martyrs — in the words of St. Jerome,[7] "Elegans in versibus scribendis"— "Elegant in writing verses." He was also a conscientious historian, because he diligently studied the traditions of the Church of Rome, and in his measured eulogies, he hands down to us precious pages from ecclesiastical history, which would otherwise have remained in oblivion. Moreover, Damasus often cites the sources of his information concerning the histories of the martyrs:

> "Percussor retulit Damaso mihi cum puer essem . . . "[8]
> "Fama refert . . . "[9]
> "Credite per Damasum . . . "

He does not hesitate to indicate caution when he is not sure of the authenticity of his information. This point is admirably shown in one of his verses:

"Haec audito refert Damasus, probat omnia Christus"— "Damasus relates these things on hearsay, Christ proves all things."[10]

It should be noted, therefore, that the information handed down to us by Damasus concerning the martyrs is of great value and authority, because he must have been very well acquainted with the historical documents of the persecutions which were preserved in the archives of the church where he passed his youth.

Damasus also composed a treatise entitled *De Virginitate* — *On Virginity* — which has not come down to us. Many of his poems have also been lost. The ancient collections of epitaphs preserve for us the texts of about forty inscriptions, which were published by Fabrizio (1562), Rivino (1652), Sarazani (1638), Merenda,[11] Migne, and recently by Ihm (1895).

The inscriptions are almost all in hexameters, although the rules of poesy are not always rigorously observed. The style is distinct and characteristic;[12] some expressions are used frequently, as for example, "rector," designating the pope; "fateor," "supplex," "mira fides." St. Jerome speaks of Damasus as "Virgilii non incuriosus" — "not unacquainted with Virgil."[13] In fact, Damasus has numerous verses which are strongly reminiscent of the *Aeneid*:

Bk. I: "Aeternumque tenet per saecula nomen." ("He had an everlasting name through the centuries.")

Damasus: "Teneat proprium per saecula nomen." ("He held his own name through the ages.")[14]

Bk. II, 39: "Scinditur incertum studia in contraria vulgus."

Damasus: "Scinditur in partes populus gliscente furore."[15]

Bk. XII, 437: " . . . Omni nunc arte magistra."

Damasus: "Non haec humanis opibus, non arte magistra."[16]

The Damasian inscriptions are engraved in marble, in very beautiful characters of a special form; and de Rossi discovered the name of the artist in whose care the execution of this work was placed. He had recognized this artist in the well-known Furius Dionysius Philocalus, mentioned on a fragment placed by Marini among the samples of pagan inscriptions in the Vatican. Later, when the inscription of Pope Eusebius was discovered in the cemetery of St. Callistus (1856), he was able to prove that this was actually the name of the secretary of Damasus. The older archeologists were wont to call any ornate letters Damasian — an error, since the truly Damasian letters have an altogether special character.[17] The ends, for example, always taper to a double curved line; the character is deeply incised and there is throughout the same proportion between the width and the height. The letter M has straight ends, while in other inscriptions these are often found inclined. In the letter R, the oblique line is separated from the vertical.[18] This hieratic paleography was reserved, as a rule, for the epitaphs of the martyrs, and only by way of exception was it employed by Damasus in other inscriptions, as for example, in that of Projecta, preserved in the Lateran Museum. Those which he had made before decorating the tombs of the martyrs were, in fact, done in characters common to the fourth century, as may be seen in the two inscriptions composed by him for his mother and sister.

Damasian inscriptions have a threefold importance: dogmatic, historical and topographical. Their value is dogmatic, because they bear witness to the faith and the dogma of the Communion of Saints; historical, because they give us authoritative information on the lives of the martyrs; and topographical, because they point out to us the places where the martyrs were buried in the Roman catacombs. The most important texts of these inscriptions have already been indicated.[19]

## 2. Inscriptions after the Time of Damasus

The style of the Damasian inscriptions was imitated especially during the pontificate of his successor, Pope Siricius. A few well-preserved and judiciously selected examples of these inscriptions were spoken of by Merenda in the words, "Damasum sapiunt" — "They remind one of Damasus." They form a group apart, being known as Sirician or pseudo-Damasian inscriptions.

We have an example of these in the cemetery of St. Hippolytus, where Damasus had placed an inscription in the historical crypt.[20] During the excavations made in that cemetery, another pseudo-Damasian acrostic was found, in which a priest by the name of Leo gives a list of the works of Damasus. The supplementary words and letters are by de Rossi.[21]

LAETA DEO PLEBS SANCTA CANAT QVOD MOENIA
   CRESCVNT
ET RENOVATA DOMVS MARTYRIS *Yppo*LITI
ORNAMENTA OPERIS SVRGVN*t auctore Dam*ASO
NATVS QVI ANTISTES SEDIS A*postolicae*
INCLITA PACIFICIS FACTA EST *haec aula triumphis*
SERVATVRA DECVS PERPETV*amque fidem*
HAEC OMNIA NOVA QVAEQVE VIDES LEO *presby*TER ORNAT

In the form of the letters of some epitaphs of Pope Siricius, we recognize an effort to imitate Pope Damasus; the same is true of an inscription of Boniface I in the crypt of St.

Felicitas, where one is forcibly reminded of the inscription of St. Agnes.[22]

The style changes with the turn of the century, as may be seen in an inscription in the basilica of St. Stephen, on the Latin Way. This epitaph is to be referred to the work of restoration carried out there under Pope Leo I after the sack of Rome under Genseric in 455:

CVM MVNDVM LI*nqu*ENS DEM*etrias* AMNIA *virgo*
CLA*ud*ERET EX*t*REMVM NON MORI*tura diem*
H*ae*C TIBI PAP*a* LEO VOTORVM EXTREMA *suorum*
Tradi*DIT u*T *sacr*AE SVRGERET AV*la domus*
M*a*ND*a*TI COMPLE*ta* FIDES SED GLOR*ia maior*
I*n*TERIVS VOTVM SOLVERE QVAM PROPA*lam*
IN*di*DERAT CVLMEN STEP*han*VS QVI PRIMVS IN OR*be*
RAPTVS MORT*e tr*VCI REGN*at* IN ARCE *poli*
P*r*AESVLIS HA*nc iuss*V TIGRINVS P*resbyter aulam*
EXCOLIT INS*ig*NIS MENTE LABO*re vigens*

To this group of inscriptions also belongs one composed by Pope Vigilius during the work of restoration undertaken after the invasion of the Goths. A fragment of it, found in the cemetery of Sts. Peter and Marcellinus, was later removed to the Lateran Museum.

The example of Vigilius was imitated by others, who, after that same calamity (537), embellished the basilica of St. Saturninus on the Salarian Way. The following inscription is given to record their labors:

PAVPERIS EX CENSV MELIVS NVNC ISTA RESVRGVNT
DIVITE SED VOTO PLVS PLACITVRA DEO
PLANGE TVVM GENS SAEVA NEFAS PERIERE FVRORES
CREVIT IN HIS TEMPLIS PER TVA DAMNA DECVS

Similar labors of restoration are also recorded in an inscription of the cemetery of St. Hippolytus, in which the deficiencies were supplied by de Rossi:[23]

> *Devastata* iTERVM SVMMOT*a plebe precantum*
> *Priscum* PERDIDERANT ANTRA *sacrata decus*
> *Nec tua iam ma*RTYR POTERANT *venerande sepulcra*
> *Huic mundo* LVCEM MITTERE *qua frueris*
> *Lux tamen ista* tVA EST QVAE NESCIT *fu*NE*ra sed quo*
> *Perpet*VO CRESCAT NEC MINVA*tur ha*BE*t*
> *Nam nigra nox* tRINVM STVPVIT PER *spe*CVLA LVMEN
> *Admittunt*QVE NOVVM CONC*av*A SAXA DIEM
> *Frustra ba*RBARICIS *fremuerunt* AVSIBVS HOSTES
> *Foedaruntque* SACRVM *tela cr*VENTA LOCVM
> *Inclyta* SED MELIVS *splendescit* MARTYRIS AVLA
> AVCTOREMQVE *gravant imp*IA FACTA SVVM
> PRAESVLE VIGILIO SVMP*serunt* ANTRA DECOREM
> PRESBYTERI ANDREAE CVR*a* PEREGIT OPVS

Toward the end of the sixth century, Pope Pelagius II restored the basilica of St. Lawrence. An inscription placed on the triumphal arch which separates the *basilica major* from that *ad corpus,* records the works of Pelagius:

PRAESVLE PELAGIO MARTYR LAVRENTIVS OLIM
   TEMPLA SIBI STATVIT TAM PRETIOSA DARI
MIRA FIDES GLADIOS HOSTILES INTER ET IRAS
   PONTIFICEM MERITIS HAEC CELEBRASSE SVIS
TV MODO SANCTORVM CVI CRESCERE CONSTAT HONORES
FAC SVB PACE COLI TECTA DICATA TIBI

A little further down we find:

✠ MARTYRIVM FLAMMIS ✆ OLIM LEVITA SVBISTI ✆
IVRE TVIS TEMPLIS ℞ LVX BENERANDA REDIT ℞

The seventh century marks a period of ignorance, which is indicated, among a multitude of other ways, by the epigraphy. Historical inscriptions become more rare, and pertain only to the popes or other important persons. Among these few, we shall cite that of Pope Honorius who lived about 630. After having restored the basilica of St. Agnes, he placed the following below the mosaic of the apse:

AVREA CONCISIS SVRGIT PICTVRA METALLIS
    ET COMPLEXA SIMVL CLAVDITVR IPSA DIES
FONTIBVS E NIBEIS CREDAS AVRORA SVBIRE
    CORREPTAS NVBES RVRIBVS ARVA RIGANS
VEL QVALEM INTER SIDERA LVCEM PROFERET IRIM
    PVRPVREVSQVE PAVO IPSE COLORE NITENS
QVI POTVIT NOCTIS VEL LVCIS REDDERE FINEM
    MARTYRVM E BVSTIS HINC REPPVLIT ILLE CHAOS
SVRSVM VERSA NVTV QVOD CVNCTIS CERNITVR VSQVE
    PRAESVL HONORIVS HAEC VOTA DICATA DEDIT
VESTIBVS ET FACTIS SIGNANTVR ILLIVS ORA
    EXCITAT ASPECTV LVCIDA CORDA GERENS

With the seventh century, ancient Christian epigraphy really comes to an end; and it is for that reason that de Rossi included in his work only the Christian inscriptions of the city of Rome older than the seventh century (*Inscriptiones Christianae Urbis Romae septimo saeculo antiquiores*).

## Chapter VIII

## THE GRAFFITI

TWO CLASSES of graffiti are distinguished: burial graffiti and the graffiti of the pilgrims. The burial graffiti, the more ancient, are nothing more than abbreviated inscriptions engraved, at the time of interment, in the fresh mortar of the chambers in which the body had been placed. Some of these express invocations analogous to the inscriptions properly so called, and therefore have a dogmatic value. Such is a graffito recently found in the cemetery of Commodilla, which contains a beautiful prayer for the repose of the soul with an invocation to the local martyrs: REFRIGERET . TIBI . DEVS . ET . CHRISTVS . ET DOMINI . NOSTRI . ADEODATVS ET FELIX. Some graffiti also give the consular dates; others, on the contrary, as those on page 262, simply indicate the day of the month. The graffiti are found in Latin as well as in Greek.

The graffiti of the visitors were not inscribed in the soft mortar but in the hard surface of the walls. For that reason they may be very easily distinguished. They often express sentiments of a prayerful nature, or invocations; or they may contain but a name. Some of them go back as far as the period of peace. During the fourth and fifth centuries, Latin and Greek names are found, but from the sixth to the ninth century, Gothic, Saxon and Lombard names are met with (for example, Arivalitus, etc.). At times the sign of the cross precedes the names; these may perhaps be the names of the priests who had celebrated Mass on the tombs of the martyrs. The name ✠ LEO, LEO PBR, is repeated in many places.

FACSIMILE OF GRAFFITI MADE BY VISITORS ON THE WALL OF THE ENTRANCE OF THE CRYPT OF THE POPES IN THE CEMETERY OF CALLISTUS.

(For a transcription, see the following page.)

The prayers expressed in the graffiti may be prayers for the dead or invocations to the martyrs. At the cemetery of St. Callistus, the entrance to the chapel of the popes is covered with such inscriptions, especially with invocations to Pope St. Sixtus II (see above and page 261).

*Maria*NVS BONIZO
///I VIV*as*

FEL*ic*I P̄B̄R̄ PECCATOR

POϒΦINA

SANCTE XVC*te*

MAXIMI     ENΘεω METαΠANTων επισκοπων

*Pri*MITI X̱ ΠONTIANE ZHCHC  SANC*ie Suste in men*
PRO  *b*INIANI       TE ABEAS IN ORATIONE
           Tε εIC MIAN

         *pe*TE*p*ROME EVSTA*chi*VM

PRIMITI NONNANI*b*C      SANTE SVSTE IN MENTE
*A*MANTI         HABEAS IN ORATIQNES
   NA      NA    AVRELIV REPENTINV

.IERVSALE CIVITAS ET

  ANASTATXA     A PETE PRO MARCIANVM ALVMNV IIM
ORNAMENTVM

      CARA MATER
MARTYR̄V̄ D NABALTARIA
 CVIVS///    BER TALLA

            SANCTE SVSTE///
             ///REPENTI*num*

SVCCESSVM RVFINVM AGAPITVM E
SANCTE XYSTE
*in me*NTE HABEAS IN HO*rationes*   SVSTE SAN*cte.*
             VT AELIBERA

SUCC/// SVM RVFINVM AGAPITVM        SA

              CROCEO
      RV ☧ FINVM ΓεΛΑCI ZH CεNε Θεω
               R.V.
  BϒΛ///       CONTRI ΛιoνϒCI ZHCεC
                     CIA
VT QVOD ITERAVI*mus*   FACER BIBAC IN Θεω
   IN P*ace*   ASTRA   PETE   TVXIC
       ELIA
  NTE      BIBAC
 E SATVR   IN ΔEO   MARCIANVM
ARANTIAM AQ
ORTA   MAX        SVCCESSVM.
   TVA     ANCTA
  VT VERICVNDVS CVM SVIS SEVERVM SPIRITA ☧

ARMEN    BENE NAVIGET
(*Figura·*   SEBATIA      SANCTA IN MENTE
*graffita*)  ☧ PATωNI     HAVETE ET OM
     XIC        NES FRATRES NOS

  AΔPIANOC AICXIONAC   LEONTIVIB*a*
ΛEO   AVIVS    TROS    IN VITA

                ☧

TRANSCRIPTION OF GRAFFITI OF THE PAPAL CRYPT.
(See facsimile on preceding page.)

In the same cemetery, there are graffiti in many places containing prayers to a certain Sophronia. The pious visitor shows that he came to these sanctuaries with a lively remembrance of Sophronia always in mind. She might have been his wife, his sister or his mother.

"Before entering into the vestibule of the principal sanctuary, he wrote: SOPHRONIA VIVAS . . . CVM TVIS — 'O Sophronia, may you live with your own.' A little further on he repeats, on the door of another chapel, the same wish in a more religious form: SOPHRONIA (*vivas*) IN DOMINO — 'O Sophronia, may you live in the Lord.' Still further on, near the arched vault on another chapel (which was as far as the pilgrims used to go at that time), he traced in wider, more religious characters, in large, monumental letters this tender expression:

1.

LATINIO D·P
VIII·KAL APRILES
INPACE

2.

XVIII KAL
IVNIAS TETIMINA
depos- ACE

3.

VERNA DP luNONAS
AVGVSTAS

4.

⊢ DT ) つ S S
X

5.

DPbd̶ʼCVCNE ʃUTIAʃ
✳IIIIKɑ̷l DETEMBRES
N

EXAMPLES OF
SEPULCHRAL GRAFFITI.

SOPHRONIA DVLCIS SEMPER VIVES IN DEO — 'My dear Sophronia, may you always live in the Lord'; and immediately beneath this, he repeated this thought once more as if he could not get the idea out of his mind: SOPHRONIA VIVES — 'Sophronia, may you live.' A tender and moving story is found on these walls, a story of the sentiments which filled the soul of this pious visitor . . . while he visited the various tombs of the martyrs. At first there is desire, love, a faithful remembrance, a tender hope; then under the sweet influences of these holy places, this hope changes to a tender confidence, it transforms itself into a certainty, it is transmuted to a cry of triumph, of love illumined by faith."[1]

FACSIMILE OF THE GRAFFITI MADE BY VISITORS,
WITH AN INVOCATION TO ST. PRISCILLA AND ST. CRESCENTION,
IN THE CEMETERY OF PRISCILLA.

In a chapel in the cemetery of Priscilla, this inscription may be seen: PAVLINA REQVIESCAS IN PACE, ET FILII TVI OMNES HABEANT DEVM PROTECTOREM — "Pauline, may you rest in peace, and may your children have God as their protector." At the entrance to the chapel of the popes, in St. Callistus' cemetery, we find: IERVSALE CIVITAS ET

ORNAMENTVM MARTYRVM DEI — "Jerusalem, the city and ornament of the martyrs of God."[2] We often meet with prayers directed to the martyrs. Thus, in a chamber of the cemetery of Priscilla, we read: CITO CVNTI SVSCIPIA*ntur* VOTIS | DOMNAE PRISCILLE BEATE . . . Above this there is an inscription: SALBA ME DOMNE CRESCENTIONE (see page 263). Oftentimes the following phrases are seen: IN MENTE HABEAS; IN MENTE HABETE; IN ORATIONIBVS TVIS PETE PRO . . . ; PETITE SPIRITA SANCTA, etc.

Even the historical crypts of Sts. Peter and Marcellinus yield many graffiti inscribed on the walls; in the midst of Greek, Latin and Lombard names is found the prayer: MARCELLINE PETRE PETITE PRO . . .; IN MENTE HABETE. And in the cemetery of Pontian, two pilgrims traced similar graffiti, using the title of sinners: EVSTATIVS HVMILIS PECCATOR . . . ; HVMILIS PECCATOR PRESBYTER VESTER. . . .

The locations of the principal groups of graffiti in the Roman catacombs are:

1. Cemetery of Priscilla, in the underground chapel, under the basilica of St. Sylvester. Here one may find the beautiful expression: LIMINA SANCTORVM — "The abode of the saints" — which indicates its great importance. Again, we find the words: SALBA ME DOMNE CRESCENTIONE — "Help me, St. Crescention";

2. Cemetery of St. Hippolytus, in the historical crypt of the martyr;

3. Cemetery of Callistus, at the entrance of the papal crypt;

4. Cemetery of Pontian, in a gallery near the tomb of Sts. Abdon and Sennen;

5. Cemetery of Sts. Peter and Marcellinus, in the historical crypt and at its entrance;

6. Cemetery called *ad catacumbas,* near St. Sebastian's. There are two groups of graffiti with invocations to the Apostles Peter and Paul. Many of these graffiti may be seen in the so-

called *triclia,* the room where the agapes were held, discovered in 1915 beneath the pavement of the church. Other graffiti were discovered in 1919 in a deep underground hiding place lying close by, which can be recognized as the place where the bodies of the two apostles were hidden for a time. The phrase most frequently employed is: PETRE ET PAVLE IN MENTE HABETE, etc.[3]

The graffiti of St. Sebastian's also record the *refrigerium* or refreshment taken close to the tomb of the apostles.

The paleography of the graffiti made by the pilgrims is different from that of the burial graffiti, because the latter are much older. This paleography is very difficult; it may be studied in the collection of the celebrated papyri of Ravenna published by Marini, and even more profitably in the modern paleographical atlases, as for example, those of Châtelain and Monaci.

But it is necessary to note, above all, the topographical importance which these graffiti possess. Almost always, in the Roman catacombs, they indicate the proximity of a historical crypt; at times they enable us to follow, step by step, the same way as the ancient visitors used when they went from the upper basilicas to the subterranean chapels which contained the most venerated tombs.[4]

# Part Five

## ANCIENT CHRISTIAN ART

---

### Chapter I

### GENERAL PRINCIPLES[1]

#### 1. Pagan and Christian Art

TODAY it is generally admitted that ancient Christian art in the Occident did not arise from Oriental art, as some have pretended, but derives its essential characteristics from classical Graeco-Roman art. Hence, it underwent the same development and suffered the same vicissitudes.

Roman art reached its apogee under the Empire, and maintained its elegance until the second century. In fact, the paintings found on the Palatine and in Pompeii are of the finest style, just as fine as are the monuments of the period of Trajan and Hadrian.

The decadence of art began under Septimius Severus. A proof of this is furnished by the triumphal arch erected in his honor in the Roman Forum, which cannot compare with the simplicity and purity of line of the arch of Titus. The same criterion could be used in comparing paintings of the third century with those discovered at Pompeii. At the time of Constantine, painting as well as sculpture was in full decay. It suffices to observe the enormous difference between the bas-reliefs at the base of the arch of Constantine and those at the top, which were taken from a monument of the time of Trajan. Only architecture still preserved all its ancient grandeur, as the mausoleums of St. Constantia and St. Helena clearly show.

But toward the end of the fourth century, under Honorius and Arcadius, the disintegration is complete.

Christian art underwent the same changes. It is customary to say that Christian art is a coarse art, a rough art; but this is not true. If many Christian monuments are coarse, this impression arises from the fact that the late Christian monuments are more numerous than those of the classical period. The most ancient Christian monuments do not yield in elegance to the pagan monuments contemporaneous with them. Christian art has a character, an inspiration and a symbolism which set it off as something distinct, artistic and individual. Even in indifferent subjects and in simple decorations, it may be distinguished "by a certain general nobility, a candor, an innocent and tranquil joy. Ancient form and style have been purified by the spirit of Christianity, its chasteness penetrating even art, which, in this period of luxury and pleasures, was often a school of immorality."[2]

## 2.   Brief Historical Remarks on Christian Art

PAINTING.[3] — Christian painting began with the origin and spread of Christianity. The custom of decorating tombs is a very ancient one, which the Romans had inherited from the Etruscans. The Christians therefore conformed to this common, universal practice.

The style and the motifs of the Christian frescoes vary with the times.

During the most primitive period, when the catacombs were private cemeteries, there were no real and, properly speaking, Christian paintings. For example, the decorations in the vestibule in the tomb of the Flavii, in the cemetery of Domitilla, belong to the end of the first century and are nothing more than geometrical ornamentations, pastoral scenes, birds — in a word, the types of subject customarily found in pagan tombs. The decorations depicted in the crypt of Ampliatus in the same cemetery recall the frescoes of Pompeii.

Symbolism made its appearance and took definite shape during the second century, as we recognize in the paintings of the Greek chapel in the cemetery of Priscilla. In the second period, the catacombs became common Christian burying grounds; this epoch corresponds with a new phase of Christian painting, which lasted until 313. In this period, the entire Christian symbolical and theological cycle was developed.

It cannot be denied that the paintings of the Sacraments in the cemetery of Callistus were inspired by a Christian teacher; such is the logical nexus deriving from the symbolic rock whence spring the waters of grace ("Petra erat Christus," "The rock was Christ"),[4] in Baptism, Penance and the Eucharist. In Christian art, because of the still prevailing discipline of secrecy, the dogmas are expressed by means of figures; but, while symbolism emerged much later, the style of the paintings becomes less elegant.

From 313 to the beginning of the fifth century, Christianity triumphed, and Christian art did not feel the need of further dissimulation. Hence symbolism tends to disappear, in order to make way for representations less mysterious. Thus the symbol of the fish becomes more rare; and whereas primitive art rarely produced portraits, or actual scenes from real life, during the fourth century scenes of this kind multiplied, so that at times even the profession of the departed is represented.

During this same period, great use was still made of subjects or topics taken from the New Testament; but little by little the images of the Saviour and the saints were modified. In the fourth century, the Saviour is still pictured as typically Roman, without a beard; in the fifth century He has already become Oriental, iconographic. Also, while up to the fourth century the nimbus or halo had been reserved to the Saviour and the angels, during the fifth century, it began to be given to the Virgin and the saints.

SCULPTURE.[5] — The art portrayed by the sarcophagi, not only of the pagans but also of the Christians, never attained a high degree of perfection, because the sarcophagi never go back before the second century, an epoch very close to the decadence of art. From the beginning of the Republic, the use of cremation had become quite general, and we have only a few of the sarcophagi of the limited number of families, such as the *gens Cornelia,* who adhered to the custom of burying their dead. These examples illustrate the fact that the sarcophagi were coarse, rough and without ornament. During this period the *columbaria* were the most frequent places of burial; that is why we have cinerary urns and pedestals in large numbers dating from this epoch. When the custom of burial was again adopted in the second century, there were sarcophagi of sufficient elegance and workmanship — as we may see from examples preserved in all museums — but these cannot in any manner compare with the decorative bas-reliefs of the first century. With this species of art, decadence was rapid, and we find the same subjects executed at times in a coarse style and with constant repetitions.

Christian sculpture began much later than painting; it was easy to depict any scene in the catacombs, and much more difficult to execute objects of a distinctly Christian nature in a public workshop where sculpturing and stone-cutting was done. Hence, Christian sculpture did not begin in earnest until the epoch of Constantine, and Christian sarcophagi, properly so called, anterior to the peace of the Church, are rare exceptions. Christians procured their sarcophagi from those who supplied everyone, avoiding only those subjects which might offend against the principles of their religion. Thus in Rome, in the cemeteries of Praetextatus, Domitilla and Callistus, sarcophagi were found adorned with genii, busts, persons, etc., which do not differ in any point from those employed by the pagans. In the third century, there are some examples of Christian sculpture, but these deal with isolated representations of the Good Shepherd, the praying figure (Orans), or the anchor. Moreover, certain general subjects readily lent themselves to a Christian signification: scenes of the pastoral life could indicate, for example, the Good Shepherd; the sea, with fish, could represent the world and the faithful; a ship was the symbol of life, etc. There have never been found either sarcophagi or inscriptions of an absolutely idolatrous character belonging in the catacombs. The rare fragments of this nature discovered there were either thrown there from above or brought from somewhere else to be used as building material.[6]

Christian burial sculpture, therefore, developed between the beginning of the fourth and the end of the fifth century; there are scarcely any remaining traces of it in the sixth. Sculpture, like painting during the same period, shows few symbols, but these always of the same subjects with equal conformity of composition. The absence of a logical connection is noteworthy — the artist groups together subjects of the most diverse nature. But even here, we see exceptions. A sarcophagus, discovered at St. Paul's outside of the Walls and preserved in the Lateran Museum, portrays a logical series of subjects representing Christian thought, from the creation of the world to the founding of the Church and the persecutions. These points will be treated in their proper place.

Today, the most acceptable theory is that Christian art arose in the Western world and may later have been modified by what was adopted from the Oriental world.

### 3.  Symbolism

Burial monuments have handed down to us priceless information concerning the beliefs of the early Christians; but it must not be imagined that it is possible to find all the dogmas and articles of belief clearly expressed, as some have asserted. This exaggerated claim in time created a reaction toward the other extreme — the disposition to maintain, without reason, that the burial monuments could not contribute anything in proof of Christian beliefs.[7] It is not necessary to claim for these funerary monuments anything more than that they afford us simple allusions. To go beyond this would be as unwarranted as to imagine that present-day burial monuments bear a clear-cut expression of all our Catholic doctrines. The predominating thought running through all these burial monuments was that of a future life and a belief in the resurrection. "Fiducia Christianorum resurrectio mortuorum" — "The belief of Christians is the resurrection of the dead."[8] Therefore it was natural that their symbols should refer almost exclusively to this central idea and that all others had only secondary importance. Dogmatic symbols thus bear witness to the faith professed by the Christians. It was with this in mind that they adorned their tombs.[9]

The sources from which these symbols were taken are: the Bible, preaching by word of mouth (for example, the *Shepherd of Hermas*), and the burial liturgy. Le Blant[10] has emphasized the great influence which this liturgy exercised on burial art. The prayers employed in recommending the soul of the departed are, in fact, often reproduced in the inscriptions, and they may even be recognized in figurative expressions used to decorate artistic monuments. The special motif was the miracle of the resurrection of Lazarus, so often represented in both painting and sculpture.

Each fresco, each sarcophagus, appears to repeat one or two of the more touching invocations which are still employed in the prayers for the dying: "Receive, O Lord, the soul of Thy servant in the place of salvation which he hopes of Thy mercy." "Free, O Lord, the soul of Thy servant, as Thou didst free Enoch and Elias from the death common to this world . . . as Thou didst free Noe from the deluge . . . as Thou didst free Job from his sufferings . . . as Thou didst free Isaac from the sacrifice and from the hands of Father Abraham . . . as Thou didst free Moses from the hands of Pharaoh, king of Egypt . . . as Thou didst free Daniel from the lions' den . . . as Thou didst free the three young men from the fiery furnace and the hands of a perverse king . . . as Thou didst free Peter and Paul from their chains . . . thus deign to free the soul of Thy servant and enable him to enjoy with Thee celestial bliss."

All Christian symbolism is incomprehensible unless it is brought into alignment with the liturgical prayers, the writings of the Fathers, and the teachings of the Church. Considered together with them, it offers a beautiful proof of the early Christian beliefs.

## 4. Technique[11]

By burial paintings are generally understood the frescoes executed on the walls of chapels and arched vaults, or on the spaces which separated tomb from tomb. These paintings are done on a plaster formed of marble dust; very fine plaster is a sign of great antiquity. Often, before the execution of the painting, a sketch or outline was traced in the plaster itself, which is sometimes still recognizable. Paintings of tempera, which are also met with, are of a later period and more coarsely done.

Burial paintings show varied styles, and we can determine their date by means of the topics or subjects employed. Even in the cemeteries we may find, as at Pompeii, examples of good paintings, along with others of the same period, of a much inferior style. Especially in the third century, there were schools of painters who preferred to work in this or that cemetery; in fact, among the paintings of a given cemetery, one may notice a certain analogy, while there may be a very noticeable difference among the various cemeteries. Just as in ancient Egypt, where each necropolis of the times of Pharaoh possessed its own artists, painters, sculptors, cutters, who lived close at hand so as to be ready to perform whatever funerary labors were required of them, so for the same laudable reasons did the Christian artists live in the vicinity of the tombs.

## Chapter II

## DECORATIVE AND ALLEGORICAL PAINTINGS[1]

CHRISTIAN art took its motifs for decoration from pagan art, avoiding only idolatrous subjects. At times it deals with architectural designs, as may be seen in the chapel of Ampliatus in the cemetery of Domitilla; again it treats of other topics, as is illustrated in the chapel of the Flavii which has already been mentioned, in the same cemetery, and in the catacombs of St. Januarius at Naples; finally, it deals with perspective views, similar to those of the so-called "house of Livia" on the Palatine. Thus, for example, in a painting in the cemetery of Domitilla, there is depicted the scene of a Roman villa with many of the characteristic details.

CHAMBER WITH DECORATIVE PAINTINGS.
Cemetery of Domitilla. First and second centuries.

Decorations at times assumed an allegorical significance. Thus, the trees, flowers, gardens, etc., were meant to represent Paradise. Among the most ancient allegories, we find those of the vineyard and the seasons of the year. The vineyard is also found in pagan burial paintings, where it had funerary significance, because the vintage expresses the end of life; in Christian art, on the contrary, it represents the mystic Vine, the Redeemer ("Ego sum vitis vera" — "I am the true Vine"),[2] and at times even the Eucharist. It is perhaps the most ancient allegory, for we find it in the vestibule of the Flavii and in the chapel of Ampliatus at the cemetery of Domitilla. It is also found later, on the vault of the mausoleum of St. Constantia (fourth century).

Even the figures of the seasons are found in pagan funerary paintings, symbolizing the vicissitudes of human life. Christian art adopted this allegory, by representing the seasons now as genii (cemetery of Domitilla), again as figures of women (cemetery of Callistus, chapel of the third century opposite that of Miltiades), and still again under the guise of the fruits of the various seasons; that is, the vineyard, laurel, ears of grain, roses (cemetery of Praetextatus in the crypt of St. Januarius).[3]

ORPHEUS.

Cemetery of Callistus. Third century.

At times this allegory is christianized by the insertion of a figure of the Good Shepherd, that is, of Him Who regulates the life of man and the course of the seasons.

Among all these allegories, the only one which can truly be said to be mythological is that of Orpheus; but this representation is not frequent and is found only in the catacombs of Domitilla, Priscilla and Callistus. Its Christian significance is very clear: just as the Orpheus of paganism had overcome the savage beasts by the music of his lyre, so the Divine Orpheus, Jesus Christ, had transformed the pagan world by the sweetness of His doctrine.

## Chapter III

### THE PASTORAL CYCLE, THE ORANS, ETC.

THE FIGURE of the Good Shepherd is the most ancient representation of the Redeemer; the isolated bust of the Saviour is probably not found earlier than the time of peace.

Some have maintained that the type of the Good Shepherd is derived directly from the pagan Mercury carrying a sheep (*criophorus*). At first sight there may be some resemblance; but these two types cannot actually be confused because, while the figure and position of Mercury are very variable, the Good Shepherd, on the other hand, is a fixed, hieratic type. It may be admitted, however, that the Christian artists received some inspiration from the pagan Mercury, just as they were inspired at times by other pagan allegories.[1]

DANIEL, THE GOOD SHEPHERD,
PRAYING FIGURES, HEADS, GENII, BIRDS.
Cemetery of Callistus. Second century.

The most natural significance of the Good Shepherd is the charity of Jesus Christ, and even repentance, because He bears on His shoulders the lost sheep; but this figure also has a funerary meaning. In the ancient liturgy, there was a prayer to the effect that the soul of the departed "might be carried on the shoulders of the Good Shepherd," which was followed by the mention of sheep and the heavenly Paradise. The Acts of St. Perpetua, as we have already seen, tell us that the saint was received by the Good Shepherd in the middle of a garden. All this concurs with what we know of the paintings of the Good Shepherd.

THE GOOD SHEPHERD IN THE MIDST OF HIS FLOCK.
Cemetery of Callistus. Third century.

Ordinarily the Good Shepherd is represented with a lamb on His shoulders, one on His right and another on His left; oftentimes He is shown in a pastoral scene, in the midst of a flock of lambs and sheep. In some representations the Good Shepherd is found united with an Orans, emblematic of the Christian soul.

A fresco of the third century, at St. Callistus' (see above), represents the Good Shepherd carrying a sheep and surrounded by others upon which two disciples are throwing water. Some of the sheep appear to listen to Him, others are moving away from Him, still others are intent on their browsing. In this painting, many have professed to see an allegory depicting the various effects produced in souls by grace and the Divine word; an explanation which, if not entirely true, is at any rate ingenious.

THE GOOD SHEPHERD.
Cemetery of St. Callistus. Second century.

In the painting reproduced above, also found in the cemetery of Callistus, the Good Shepherd carries a pail of milk, symbolizing the Eucharist. In the crypts of Lucina, the pail of milk is placed on a small altar guarded by two sheep (see page 278).

Sometimes in these pastoral scenes, the Christian artists have departed considerably from the hieratic type, the better to

imitate pagan paintings. For example, they have placed the
Good Shepherd in the midst of His flock, in the attitude of
playing the flute. To this category belong the shepherds depicted on the angles of the lid of the great sarcophagus ascribed
to Pope Miltiades in the cemetery of Callistus.

To this series of compositions should be added the lamb,
emblem of the Christian and of Jesus Christ Himself: "Ecce
Agnus Dei" — "Behold the Lamb of God."[2]

VESSEL OF MILK GUARDED BY SHEEP.
Cemetery of Callistus. Second century.

Symbolism of this kind is extremely old. In the crypt of
Lucina, in fact, there is a very ancient inscription (reproduced
on page 279) in which an anchor with a lamb beneath is depicted, along with the dove. A veiled crucifix may also be seen.
St. Paulinus of Nola tells us that in the basilica of this city, and
in Fondi, similar images existed, which could be explained by
the following inscription: SVB CRVCE SANGVINEA NIVEO
STAT CRISTVS IN AGNO — "Under the bloody cross is
Christ as a snowy white lamb."[3]

This same symbol, which is also repeated in the cemetery
of Domitilla, took on a different form later — that of a lamb

on a small hill, whence arise the four rivers of the Gospels. This new composition was developed especially in mosaics, but it is prior to the sixth century. There is an example of it dating from the fourth century to be found in the cemetery of St. Sebastian.

To the figure of the Good Shepherd we should add that of the Orans, or praying figure, which often completes the picture. It is said by some that the Orans is derived from the pagan *Pietas,* a beautiful statue of which is preserved in the Vatican. Certainly there is some resemblance between the two figures, and it may even be supposed that the Christian artists were assisted and inspired by a type which was already known to them. The point that they imitated this figure in reality is by no means proved, because the attitude of the Orans is common to both the Romans and the Orientals. According to St. Ambrose, this attitude recalls that of the Redeemer on the cross; this is a pious interpretation which may not have been the actual intention of the artists.

Cemetery of Callistus. Second century.

Two kinds of praying figures may be distinguished: the Biblical and the isolated. Almost all the figures used by the Christian artists are made to assume this posture — for example, Noe, Isaac, the three young men in the furnace, etc. The solitary Orans is sculptured on the burial stones, depicted on the ceilings, on the arched vaults, and on the graves.

Some have sought to maintain that it is intended as the portrait of the departed; and it is in fact not unusual to find the name of the deceased close to the figure of an Orans. We can recognize this on the tomb of Veneranda in the cemetery of Domitilla, and in the chapel known as the Five Saints in the cemetery of Callistus; in both cases, it may be believed that the Orans is a portrait (see next page and 311). Generally how-

AN ORANS OR PRAYING FIGURE.
Cemetery of Callistus. Third century.

ever, it is a symbolic figure of the soul. Thus it is usually a feminine figure, even when united with the name of a man. At times, we will find, close to the figure of an Orans, the words: ANIMA DVLCIS; ANIMA TVA IN PACE. A devotional medal preserved in the Christian Museum of the Vatican Library shows St. Lawrence on the gridiron, and his soul taking flight pictured by an Orans. The Acts of Sts. Peter and Marcellinus inform us that the souls of the two martyrs were seen flying toward heaven under the form of two maidens richly dressed.

But the Orans, even when it is a portrait, is highly spiritualized. Thus, for example, the five saints of the cemetery of Callistus are placed in the midst of flowers and birds, emblems of heaven. In the fourth century, the Orans assumed more realistic forms; such is the richly dressed Orans of the cemetery of Thraso. Later on, however, as we may conclude from the picture of St. Cecilia (see page 282), the Orans became typically Byzantine.

At times the Orans was used even as a representation of the Virgin Mary or of the Church; some of these praying figures have the name MARIA or MARA attached to them, as may be seen on the gilded glass examples in the Vatican Museum. The female figures of the mosaic of St. Sabina's, which goes back to the pontificate of Celestine I (beginning of the fifth century), are designated: ECCLESIA EX GENTIBVS, ECCLESIA EX CIRCVMCISIONE. But ordinarily it is not an easy matter to determine if the intention was really to give an Orans any of these symbolic significations.

THE FIVE SAINTS.

Cemetery of Callistus. Beginning of fourth century.

## Chapter IV

### BIRDS — PARADISE

THE FIGURES of birds, whether symbolic or decorative, are numerous. This symbol is very old and is perhaps derived from Egypt; in Egyptian art of the period of the Pharaohs, the soul was represented by a bird called Ba.

The commonest figure is that of the dove, a very natural emblem for the Christian to use in portraying the innocence of the soul of the faithful departed. It represented, in fact, the soul freed from its corporeal bonds. At times this figure was found in union with an Orans, or accompanied by proper names or words which could be applied only to a person: ANIMA INNO-CENTISSIMA; PALVMBA; PALVMBA SINE FELLE — "Most innocent soul"; "Dove"; "Dove without guile."

ST. CECILIA AMONG THE FLOWERS OF PARADISE.

Cemetery of Callistus. Byzantine period.

The dove also signified the Holy Spirit. This is its use in the scene in the crypts of Lucina, and in an inscription already mentioned, from Caesarea in Mauritania.[1]

When the dove is pictured in the midst of flowers and trees in the garden of Paradise, or as resting on a vase or in the act of pecking at a bunch of grapes, it is the emblem of the joy of heaven, or it may even be a Eucharistic symbol.

In the crypts of Lucina, facing the scene of the two sheep turned toward a pillar upon which rests a pail of milk, two doves are pictured guarding a small tree. These scenes apparently contain a twofold parallel symbolism. The first picture may signify the faithful nourished by the Eucharist during earthly existence; the second, the souls released from their bodily bonds and saved in virtue of the cross. An analogous scene is found on an arched vault in the cemetery of Callistus, in which the cross, formed of flowers, is still concealed, but more easily recognizable.

Finally, the same idea is manifested with greater clearness during the fifth century, when the cross was represented with a dove on each arm. We have numerous examples of this on sarcophagi. Other birds generally have the same meaning as the dove, and are an image of the soul. The peacock and the phoenix are also represented on many monuments. The first

DOVES IN THE HEAVENLY GARDEN.
Cemetery of Callistus. Second century.

was employed frequently during the third century as a symbol of eternal life, because its flesh was presumed to be incorruptible. The phoenix emblemized the resurrection and eternity. It is still found in basilicas of the Middle Ages, but it is not very common on monuments which are of any great antiquity.

Birds were generally represented in flower gardens, which for the early Chrisitians were symbols of heaven. In fact, the liturgical prayers and the Acts of the first martyrs describe eternal happiness as a refreshment and a repose; all of which merely utilized an idea taken from daily life to express a more sublime concept.

Another symbol of Paradise is the starred vault. There is a fine example of this in the underground chapel of the Acilii in the cemetery of Priscilla.

This method of representing the heavens was employed until the fourth century. In the mausoleum of St. Constantia, important traces of a decoration in mosaic showing the Constantinian monogram have been discovered — a monument of the triumph of Christianity in the midst of a starry heaven. This is perhaps a symbolic record of the vision of Constantine. At any rate, the symbol is much rarer than that already described as denoting heaven — a garden with flowers, praying figures, fruits and doves.

All of this symbolism was only the representation in figures of the funerary inscriptions and prayers: SPIRITVS TVVS IN PACE; SPIRITVS TVVS IN BONO; DEVS SVSCIPIAT ANIMAM TVAM; DEVS PERDVCAT TE IN PARADISVM. ("May your spirit be at peace"; "May God receive your soul"; "May God lead you to Paradise.")

## Chapter V

## THE SACRAMENTS

THE IMPORTANT paintings which adorn the series of burial chambers known as the "chambers of the Sacraments," in the cemetery of Callistus, are not later than the third century, and therefore belong to the period of Callistus, Zephyrin and Tertullian. They show us that a great development of Christian symbolism concerning the Sacraments took place in this period. In no other cemetery have so many paintings relating to the same subject, and so well connected with one another, been found.

## 1.  Grace — Baptism

The first scene represents Moses striking the rock, a symbol
of the authority of the Church which causes the waters of grace
to flow from the rock which is Jesus Christ.[1] In general the
type used for Moses is that of an idealized youth, but at times
he is represented more realistically as a bearded man, recalling
the figure of St. Peter. We know with certainty that the early
artists intentionally represented St. Peter in the guise of Moses.
In fact, a plate of the fourth century, found at Podgoritza in

PLATE OF PODGORITZA.
Fourth century.

Illyria, shows Moses striking the rock and bears the following
commentary: PETRVS VIRGA PERQVODSET (*percussit*);
FONTIS CIPERVNT QVORERE (*fontes coeperunt currere*)

— "Peter struck with the rod; waters began to flow." Two gilded cups in the Vatican Museum also show the same scene with the word PETRVS. This conforms with the tradition handed down to us, since the Fathers often compare Moses with Peter, and the water flowing from the rock to satisfy the thirst of all Israel, with the confession of Peter which gave new life to the world.

In the paintings we are discussing, in the chambers of the Sacraments, the idea of the artist is developed logically. Facing

Cemetery of Callistus.  Beginning of the third century.

Moses stands the Samaritan woman: it is not enough that grace is produced; it is necessary to get to the very fountain-head opened up by the Saviour.

Following the scene of Moses comes one of the miraculous draught of fishes. Tertullian's description of the symbolism of the fish — "Nos pisciculi sumus secundum IXΘYN nostrum Iesum Christum"[3] — was graphically reproduced by the early Christian artists, who represented the fish swimming toward the anchor or the Eucharistic Bread. The draught of small fishes is an image of Baptism, the anchor is a veiled symbol of the cross, although it may also refer to the sea and the waters of Baptism.

In the chambers of the Sacraments there is also a scene depicting real Baptism by immersion and aspersion. One person stands with a part of his body immersed, another pours water

on him. This picture is completed by another close by representing the paralytic in the Pool.[4] The same allusion is found on a
fresco of the so-called region of St. Soter, where the disciples
of the Good Shepherd pour water on the heads of the sheep.[5]

BAPTISM.
Cemetery of Callistus. Beginning of the third century.

Another symbolic representation of Baptism is that of
Noe and the Ark; this symbol is very ancient, since it is found
among the paintings of the Greek chapel in the cemetery of
Priscilla.

Among the other monuments which figure Baptism, we
recall an inscription from Aquileia, and a cup of the fourth
century, found in the hospice of Pammachius at Porto and now
preserved in the Vatican Museum.[6]

Baptism naturally reminds us of Penance. De Rossi sees
a symbol of this sacrament in the paralytic, on the walls of the
tombs of the cemetery of Callistus. This, in his opinion, is the
paralytic of Capharnaum. But the place occupied by this painting has induced other archeologists to conclude that it represents the paralytic of the Pool of Bethesda. On the whole, this
symbol is not encountered often and even the Sacrament of
Penance is very rarely represented. Father Marchi is inclined
to see in the chair of the Greater Cemetery of St. Agnes an
indication of sacramental confession; but this hypothesis is
inadmissible because such chairs served merely as appurtenances
during liturgical ceremonies. The true symbol of Penance in
the cemeteries is the Good Shepherd.

INSCRIPTION OF AQUILEIA, WITH A SCENE OF BAPTISM.
Fourth century.

## 2.  The Eucharist

The Eucharistic prayers must have been recited after the agape. This is an indication of their great antiquity, because the custom of celebrating the liturgical agape[7] along with the Eucharist[8] had already fallen into disuse in the second century. In fact, the letter of Pliny to Trajan speaks of two different meetings which the Christians had each Sunday, one of which was held for the purpose of eating a meal in common.[9] St. Ignatius of Antioch[10] says that the Eucharist could be celebrated without the bishop but not so the agape: "Valida Eucharistia habeatur illa, quae sub episcopo peragitur, vel sub eo cui ipse concesserit . . . Non licet sine episcopo neque baptizare neque agapen celebrare." ("That Eucharist is valid which is held with the bishop or with the one who has received permission from him . . . It is not allowed to baptize or celebrate the agape without the bishop.")  The same distinction is made in the first *Apology* of St. Justin.  Hence, about the year 110, at least in numerous churches, the Eucharist had been separated from the agape. From this it must be concluded that the Διδαχή is at the latest from the end of the first century, a period when the ecclesiastical hierarchy had not yet become well developed, since the Διδαχή speaks only of the bishop, deacons and prophets.

The celebrated *Apology* of St. Justin gives a more complete description of the Eucharistic liturgy practised about the year 155. In this work, the Eucharist is called the heavenly nourishment of the Body of Jesus Christ, and mention is made of the mixing of wine with water under the term of κέρασμα. St. Justin refers to the consecration almost in the same words as St. Paul, and we may conclude from his description that the discipline of the secret had slightly relaxed during the periods of tranquillity. He records the prayers which precede and follow communion, and mentions the kiss of peace; but he does not refer to the communion itself. However, it is spoken of in other documents which have come down to us, especially in the writings of Tertullian,[11] who says that Christians should not make statues of idols with hands that touched the Body of the Lord: "Eas manus admovere corpori Domini, quae daemonis corpora conferant." He tells us that upon receiving communion the recipient answered "Amen."[12]

A celebrated passage in St. Irenaeus speaks of a heretic who, employing white wine, colored it red to indicate the change of the substance of wine into the blood of Jesus Christ.[13]

All these texts of the Fathers serve to shed light on the evidence found in the cemeteries.

According to de Rossi, the most ancient painting of the Eucharist is that of the crypt of Lucina, which is entirely symbolic and hence belongs to a period anterior to that of the *Fractio panis* of the cemetery of Priscilla. It consists of two symmetrical representations of a fish, placed on a background colored green, and carrying on its back a basket of wine and bread. A better method of showing the compenetration of the Eucharistic elements with the Body of the Redeemer could not have been chosen;[14] one cannot doubt that this treats of the Eucharist. The body of Jesus Christ in the Eucharist is called by St. Paulinus: "Panis verus et aquae vivae piscis" ("True bread and water of the true fish").[15] We know that poor churches employed baskets to carry the Eucharist: "Nihil illo ditius qui corpus Domini in canistro vimineo et sanguinem portat in vitro." ("Nothing is more precious than the wicker basket which carries the Body of the Lord and the glass vessel

THE EMBLEMATIC FISH UNITED WITH THE
TWO EUCHARISTIC SPECIES.
Cemetery of Callistus. Second century.

which carries His Blood.") With respect to the fish, it was
certainly used as a symbol of the Saviour from the time
of the second century, and the well-known acrostic ΙΧΘΥC
contributed much to render this increasingly common.[17] Renan
pretended to see in this painting only an allusion to the fish
eaten by Jesus and His disciples at the lake of Tiberias, but
de Rossi has shown that that episode has nothing to do with
this group, but must be referred to the paintings of banquets
in the cemetery of Callistus which are much later than the frescoes of the crypt of Lucina. Others have seen in this painting
an allusion to the multiplication of the loaves and fishes. However, if this sense alone were intended, the presence of a vial
of red wine could not be explained.

The Eucharistic symbol is repeated very often in the art

THE BREAKING OF BREAD (Eucharistic Communion).
Cemetery of Priscilla. Second century.

of the cemeteries. In the cemetery of Priscilla there is the painting of the *Breaking of Bread* (*Fractio panis*), which goes back
to the time of the reign of Hadrian or Antoninus Pius, that is,
the period of St. Justin. For this reason, the Greek chapel in
which this painting is to be found may be considered the oldest
church of Rome. The fresco, which was discovered during the

cutting of a calcareous stratum,[18] represents the liturgical act of
the breaking of bread. At the left can be seen the priest or
bishop who divides the bread; in front of him stands a chalice.
Six other persons, including a feminine figure, are seated around
a table, on which are placed loaves of bread and fishes. According to Wilpert, this is a vivid and real representation of the

EUCHARISTIC OBLATION.
Cemetery of Callistus. Beginning of third century.

Eucharistic rite celebrated there during the second century. It
is a fact that the persons are depicted with a realistic expression
seldom seen elsewhere. But we cannot say that all is real,
because the baskets at each place, as in the scene of the multiplication of the loaves, evidently have a symbolical meaning.
Moreover, the priest has raised his feet to the height of the
table, a thing certainly inadmissible in reality. Finally, this is
a case where the agape was united with the Eucharist, which
we have seen was no longer the custom in the second century.

Hence, this painting may be said to combine reality with symbolism; the most realistic thing depicted in it is the action of the priest.

Another Eucharistic painting is that of the tripod with bread and fish. There are two examples of this in the chambers of the Sacraments. In one of them, the tripod can be seen in the midst of seven baskets, representing the multiplication of the loaves. The other depicts a man extending his hand as if to bless, while a praying figure assists at the ceremony (see page 292). De Rossi recognized in this scene the very act of consecration. The tripod is the *mensa Domini* ("table of the

EUCHARISTIC BANQUET.
Cemetery of Callistus. Beginning of third century.

Lord"), and has the same form as a dining table, the common form of primitive altars. The position the picture occupies, between those representing Baptism and the Eucharistic Banquet helps to make its significance yet more clear. The Orans calls to mind the Church, which prays before the Consecrated Species. Wilpert believes he recognizes in this painting an illustration of the multiplication of the loaves; but this would not allow of any explanation either of the presence of the table or of the absence of the baskets. The sacrifice of Abraham, pictured next to it, would rather appear to indicate that some allusion to sacrifice was intended.

Representations of isolated tables are rare, although paintings of banquets are frequent, especially during the third century. The fish is always shown on the table and the number of persons is invariably seven. On one of the tombs in the chapel of the Sacraments, near the painting of the table with bread and fish, there is depicted a conventional scene with ideal figures, recording the banquet at the lake of Tiberias. There is no longer any doubt here concerning the signification of the fish: "Piscis assus Christus est passus."[19] St. Prosper of Aquitania[20] tells us that the Redeemer offered Himself to all as "a saving fish which illumines and nourishes all each day." This sentence is perhaps a reference to the fish which cured blind Tobias and restored his sight.

The baskets of loaves, among the oldest representations of the Eucharist, are also found in the painting of the *Breaking of Bread* in the cemetery of Priscilla. Even the representation of the miracle of the multiplication of loaves, to which they allude, belongs to a later period. In the same cycle belongs the depiction of the miracle of the marriage feast at Cana, a scene rather common on sarcophagi but rare in paintings. Wilpert has found an example of it in the cemetery of Sts. Peter and Marcellinus.[21] In that catacomb and in some others may be seen paintings of banquets, which must be carefully distinguished from those already spoken of. In these others, the number of persons is not always seven. Some have imagined that they represent scenes of the agapes, but this interpretation is not plausible because primitive Christian art scarcely ever made use of scenes from real life. It seems more probable that they treat of the celestial banquet promised by the Redeemer,[22] that is, of that which He called "mensa Patris Mei," "My

Father's table." It may be observed here that on some pagan tombs one often finds banquet scenes almost identical with those just described, in which bread and fish figure; but they are nothing more than representations of funeral banquets, and the fish indicates nothing more than a certain degree of sumptuousness.

A beautiful painting of the heavenly feast is that to be seen in the vestibule of the cemetery of Domitilla. Even though it is much damaged, there are still visible two persons seated in front of a table with the fish and some loaves of bread on it; at one side stands the servant or waiter, the *dapifer,* holding a plate. The painting belongs to the second century. The scenes

THE HEAVENLY FEAST.
Cemetery of Sts. Peter and Marcellinus. Beginning of the fourth century.

of the feast are reproduced six or seven times in the cemetery of Sts. Peter and Marcellinus, and go back to the third and fourth centuries (see accompanying figure). Close to the table there are always two women who preside at the feast, and the inscription indicates that they are personifications of peace and charity: IRENE DA CALDA, AGAPE MISCE MI. The word MISCE recalls the custom of mixing wine with water, characteristic of the ancient feasts and also of the Eucharistic Sacrifice. The inscription of Abercius also contains an expression of the same kind.

The feast of the five Wise Virgins is represented more rarely. An example of it has been found on an arched vault in the Greater Cemetery of St. Agnes. In the midst of the Virgins is a praying figure, then come the five with lighted lamps; at the other side four Virgins are seated at a table, and the fifth is represented by the praying figure. In this picture one may recognize the marriage feast of the Heavenly Spouse.[23] On a fresco of the cemetery of Cyriaca the five Virgins are pictured, without the table.

The pitcher containing milk is also an emblem of the Eucharist, and we have a proof of this in one of the celebrated visions of the martyr Perpetua, already related. (See page 45 f.) The Good Shepherd appeared to the saint in a garden, surrounded by His flock and a number of other shepherds. He was milking, and He gave a little coagulated milk to her, while all those standing about bowed their heads and exclaimed: "Amen."

We have also mentioned the paintings of the cemetery of Callistus, one representing the Good Shepherd with a pitcher of milk, and the other showing the pail of milk between two sheep.[24] In the cemetery of Domitilla a sheep is depicted near a pail of milk, and attached to a stake — a symbol of the Good Shepherd. This same scene is repeated in front of the altar of Sts. John and Paul, whence it seems that the symbol was employed even in the fourth century.

A bunch of grapes has the same signification. It is scarcely ever painted, but it is often found cut into the burial stones. Manna, figure of the Eucharist,[25] is to be seen on an arched vault in the cemetery of Cyriaca.

To confirm the interpretation given to these cemetery paintings, the renowned Eucharistic burial inscriptions of Pectorius and Abercius may be cited.

The inscription of Pectorius, found at Autun in 1839, was published with a commentary by Pitra.[26] It is a priceless monument harking back perhaps to the beginning of the third century, which contains the following expressions, of great dogmatic importance:

Ἰχθὺς ο[ὐρανίου θε]ῖον γένος ἤτορι σεμνῷ
Χρῆσε λαβὼ[ν πηγὴ]ν ἄμβροτον ἐν βροτέοις
Θεσπεσίον ὑδάτ[ω]ν τὴν σὴν φίλε θάλπεο ψυχ[ήν]
Ὕδασιν ἀεινάοις πλουτοδότου σοφίης
Σωτῆρος δὲ ἁγίων μελιηδέα λάμβαν[ε βρῶσιν]
Ἔσθιε πινάων ἰχθὺν ἔχων παλάμαις.

"Piscis caelestis divinum genus corde puro utere, hausta inter mortales immortali fonte aquarum divinitus manantium.

FRAGMENT OF THE INSCRIPTION OF ABERCIUS.
Later. Museum. Second century.

Tuam, amice, foveto animam aquis perennibus sapientiae largientis divitias. Salvatoris sanctorum dulcem sume cibum; manduca esuriens piscem tenens manibus."

The faithful, in a word, are invited to nourish themselves by means of a holy food and to receive in their hands the Consecrated Species, according to ancient liturgical usage.

The inscription of Abercius, Bishop of Hieropolis in Phrygia,[27] was already known from his Acts, when, in 1882, Ramsay discovered an identical inscription in Phrygia which, however, contained another name. It bore the date of the year 300 of the Phrygian era (216 of our era).[28] This is undoubtedly an imitation of the inscription of Abercius, because one verse does not correspond to the meter otherwise employed, on account of the substitution of the name ΑΛΕΞΑΝΔΡΟΣ for ΑΒΕΡΚΙΟΣ.

Ramsay also found two other fragments a few years later, which were presented to Leo XIII on the occasion of his sacerdotal Jubilee, one by the sultan, the other by Ramsay himself.

The inscription was cut on three sides of a burial pillar,[29] and composed of twenty-two verses, each of which occupied two lines. In the reproduction given here, the capital letters indicate the portion preserved in the Lateran Museum.[30]

1 Ἐκλεκτῆς πόλεως ὁ πολεί
   τῆς τοῦτ᾽ ἐποίησα
2 ζῶν ἵν᾽ ἔχω καιρ . . .
   σώματος ἔθα θέσιν
3 οὔνομ᾽ Ἀβέρκιοσ ὤν ὁ
   μαθητὴς ποιμένος ἀγνοῦ
4 ὃς βόσκει κροβάτων ἀγέλας
   ὄρεσιν πεδίοις τε
5 ὀφθαλμοὺς ὃς ἔχει μεγάλους
   πάντη καθορῶντας
6 οὖνος γὰρ μ᾽ ἐδίδαξε
   [τὰ ζωῆς] γράμματα πιστά

Electae civitatis hoc feci
Vivens ut habeam [cum tempus erit] corporis hic sedem
Nomen mihi Abercius discipulus [sum] pastoris casti
Qui pascit ovium greges in montibus et agris
Cui oculi sunt grandes ubique conspicientes
Is me docuit litteras fideles [vitae].

7 ΕΙΣ ΡΩΜΗν ἔπεμψεν
   ΕΜΕΝ ΒΑΣΙΛείαν ἀθρῆσαι
8 ΚΑΙ ΒΑΣΙΛΙΣσαν ἰδεῖν χρυσός
   ΤΟΛΟΝ ΧΡυσοπέδιλον
9 ΛΑΟΝ ΔΕΙΔΟΝ ἐκεῖ λαμπράν
   ΣΦΡΑΓΕΙΔΑΝΕχοντα
10 ΚΑΙΣΥΡΙΗΣΠ ΗΕδον ᵀειδα
   ΚΑΙΑΣΤΕΑΠΑντα Ν'σιβιν

Qui Romam me misit regnum contemplaturum
Visurumque reginam aurea stola aureis calceis decoram
Ibique vidi populum splendido sigillo insignem
Et Syriae vidi campos urbesque cunctas Nisibin quoque

11 ΕΥΦΡΑΤΗΝΔΙΑθας παν
   ΤΗΔΕΣΧΟΝΣΥΝΟμίλους
12 ΠΑΥΛΟΝΕΧΟΝΕΠΟ ....
   ΠΙΣΤΙΣ πάντη δὲ προῆγε
13 ΚΑΙΠΑΡΗΘΗΚΕτροφήν
   ΠΑΝΤΗΙΧθΥΝΑπὸ πηγῆς
14 ΠΑΝΜΕΓΕΘΗΣΑΘαρον ὅν
   ΕΔΡΑΣΑΤΟΠΑΡΘενὸς ἁγνή
15 ΚΑΙΤΟΥΤΟΝΕΠΕδωκε φι
   ΛΟΙΣΕΣΘίειν διὰ παντός
16 οἶνον χρηστον ἔχουσα
   κέρασμα διδοῦσα μετ' ἄρτου

Transgresso Euphrate. Ubique vero nactus sum [familiariter] colloquentes
Paulum habens ....
Fides vero ubique mihi dux fuit
Praebuitque ubique cibum piscem e fonte
Ingentem purum quem prehendit virgo casta
Deditque amicis perpetuo edendum
Vinum optimum habens ministrans [vinum aquae] mixtum cum pane.

17 ταῦτα παρεστὼς εἶπον
   'Αβέρκιος ὧδε γραφῆναι
18 ἑβδομήκοστον ἔτος καὶ
   δεύτερον ἦγον ἀληθῶς
19 ταῦθ' ὁ νοῶν εὔξαιτο ὑπέρ
   'Αβερκίου πᾶς ὁ συνῳδός
20 οὐ μέντοι τύμβῳ τις ἐμῷ
   ἕτερόν τινα θήσει
21 εἰ δ' οὖν 'Ρωμαίων ταμείῳ
   θήσει δισχίλια χρυσᾶ
22 καὶ χρηστῇ πατρίδι 'Ιερο
   πόλει χίλια χρυσᾶ

Haec adstans Abercius dictavi heic inscribenda
Annum agens vere septuagesimum secundum
Haec qui intelligit quique eadem sentit oret pro Abercio
Neque quisquam sepulcro meo alterum superimponat
Sin autem inferat aerario Romanorum aureos bis mille.
Et optimae patriae Hieropoli aureos mille.

The following is a free rendering:

*On the first side of the pillar:*

As a member of the chosen city have I done this,
While still alive, while there is yet time,
In order that I might have a place for my body.
My name is Abercius and I am a follower of the Good Shepherd
Who pastures His flocks of sheep on the mountains
And in the meadows,
Whose eyes are large, seeing everywhere;
He has taught me the saving doctrines of life.

*On the second side*:
(In the Lateran Museum)

He sent me to Rome to contemplate His kingdom,
And to behold the queen bedecked in a golden stole and golden sandals.
There I saw a renowned people, with a shining record,
And I saw all the plains and cities of Syria and Nisibis also.

Having crossed the Euphrates, I went everywhere,
They discussed things with me in a familiar manner
Having Paul . . . . . . . . . . . .
Faith, indeed, was my guide everywhere
And she gave me at all times the great and pure Fish from the deep
For food, Whom the Chaste Virgin conceived and gave to friends
To be eaten perpetually,
Having the finest wine which was served combined with water
and bread.

*On the third side*:

These things did Abercius dictate while present in person,
And ordered them to be inscribed on this,
During the seventy-second year of his life.
Let him who understands these things
And grasps their meaning, pray for Abercius,
Nor let anyone place another in my tomb,
Unless he pays two thousand gold pieces to the Roman treasury,
And one thousand gold pieces to our best-beloved fatherland Hieropolis.

To those who understand the language of early Christian symbolism, the sense is obvious. The Chaste Shepherd is He of the Gospels Who "gives His life for His sheep."[31] The ΙΧΘΥΣ ΠΑΝΜΕΓΕΘΗΣ is the "great Fish" of which Tertullian speaks: "We are little fish born in water according to ἰχθύν our Christ Jesus."[32] The queen whom Abercius saw in Rome is the Christian community of Rome, the Church renowned among all the brethren not only because of its founders but also because of its faith.[33] The Chaste Virgin who has taken the fish from the waters signifies the Blessed Virgin Mary who conceived our Saviour. The discipline of the secret made it necessary to use this cryptic and symbolic language, but the initiates understood it perfectly: "Haec qui intelligit quique eadem sentit" — "Who understands these things will appreciate them also."[34]

Dr. Gerhard Ficker, of Halle, denied this interpretation some years ago, claiming that the inscription is pagan, and that Abercius was actually a priest of Cybele. But his argument is valueless. His first objection refers to the form of the monument; but there is no question that even in Christian cemeteries above ground there were monuments in the form of pillars.[35] He next maintains that in a Christian inscription of the second century there should be found some reference to the dogma of the Resurrection. But is there not actually such an allusion in the recommendation of the soul to the prayers of the living? On the whole, the word "resurrection" is rather rare in burial inscriptions.

The positive part of Ficker's argument has even less substance, for he builds it up on a number of fantastic hypotheses, identifying Cybele with the Chaste Virgin and Attis with the Shepherd. Now, one of the duties imposed on the worshippers of Cybele was precisely abstinence from fish; how then could Abercius have advocated the violation of this obligation during his religious journey?[36] Finally, it is simply beyond the imaginable that the Christians, who certainly honored Abercius, should have chosen as their bishop a priest of Cybele. "How can one treat with seriousness," exclaims de Rossi in commenting on the argument, "and discuss as worthy of scientific controversy, troubled dreams of this sort?"[37]

The majority of scholars hold that the inscription of Abercius is a Christian inscription — in fact, "the queen of Christian inscriptions," and perhaps the most important of all from the dogmatic point of view. It refers to the Divinity of Christ and to the Eucharist; it alludes to the veneration of the Virgin Mary; it attests the Communion of Saints by expressing an invitation to the faithful to pray for Abercius; and it contains the concept of the primacy of the Roman Church.[38]

## Chapter VI

## BIBLICAL SCENES[1]

### 1.  Scenes from the Old Testament

ADAM AND EVE NEAR THE TREE OF SIN. — This scene, very frequent on sarcophagi, is rather rare in paintings. We have an example of it in the cemetery of Domitilla. The scene points to a belief in the Redemption.

NOE.

Cemetery of Priscilla.
First half of second century.

NOE LEAVING THE ARK. — Represented under the figure of an Orans, covered almost to the middle of the body by a kind of square box. Near him is seen a dove with an olive branch. It is a symbol of Baptism, and also of the peace bestowed on the soul after the hardships of this earthly life.

The symbolism of Baptism in paintings representing the Noetic Deluge is based upon the words of one of St. Peter's Epistles.[2]

THE SACRIFICE OF ABRAHAM.[3] — This is often found portrayed in paintings; at times it has a dogmatic signification, as in the chapel of the Sacraments, where it accompanies and completes the representation of the Eucharistic Sacrifice.  In general, however, it illustrates prayers said for the souls of the departed: "Libera, Domine, animam servi tui, sicut liberasti Isaac de hostia et de manu patris sui Abrahae" — "Free, O Lord, the soul of Thy servant, as Thou didst free Isaac from immolation and the hands of his father Abraham."

MOSES STRIKING THE ROCK. — This scene, whenever it is historical, refers to the waters of grace and especially, as already said, to the Sacrament of Baptism.

JONAS. — The story of the prophet Jonas is often represented.[4] Three scenes are shown, and they are seen together or
separately: Jonas swallowed by the
sea monster; Jonas cast upon the
shore; Jonas under the pumpkin-vine.
The monster always has the same
bizarre form, which is not that of a
whale. The symbolism of the first
two scenes is very clear; in fact, it
was explained by Christ Himself.[5]
The third scene, Jonas resting under
the pumpkin-vine, may be a picture
of the sleep of death or of the vanity
of human life which passes with the
same rapidity as the plant that with-
ers in a day. The use by the Christian artists of this plant shows that
they had recourse to the ancient
Italic Version of the Old Testament
for their inspiration, for St. Jerome
rendered the word as "ivy." Rufinus,
taking him to task for this innova-
tion, based his argument on the representations in the catacombs, and
on St. Augustine.[6]

THE CYCLE OF JONAS.
Cemetery of Callistus. Beginning of the third century.

JOB. — Representations of Job always picture him in pain. At times
his wife is shown standing before
him. This is interpreted as a belief
in the resurrection and prayer for
the liberation of the soul. There is
an important example of this scene in an underground Gnostic
chapel of the Aurelii recently discovered in the Manzoni Road.[7]

THE THREE YOUTHS OF THE BOOK OF DANIEL. — The
story of their refusal to adore the statue of Nabuchodonosor
is taken from the protocanonical part of this Book; the statue
of Nabuchodonosor always consists of a column surmounted

by a bust, as may be seen in a painting of the cemetery of Priscilla.[8] From the deuterocanonical portion has been repro-

THE THREE YOUTHS REFUSE TO ADORE
THE STATUE OF NABUCHODONOSOR.
Cemetery of Priscilla.  Beginning of fourth century.

duced the scene of the young men in the furnace. This scene is found depicted in the Greek chapel (second century) in the cemetery of Priscilla, again in the cemetery of Callistus, and elsewhere.

LAZARUS.  A VEILED ORANS.
THE THREE YOUNG MEN IN THE FIERY FURNACE.
Cemetery of Callistus.  Third century.

DANIEL IN THE LIONS' DEN. — This scene is generally based on the protocanonical portion of the Book of Daniel, but at times it is based on the deuterocanonical portion, with the added presence of the prophet Habacuc.  ·

SUSANNA. — Her story is pictured on the side walls of the Greek chapel of Priscilla. Susanna is in the act of praying in this representation.

DANIEL DEFENDING SUSANNA.
Cemetery of Callistus. Third century.

In a picture of the cemetery of Callistus, de Rossi sees a reproduction of the judgment of a martyr. Wilpert,[9] on the other hand, recognizes it as the scene from the sacred text, in which Susanna is vindicated; she is shown facing Daniel, who interrogates and confutes the two old men separately. In the cemetery of Sts. Peter and Marcellinus, Susanna is represented in a garden, between the two old men, and in that of Praetextatus, her name is written over the figure of a lamb, between two wolves designated by the name "seniores" ("old men"). These various frescoes prove that, from the third century, the Christians used not only the protocanonical books of the Scriptures, but the deuterocanonical books as well. All these ideas are to be referred to the concept of prayer for the repose of the soul.

TOBIAS. — One painting of the cemetery of Thraso represents Tobias offering the angel Raphael the fish caught in the river Tigris. In this scene, we are to recognize the symbol of the divine fish, that is, Christ, Who enlightens and heals.

TOBIAS.
Cemetery of Thraso. Fourth century.

## 2.   Scenes from the New Testament

In these paintings, as in those of the Old Testament, we can at times recognize a solemn profession of Christian beliefs.

THE ANNUNCIATION. — This is a subject only rarely treated and the existing representations in the cemeteries of Priscilla and Callistus are in a very bad state of preservation.

THE CRIB. — There is only one known painting of this, in the cemetery of St. Sebastian. It adorns the vault of an *arcosolium* of the fourth century, at the base of which is traced the monogram. The Infant Jesus is lying on a table and at His side may be seen an ox and ass. Above the Infant is a bust of the Saviour. Unfortunately, the painting was recently washed by an inexpert hand and at present is in such a state of ruin as to be scarcely visible.

MOSES. THE CRIB. AN ORANS.
Cemetery of St. Sebastian. Fourth century.

The same Christian subject, however, was often reproduced on the sarcophagi, as can be seen from examples in the Lateran Museum. De Rossi published the designs of a fragment of a sarcophagus with this scene, dating from the year 343. In these representations, St. Joseph almost always has the appearance of a young man.

THE EPIPHANY. — This is one of the subjects most often represented. During the second century, it is to be found in the Greek chapel of Priscilla, and during the third and fourth in numerous others. The number of the Magi is not constant; there are two, three, four or even more. On a vase in the Kircher Museum there are eight, but the most frequent number is the traditional three. The Magi are not dressed in royal clothes, but have Phrygian caps and the costumes of great Persian personages, like Sts. Abdon and Sennen in a painting of the cemetery of Pontian. The Romans would presumably have a special preference for this scene because it records the calling of the Gentiles to Christianity.

THE BAPTISM OF THE SAVIOUR. — There is one painting of this scene in the crypts of Lucina in the cemetery of Callistus. The presence of the dove proves that the picture refers to the Baptism of the Saviour and not to that of one of the faithful.

In a painting of the cemetery of Praetextatus, believed
by some, though without
reason, to be the Crowning
with Thorns, one may recognize the scene of the testimony of John the Baptist
which has a relation with the
Baptism of the Saviour.

THE GOSPEL MIRACLES. —
The miracles found repre-
sented in the catacombs are:
the multiplication of the

THE BAPTISM OF THE SAVIOUR.
Cemetery of Callistus. Second century.

loaves, the marriage feast at Cana, the cure of the man born blind (more frequent on sarcophagi than in paintings). Re-cently there has also been found a painting showing the scene of the woman bowed together, mentioned in the Gospel of St. Luke.[10] The commonest subject of all is the raising of Lazarus from the dead. This is found from the beginning of the second century in the cemetery of Priscilla. The picturing of this miracle in the art of the catacombs demonstrates that from the second century, the Gospel of St. John was considered as canonical as the three synoptics; it is the only Gospel which recounts this episode. In the details, however, the paintings of the catacombs are not based on the account of St. John. The story of the raising of Lazarus from the dead was given to the Christians as the most beautiful symbol of our future resurrection and of the promised salvation of the Redeemer. In this sense, it was invoked in the funeral liturgies. The use of this scene in the catacombs is also symbolical. Here, in fact, details are superfluous; two persons suffice to render the scene recognizable — Jesus Christ and Lazarus. Christ, the Wonderworker, is characterized by the rod in His hand, a symbol among the ancients and in the Bible of a beneficent power and strength which came from God. The tomb, on the other hand, typifies Lazarus. Instead of the cave which St. John mentions, the painters of the catacombs depicted a mausoleum in the form of a temple, a *heroon,* because this could be drawn with greater ease and simplicity and was easier to understand. However, it assumes the most varied forms; at times it is only a few steps and a door on high; again it appears to be a small basilica with its own stairway, columns forming a triangular front and a nave with windows. Two frescoes of the third century in the cemetery of Callistus show us the second act of the drama: the risen Lazarus, clothed in a tight-fitting tunic, coming out of the tomb in obedience to the command of the Redeemer. The usual style of representation shows Lazarus as a child, wrapped in the winding cloths used for the dead (as in the case of Egyptian or Jewish mummies), rising to the outside level of the tomb.[11] This is related to the Passion of Christ; we will speak of it in the section reserved for the images of the Redeemer.

### 3.   Scenes Referring to the Soul of the Deceased

The scene of the particular judgment of the soul, sometimes difficult to recognize, sometimes more evident, belongs almost always to the third and fourth centuries. There is an example of it in the cemetery of St. Hermes, in a painting thought for a long time to depict "a sacred ordination" (see page 309). In the center is a seated figure; two others assist on the right and on the left; an Orans stands in front, at the foot of the group. The scene recalls an inscription of Vercelli in which a soul is congratulated because it is assisted at the judgment seat by two martyrs:

O FELIX GEMINO MERVIT QVI MARTIRE DVCI, etc.

In this painting of the cemetery of St. Hermes the two martyrs are the local saints, Protus and Hyacinth.

At other times, for example, on an *arcosolium* of the cemetery of Cyriaca, the soul is pictured as a woman who stands alone in front of the Divine Judge. In the cemetery of Sts. Peter and Marcellinus also, the soul is shown at the judgment-seat, in the vault of a cubicle where the decoration has been made to follow this logical order: the Annunciation, the Epiphany, the Baptism of the Saviour, the Good Shepherd and the Orans. The cycle is completed by the miracles of the Saviour, namely, the curing of the paralytic, the man born blind and the woman with a flow of blood, and the scene of the Samaritan woman at the well.[12] All these scenes are the expression of the faith of the departed and a reinforcement of those burial inscriptions which so often repeat "Credidit in Deo," "Credidit in Christo," "Credidit in Deo Christo": "He believed in God," "He believed in Christ," "He believed in God Christ."

THE JUDGMENT OF A SOUL.
Cemetery of St. Hermes. Fourth century.

These paintings often represent heaven and the saints who assist the deceased to enter heaven. At times, the heavenly

mansion is substituted for the heavenly garden. A fresco of the
cemetery of Cyriaca shows the entrance to a house, and a martyr
lifting the latch of a door; a fragment of an inscription of the
Lateran Museum shows the interior with some columns. Thus
a crypt of the cemetery of Domitilla shows St. Petronilla, who
seems to be leading the matron Veneranda into heaven (see
page 311). All these scenes illustrate the words of the Redeemer: "In My Father's house there are many mansions,"[13]
and also express the belief that the saints would accompany
the soul to heaven. At times, the Orans is surrounded by can-

*ARCOSOLIUM* IN THE CEMETERY OF CYRIACA.   Fourth century.

The Saviour among the Wise Virgins. The soul received by the saints.
The denial of St. Peter. The miracle of the manna.

delabra, lamps, symbols of the eternal light or of the knowledge which leads to heaven: "Thy word, O Lord, is a light to my feet."[14]

The scrolls which are seen in the hands of the Saviour, the martyrs or the departed are important for the history of the New Testament, for they certainly represent the Sacred Scriptures. They figure in the paintings prior to the time of Constantine; in those of a later date, there are found instead the *codex* and the book, which began to be used in the second half of the third century, and at the beginning of the fourth were employed for the Holy Scriptures. The Vatican manuscript (Codex B) belongs to this epoch. During the fifth century, in the mosaics of St. Pudentiana's and St. Sabina's, the book definitely takes the place of the scroll.

ST. PETRONILLA INTRODUCING A SOUL INTO HEAVEN.
Cemetery of Domitilla. Fourth century.

Zahn and Schultze have observed that when the scroll was used there could be no thought of order in the classification of the Gospels, because each scroll contained only one of them. The order of the Gospels in use nowadays is certainly very old, and seems to have been that of the Canon of Muratori. Schultze thinks that it was taken from the illustrated monuments; but up to the end of the third century, the combinations vary greatly.

## Chapter VII

## PICTURES OF THE SAVIOUR AND THE SAINTS

### 1.  Pictures of the Saviour

ANCIENT Christian art represented the Saviour under the image of the Good Shepherd or of the Master, always picturing Him as an ideal type, a type of the classical Roman. Perhaps the Romans, who despised the Oriental races, wished thus to express their belief that the Saviour had not come only for the Hebrew people.

Throughout the Orient there were images of the Redeemer which were held to be authentic portraits.  In proof of this, a letter was cited which Publius Lentulus, procurator of Judea, was said to have sent to the Roman Senate, giving an account of the Passion of Christ and a description of His Countenance.[1] This letter is apocryphal, as are all the pictures called *achero-pite* and those attributed to Nicodemus and St. Luke.[2] The same is true of the letter Christ is supposed to have sent, along with His picture, to Abgar, king of Edessa.[3] This was declared apocryphal in a council held under Pope Gelasius in 494.[4] The picture mentioned above is cited for the first time by Evagrius.[5]

Eusebius speaks of a statue which, according to an ancient tradition, was supposed to have been erected by the woman mentioned in the Gospel as cured of a flow of blood, and which still existed in his time, at Paneas in Palestine.[6]  Some historians have claimed that this statue represented one of the Roman emperors, seeing the personification of a province in the figure at the statue's base which rendered him homage under the title of its "Saviour." The word ΣΩΤΗΡΙ must have produced this confusion, but the opinion is inadmissible; no one can imagine that Eusebius committed such an egregious error. This statue, which was held in great veneration at the beginning of the fourth century, must have had a certain resemblance to the real type of the Saviour, and served as a model for the Oriental pictures and those introduced into the Occident toward the end of the same century. In these paintings, the Saviour is represented as having a beard. In the most ancient He has a sweet and beautiful countenance; later, from the fourth century onward, His expression becomes somewhat severe.

From these types the ancient iconographic pictures of Christ were derived — bearded images with long, flowing hair, such as may be seen in some paintings dating from the time of peace.

From this period on, this type began to spread throughout the Occident. However, it must be remembered that the oldest type, and the one commonly employed in the Occident, was that of the Good Shepherd. A fourth-century bust of the Saviour, with a beard, is shown in the cemetery of Domitilla.[7]

To these images there was soon added, as a sign of distinction, the nimbus or halo. In ancient art it was a mark of power, and at times it was given to the pagan divinities.

Cemetery of Pontian. Sixth century.

It had its origin in the disc of metal which was placed over the statue to protect it from the inclemencies of the weather. The emperor's image on coins was at times set off by a halo; hence this sign later became a symbol of a superior being.

Thus it happened that the nimbus was first given to the Saviour, then to the angels and the Blessed Virgin, and finally to the saints. It was formed, successively, of a circle, several circles, and later, a circle cut by a cross. This last type of halo (see accompanying cut) was reserved for the Saviour.

Cemetery of Generosa.  Seventh century.

THE VIRGIN. THE SAVIOUR. ST. SMARAGDUS.
Catacombs of Albano.  Seventh century.

The pictures of Christ crucified are not by any means as old, because early Christian art always avoided representing any of the episodes of the Passion[8] in a manner which would reveal their stark reality. No painting in the catacombs of the first centuries does so.

The effort to hide the scenes of the Passion can be observed on a beautiful sarcophagus of the fourth century in the Christian Museum of the Lateran.[9] Even the cross was not clearly shown until the fifth century. Before this period, it was very rarely represented in the catacombs.[10] It was customarily symbolized by an anchor, by a lamb beneath an anchor, by a dolphin over a trident, etc., as shown in the inserted figure.

The abolition of the penalty of crucifixion by the command of Constantine was not sufficient to overcome all the repugnance of the Christians. During the fourth century, the monogrammatic cross is found; but the cross alone shows

THE BAPTISM OF THE SAVIOUR.
Cemetery of Pontian.  Sixth century.

itself only during the reign of Theodosius, when the Christian religion became the religion of the Empire. It may be supposed, however, that the Christians used the cross and even the crucifix in their private devotions, as is indicated by the celebrated crucifix discovered on the Palatine.[11]

In the first representations, the cross, being adorned with flowers and gems, is called the *gemmed cross* (*crux gemmata*).

GEMMED CROSS.
Cemetery of Pontian.   Sixth century.

There are numerous examples of this still to be seen not only in paintings but also in mosaics. In the baptistery of the cemetery of Pontian, beneath the scene of the Baptism, there is depicted a gemmed cross which seems to arise from the water (see cut above). It is entirely surrounded by flowers, candelabra are upon its arms, and suspended therefrom are the letters A and Ω.  The Syrian Evangelary of the Laurentian library of Florence (sixth century) has an image of the crucifix.

A mosaic of the seventh century, at St. Stephen Rotondo's in Rome, represents a cross surmounted by a bust of the Saviour. On a vial of the priest John, preserved in the treasury of Monza, the Redeemer appears to pray between two figures, possibly the thieves, though the cross is hidden.  A like scene is found in the sculpture in wood on the door of St. Sabina's, a work of the fifth century.

CRUCIFIX WITH ST. JOHN THE EVANGELIST.
Cemetery of St. Valentine.  Seventh century.

Thus it is apparent that up to the seventh century there were no real pictures of the crucifixion. They probably appeared first in miniature, to illustrate manuscripts; later on they were used on public monuments.  The cemetery of St. Valentine has the only crucifix found in the Catacombs of Rome (seventh century). It was seen and copied by Bosio.[12] In his sketch, Christ is clothed in a long garment and His hands and feet are held to the cross by four nails, a number conformable with tradition, as St. Gregory of Tours expressly declares: "Clavorum ergo dominicorum gratia quod quatuor fuerint haec est ratio: duo sunt affixi in palmis, et duo in plantis."[13]

A painting in the subterranean church of Sts. John and Paul is analogous to that in St. Valentine's. The same may be said of Old St. Mary's (eighth century). In the basilica of St.

CRUCIFIX OF OLD ST. MARY'S.
Eighth century.

Clement, the Crucified is represented naked with a loin cloth and four nails (middle of the n i n t h century). The modern representation of the crucifix with three nails was not introduced until about the twelfth century. At that time, Christ was represented very realistically. His feet were pierced by one nail instead of two in order to give the body a more artistic finish and an aspect which was more effective in moving or impressing the faithful.[14]

With respect to the painting in Old St. Mary's it may be pertinent to recount an incident communicated to the author by Cav. Romolo Ducci. In company with the late lamented Joseph Gatti, he observed, some days after the discovery of this fresco, that "from the pierced side of Christ, a drop of blood flowed and fell exactly on the eyes of Longinus." He believes that this should be viewed in connection with the legend which says that Longinus became blind after having pierced the side of the Saviour.

## 2. Pictures of the Blessed Virgin

The Virgin was ordinarily represented in the paintings of the catacombs in a seated position, with the Infant Jesus on her lap or at her breast, as may be seen in the paintings of the Epiphany showing the Magi. At times the presence of a prophet indicates that the woman represented is Mary. In the one painting of the cemeteries showing the crib, the Blessed Virgin is not included, though she appears in sculpture. She was frequently shown in the guise of an Orans, as may be seen on the gilded glass of the third and fourth centuries, in which she is often specifically named, even though she may be portrayed in the midst of other saints: MARA or MARIA, AGNE MARIA, PETRVS, MARIA, PAVLVS.

On the glass bearing these last names, a scroll may be seen to the right and left of the Virgin, an emblem of the Law and the Two Testaments. A monument of St. Maximinus in Provence shows the Virgin as an Orans with the following inscription: MARIA VIRGO MINESTER DE TEMPLVO GEROSALE. It has already been noted that the Orans near the Good Shepherd at times represents the Virgin.[15] However, it is not easy to guess when the artist had this in mind; in general, the Orans represents rather the soul of the departed. The symbol of the Church is often united to that of the Virgin: "Quam pulchra illa quae in figura Ecclesiae de Maria prophetata sunt."[16] When there are no guiding inscriptions, it is difficult to decide with certainty whether the Orans pictures the Virgin or the Church.

There are no traditional types of the Virgin; hence as far back as the fourth century, St. Augustine could say: "Neque enim novimus faciem Virginis Mariae" — "We do not know what the countenance of the Virgin Mary looked like."[17]

A list is given here of the most important paintings of the Virgin known at present in the Roman catacombs, some of which will be reproduced with explanatory remarks. There are many works which may be consulted by anyone desiring more information on this point.

Cemetery of Priscilla (a picture of the second and one of the third century).

Cemetery of Domitilla (third century).

Cemetery of Callistus (third century).

Cemetery of Sts. Peter and Marcellinus (third century).

THE OLDEST PICTURE OF THE BLESSED VIRGIN.
Cemetery of Priscilla. First half of the second century.

Greater Cemetery of St. Agnes (fourth century).

Cemetery of Commodilla (sixth century).

Cemetery of St. Valentine (seventh century).

De Rossi was the first to give a chronological account of the pictures of the Blessed Virgin found in the catacombs.[18] The principal examples of these pictures are of great interest:

THE CEMETERY OF PRISCILLA.[19] — This contains the oldest
of the pictures of the Blessed Virgin, which forms part of the
decoration of a tomb in an ancient subterranean chamber (page
320). In the center of the painting is seen the Good Shepherd
in stucco; to the left, a man, a woman and a child, each in the
attire of an Orans, form a group representing the family which
owned the chamber. To the right we see the Virgin, seated,
with the Infant Jesus at her breast. A figure in the foreground
probably represents a prophet; a star placed above allows the

MOSES. THE VIRGIN WITH THE MAGI. NOE.
Cemetery of Sts. Peter and Marcellinus. Third century.

impression of its being Isaias, who communicates the divine
light; or it may be Micheas or Balaam.[20] This scene does not
represent the members of an actual family; the reproduction of
domestic scenes is very rare in ancient Christian art, and it is
certain, on the other hand, that all the decorations used on this
tomb were symbolic and of a sacred nature. The classical Pompeian style of painting permits us to place its date at the beginning of the second century, a judgment which has been accepted
by some critics not of our faith. For the rest, the chapel is
situated in the oldest section of the cemetery, a short distance

from the primitive inscriptions, and recent excavations have brought to light, below its actual level, a number of tombs with very ancient inscriptions; yet these tombs were dug after the graves lying above, and hence are later than the painting. In the light of all this, we see how untenable are the opinions of certain foreign archeologists who attribute this painting to the sixth century.

CONSECRATION OF A VIRGIN. AN ORANS. THE BLESSED VIRGIN.
Cemetery of Priscilla. Third century.

In the Greek chapel of the same cemetery is to be found the oldest painting of the Epiphany, which is likewise of the second century.

Another painting of this cemetery represents the person buried there in the form of an Orans; to the left is seen a bishop, assisted by a deacon, giving the veil to a holy virgin and showing to her the Blessed Virgin as her model. The Blessed Virgin is represented with the Infant Jesus on her lap. The painting has been interpreted as a reproduction of a scene of real life, but this is inacceptable. The opinion above is more natural and logical (see cut above). This group is of the greatest importance because it proves that the Virgin Mary was represented by the first Christians not only as a subject of veneration, but also as a model of virtue to be imitated.

It is noteworthy that these three most important pictures of the Virgin are found in the oldest Christian cemetery of Rome, namely, that of Priscilla, which goes back to apostolic times.

CEMETERY OF DOMITILLA.[21] — This contains a third-century painting on the wall of a corridor between two tombs, dealing with the Epiphany. The Virgin is veiled and seated on a chair with the Infant Jesus on her knees. The Magi number

THE EPIPHANY.
Cemetery of Domitilla. End of the third century.

four, though on another fresco of the same cemetery their number is three (see page 324), which is more common.

CEMETERY OF STS. PETER AND MARCELLINUS.[22] — This cemetery also contains a scene of the Epiphany. There are only two Magi shown. The Virgin is pictured bareheaded. It is known that the veil, distinctive of the Roman matron, was also given to consecrated virgins, as spouses of the Divine Lamb; but in this painting there is an allusion to the virginal integrity of Mary, who is therefore represented as a maiden (see page 321).

CEMETERY OF CALLISTUS.[23] — A scene of the Epiphany with three Magi is found in this cemetery.

GREATER CEMETERY OF ST. AGNES.[24] — On an *arcosolium* of the fourth century, Fr. Marchi recognized a picture of the Blessed Virgin with the Child Jesus (see page 325); to the right and left may be seen the Constantinian monogram turned toward the Infant, to indicate that it is Christ.[25]

This new type of the Virgin was not a solitary example, but continued to be employed until the early Middle Ages.

It is also preserved for us in pictures of the Byzantine style so common in the Orient.

CEMETERY OF COMMODILLA.[26] — In the historical crypts of Sts. Felix and Adauctus, discovered in 1904, there was found a remarkable painting in an excellent state of preservation, showing the Virgin Mary seated upon a gem-studded throne as a queen, with the Child Jesus on her knees. The Infant holds a

RAISING OF LAZARUS FROM THE DEAD.
THE EPIPHANY WITH THE THREE MAGI. THE PARALYTIC.
Cemetery of Domitilla. Fourth century.

scroll in His hands. At the sides may be seen the figures of Sts. Felix and Adauctus, the first rolling a scroll, the other presenting a woman (the person buried in the tomb) with a volume of the law. This painting is not later than Pope John (523-526) who decorated this cemetery (see page 326).

CEMETERY OF ST. VALENTINE.[27] — This also contains a picture of the Virgin in Byzantine style. It is of the seventh century. That it is the Virgin is indicated by what is left of the inscription: SCA DEI GENETRIX,[28] "Mother of God."

To understand the significance of these pictures, against which Protestant archeologists, especially Roller, have raised objections which are more specious than solid, it is necessary to remember that the saints, the martyrs, were represented on the burial monuments as the advocates of the departed.[29] Hence, the Virgin is the advocate par excellence. "Advocata," in fact, is what St. Irenaeus (second century) actually calls her. For that reason she is represented at all times as occupying the position of honor, seated on a chair, which is the symbol at one and the same time of her power and her dignity.

THE BLESSED VIRGIN WITH THE CHILD JESUS.
Greater Cemetery of St. Agnes. Fourth century.

Finally, the symbolism of these paintings cannot be denied, but its explanation must be sought, as has been said, in the liturgical prayers of the Church. In some ancient inscriptions is to be found the formula: "Refrigeret tibi domnus Ippolitus," etc. — "May St. Hippolytus refresh thee," etc. The analogous prayer "Refrigeret tibi domna Maria" has not yet been found, but the thought is already conveyed by these pictures.

If the Christians had not a sentiment of veneration for the Blessed Virgin, how can we explain the presence of the many pictures of her found upon the walls of the catacombs, on gilt glass and on the sarcophagi? And there would be many more if numerous monuments had not been destroyed, or if all those still hidden by ruins were known.

These monuments, therefore, supplemented by the ancient liturgical prayers and the writings of the Fathers, all agree that, long before the Council of Ephesus, the Christians well knew how to worship Christ by venerating and honoring His mother, the Blessed Virgin Mary.

ST. ADAUCTUS. THE BLESSED VIRGIN. ST. FELIX.
Cemetery of Commodilla. Sixth century.

### 3.  Pictures of the Saints

Paintings of the particular judgment and the justification of the soul have already shown us the saints as intercessors, as advocates.[30]

The Orans, in general, figures the soul of one departed, who prays in heaven for those who are still living. It expresses the faith of the early Christians in the Communion of Saints.

Paintings of the martyrs have a special importance at times; this may arise from the locality in which the martyr was buried, or from the great veneration paid to him. There is an example of this in a painting in the crypt of St. Cecilia which represents three saints buried elsewhere: St. Sebastian, St. Quirinus and St. Policamus. The last-named is unknown; the other two had been interred in the cemetery known as *ad Catacumbas*.

Portraits of the saints are more frequent on stained glass than in paintings. The pictures of St. Agnes, St. Sixtus, St. Peter and St. Paul are often found on stained-glass objects. Numbers of these articles are from the third century; they were employed in the agapes and later given away as gifts. It is noteworthy that many of these glass objects contain the pictures of Peter and Paul, a fact which confirms the tradition of their common apostolate in Rome.

The pictures of the two apostles agree in type with the description given in the *Clementine Books* which, though apocryphal, date from great antiquity. The earliest article exhibiting this type is a medal found in the cemetery of Domitilla which de Rossi judged to be no later than the third century, on the basis of a comparison with another of the time of Alexander Severus.

Besides these isolated figures, Christian art presented groups of saints. One of the columns of the altar of the basilica of St. Petronilla carries in relief the scene of the martyrdom of St. Achilleus; the other column must evidently have shown a corresponding scene of the martyrdom of St. Nereus. Prudentius describes two scenes of martyrdom which he saw depicted, one in the chapel of St. Hippolytus on the Tiburtine Way and the other on the tomb of St. Cassian, martyr of Imola.[31] According to St. Paulinus, analogous paintings adorned the basilica of St. Felix at Nola.[32]

It is true that Protestant objectors have cited a decree of the Council of Elvira (305): "Placuit picturas in ecclesiis esse non debere"—"There should be no paintings in churches." But this prohibition was local, and only temporary besides, being due to the circumstance of the persecution of Diocletian. The council had in mind those churches which were accessible to pagans, of which there were even then quite a number, in Spain and elsewhere. It would have been extremely dangerous had paintings in such churches given the pagans the least idea of an idolatrous worship on the part of Christians. Hence the prohibition of paintings.

Cemetery of Domitilla.

At the time of the peace of the Church, these paintings increase, beginning with representations of the triumph of the martyrs who offer their crowns to Christ or receive them from His hands.[33] In the fifth century, the saints are shown with a halo as a mark of distinction, but neither the cross nor the monogram is included.

Following this epoch, great compositions were begun after the fashion of those made in mosaics. The great fresco in the cemetery of Sts. Peter and Marcellinus, for instance, representing the Saviour seated amid Sts. Peter and Paul and five local martyrs, dates from the fifth century. At the base of the painting may be seen a lamb on a hillock whence the four symbolical streams are depicted as flowing.

Again, in the cemetery of Domitilla, there is a magnificent fresco of the fourth century in the style usually found in basilicas, representing the Saviour in the midst of His apostles.

In the cemetery of Felicitas, on the Salarian Way, may be observed a painting of the Saviour, with a halo, crowning St. Felicitas and her children, who hold other crowns in their hands. Their names are written close to their pictures:P*hilip*
PVS, MARTIA*lis,* S*ilanus,* IaNVA*rius, Felix, Vitalis, Alex-*

*ander.* This style of composition is very frequent during the fifth and sixth centuries. Later on appears the Byzantine style to which belong the pictures of St. Cecilia and Sts. Cornelius and Cyprian in the cemetery of Callistus (see below and page 282). In this same category fall the paintings found in the cemetery

ST. CORNELIUS AND ST. CYPRIAN.
Cemetery of Callistus. Sixth century.

of St. Valentine. It must be noted, however, that the decorations of the underground chapel of St. Valentine were made after the removal of the body of the saint to the external basilica. This was restored by Honorius. Hence his picture was placed here for purposes of veneration by the devout, as was the picture of St. Cyprian in the crypt of St. Cornelius. These Byzantine paintings of the historical crypt were the last to be executed in the catacombs before their final abandonment.

---

To complete the section on the paintings in the catacombs, a word may be said concerning paintings made from real life. The few which have come down to us belong entirely to the period in which peace was granted to the Church, and are less elegant than the contemporary paintings of the same topics in pagan art. In general, they represent the professions of the departed. Thus, in the cemetery of Callistus, de Rossi found the painting of a seller of herbs; in that of Domitilla, Wilpert ascribed certain paintings to scenes taken from the lives of bakers (*corpus pistorum*). In the cemetery of Priscilla and in the Greater Cemetery of St. Agnes may be seen paintings dating from the fourth century, representing wine merchants.

## Chapter VIII

## EARLY CHRISTIAN SCULPTURE

EARLY Christian sculpture is represented by many sarcophagi, but by very few statues.

### 1. Sarcophagi[1]

Christians made use of sarcophagi from the earliest times. Fragments of them are found in the oldest underground chapel of the Acilii in the cemetery of Priscilla. In the vestibule of the cemetery of Domitilla there is to be seen a grave of special form, consisting of a false sarcophagus made of stucco. Generally, as has been said, the primitive sarcophagi, purchased from those who served the population as a whole, did not possess any specific Christian characteristics, but were adorned like those of the pagans, with lines, lions' heads, marine subjects and topics suggested by the hunt. They of course do not show sculptures which would be actually repugnant to Christian principles.

On the other hand, it is certain that even before the epoch of peace there were Christian sculptors. As an example, there may be seen in the Museum at Urbino an inscription of the sculptor Eutropius. He is here represented in the attire of an Orans, with a dove. Beneath the inscription is a scene showing the making of a sarcophagus and the sculptor chiseling lions' heads.

EUTROPIUS, A CHRISTIAN SCULPTOR.

The inscription reads: "Blessed Eutropius, a worshipper of God, may you rest in peace. Made by his son. Buried ten days before the calends of September."

Only rarely did even these sculptors execute Christian topics on their sarcophagi. On the sarcophagus of Livia Primi-

Louvre Museum. Third century.

tiva (belonging to the apostolic cemetery of the Vatican, but at present in the Louvre) one may observe a scene of the Good Shepherd, the anchor and the fish. Very important and of the greatest antiquity is another sarcophagus, found on the Salarian Way and at present preserved in the Lateran Museum. This has figures, cut in the classical style, of the Good Shepherd and an Orans. Both these sarcophagi are perhaps prior to the third century. Other sarcophagi and fragments may be ascribed to the third century, but the greater part belong to the fourth and fifth centuries.

After the peace of the Church, Christian sculpture developed freely and took its inspiration and subjects from the paintings in the catacombs. But as art was already in its de-

SARCOPHAGUS FROM THE SALARIAN WAY.
Later. Museum. Third century.

cadence, it follows that the sarcophagi of the fourth and fifth centuries are of a rather rough, coarse style. After the fifth century, they are no longer figured, but carry only a few simple decorations, such as crosses, lines, etc.

Sarcophagi showing Christian subjects were employed at times in the subterranean cemeteries, but more often in oratories near the great basilicas, in the cemeteries above ground, etc. Hence it is easy to see why the greater part of such collections come from this source. Oftentimes such structures were covered by a small roof or *tegurium,* as may be seen, for instance, in the vestibule of St. Lawrence's outside the Walls.

Christian sarcophagi are found everywhere and Rome possesses a large number. These are preserved in the Vatican Grottoes, in St. Lawrence's outside the Walls, in the cloister of St. John Lateran, in the National Museum of Rome, etc., but the most remarkable collection is that of the Lateran, arranged by Father Marchi.[2]

These sarcophagi almost always show the same subjects, generally without logical or chronological order. The artists followed their own ideas, without that rational direction which the paintings of the catacombs indicate. At times, it is true, certain scenes evince a logical order. Thus, one of the better sarcophagi of the Lateran, known as the Theological, contains a compendium of the Bible in figures. At the top, to the left, may be seen the creation of man and woman by the Holy

THE SO-CALLED THEOLOGICAL SARCOPHAGUS.
Later. Museum No. 104.  Fourth century.

Trinity; then the fall of Adam and Eve, and a figure of the Word Who makes a distribution of labor, giving man a head of grain and woman a lamb to be shorn of its wool. Beneath this is portrayed the Epiphany, and then a series of miracles which demonstrate the divine mission of Jesus Christ. The first represents the cure of the man gone blind; at the top, to the right, there is the changing of water into wine, followed by the multiplication of the loaves, the raising of Lazarus from the dead and the cure of the woman with a flow of blood. Beneath this, as a remembrance of Christ's Passion, is the three-fold denial of Peter, then St. Peter led to prison, in allusion to the persecution suffered by Christians,[3] and Moses striking the rock, symbol of St. Peter and the authority of the Church. In

ELIAS IN THE CHARIOT.
Later. Museum, No. 149. Fourth century.

the center at the top, in the shield, is a bust of the departed couple, beneath which is seen the praying figure of Daniel in the midst of lions, referring to the prayers for the repose of the soul.

Among the other sarcophagi preserved at the Lateran,[4] No. 149, with the rare subject of the prophet Elias, is reproduced here. Elias is shown on a chariot riding toward heaven, leaving

Later. Museum, No. 171. Fourth century.

his mantle to Eliseus. No. 171 pictures the Redeemer before
Pilate, who washes his hands; the Crowning with Thorns; and
the journey to Calvary. In the center the Resurrection is shown
by featuring the triumphal monogram inside a wreath placed
above a Greek Tau, amidst sleeping soldiers. No. 174 shows
Christ in glory. In the center is a figure of the Saviour, without a beard, seated on a veil figuring the heavenly firma-

Later. Museum, No. 174. Fourth century.

Later. Museum, No. 177. Fourth century.

ment, giving St. Peter and the other apostles the Book
of the Laws. To His left is shown the denial of Peter, the
cure of the woman with a flow of blood and the sacrifice of
Abraham. On sarcophagus No. 177 may be seen a figure
of the Good Shepherd among the twelve sheep; behind the
sheep stand the apostles; to the right stands St. Peter, in the

first place, and the Saviour strokes the sheep before Him. This is an allusion to the words "Feed My sheep." On No. 199 are shown the three Magi with a camel, approaching the crib.

THE CRIB.
Later. Museum, No. 199. Fourth century.
The part on the left after the figures of the Magi is modern.

Near the cradle of the Infant are shown the oxen and the ass. Beyond may be seen the figures of St. Joseph and the Blessed Virgin Mary.

In the Vatican Grottoes is preserved the sarcophagus of Junius Bassus, dating from 359. Beneath the inscription are the customary scenes in two rows. Above the dividing lines may be

SARCOPHAGUS OF JUNIUS BASSUS. Vat. Grot. 359 A. D.

The first group to the left and in the lower row represents Job reproved by his wife. The second group to the left above is the imprisonment of St. Peter. The last group below shows St. Paul led to his martyr-dom. The others are easily recognized and explained.

seen, in miniature, the Divine Lamb resuscitating Lazarus, multiplying the loaves and baptizing.[5]

In connection with sarcophagi, it may not be amiss to mention a few other monuments which are analogous to them. One of these is the door of St. Sabina's, long ascribed to the eleventh century, but shown by Kondakoff to belong to the first half of the fifth — that is, to the same period as the basilica itself.[6] The sculpture of this door (figures, style, costumes) is identical with that of the sarcophagi. It shows episodes of the Old and New Testaments: Adam and Eve, the passage of the Red Sea, the multiplication of the loaves, and a scene from the Passion (the crucifixion represented by Christ praying between two thieves), the scene of the prodigy of Emmaus, etc.

CHRIST IN THE BOAT WITH THE EVANGELISTS.
De Rossi collection. Fourth century.

The Municipal Museum of Brescia possesses a beautiful reliquary which plainly shows the style of the sarcophagi and the door of St. Sabina's. Many resemblances may also be seen in the coverings of the Gospel-books of the fifth century. Thus, on an example in the Vatican, may be seen the Saviour as a youth, seated between two angels; beneath is a representation of the Epiphany. In the National Museum of Rome, two fragments of sarcophagi are noteworthy: one with traces of gilt represents the Sermon on the Mount, the other the scene of Emmaus, a rare thing in Christian sculpture.

In the private collection of de Rossi there is preserved a sarcophagus of the fourth century, containing a representation of a ship, symbol of the Church, piloted by Christ and His Evangelists (see page 337). Outside of Rome there may be mentioned the well-known sarcophagus of Salona (fourth century), at present preserved in the Museum at Spalato, depicting the Good Shepherd in the midst of sheep, and two spouses surrounded by a multitude of young people.

At Ravenna, in the church of St. Apollinaris, are to be found sarcophagi also belonging to the fourth century. At Tolentino, the magnificent sarcophagus of St. Catervus is ornamented with many symbols. Finally, the beautiful collection of sarcophagi of Arles which was studied by Le Blant should be recorded, and those from Roman Africa. All these monuments present the same style as those of Rome and belong to the same period.

## 2.  Statues

During the first three centuries, statues were rare among Christians. The earliest example is the group of Paneas.[7] In the Occident, information concerning statues begins with one of the Good Shepherd. This beautiful work was referred by Mariotti, its first possessor (it is now preserved in the Lateran Museum), to the third century. Its antiquity and its Christian character are indisputable (see page 339). The type of the Good Shepherd has been likened by some to the conventional representation of Mercury carrying a sheep, to which, in fact, it does present certain analogies; we have already noted the fact that the first Christians used pagan models for their own topics and inspiration. However, the attire of the Good Shepherd and the sweetness of His countenance, clearly evident in the Lateran statue, make something quite different from the pagan model. Among the few statues of the Good Shepherd that have come down to us, de Rossi distinguishes two types: the first is the older, the second follows the time of Constantine. The statue under discussion belongs to the first type;[8]

it recalls the style of paintings found in the crypts of Lucina and the sculpturing on the oldest sarcophagi.

We know from Eusebius[9] that Constantine placed statues of the Good Shepherd in bronze on the fountains in public squares of his capital city. An example of this type of statue is preserved in the museum at Constantinople. Generally, the Good Shepherd is represent-ed without a beard, althoug'n there are some figures of the fourth century which are bearded.

The Christians often erect-ed statues to persons whom they held in high veneration. An example is the statue of St. Hippolytus, discovered in 1551 among the ruins of an oratory near an anonymous cemetery on the Tiburtine Way. It was first taken to the Vatican Library and later transferred to the Lateran Museum. The statue belongs to the third century, but the head, hands and chest are of modern workmanship. On the sides of the chair may be seen two long inscriptions in Greek, one containing the Paschal Cycle composed by Hippolytus himself, and the other a list of his writ-ings (see page 340).

THE GOOD SHEPHERD.

Later. Museum. Third century.

The statue of St. Peter in the Vatican is also very old and important, although we lack any definite information concern-ing this outstanding monument. During the time of the icono-

clasts, there is an allusion to a statue of St. Peter held in great
veneration by the Roman people. In the ancient basilica, the
statue in bronze stood in the oratory of St. Martin; Paul V
placed it in its present position. Some archeologists have imagined that this statue is the work of the thirteenth century; but
it is truly classical and according to the more common opinion,
should be ascribed to the fifth. There is absolutely no reason
why it should be compared to the statue of Charles of Anjou
preserved in the Capitoline Museum.

ST. HIPPOLYTUS.

Later. Museum. Third century.

## Chapter IX

## SMALL OBJECTS FOUND IN THE CATACOMBS

THE Christian Museum of the Vatican Library contains a beautiful collection of small objects found either in the tombs or in the mortar used to enclose the burial vaults. The most usual articles are lamps, stained glass, coins, medals, cut stones, and small trinkets for domestic use.

### 1. Stained Glass[1]

Stained-glass relics of the catacombs were made the object of special study in the eighteenth century by Buonarroti, and in the nineteenth by Father Garrucci, the archeologist de Rossi, and more recently, Volpel. They are generally composed of two discs of glass fused together by fire; in the center, on a stained surface, there is depicted or scratched a scene or an inscription. These glasses often formed the bases of cups of which other fragments have been found. They were employed for decorative purposes, or for religious or domestic use, or they were given as gifts on the occasions of marriages or other solemnities. Christians used them also to decorate their tombs.

Sometimes the inscriptions tell us which formed parts of cups: BIBAS, BIBE, "May you drink," "Drink," etc., ΠΙΕ ΖΗΘΗΘ. Whenever religious or symbolic subjects are represented, we may suppose that the cups were used at sacred banquets or perhaps at liturgical functions, because chalices have been found which have the same form as that depicted in the *Breaking of Bread* (see page 291). To this category belong those glass relics which are adorned with the figures of the Redeemer, the Blessed Virgin and the saints, the depiction of Baptism, etc.; while those destined for use at a banquet or marriage or some other civil feast contain only pictures and good wishes, with at times the Saviour in the act of placing a crown on the heads of the married couple. Among the stained-glass objects, the one found at Podgoritza is noteworthy. This plate, which goes back to the fourth century, contains numerous Biblical scenes and inscriptions in cursive characters.[2]  As a rule such glass objects are of the third and fourth centuries, and are very important for the proper study of the symbolism of ancient Christian art.

Some of these glass cups may have served in the sacred agapes and in the funeral rites of the so-called *refrigerium* held in intercession of the departed and in honor of the martyrs.

A painting in one of the chambers discovered in the cemetery of St. Hermes near the chapel of Sts. Protus and Hyacinth, portrays a woman holding a vase, which she is clearly in the act of placing on a grave for the ceremony of the *refrigerium*. This usage might also have had a symbolical meaning: the vase being an emblem of good works, the placing of it on a tomb was an allusion to the reputation which follows the Christian's good deeds. It is likewise probable that this refers to the following passage of the Apocalypse: "Habentes phialas aureas plenas odoramentorum quae sunt orationes sanctorum."[3]

Glass objects buried in the mortar of the tombs in the catacombs are nothing more, for the most part, than the bases of urns or cups placed on the tombs for purposes of decoration. They have nothing in common with the vials of blood, which were rather placed inside the tombs. Le Blant maintains otherwise; but his contention that the outside vials contained the blood of the persons buried in the tombs is arbitrary and inadmissible. In the majority of cases, these vials held balsam and other varieties of perfume.

On the glass objects forming the Vatican collection, various scenes of the Old and New Testament are pictured, such as: (1) Adam and Eve at the Fall, with the inscription PIE; (2) the sacrifice of Abraham, with the sentence ZEZES CVM TVIS SPES HILARIS ("It is our own fervent hope that thou wilt drink with thine own"); (3) Jonas; (4) the raising of Lazarus from the dead, and the multiplication of the loaves, with the inscription: ZESVS CRISTVS; (two others represent the raising of Lazarus, and four the multiplication of loaves); (5) the Good Shepherd, with the words

DIGNITAS AMICORVM PIE ZESES; (6) Jesus in the midst of His apostles; (7) Jesus crowning two spouses, with the in-

PETER AS MOSES.
Glass of the Christian Museum of the Vatican Library.

scription PIE ZESES — DVLCIS ANIMA VIVAS. There are also numerous glass objects which show the Apostles Peter and Paul together, the one at the right and the other at the left. On other glass relics, however, they are only seen singly. One of the two objects reproduced herewith represents St. Peter alone in the act of striking the rock; the other shows St. Paul.

ST. PAUL.
Christian Museum
of the Vatican Library.

Some of these glass objects depict the Blessed Virgin, with the name MARA or MARIA. There are also three glass objects with the picture of St. Agnes between St. Peter and St. Paul, and other examples with figures of various saints, such as St. John the Evangelist, St. Luke, St. Damasus, St. Cyprian, St. Lawrence, St. Genesius, St. Callistus, etc. Some of these bear portraits of persons, alive or dead, the most beautiful example carrying the inscription: EVSEBI ANIMA DVLCIS. Finally there are several glass objects on which are depicted a number of workmen, a workshop and the man in charge, with the inscription: PIE ZESES TV CVM TVIS SEMPER REFRIGERES IN PACE DEI, etc.

A few pagan objects of glass have also been found, but their number is very small. The Vatican Museum likewise possesses four examples of Hebrew glasswork, of which three show the candelabrum with seven candlesticks, and the fourth a view of the temple at Jerusalem. This last probably came from the ancient Jewish cemetery on the Labican Way, because it was found in the vicinity of the cemetery of Sts. Peter and Marcellinus.

## 2.  Lamps[4]

Christian lamps have the same form as those of the pagans, and what was said of sarcophagi also applies to them. There are pagan funerary lamps, others of an absolute Christian character and still others of indifferent character, which were used by Christians. Generally the oldest are artistic and light, while those of a later period are coarse and heavy.

Lamps which are definitely Christian belong especially to the periods of peace; but many showing scenes with the Good Shepherd have been found dating from the third century. Some carry the name of the maker, ANNISER, and Dressel showed that this name should read *Annius Serapiodorus*,[5] the name of a Christian manufacturer who had his workshop in Ostia. This workshop lasted to the fourth century.

In the underground cemeteries, the lamps were used to illumine the galleries and tombs, and were lit especially on the occasions of the anniversaries. Ordinarily they were placed in small niches or fixed in the mortar of the tombs. Besides its usefulness, this light had a symbolical meaning, which may be referred to the words of the Psalm: "Thy word is a lamp unto my feet." The lamp fastened to the tomb signified the lamp of heaven which was invoked when the departed was spoken of: "locum refrigerii, lucis et pacis" — " a place of rest, light and peace."

Christian Museum of the Vatican Library.

Two lamps (one found in an oratory of Tebessa in Africa, now in the Christian museum of the German cemetery of Rome; the other in the Zurla Collection, at present in the Roman seminary) represent the same scene: two Jews carrying a bunch of grapes from the Promised Land. The grapes are evidently a symbol of the Eucharist, just as the vine is an emblem of the cross: "Ipse est bothrus ille qui pependit in ligno" — "He is the grape Who hung on the cross."[6] Evagrius expresses himself in the same manner: "Age nunc, intellige racemum illum ...quem in terra repromissionis duo vectantes reportabant, quod utique figura fuit Christi pendentis in ligno"—"For that reason we are to understand that the bunch of grapes carried by two from the Land of Promise was a figure of Christ hanging on the cross."[7] In the fifth century, Eucherius of Lyons spoke as follows: "Bothrus Ecclesia, sive corpus Domini"— "The bunch of grapes signifies the Church or the Body of Christ."[8] These lamps, presenting such veiled symbolism, may be from a period earlier than the beginning of the peace of the Christ."[8] These lamps, presenting such veiled symbolism, may purposes.

The lamps spoken of thus far are of terra cotta. The

pagans made extensive use of lamps and candelabra of bronze, as may be seen from the large number discovered at Pompeii, and the Christians also employed them. The Vatican Library possesses an example which comes from the *Xenodochium* of Pammachius of Porto; it has the form of a monster biting a fruit and carrying the monogrammatic cross on its head. This symbolizes a victory of Jesus Christ over the demon (see page 345). Another lamp of the fourth century, belonging to the Basilewsky Collection, reproduces the form of a Christian basilica.[9] Still another, found at Rome on the Caelian near the place where the patrician palace of the Valerii stood, and at present preserved in the collection of the Uffizi Gallery at Florence, represents a nave with a veil and carries the following inscription: DOMINVS LEGEM DAT VALERIO SEVERO EVTROPI VIVAS.

### 3.  Medals[10]

An excellent study was made of medals by de Rossi. We divide them, with him, into six principal groups: (1) stamps with signs of Christianity; (2) commemorative coins, which were used as necklaces: (3) discs with figures on them; (4) phylacteries, that is, amulets which are evidence of superstitious practices and often refer to Gnosticism;[11] (5) Byzantine coins furnished with Christian emblems; (6) medals properly so called, used as objects of devotion. Bronze discs were often suspended about the neck; or those of great size were simply kept in the home. Byzantine coins used as medals are generally of the ninth or tenth centuries.

True medals of devotion were round, and pierced by a small hole; they were struck especially on the occasion of Baptism. In the Christian Museum of the Vatican there is a medal, reproduced by de Rossi, which represents the martyrdom of St. Lawrence. There is also another medal of the Zurla Collection depicting this same martyrdom, which shows St. Lawrence in the act of carrying the cross and crushing the serpent beneath his feet.

The custom of carrying devotional objects around the neck is very ancient. In several tombs, objects intended for this usage, dating from the third century, have been found, as for example, small fish in metal, in pewter and in terra cotta. Some of these are preserved in the Christian Museum of the Vatican Library.

MARTYRDOM OF ST. LAWRENCE.
Tomb of St. Lawrence.

## 4.  Miscellaneous Objects[12]

Christian tombs contain a quantity of various objects, for example, articles of domestic use, children's rattles, triumphal symbols, etc. In the Christian Museum of the Vatican, there is a kind of crown in stone in the center of which may be seen a mosaic with the Constantinian monogram and inscription: IN HOC SIGNO SIRICI . . . Evidently this deals with a reproduction of the labarum, applying to the departed Siricius the words read by Constantine: "In hoc signo vinces (or vives)," "In this sign thou shalt conquer (or live)." Some traces of signs resembling this were observed in the mortar of the tombs, and de Rossi was inclined to think that the early Christians had small reproductions made of the labarum which were kept in their homes, or used to decorate their tombs.

The large bronze medallion with the busts of the Apostles Peter and Paul, from the cemetery of Domitilla, has already been shown (see page 327). It will be of interest to mention a few other objects which are found in the early Christian cemeteries.

At times coins of the first, second, third and fourth centuries may be found in the mortar of the tombs in the catacombs. De Rossi has shown a beautiful coin of Severina Augusta, wife of the Emperor Aurelian, found embedded in a tomb in the crypts of Lucina.[13]

There are also glass cups with figures scratched on them or cut in, of a quality very much like that of the plate of Podgoritza. Numerous examples may be seen in the Vatican Museum. A fragment found on the Esquiline shows Biblical scenes with Habacuc, Isaac, the Hebrews in the desert guided by a cloud, and two lions which must have accompanied a picture of Daniel.[14]

In the excavations carried on at Porto, other fragments were brought to light containing pastoral scenes, with the Saviour between two saints, and again between St. Paul and St. Peter, to whom He gives the Book of the Laws.[15] In Sicily a valuable glass cup was found still intact, showing rough scenes representing the raising of Lazarus from the dead. This cup was ascribed by de Rossi to the fourth century.[16]

Examples of painted glass are rather rare, but two samples may be mentioned: one preserved in the Christian Museum in Brescia showing three portraits — according to Odorici and Sala, Galla Placidia and her sons Valentinian and Honorius, but according to others, Ausa with the youths Aderchius and Angilsperga.[17] The other glass relic, with a splendid painting showing scenes of birds and fruits, may be seen still standing on a tomb in a cemetery of the New Salarian Way. It has been reproduced by de Rossi.[18]

There are also found in cemeteries various kinds of glass urns and vases, known as *vasa diatreta* because they are composed of an ovoidal cup surrounded by a glass network. One of these vases was discovered in the cemetery of Priscilla, near the baptistery, a few years ago.[19]

Christians substituted rings with Christian representations and symbols for those of pagan make showing idolatrous or profane subjects. In fact, the catacombs have yielded precious rings of gold and silver with gems and cameos, rings of pewter, of iron and of glass with symbols of the palm, the anchor, the fish with the word IXΘΥC, the dove, the Apocalyptic letters A and Ω, the Constantinian monogram, and even with short inscriptions like: SPES IN DEO ⳨ ; VIVAT or VIVAS IN DEO; VTERE FELIX, etc.[20]

# Part Six

## CHRISTIAN BASILICAS[1]

### Chapter I

### ORIGIN OF THE FORM OF BASILICAS

THE CHRISTIAN basilica has almost always the form of an elongated rectangle with one of the smaller sides terminating in a semicircle.

It is often divided by columns along its greater length so as to give an uneven number of naves. The central nave is covered by an elevated roof with which the two roofs of the naves form an angle.

Some authors pretend that the Christian basilica may have been derived from pagan temple architecture, but this cannot be admitted. Roman temples, built in imitation of Greek temples, were generally small and intended to house only the altar or a statue of some divinity; sacrifices were offered on another altar built outside the temple. If some temples (for example, that of Venus in Rome) showed great proportions, this was due to the amplitude of their porticoes. Pagan temples were ordinarily surrounded by a row of columns (*peripteros*) or two such rows (*dipteros*); the facade might have four, six, eight or even more columns (*tetrastylum, hexastylum,* etc.). Edifices of this sort were not adapted to Christian ceremonies which were performed before a large number of the faithful. It was for this reason that, during the sixth century, no temples were transformed into churches; Christian basilicas were already in existence.

Christian basilicas did not take their interior form from the civil basilicas, the so-called *basilicae forenses.*

The civil basilica arose in Greece, where it was called βασιλική στοά or στοά βασιλέως — the place where the first archon — the ἄρχων βασιλεύς — meted out justice. We do not know exactly what the form of these basilicas was because Vitruvius speaks only of Roman basilicas; but we can imagine that they were like a kind of gallery, as for example, the Loggia of the Lanzi on the Piazza of the Signoria at Florence. The Roman basilicas also served as tribunals, marketplaces and sidewalks.[2] There are some inscriptions which record the specific nature of the business transacted, for example the *nummularii de basilica Iulia.* The basilicas made their appearance during the sixth century of Rome. Titus Livius, in speaking of the year 542, observed: "Neque enim tunc basilicae erant"[3] — "For there were no basilicas at that time." The first was the *basilica Porcia,* near the Comitium, perhaps in the beginning a simple private basilica. Later came the *basilica Aemilia* to the north of the Forum; the *Sempronia* to the south; the *Julia* almost in the same locality; the *Ulpia* in the Forum of Trajan; and the *Constantiniana* near the Forum of Peace.[4] Their form is known from ruins which still remain and from coins of that period bearing their images. It is through coins of the *gens Aemilia* and of Trajan that we know that the basilicas of Aemilia and Ulpia each had two stories. The Julian and Ulpian basilicas are pictured on the arch of Septimius Severus.

The Constantinian basilica in the Forum had great arches, much after the fashion of those of the Vatican basilica. In the beginning it also had an apse facing the principal entrance which was located on the side of the Flavian Amphitheater. The statue of the emperor must have stood in the body of the apse. However, not all the civil basilicas possessed the same form; some of them were open, others closed; some had apses, others had not. Many, such as the basilicas of Julia and Ulpia, had upper galleries. For this reason, the old theory, followed by Nibby, Ciampini and Canina, who claimed that the Christian basilicas were derived from this basilica only, must be greatly modified.[5]

Christian basilicas were not even derived from the *basilica equestris exercitatoria,* which was a species of riding school.

In 1886 Brown advanced the opinion that they might have been derived from the oratories built in the ancient cemeteries, basing his contention especially on the resemblance offered by the *cella trichora.*[6] Against this theory may be urged that the basilicas almost never had this form, analogous to the Greek Cross, which is often used as a model for modern churches.

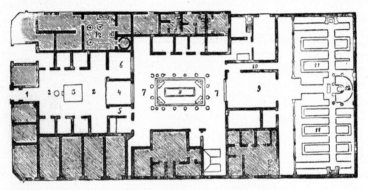

THE HOME OF PANSA (Pompeii).

The most acceptable theory is that the Christian basilica, considered generally, may be an imitation of a Roman home, where the first reunions must have been held, and that in time it reproduced some part of the civil basilica, whether public or private. This conclusion is strengthened by a comparative study of various monuments.[7]

As may be seen from the many examples furnished by the excavations at Pompeii, the arrangement of Roman houses was almost always the same (see cut above): a vestibule (1) at the entrance, flanked by walls, followed immediately by a first court-yard or *atrium* (2) and some rooms, the kitchen, *lararium,* etc., and then by a second courtyard surrounded by columns, the so-called *peristylium* (7). In the middle of each courtyard there was a basin, the *impluvium* (3, 8); in the body of the *peri-*

*stylium* was the salon or reception room, the *tablinum* (9) and leading off from it were corridors, the *fauces* (5, 10) which often led to a second peristyle or rather to a *viradarium* or garden.

This general arrangement is also found in Christian basilicas; they have a vestibule, an *atrium* with a fountain, a peristyle with columns and finally, the nave, which corresponds to the *tablinum*.

The style of the churches is almost the same as that of a public or private basilica. The basilica of Constantine, for example, might have been transformed into a Christian church with almost no modifications.

Vitruvius expressly speaks of rich homes which had true private basilicas. These were found among the magistrates, in the imperial palaces, etc., which served for the administration of justice.[8] The basilica of the home of the Flavii

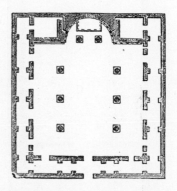

PRIVATE BASILICA OF THE
HOUSE OF THE FLAVII
ON THE PALATINE.

on the Palatine is well known, and presents a very close analogy to Christian basilicas. This adaptation of the classical forms to Christian liturgical usages did not arise only at the time of peace, for we already find important examples of architecture of the style of the basilicas in the catacombs which are perhaps prior to the time of Constantine.[9]

## Chapter II

## PARTS OF A BASILICA

AFTER passing through the vestibule and the *atrium* (A), when this existed, one had to go through a corridor or *narthex* (B), where the catechumens and penitents, who had not the right to assist at Mass, remained; from this point one could easily get to the interior of the basilica. Toward the end of

the central nave could be found the choir (*schola cantorum*),
surrounded by lattice work (G) with the ambones for the

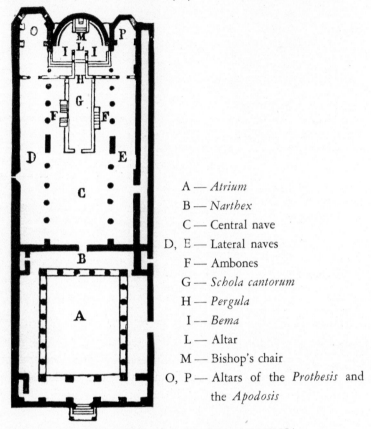

A — *Atrium*

B — *Narthex*

C — Central nave

D, E — Lateral naves

F — Ambones

G — *Schola cantorum*

H — *Pergula*

I — *Bema*

L — Altar

M — Bishop's chair

O, P — Altars of the *Prothesis* and
the *Apodosis*

GENERAL TYPE OF A CHRISTIAN BASILICA.

Epistle and Gospel on the right and left (F). Higher up were
situated the *bema* (I) and the altar (L), and beyond these
were the apse with seating for the clergy and the bishop's
chair (M).

Basilicas sometimes have but one nave, though as a rule
they have three or five — rarely a larger number.[1]

The altar was constructed over the tomb of a martyr, or
it was simply a memorial, depending on whether the basilica
was in the city or in the catacombs.[2] In the Lateran basilica, in
place of the tomb there was a modern altar, on which, accord-

ing to a tradition, St. Peter is supposed to have said Mass. In some localities altars were consecrated with the so-called *patrocinia sanctorum,* or with beams touching the tombs of the martyrs. Following the removal of the bodies of the martyrs into the city, confessionals in imitation of the galleries of the catacombs were built. This is exemplified in the basilica of St. Praxedes. The isolated altar was covered by a *ciborium* or tabernacle with four columns, from which were suspended two veils and a dove of precious metal containing the Eucharist.

The pergola, corresponding to the *iconostasis* of the Greeks, separated the altar from the choir. It was composed of an architrave of marble or of wood supported by columns; lamps hung down from it as well as ex-voto gifts, etc.[3] The *plutei* or partitions which closed off the choir or the space reserved for the singers were often sculptured with ornaments of a symbolic or decorative character.

The bishop's chair (throne) and the seats for the clergy were generally in the body of the apse; but at times there were exceptions to this. Thus in the basilica of Parenzo, later transformed, the body of the apse was originally occupied by the tomb of the local martyr and the bishop's chair was placed ahead.[4] Sometimes the apse, instead of being closed, ended with arches which gave access to a gallery for women, as in the basilica of St. Severus in Naples, and in those of Sts. Cosmas and Damian, St. Sebastian and St. Mary Major, in Rome. The basilica of St. John Lateran showed this same feature until recently, when it was destroyed by works of renovation and reconstruction.

In some basilicas, especially in Rome, a transverse nave cut across the principal one, and in the body of the apse with which it terminated, two small altars were erected where the sacrificial oblation began and ended, a practice remaining in some Oriental rites. The altar where the sacrifice was prepared was called the *prothesis.* At times, there was also another altar where the Sacred Species were consumed, as is still the rite among the Greeks. This arrangement may be seen in Rome in the ruins of the basilica of St. Valentine on the Flaminian Way.[5]

The space reserved for the faithful was divided between the men and women. Until the time of the meetings in the catacombs,[6] the two sexes were separated. An inscription in the ancient basilica of the Vatican records that "the left side is for the men."[7] For the great, there were reserved places called respectively *matroneum* and *senatorium;* the *matroneum* did not comprise only the upper gallery, corresponding to our tribunal and the *matroneum* in civil basilicas, because it existed in all Christian basilicas, while the special gallery was found only in some. These two separate places were to be found at the ends of the parts reserved for each sex, that is, near the sanctuary.

The different parts of the basilica were separated by veils, and may still be traced by the heads of the nails once used to fasten them in place. This is especially noticeable on the columns of the basilica of Liberius.[8]

Light was admitted into the churches through windows of different sizes and varying numbers. Glass was already known, but slabs of marble of the most varied designs were used for these windows, as may be seen from the reproduction below.

 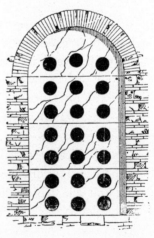

To conclude this brief description, two very singular monuments are reproduced, both of African origin. One is a lamp in bronze found near Orléansville and the other a mosaic recently discovered at Thabraca (pages 357-8). The lamp repro-

duces the external part of a Christian basilica and the mosaic
shows us the inside of a basilica with all its various parts. These
reproductions were undoubtedly made for some symbolical

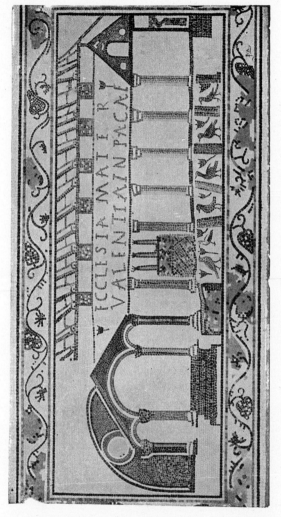

AFRICAN BURIAL MOSAIC REPRESENTING THE INTERIOR
OF AN ANCIENT CHRISTIAN BASILICA. FOURTH CENTURY.

The entrance is to the right of the observer; the apse with the presbytery is to the left. In front
of the apse may be seen the altar with three lighted candles.

reason. The lamp represents the idea that the Church is the
agent bringing the true light of the Gospel to the world; the
mosaic, which was built on a tomb, expresses the hope that
the departed woman would enjoy peace because she had been
a member of the true Church.

Paintings, sculptures and mosaics completed the ornamentations of a basilica. The following chapter will treat
of these.

THE AFRICAN LAMP IN THE FORM OF A BASILICA.

## Chapter III

## THE DECORATION OF BASILICAS

I. — MOSAICS go back to the remotest antiquity, and are
even mentioned in the Bible: "pavimentum smaragdino et pario
stratum lapide."[1] Pliny tells us that a kind of work of this sort,
which he called "lithostroton," was known to the Romans as
far back as the time of Silla: "Lithostrota coeptavere iam sub
Silla parvulis certe crustis: exstat hodie quod in Fortunae de-
lubro Praeneste fecit."[2] The true mosaic (*opus tessellatum, opus
musivum*, later corrupted into the present name) is composed
of small regular cubes of marble, and should be distinguished
from the *opus sectile* which is formed of much larger fragments
or pieces. The so-called *opus sectile* is known as *Alexandrinum*,
after the Emperor Alexander Severus. There are remnants of it
on the Palatine, in the pavement of the apse of the palace of
the Flavii, and on the Esquiline, in the basilica of Junius Bassus.
In the fourth century it was also employed in the apse of the
basilica at Parenzo.

Christians also used mosaics, and there are a few rare examples in the catacombs; but this chapter deals with the decorative mosaics of the fourth century.[3] In the catacombs of St. Hermes may be seen a mosaic with the picture of a departed individual and of Daniel in the midst of lions; in the catacombs of St. Agnes there was a portrait of a woman named Tranquillina;[4] in the cemetery of Cyriaca were to be found the portraits in mosaic of a man and his wife, dating from the fourth century — Maria Simplicia and Fl. Julius Julianus. This mosaic was later removed to the Christian Museum in the Lateran.

A beautiful mosaic pavement may be seen in an underground chapel in the catacombs of Sts. Peter and Marcellinus. This was believed by Visconti and Marchi to be Christian, because the mosaic contains the image of a dove and the tombs have the form of *loculi;* but it is also possible that this underground structure was pagan.[5] Splendid mosaic compositions may be found, however, especially in the Constantinian basilicas of Rome, Constantinople[6] and Ravenna, where the most ancient are from the period of Bishop Ursus (fifth century).

A brief list of the principal Christian mosaics still preserved will be useful at this point, with particularized remarks on the mosaics found in Rome itself. To the time of the persecutions belongs a mosaic of Parenzo. It is certain that at that time Parenzo possessed a domestic church, destroyed under Diocletian, rebuilt after the granting of peace and enlarged in the sixth century under Bishop Euphrasius. There still remains a mosaic pavement of the primitive edifice showing the symbolical decoration of the fish which goes back to the earliest days of the Church. On this mosaic are found traces of columns which supported the altar. A basilica was later erected in this place during the period of peace, and in it may be seen other mosaics with the names of the donors on the various squares.[7]

Another outstanding Christian mosaic is the one discovered a few years ago at Madaba, in Palestine, in which the Holy Land is represented geographically, along with a perspective view of the city of Jerusalem.[8] Very important is the mosaic pavement of the duomo of Aquileia which contains Biblical and

symbolical figures made during the time of Bishop Theodore
(fourth century).

The mosaic decoration of St. Constantia's in Rome also
goes back to the fourth century. It was formerly believed that
this monument was an ancient pagan temple, because the
decorations show figures of the vintage, of small, winged genii,
etc., and for this reason it was called a "temple of Bacchus."
It is certain, however, that it is none other than the mausoleum
of the family of Constantine. The style of the mosaic of the
vault is different from the mosaics of the lateral apses, in
which are shown God giving the Law to Moses and the Saviour
giving the Law to Peter. In the body is painted a starry firmament, in the midst of which shines the Constantinian monogram.[9] The other mausoleum of the imperial family, that of
St. Helena on the Labican Way, was also adorned with mosaics,
seen by Bosio, but today entirely lost. The mosaic of St.
Pudentiana's also belongs to the fourth century, having been
executed under Pope Siricius. It shows the Saviour seated among
His apostles, holding a volume of the Law and an inscription,
DOMINVS CONSERVATOR ECCLESIAE PVDENTIANAE,
with a group of local buildings in the background (see opposite). There are other examples of mosaics in Rome, Carthage,
Milan, etc.

The mosaics of St. Mary Major's were executed during the
reign of Sixtus III, in the fifth century, with the exception of
the apse which belongs to the thirteenth; the large mosaic may
perhaps date from the time of Pope Liberius. The mosaic
found in St. Sabina's also belongs to the fifth century, and was
completed under Celestine I. It contains figures which personify
the Church: ECCLESIA EX GENTIBVS; ECCLESIA EX CIR-
CVMCISIONE. The mosaic of the Baptistery of the Lateran
is of the time of Pope Hilary.

There are many mosaics of the sixth century in Ravenna[10]
(see page 362). Those of the church of Sts. Cosmas and
Damian in Rome (see page 363) and of the basilica of St.
Lawrence (time of Pope Pelagius II — see page 364) are also
of the sixth century.

In the mosaic of the church of Cosmas and Damian, restored at the time of Urban VIII, the Gothic type could be discerned, according to Gregorovius. During this period, the Roman style began to disappear to make way for the Byzantine.

MOSAIC IN THE APSE OF THE BASILICA OF ST. PUDENTIANA.
End of the fourth century.

Of the seventh century are the mosaics of St. Agnes' outside the Walls, in which the saint may be seen between Popes Symmachus and Honorius (see page 365); those of the oratory of St. Venantius (time of Pope John IV), with the figures of sainted Slavs; that of St. Stephen Rotondo's in which for the first time the Saviour is pictured with the cross; and the St. Sebastian mosaic of the church of St. Peter in Chains, an ex-voto offering of the Romans following a pestilence.

To the eighth century belong the mosaics of the oratory of the Virgin on the Vatican, executed under John VII and destroyed under Paul V; the fragments are partly preserved in the Vatican Grottoes, partly at St. Mary's *in Cosmedin,* and partly at St. Mark's in Florence. To this group must be added the mosaics of Sts. Nereus and Achilleus from the time of Leo III, and the one of the *Triclinium Leonianum,* which formed part of the Lateran Palace, but later was demolished. The mosaic at present near the Scala Santa is a copy made under Benedict XIV from an ancient design, representing the Saviour with the apostles; at one side stands St. Peter with Charlemagne, at the other St. Sylvester with Constantine.

ST. APOLLINARIS IN THE MIDST OF HIS FLOCK.
Mosaic of Ravenna. Sixth century.

The mosaics of St. Cecilia's, St. Praxedes' and St. Mary's
*in Dominica* must be ascribed to the ninth century. They were
finished under Pope Paschal I.[11] The mosaic of St. Mark's (see
page 366) is from the time of Pope Gregory IV.

MOSAIC IN THE APSE OF THE BASILICA
OF STS. COSMAS AND DAMIAN. Sixth century.

The art of making mosaics fell into oblivion from the tenth
to the twelfth century, a very dark and unsettled period for all
art. During the twelfth century mosaics returned, but in an

entirely new style, neither classical Roman nor Byzantine. To
this first renaissance of Italian art must be ascribed the mosaics
of St. Clement's (see page 367) and of New St. Mary's.

The apses of St. Mary Major's and St. Mary's in Transtevere belong to the thirteenth century; that of St. Paul's (see
page 368) and the mosaic of Innocent III in the Vatican, of
which some fragments are preserved in the Torlonia Villa at
Poli, also date from this period. The new taste of the fifteenth
and successive centuries underestimated this art, as it was considered mediaeval. Mosaics also became rarer because artists,
increasingly independent in their work, preferred to produce
compositions which required less time and expense.

MOSAICS IN THE APSE OF THE BASILICA OF ST. LAWRENCE.
Sixth century.

II. — Sculpture served, in the basilicas, principally to
decorate the altars, the tabernacles and the ambones. There are
some samples of this work which may go back to the fourth
century, as for example, a portion of a column showing the
martyrdom of St. Achilleus, in the basilica of St. Petronilla,[12]

and some ruins of the basilica of St. Agnes on which may be
seen a praying figure of the saint.

The greater portion of ancient sculpture which has come
down to us consists of the partitions of basilicas. During the
fifth and sixth centuries, these were adorned with crosses,

MOSAIC IN THE APSE OF THE BASILICA OF ST. AGNES
OUTSIDE THE WALLS. Seventh century.

monograms, etc. The partition of St. Clement's, for instance,
bears the monogram of John II (sixth century).

Decorations became more complicated during the eighth
and ninth centuries, as may be seen in the ambo of Nepi, dating
from the time of Gregory IV (see page 370).

Another decoration pertaining to basilicas was that used to
adorn the bishop's throne. We may arrive at some idea of this
from the wooden chair attributed to St. Peter and preserved in
the Vatican basilica, as well as from the renowned chair
Maximian kept at Ravenna (see pages 371, 372).

III. — Later on a new work, similar to sculpture and
mosaic, made its appearance. This was the product of a true

school of Roman marble-workers, which is found scattered throughout many basilicas. *Opus Alexandrinum* is a misnomer for it, since the phrase properly refers only to articles made during the time of Alexander Severus, as has already been stated. Examples of it have also been called *opera Cosmatesca*,[13]

MOSAIC IN THE APSE OF THE BASILICA OF ST. MARK.
Ninth century.

but the Cosmati were not its inventors; others before them had employed it. The true name is furnished by an inscription of the cloister of Sassovivo, near Foligno,[14] which states that the cloister was made according to the "romano opere et maestria." Thus also, in an inscription at Civita Castellana, the articles are called "magistri doctissimi romani."[15] The works of the Roman artists may be seen at Rome, Venice, Ravenna, in Northern Italy, in Sicily and even in England.

In these decorations one may sense the Byzantine influence. This should not surprise us because we know, from the chronicle of Leo of Ostia, that an abbott of Monte Cassino had a number of artists come from Constantinople to decorate the church.

De Rossi, while studying the mosaics of the church of St. Mary in Castello, at Corneto, was able to reconstruct the genealogy of one of the first families of marble-workers which flourished in the twelfth and thirteenth centuries:[16]

MOSAIC IN THE APSE OF THE BASILICA OF ST. CLEMENT.
Twelfth century.

"Petrus et Nicolaus Ranucii romanus" (1143);
"Iohannes [son of Nicolaus] et Guitton" (1168);
"Ioannes Guittonius (filius) civis romanus" (1209).

A second group is formed of the family of the marble-worker Paul, who decorated the tabernacle of St. Lawrence's

MOSAIC IN THE APSE OF THE BASILICA OF ST. PAUL.
Thirteenth century.

outside the Walls by the order of Abbot Hugh (1148). He worked in conjunction with his sons John, Peter, Angelo and Sasso. The same group worked on the tabernacle of St. Mark's, as may be seen from an inscription copied by De Winghe,[17] and a manuscript from the Chigi Library:[18] IN N. D. MAGISTER GILbertus PR. CARD. S. MARCI IVSSIT HOC FIERI PRO REDEMPTIONE ANIME SVE ANN. DNI M. C. L. IIII, IND. II FACTVM EST PER MANVS IOHIS PETRI ANGELI ET SASSONIS FILIOR.

AMBO AND CANDLESTICK FOR THE PASCHAL CANDLE
IN THE BASILICA OF ST. CLEMENT. Twelfth century.

Three of these men made the tabernacle of the church of the Holy Cross in Jerusalem: IOHANNES DE PAVLO CVM

FRATRIBVS SVIS ANGELO ET SASSO HVIVS OPERIS
MAGISTRI FVERVNT.[19] Finally, the name of the father of
the artist only is found on a mosaic in the Casino of Pius IV on
the Vatican:

✠NVNC OPERIS QVIDQVID CHORVS ECCE NITET PRETIOSI
ARTIFICIS SCVLTRIS COMSIT BONA DEXTERA PAVLI.

The Cosmati were successors of the sons of Paul, and their
head was Lawrence, father of James and uncle of the first
Cosmas.

AMBO OF NEPI.
Eighth century.

Lawrence lived toward the end of the twelfth and the
beginning of the thirteenth century. The inscription relating to
him, in Civita Castellana, is as follows: LAVRENTIVS CVM
IACOBO FILIO SVO MAGISTRI DOCTISSIMI ROMANI
HOC OPVS FECERVNT. MAGISTER IACOBVS CIVIS
ROMANVS CVM COSMA FILIO SVO CARISSIMO FECIT
HOC OPVS A. D̅N̅I̅ MCCX. Peter Sabinus transcribed the
following inscription from St. Peter's on the Vatican in Leonine verses:

HOC OPVS EX AVRO VITRIS LAVRENTIVS EGIT
CVM IACOBO NATO SCVLPSIT SIMVL ATQVE PEREGIT.

Inscriptions analogous to this may be read in the church of
Ara Coeli:[20] LAVRENTIVS CVM IACOBO FILIO SVO
HVIVS OPERIS MAGISTER FVIT; in St. Thomas' *in Formis,*
on the door of the monastery:
MAGISTER IACOBVS CVM
FILIO SVO COSMATO FECIT
HOC OPVS; at the church of
Sts. John and Paul: ✠MA-
GISTER C O S M A S FECIT
HOC OPVS.[21] The last of the
family must have been Deo-
datus whose name may be read
on the tabernacle of the church
of St. Mary *in Cosmedin* —
✠DEODATVS ME FECIT —
and on a beautiful fragment of
a tabernacle, preserved in the
cloister of St. John Lateran's.

Page 373 shows a sample of
the letters employed in these
inscriptions.

The same artists worked at
Subiaco where, in the cloister
of St. Scholastica's, may be seen
the names of Cosmas, Luke and
John, and on the inside door of
the monastery of St. Benedict,
the inscription: ✠LAVREN-
TIVS CVM IACOBO FILIO SVO FECIT HOC OPVS.

CHAIR OF MAXIMIAN
IN RAVENNA.

At the same time there flourished another school, that of
the Vassalletti, makers of the cloister of St. John Lateran. The
following inscription, first seen by Sirmondo,[22] may be found:

NOBILIS ET DOCTVS HAC VASSALLECTVS IN ARTE
CVM PATRE CEPIT OPVS QVOD SOLVS PERFECIT IPSE.

This cloister dates from the beginning of the thirteenth century, as we know because that of St. Paul, which is an evident imitation, was completed during the last year of the Abbot John of Ardea, who died in 1241.

CHAIR OF ST. PETER IN ROME.

The chair in the cathedral of Anagni was also built by one of the Vassalletti, VASALET DE ROMA, and the candelabrum of the same church has these words: VASALETO ME FECIT. Reference is also found on the tabernacle for the holy oils in the church of St. Francis at Viterbo — BASSALLECTVS ME FECIT; on the lion placed at the entrance of the church of the Holy Apostles in Rome — ✠BASSALLECTVS; on the candelabrum of St. Paul's outside the walls:

EGO NICOLAVS DE ANGELO CVM PETRO
BASSALLETTO HOC OPVS COMPLEVI.

One may even believe that the signature on a statue of Aesculapius, preserved in the palace of the Verospi, is that of Vassalletto: ASALECTVS. Winkelmann believed that he recognized the name of a Greek artist called Ασσαλεκτος, but

Marucchi is of the opinion that the inscription shows that the statue may have served as a model for this mediaeval artist.[23]

Grisar has been able to ascertain the name of another school of artists who worked in Umbria, especially at Spoleto, during the twelfth century.[24]

Finally, in addition to these families of artists, there were also individual artists like Paschal, who made the candelabrum of St. Mary's *in Cosmedin*:

VIR DOCTVS ET PROBVS PASCALIS RITE VOCATVS
SVMMO CVM STVDIO CONDIDIT HVNC CEREVM.

There were other independent artists such as Dudus de Trivio,[25] and a certain Ivo magister, artificer of a tabernacle of Sts. Cosmas and Damian (now destroyed), near Vicovaro: QVAE VIDETIS IVO ME FECIT.[26]

Unfortunately, however, in order to make their decorations and ornaments, these artists used a very free hand with respect to the stones of the catacombs, which were easy to work to any form required by their art. We see an example of this in an ambo of St. Lawrence's outside the walls, where an ancient inscription of a priest of the title of Nicomedes was employed. Such inscriptions were even taken away from Rome, as may be seen at Genazzano, Corneto, and even as far away as Westminster.[27]

CLOISTER OF ST. JOHN LATERAN'S.
Thirteenth century.

## Chapter IV

## THE ANCIENT LITURGY OF BASILICAS

AFTER having treated of the origin of Christian basilicas, and their design and ornamentation, it seems proper to say something on the use to which these structures were put, that is, their liturgy. Unfortunately the shortness of the space available reduces this section to a few brief, essential remarks.

The liturgy of the basilicas had its origin in the mani-
festations of Christian worship during the period of the persecutions and of the Apostolic Age itself.[1] The earliest documents
are few and very brief — a few passages from the Epistles of
St. Paul and St. Clement, the Διδαχὴ τῶν δώδεκα ἀποστόλων, the
writings of St. Justin, St. Irenaeus, Tertullian and St. Cyprian,
in addition to the information which may be derived from the
*Book of the Popes.*

Baptism, which is the Sacrament of Christian initiation,
was administered at the same time as Confirmation, in a special
place connected with the basilica (baptistery and consignatory);
the baptismal rite, very simple in the earliest times, was united
at the period of peace with those mystical ceremonies which in
great measure are preserved to this day, at least in the baptism
of adults.[2] But the most solemn act of the liturgy was always
the Eucharistic Sacrifice, the Mass.

The oldest name given to the Eucharistic liturgy was
"Fractio panis"[3] ("the Breaking of Bread"). St. Paul also calls
it "coena Dominica,"[4] "the Lord's Supper." It was likewise
known as "liturgy" and "oblation." The day chosen for the
liturgical reunion was usually Sunday. According to St. Justin's
first *Apology,* and other ancient documents, it began with the
recitation of some psalms and the reading of apostolic or
prophetical books. The presiding officer of the reunion, ordinarily the bishop, addressed the assembly by commenting on
the words just read; then all arose for common prayer. At this
point the Mass of the Catechumens ended, and the Mass of the
Faithful, at which only they could assist, began. The presenta-
tion of the offering of bread and wine was performed by the
faithful themselves; remnants of this rite may still be seen in
the liturgy of the consecration of a bishop and the solemn
canonization of the saints. Then ensued a more solemn and
secret part of the ritual — namely, the recitation of the canonical prayer (the Canon of the Mass) which comprised the consecration. After other prayers, all the faithful recited the Lord's
Prayer and partook of the Eucharist under both Species. The
Eucharistic liturgy ended with solemn prayers of thanksgiving,
and was often followed by a fraternal banquet of love (the

agape), which in the earliest days was intimately connected with the Eucharist. This custom, as we have already seen, persisted until the second century, when the agape was separated from the Eucharist, often to be performed in the evening.[5]

It is evident, therefore, from a study of these ancient documents, that our modern Mass is directly derived from the Eucharistic liturgy of the first centuries, and that in its principal parts it had, at least at the end of the first half of the second century, the form which it has always essentially preserved.

The ordinary ancient liturgy corresponded to that which we nowadays call "solemn"; while the abbreviated form, which we customarily call the "reading of Mass," had a rather private character, and was used during those reunions at which there was only a small group present. This may have occurred either to celebrate the feast of a martyr at his tomb or to commemorate the anniversary of one of the departed. Hence, the distinction of *Missa ad corpus* and of *Missa major.* The word *Mass* itself is very ancient and is derived from the usage of requesting the catechumens, who could not attend beyond the first part of the liturgical functions, to leave before the time of the Offertory. The deacon then said: "Fit dismissio cathecumenis, manebunt fideles"—"Let the catechumens be dismissed, the faithful remain." The Greek liturgy still retains this custom of the *dismissio cathecumenorum,* but in the Latin liturgy there remains only the dismissal of all the faithful after the completion of the rite, which the deacon performs by uttering the words: "Ite, missa est" — "Go, the Mass has been said."

We know nothing concerning the altars on which the liturgy was performed in the domestic oratories, or titles, of the first centuries, nor of the altars used in these early days in the catacombs near the tombs of the martyrs, and in the underground chapels. Some ruins of altars in catacombs have been found, but they date from the time of peace.

In ancient basilicas, as the altar stood by itself, there were no pictures, images, etc., as there are on modern altars which are placed against the wall. There was only some sort of emblem, such as a cross or monogram, attached to the *pergula,* from which lamps also hung.

The pictures in an ancient Christian basilica were almost without exception worked in mosaic in the apse or painted on the walls. They were placed there especially for the instruction and edification of the faithful.

In the Greek Church, however, the iconoclastic heresy produced, as a natural reaction, an altogether disproportionate veneration of images. It was due to this that there was a special place set aside facing the altar where images, pictures, etc., could be gathered. This, called the *iconostasis,* is still found in all Greek churches. Thus it is that the acts of veneration which, in the ancient basilicas, were performed toward the tomb of the martyr represented by the altar, and which in the Latin liturgy are preserved in the ceremony of incensing the altar and the relics placed above or below it, in the Greek Church are directed especially toward the pictures, images, etc., of the *iconostasis.* This remains the practice in all Oriental churches.

From ancient times the altar was of small size and supported only the candles, as may be seen, for example, in the mosaic of Thabraca (see page 357). It was not until relatively late that the usage of placing a cross upon it came into practice. Later still — certainly not before the sixth century — the crucifix was placed upon it, but only in the form of a living Christ, dressed in a tunic and pierced by four nails.

The narrow space between the altar and the apse was reserved for the clergy surrounding the bishop's throne, which was located in the body of the apse itself. Facing the altar there was a place for the singers (*schola cantorum*), with two ambones from which the Epistle and Gospel were read aloud, since, according to the intention of the Church, the Sacred Books were to be heard and understood by all for their common instruction and edification. The naves of the basilica were destined for the use of the faithful who assisted at the services. As we have seen, men and women were in different sections; and moreover, all the faithful who took part in the sacred rites were separated from those not in union with the Church. These latter had no right to come close to the altar during the time of liturgical functions.

It is desirable that even in modern churches, such of these practices as are possible of imitation be followed out, and that the clergy employ every means at their disposal to ensure that the faithful do not remain aloof and indifferent spectators of these sacred ceremonies, but take a lively part in them, as did the early Christians. A realization of this need is one of the practical results which young men aspiring to the priesthood should derive from the study of Christian archeology.

A few words may be said here concerning Eucharistic worship, a devotion which is intimately associated with the altar and the basilica.

Although this worship began with Christianity (its antiquity has been shown in a special chapter), it was not as developed nor as widespread either in the years of persecution or in the periods of peace as it became later on. This was because, in the earliest times, in both Orient and Occident, it was restricted almost exclusively to the adoration of the Sacred Species during the celebration of the liturgy or Mass. Later, as already noted, in the Orient, where the iconoclastic heresy raged during the eighth century, the veneration of sacred images was accentuated, and entered into the liturgy itself. In the Occident, on the other hand, the impugning of the dogma of the Eucharistic Presence by Berengarius, in the eleventh century, added to the gradual growth of understanding and devotion, resulted in a reaction in its favor; and hence the worship of the Blessed Sacrament steadily developed, spread and unfolded, while in the Orient, the ancient form was retained. After the eleventh century, the custom of exposing the Sacred Species gradually began, and finally the use of the monstrance arose.

This period also saw the introduction of architectural changes in the churches; lateral oratories, already under way, began to increase in numbers and altars were multiplied, for the saying of more Masses. In this fashion, gradually and almost imperceptibly, we find coming into being the new forms which characterize the churches of the Renaissance and finally those of our own times.

## Chapter V

## NAMES AND DERIVATIONS
## OF THE LITURGICAL VESTMENTS[1]

THE LITURGICAL vestments preserve, in part, the names and the forms of the ancient Roman dress from which they were derived.

The *Alb* took its origin from the tunic, a garment used by the ancients at all periods — especially from the *tunica talaris,* which reached to the ankles.

The *Cincture* (*cingulum*) arose from the *zona* or *balteum,* a belt which held garments in place on the body.

The *Maniple* (*manipulum* or *mappula*) was a sort of handkerchief which was carried on the arm.

The *Stole* (*stola*) was a woman's garment, as the toga was properly the dress of men. The stole was ornamented by a costly band, and this, separated from the garment, is what has become one of the sacred vestments. It was also called the *orarium,* from its indicated origin.

The *Chasuble* (*casula*) is taken from the *penula* of the Greeks and Romans, although it is preserved in ampler form similar to the ancient dress of the Orientals. In the Occident, from the fifteenth century on, it became smaller until it reached its present form, which retains practically nothing of its ancient origin.

The liturgical *Pallium* is derived from the civil pallium which, in imperial times, was often worn in place of the toga. It was preferred by the Christians, in opposition to the toga, an exclusively Roman garment, as representing a philosophical dress. This garment was later altered (*contabulatum*) because, during the fourth century, the use of the chasuble began to prevail, finally reducing the pallium to a mere band or stripe. The sacred pallium was from its very origin the token of episcopal authority.

The *Dalmatic* was a special tunic with wide sleeves, in vogue during the third century of our era. It takes its name from Dalmatia, the country in which its use began. It was worn at times under the chasuble, and that is why the bishop puts it on during solemn functions. It soon became the distinctive dress of deacons.

The *Pluvial* (*pluviale*) was a covering used in the open to guard against rain; it is employed in those functions which necessitate going out of the church, in processions, etc.

The other liturgical vestments may be considered as derivatives of these main articles of wear during the celebration or performance of sacred functions.

## Chapter VI

## ANCIENT ECCLESIASTICAL TITLES[1]

IN THE beginning the Christians held their meetings in the rooms of private homes; of such a character were the Cenacle of Jerusalem,[2] and the places of reunion recorded in the Acts of the Apostles.[3] For this reason, the oldest oratories or chapels are called *ecclesiae domesticae* ("domestic churches"), and St. Paul speaks of those in Corinth and in Rome, in the home of the two Jewish converts, Aquila and Prisca.[4]

Thus, according to tradition, there were such oratories in Rome in apostolic times: the home of Aquila and Prisca on the Aventine, and the *ecclesia* of Pudens on the Viminal. The documents which speak of these, though partly legendary,[5] are nevertheless very ancient and are confirmed in substance by archeological monuments and proofs. A mosaic of the fourth century, representing St. Peter in the midst of his flock,[6] existing in the title of Pudens, confirms the fact that there was a chapel here where the apostle had gathered together the first Christians. This church was in close touch with that of St. Prisca, because as we have seen a certificate was found in the latter, of the beginning of the third century, conferred on one Caius Marius Pudens Cornelianus, who must have lived in the place. Moreover, both these titles had one cemetery in common known as the cemetery of St. Priscilla, in which were deposited the bodies of Aquila and Prisca, Pudens, Pudentiana and Praxedes. It was here, too, that there was a venerated and well-known chapel dedicated to the first preaching of St. Peter.[7]

These were certainly not the only centers of liturgical re-union. The titles designated by the names of the founders of other centers are also very ancient: *titulus Lucinae, Sabinae, Vestinae,* etc.

The word *titulus* is derived from the inscriptions placed on the houses of the ancients to indicate the names of their owners or proprietors.

As we have seen, the primitive churches were ordinary homes, set aside for Christian worship or rather for the common needs of the Christian community. The homes of the ancients were well adapted to such purposes, because they generally had an entrance on the public street, a courtyard surrounded by porticoes (*atria*), and in the rear a room with bath, sleeping quarters (*cubicula*) and other domestic appurtenances. This was very convenient whenever there was need of taking care of any of the different groups who composed the Christian as-semblage: the catechumens, the faithful, the penitents, etc. There would be need of a place for the bishop and the clergy who assisted in the administration of the ritual. Valuable papers had to be kept safely, books, sacred vessels, vestments, as well as the various objects needed for the poor and for pilgrims, had to be provided for.

A *domus Ecclesiae,* in those days, had to provide all this, to serve as a church, episcopal residence, refectory, dispensary, hospice and hospital.[8]

As time went on, the part of the building reserved for worship took on a special character. The *domus Ecclesiae* be-came the *domus Dei* ("the house of God"): the place, namely, where Christians prayed to the Lord.[9]

Such churches were called *tituli* ("titles"), as has been ex-plained, because they bore the titles of their founders. The antiquity of the name is shown by the fact that, during the fourth century it had already been given to twenty-five churches;[10] while in the sixth century, we find twenty-eight churches bearing this designation, as recorded in the Acts of the Council held in Rome under Symmachus in 499 A. D., and in the writings of St. Gregory the Great (595). These documents contain the signatures of the priests of each title and are there- fore of great importance in understanding the point under discussion.[11]

It will be of interest to list these titles. All are still in existence with the exception of those of Nicomedes and Emili- ana, which are unknown, and that of St. Cyriacus, transferred to St. Mary's *in via Lata*: *Titulus Praxedes, Vestinae* (St. Vitalis), *Sanctae Caeciliae, Pammachii, Byzantis* (Sts. John and Paul), *Clementis, Julii, Calixti* (St. Martin at the Moun- tain), *Damasi* (St. Lawrence *in Damaso*), *Matthei* (later Sts. Peter and Marcellinus), *Eusebii, Tigridis, Crescentianae* (St. Sixtus), *Susannae, Gaii, Romani* (probably St. Marcellus),[12] *Sanctorum Apostolorum, Eudoxiae* (St. Peter in Chains), *Fasciolae* (Sts. Nereus and Achilleus), *Priscae, Lucinae* (St. Lawrence *in Lucina*), *Marci* also called *Pallacinae, in Palla- cina, juxta Pallacinas.*

In general these titles do not carry the appellation of "Saint" in the Acts of the Roman Councils. This is a sign of their antiquity; in their origin they were connected with the or- ganization and development of the catacombs during the third century. Their antiquity is confirmed by the work of restoration and reconstruction in many of these churches in very ancient times.

In general, the titles were not situated in the most popu- lous regions of the city; there was none on the Palatine or the Capitoline, none in the Forum or the center of Rome. Further- more, none was ever established in the ancient temples or other pagan structures of Rome. The deaneries (establishments for charitable works) were, however, located in ancient edifices, as for example, in the *templum sacrae Urbis* (Sts. Cosmas and Damian), and in *horrea* (St. Mary *in Cosmedin*), etc.

We do not know whether these titles were confiscated along with the cemeteries, in 258, under the Emperor Valerian; but they certainly were under Diocletian, in 304, because Euse- bius tells us that Constantine had the places of reunion and whatever appertained to their cemeteries restored to the Chris- tian community.[13]

Along with these titles, there is mention of other churches later raised to the same dignity. At first there were churches connected with the catacombs outside the city, built on the tombs of the martyrs and depending on these titles, as did the cemeteries themselves.[14] Then, during the Constantinian period, other basilicas were built: that of the Lateran, a church of the palace given by Constantine to Miltiades, who established his residence there; the Liberian basilica, founded by Pope Liberius; the Sessorian basilica (Holy Cross *in Gerusalemme*), in the palace of the Sessorium; the basilica of Junius Bassus, consecrated to Christian worship during the fifth century, restored by the barbarian patrician Valila (471), and therefore called *cata barbarum patricium;* the basilica *Julia,* constructed under Julius I and dedicated first to Sts. Philip and James and later to the Twelve Apostles; St. Stephen's on the Caelian, erected in the grand salon of the "great market" (*macellum magnum*); St. Bibiana's, built in a room of the palace of Gallienus; St. Agatha's of the Goths, an Arian church, founded during the fifth century by the barbarian Ricimer and turned over to the Catholics by Gregory the Great; and so on.

Each title had its own regularly organized clergy. A passage from a letter addressed to St. Cyprian proves that there were at least two priests assigned to each title: "Felix qui presbyterium administrabat sub Decimo . . . " This passage refers to Africa.[15]

The same conditions obtained in Rome under Pope Hormisdas, because an inscription of St. Clement speaks of a priest by the name of Mercurius and his associates ("socii"). A decretal of Innocent I makes a distinction between those priests "constituiti ad coemeteria" ("detailed for duty in the catacombs") and those who labored "intra civitatem" ("in the city").[16] The same may be seen in a long inscription of the sixth century in which the entire order and arrangement is mentioned in speaking of a tomb acquired "a presbyteris tituli Sancti Chrysogoni, id est Petro priore, Chrysogono secundo, Catello tertio, Gaudioso quarto, vel a Philippo praeposito B. mart. Pancratii sub praesentia Nonnes Cutties, ancillae Dei vel sub praesentia Iohannitis virginis."[17]

The first priest was the titulary, the others were associates. When, during the fifth century, the churches of the catacombs acquired a certain autonomy, the guardians (*praepositi*) who were entrusted with the administration and especially the care *ad luminaria sepulchrorum martyrum,* freed themselves step by step of the authority of the titularies. The deaneries were held by the deacons. The priests as well as the deacons were assisted by clerics who lived in edifices connected with the church and were called *mansionarii* (from *manere,* "to remain").

It is to be noted, finally, that the priests of the ancient titles and the deacons of the ancient deaneries formed the higher clergy of Rome. They later became what we call at the present time the Sacred College of Cardinals: cardinal priests and cardinal deacons.

## Chapter VII

### THE ANCIENT ECCLESIASTICAL REGIONS OF ROME

FROM the very beginning of the Church, there must have been ecclesiastical divisions, analogous to the fourteen civil regions of Augustus, for the purpose of controlling and regulating the reunions and the funerary ceremonies of the Christians.

The first document which speaks of them is the *Book of the Popes,* in the section on the life of Pope Fabian (✠250): "Regiones divisit diaconibus." As there were seven deacons, there were seven regions, each of which comprised two civil regions. But there was not an exact correspondence between the ecclesiastical and civil divisions, and we do not know the precise limits of the former. At times, one ecclesiastical region comprised more than two of the civil. This question was thoroughly studied in the seventeenth century by Nardini in his *Roma antica,*[1] by Nibby,[2] de Rossi[3] and Duchesne,[4] but there are many points which still remain unsolved.

The first ecclesiastical region, it is known, corresponded at least in part to civil regions I, XII and XIII of Augustus and embraced the entire burial region of the Appian, Ardeatine and Ostian Ways. In fact, in all these catacombs, inscriptions were found bearing the names of priests and lectors belonging to the titles of Prisca, Fasciola (Sts. Nereus and Achilleus) and Balbina.

The second division comprised the Caelian and the Forum (regions II and VIII of Augustus); to it belonged the catacombs of the Latin Way and perhaps some of the Appian Way.

The third covered civil regions III and VI. It extended from St. Clement's to the Tiburtine and Labican gates. Hence it took in all the Esquiline and a part of the Caelian. The catacombs which depended upon it were those of Cyriaca, St. Hippolytus and Sts. Peter and Marcellinus.

To the fourth belonged the Quirinal and the Viminal (civil divisions IV and VI); consequently it took in the catacombs of the Nomentan Way.

The fifth corresponded to region VII of Augustus (*via Lata*) and a part of region IX, controlling the catacombs of the Salarian, Pincian and Flaminian Ways.

To the sixth belonged civil division IX, which was the most extensive.

Finally, the seventh region (Transtevere) comprised the catacombs of the Vatican and the Portuan and Aurelian Ways.

This division subsequently underwent numerous modifications, beginning in the sixth century with the invasion of the barbarians. The *Book of the Popes* tells us that under Pope John III (559-572) the services of the catacombs were carried out at the expense of the pontifical palace. It seems evident, therefore, that there no longer existed any connection between the catacombs and the titles.

Toward the end of the sixth century, the suburban catacombs began to be abandoned. The open-air cemeteries were also neglected because the people preferred to bury their dead within the city. This custom necessarily carried with it a change in the religious divisions and their arrangement. Officially, however, the ancient division was probably retained until the tenth century.

During that period, following the modifications introduced into the city administration, there were ten regions, whose limits are difficult to determine, although Nibby and Nardini have given us their names. Thus the civil districts and the ecclesiastical divisions and churches were divided off in another way. During the twelfth and thirteenth centuries, we find records of the "first partition," the "second partition," etc. To each of these there must have been assigned a special group of the clergy; but this division lasted only during the Middle Ages.

These general remarks concerning the ancient basilicas and titles refer especially to the churches of Rome, which are the most important and concerning which we have the most information. But they may also be applied to the ancient Christian churches of other regions. It is certain that the sacred edifices had the same origin everywhere, and must everywhere have been of two kinds: urban churches, and churches erected over the tombs of the martyrs or in the catacombs (basilicas of the catacombs).

## Chapter VIII

## PARTIAL LIST
## OF ANCIENT CHRISTIAN BASILICAS[1]

## ITALY

ALBANO. — A Constantinian basilica.[2]

BOVILLAE. — Basilica of St. Euphemia.[3]

BRESCIA. — Church of St. Julia.[4]

CASTEL SANT' ELIA. — A basilica.[5]

CLITUNNO (near Spoleto). — Church of the Angels.[6]

COMO. — Basilica of St. Abundius.[7]

GROTTAFERRATA. — A basilica. Close by there are St. Peter's *in Meruli* and St. Mary's *in Diaconia*.[8]

LUCCA. — The Basilica *Langobardorum* (St. Fredian's) and St. Alexander's.[9]

MARINO. — Basilica of St. Mary *in Moreni*.[10]

MILAN. — Basilicas of St. Ambrose, St. Nazarius the Great, Sts. Nabor and Felix, the Holy Sepulchre and St. Valeria.[11]

MURANO (near Venice). — Basilica of St. Donatus.[12]

NAPLES. — St. John *in Fonte* and St. Restituta.[13]

NOLA. — St. Felix's.[14]

OSTIA. — Constantinian church of Sts. Peter and Paul.[15]

PALESTRINA. — Basilica of St. Agapitus.[16]

PARENZO. — Basilica of Euphrasius.[17]

PORTO. — Basilicas of St. Hippolytus and St. Mary.[18]

RAVENNA. — Basilicas of St. Agatha, St. Vitalis, St. Appollinaris, New St. Apollinaris, *Sanctae Crucis, Ecclesia Petriana,* St. John the Evangelist, St. John the Baptist, St. Lawrence *in Classe*.[19]

ROME.[20] — Basilicas of St. Anselm, St. Balbina, St. Caesarius *in Palatio,* St. Caesarius *in Turrim,* St. Clement, Sts. Cosmas and Damian, St. Constantia, St. George *in Velabro,* St. John before the Latin Gate, Sts. John and Paul, the Lateran, St. Mark, St. Mary *in Aracoeli,* St. Mary *ad Martyres,* St. Mary *in Cosmedin,* St. Mary *in Dominica,* St. Mary *in via Lata,* St. Mary *in Transtevere,* St. Mary (old), St. Mary Major (new), Sts. Nereus and Achilleus, St. Peter in Chains, *Santi Quattuor Coronati,* St. Praxedes, St. Prisca, St. Pudentiana, St. Saba, St. Sabina, St. Sebastian *in Palatio,* Sts. Sylvester and Martin *ai Monti,* St. Sylvester *in Capite,* St. Stephen Rotondo, St. Theodore, St. Urban *alla Caffarella,* Sts. Vincent and Anastasius at the Three Fountains.

SPOLETO. — Basilicas of St. Augustine, the Saviour (called the Crucifix), St. Michael, St. Donatus.[21]

TARQUINIA (Corneto Tarquinia). — Basilicas of St. Mary *in Castello* and St. Restituta.[22]

THARROS (in Sardinia). — A basilica of the fourth century.[23]

TRIESTE. — St. Justus'.[24]

VENICE. — San Giacometto *in Rialto*.[25]
VERONA. — St. Lawrence's.[26]

## DALMATIA

SALONA. — Christian basilicas.[27]

## FRANCE

ARLES. — Basilica of St. Trophimus.[28]
DIGNE. — Ancient Christian church.[29]
MARSEILLES. — An ancient duomo.[30]
REGIMONT (near Béziers). — Basilica of Sts. Vincent,
Agnes and Eulalia.[31]
TOULOUSE. — A duomo.[32]
TOURS. — Basilica of St. Martin.[33]
VIENNE. — St. Peter's.[34]

## GERMANY

TREVES. — Basilica of St. Victor.

## SPAIN

BEGASTRI. — A cathedral.[35]
BALEARIC ISLES. — Christian basilicas.[36]
LOJA. — Christian basilica.[37]

## ROMAN AFRICA

CARTHAGE. — Basilicas of St. Perpetua, Celerina, the Mar-
tyrs of Scillitan, Theophrasiana, St. Theodore and Gratianus,
two basilicas dedicated to St. Cyprian, etc.[38]
COSTANTINE (Cirta). — Ruins of a church.[39]
DAMOUS-EL-KARITA. — A large basilica.[40]
HIDRA (the ancient Hammedera). — Two basilicas.[41]
LAMBAESIS — Christian basilica.[42]

MATIFOU. — A large basilica.

ORLEANSVILLE (Castellum Tingitanum). — Basilica of St. Reparatus.[43]

PHILLIPPEVILLE. — Church of St. Degna.[44]

TEBESSA. — Ancient Christian basilica.[45]

THABRACA. — Christian churches.[46]

TIGZIOT. — A large basilica.

TIPASA. — Basilica built by Bishop Alexander, and the basilica of St. Salsa.

For information concerning all these basilicas, consult the *Dictionnaire d'Arch. chrét.*, of Cabrol and Leclercq: article "Africa" ("Archéologie").

# EGYPT

ALEXANDRIA. — Church of St. Mark, temple of Caesareum.[47]

ANTINOE (Antinopolis). — Christian churches.[48]

BAGAOUAT. — Christian churches.[49]

BAOUIT. — Christian churches.[50]

CAIRO. — Church of St. Sergius.

DENDERAH. — Ruins of Christian churches.[51]

PHYLAE. — A Christian basilica.[52]

# ASIA MINOR

APHRODISIAS. — A church in the temple of Venus.[53]

ANDABALIS. — A Constantinian church.[54]

ANCYRA. — Church of St. Clement, a church in the temple of Augustus.[55]

ANTIOCH. — Christian churches.[56]

HELIOPOLIS. — Constantinian church.[57]

NICOMEDIA. — Church of S. Salvator.[58]

# PALESTINE

BETHLEHEM. — Constantinian basilica of the Nativity.[59]

JERUSALEM. — Basilica of the Holy Sepulchre (Anastasis), churches of St. Mary and St. Simon Stylites.[60]

MADABA. — Ancient Christian basilicas.[61]

NAZARETH. — Christian basilica.[62]

## SYRIA

ABOU-HANAJA. — Ruins of a basilica.[63]

BAALBEK (Heliopolis). — Christian basilica.[64]

BABIRKA. — Christian church.[65]

BABISKA. — Christian churches.[66]

BABOUDA. — Christian church.[67]

BAKIRHA. — Christian churches.[68]

KENNATHA. — Christian basilicas.[69]

KALAT-SEMAN. — Church of St. Simon Stylites.[70]

## PONTINE REGION

CONSTANTINOPLE. — Basilicas of St. Sophia (Holy Wisdom), St. Mennas, St. Irene, St. Thecla, St. Euphemia, Holy Cross, St. Agathonicus, St. Stephen, Sts. Sergius and Bacchus, St. Theodore, St. Michael, etc.[71]

SEBASTOPOL. — Ruins of Christian churches.[72]

# Footnotes

## PART ONE

### CHAPTER I

1. Batiffol, *Anciennes littérat. chrét.*: *La Litt. grecque,* pp. 11-13, 47-49, 64-65; Bardenhewer, *Patrologia,* Desclée, 1903, Vol. I, p. 33-38.
2. *Hist. eccles.,* III, 25 (*P. G.,* Vol. XX, col. 269).
3. *Ep. fest.,* 39 (*P. G.,* Vol. XXVI, col. 1177).
4. Paolo Savi, *La "Dottrina degli apostoli"; ricerche critiche sull'origine del testo con una nota intorno all'Eucaristia,* Rome, 1893; Batiffol, op. cit., Vol. I, p. 24-28.
5. *Apol.,* I, 65-67 (*P. G.,* Vol. VI, col. 428-429).
6. Batiffol, op. cit., p. 62-64; Bardenhewer, op. cit., p. 48-55.
7. Batiffol, op. cit., p. 84-87; Bardenhewer, op. cit., p. 55-56.
8. Batiffol, op. cit., p. 13-17; Bardenhewer, op. cit., p. 38-45. On the authenticity of the epistles of St. Ignatius, cf. Duchesne, *Les origines chrétiennes,* pp. 63-68.
9. Batiffol, op. cit., p. 95-98; Bardenhewer, op. cit., p. 62-73; Rivière, *Saint Justin et les apologistes du IIe siècle,* Paris, Bloud, 1907.
10. Batiffol, op. cit., p. 87; Bardenhewer, op. cit., p. 59.
11. Batiffol, op. cit., p. 87-88; Bardenhewer, op. cit., p. 59-61.
12. Batiffol, op. cit., p. 99-101; Bardenhewer, op. cit., p. 79-81.
13. Batiffol, op. cit., p. 99; Bardenhewer, op. cit., p. 78-79.
14. Batiffol, op. cit., p. 90-91; Bardenhewer, op. cit., p. 73-78.
15. Batiffol, op. cit., p. 93; Bardenhewer, op. cit., p. 81-84.
16. Batiffol, op. cit., p. 101-102; Bardenhewer, op. cit., p. 84-86.
17. Batiffol, op. cit., p. 94-95; Bardenhewer, op. cit., p. 88-89.
18. Batiffol, op. cit., p. 104-107; Bardenhewer, op. cit., p. 149-155; Dufourcq, *Sant'Ireneo,* Desclée, 1906.
19. Bardenhewer, op. cit., p. 220-275; Turmel, *Tertullien,* Paris, Bloud, 1906.
20. Bardenhewer, op. cit., p. 257-271; de Rossi, *Bull. d'Arch. crist.,* 1881, p. 5-55; 1882, p. 9-76; 1883, p. 60-65.
21. Bardenhewer, op. cit., p. 235-248.
22. Ibid., p. 89-91.
23. Ibid., p. 160-169.
24. Ibid., p. 170-190; Prat, *Origène,* Paris, Bloud, 1906.
25. De Rossi attributes the *Philosophumena* to Tertullian instead

(*Bull. d'Arch. crist.,* 1866, pp. 23-33, 65-97) ; others, after the example of Duchesne (*Histoire ancienne de l'Eglise,* Vol. I, p. 312 seq.) maintain that they are the work of Hippolytus; this is the most likely opinion.

26. Bardenhewer, op. cit., p. 250-257.
27. Ibid., Vol. II, p. 14-24.
28. Bardenhewer, ibid., p. 301-341; Hatzfeld, *Sant'Agostino,* Desclée, 1907.
29. Bardenhewer, op. cit., p. 247-261; De Broglie, *Sant'Ambrogio,* Desclée, 1906.
30. Bardenhewer, op. cit., p. 278-301; Turmel, *Saint Jérôme,* Paris, Bloud, 1906; Largent, *San Girolamo,* Desclée, 1905.
31. Bardenhewer, op. cit., p. 263-267.

## CHAPTER II

1. Cfr. Kaufmann, *Handbuch der christlichen Archäologie,* 1905, p. 52; Leclercq, *Manual d'archéologie chrétienne,* 1907, Vol. I, p. 66.
2. Cfr. D. Ruinart, *Acta primorum martyrum sincera et selecta;* Le Blant, *Les Actes des martyrs, supplément aux "Acta sincera" de D. Ruinart,* Paris, 1882; *Les "Acta martyrum" et leurs sources,* in his collection, *Les persécuteurs et les martyrs,* Paris, 1893; D. Leclercq, *Les martyrs,* 1903. Dufourcq (*Etude sur les "Gesta martyrum" romains* et *De manicheismo apud Latinos quinto sextoque saeculo atque de Latinis apocryphis libris,* Paris, 1900) pretends to show that Acts of the Martyrs were entirely apocryphal, having been composed in Rome in the sixth century to encourage Catholics to resist the Manichean heresy, which was being spread especially by means of books; that to combat this same force, a list was made and collected, *De recipiendis et non recipiendis,* attributed to Pope Gelasius I. This point is too general and certainly an evident exaggeration. Cf. the recent article of Leclercq which assumes the same: *Actes des martyrs,* in *Dictionnaire d'Arch. chrét. et de Liturgie,* Vol. I, col. 373-446.
3. *Breviculus collationis cum Donatistis,* col. 3, c. XI (*P. L.,* Vol. XLIII, col. 636).
4. *Supplément aux "Acta sincera" de D. Ruinart.*
5. *Acta Conc. Rom.,* I (*P. L.,* Vol. LIX, col. 160). The authenticity of this document, placed in doubt by many, is still defended by numerous reputable critics, some of whom would have this begin in part with St. Damasus. Cf. Grisar, *Anal. Rom.* Vol. I., p. 46.
6. These legends have certainly served as foundation for popular traditions more than once. It is known how easily the people accept facts which have a marvelous character, and thus new devotions are born. Benedict XIV (*De servorum Dei beatificatione* etc. IV, p. 2, c. XXVII, 14), and secondly Mabillon (*Iter Italicum,* p. 143), tell the story of a request sent to Urban VIII by a church in Spain which supposed it had the body of a St. Viar and asked for indulgences for the feast of the saint. From an investigation, it was found out that this devotion was uniquely founded on a fragment of an inscription com-

posed of the letters S VIAR, which, instead of forming the name of a saint, were the end and the beginning of the words "praefectuS VIARum." Other examples could be cited, of inscriptions which have been wrongly interpreted and thus have given rise to strange legends, as that of a St. Canellius, whose name was pieced together from fragments which really made up the inscription "ad S. Cornelium," and another very well-known epigraph of St. Philomena, in which the simple signs of punctuation were taken to be the instruments of torture used during her martyrdom. Cf. also Delehaye, *Les légendes hagiographiques*, Brussels, 1905.

7. Duchesne, *Origines du culte chrétien*, c. VIII, para. 5. Cf. the article by the same author on *Les sources du Martyrologe Hiéronymien*, in *Mélanges de l'Ecole Française*, 1885, and his edition of the *Liber pontificalis*, Vol. I, p. IX, CXLVIII; de Rossi, *Roma sotterranea*, Vol. II, p. X-XXI; Grisar, *Anal. Rom.*, Vol. I, dissert. V.

8. *Acta Ss. Novembr.*, Vol. II, Brussels, 1894. This is the last work of de Rossi, who corrected the proofs a few months before his death.

9. Quentin, *Les Martyrologes historiques du moyen-âge. Etude sur la formation du Martyrologe Romain*, Paris, 1908.

10. *P. L.*, I, Vol. XCIV, col. 799 seq.

11. *P. L.*, I, Vol. CX, col. 1122 seq.

12. *P. L.*, I, Vol. CXXIII, col. 202 seq.

13. *P. L.*, I, Vol. CXXIII-CXXIV, col. 559 seq.

14. *De Lazaro, concio*, IV (*P. G.*, Vol. XLVIII, col. 1097).

15. *De servorum Dei beatificatione et sanctorum canonizatione*, IV, p. 2, CXVII, 9. A few words might be said on the lessons of the Breviary. The same pope condemned with equal force those who attempt to show that "id fabulis esse repletum ejusque auctoritatem in factis historicis esse omnino spernendam," and others who, exaggerating the opposite view, maintain that "adversus Ecclesiae Romanae sensum, impium esse et quasi haereticum de factis historicis in Breviario Romano relatio dubitare, et multo magis iis refragari" (ibid., c. XIII, 7).

16. Duchesne, *Etude sur le "Liber pontificalis,"* Paris, 1877; id., *Liber pontificalis*, Paris, 1886; Grisar. *Anal. Rom.*, Vol. I.

17. Bianchini's edition is reproduced in Migne, *P. L.*, Vols. CXXVII-CXXVIII.

18. According to Fr. Grisar (*Annal. Rom.*, Vol. I, dissert. I), under the pontificate of Boniface II (530-532).

19. Cf. Duchesne, *Origines du culte chrétien*, c. V, para. I.

20. *P. L.*, Vol. LV.

21. "VI id. iul. natale ss. Felicis, Philippi in cymiterio Priscillae; Vitalis et Martialis, in cymiterio Iordanorum; et Silani in cymiterio Maximi, via Salaria; et Ianuarii, in cymiterio Praetextati, via Appia. III non, aug. Natale s. Stephani, in cymiterio Calisti, via Appia. VIII id. aug. Natale s. Xysti in cymiterio Calisti; et Felicissimi et Agapiti, in cymiterio Praetextati, via Appia — Prid. kal. oct. Natale basilicae Angeli in Salaria," etc.

22. *P. L.*, Vol. LXXIV, col. 1055 seq.

23. *S. Greg. Magni vita,* II (*P. L.,* Vol., LXXV, col. 94).
24. Migne (*P. L.,* Vol. LXXVIII, col. 25 seq.) has reproduced the edition of D. Hugues Ménard (1642).
25. Cf. Muratori's edition *Liturgia Romana vetus,* Vol. II.
26. *Epist. et dissert.,* Hamburg, 1720.
27. *Thesaurus novus anecdotorum,* 1717, Vol. V.
28. *Op.,* Vol. II.
29. *Liturgia Rom. pont.,* Vol. III.
30. Cf. Kaufmann, *Handbuch der christlichen Archäologie,* p. 9-51; Leclercq, *Manuel d'Archéol. chrét.,* I, p. 1-59.
31. Cf. Perini, *Onofrio Panvinio e le sue opere,* Rome, 1898.
32. Cf. Fabi-Montani, *Della cultura scientifica di San Filippo Neri e dell'impulso da lui dato agli studi ecclesiastici,* Rome, 1854.
33. *Roma sott.,* Vol. I, p. 12.
34. Recently (Dec., 1921) several galleries of this cemetery were found, revealing important paintings and inscriptions.
35. Fr. Garrucci published the *Hagioglypta sive picturae et sculpturae sacrae antiquiores, praesertim quae Romae reperiuntur, explicatae a Ioanne l'Heureux,* Paris, 1856.
36. *Historia delle stazioni di Roma,* 1588.
37. Cf. Valeri, *Cenni biografici di Antonio Bosio,* Rome, 1900.
38. *Roma sott.,* III, c. 23.
39. Cf. O. Marucchi, *G. B. de Rossi,* Rome, 1901.
40. The complete list, drawn up in 1892 by Gatti for *Albo dei sottoscrittori pel busto marmoreo del comm. G. B. de Rossi,* comprised 145 numbers, to which should be added the published works of the years 1893-1894.

## PART TWO

### CHAPTER I

1. *Apol.,* 21.
2. I Machab., VIII.
3. *Pro Flacco.*
4. *Caesar,* 84.
5. Suetonius, *Tiber.,* 36.
6. Suetonius, *Claud.,* 25; cf. Fouard, *St. Pierre,* n. XIV.
7. *Hist. des Romains,* IV, p. 406.
8. Cf. de Rossi, *Bull. d'Arch. crist.,* 1864, p. 69-72; 1873, p. 21.
9. *Roma sott.,* p. 142.
10. Cf. O. Marucchi, *Di uno nuovo Cimitero giudaico scoperto sulla via Labicana,* in the *Atti della pontif. Accad. Rom. d'Arch.,* 1887.
11. V. *Notizie degli scavi,* 1920; N. *Bull. d'Arch. crist.,* 1920, p. 55.
12. Acts X.
13. Cf. O. Marucchi, *Le memorie dei ss. Apostoli Pietro e Paolo nella città di Roma,* 1894 and 1900; Duchesne, *Les origines chrétiennes,* c. VII; De Smedt, *Dissertat. sel.,* diss. I, *De Rom. s. Petri pontificatu:*

Fr. Martin, *St. Pierre, sa venue et son martyre à Rome,* in the *Revue des questions historiques,* Vol. XIII, pp. 5 seq.; Vol. XV, pp. 5 seq.; Vol. XVIII, pp. 202 seq.

14. St. Jerome, in his rendering into the Latin of the *Chronicle* of Eusebius (*Patr. Lat.,* Vol. XXVII, col. 578).

15. Eusebius, *Hist. eccl.,* V, 6 (*P. G.,* Vol. XX, col. 445).

16. Gebhardt-Harnack, *Clementis Romani ad Corinthios quae dicuntur epistolae,* Leipzig, 1876; Funk, *Op. patr. apost.,* Vol., I; Cf. Duchesne, *Les nouveaux textes de saint Clément de Rome,* in the *Revue du monde catholique,* 1877; D. Germain Morin, O. S. B., published an ancient Latin version of this epistle from a manuscript of the Seminary of Namur, *S. Clementis Romani ad Corinthios epistolae versio Latina antiquissima,* Maredsous, 1894.

17. I ad Cor., VI (*P. G.,* Vol. I, col. 220).

18. Ad Rom., IV (*P. G.,* Vol. V, col. 689).

19. Eusebius' version, *Hist. eccl.,* V, 8 (*P. G.,* Vol. XX, col. 450); cf. Cozza-Luzzi, *Sant'Ireneo. Dell'autorità del romano Pontefice nella Chiesa,* Rome, 1896.

20. Eusebius' version, ibid., II, 25 (*P. G.,* Vol. XX, col. 210).

21. Ibid.

22. *De praescr.* 39 (*P. L.,* Vol. XX, col. 49).

23. Eusebius, op. cit., III, I (*P. G.,* Vol. XX, col. 216).

24. *De schismate Donatistarum,* II, 2 (*P. L.,* Vol. XI, col. 947).

25. *De script. eccles.,* I (*P. L.,* Vol. XXIII, col. 607, 609).

26. *Peristeph.,* hymn. xii (*P. L.,* Vol. LX, col. 356 seq.).

27. *De script. eccles.,* loc. cit.

28. De Rossi, *Bull. d'Arch. crist.,* 1867, p. 53-60.

29. St. Paul salutes him in his Epistle to the Romans, XVI, 3-5; he had been treated as a guest in their home (I Cor., xvi, 19).

30. Orelli, *Inscript. select.,* 956.

31. Cf. de Rossi, *Bull. d'Arch. crist.,* 1867, p. 49 seq.

32. Cf. de Rossi op. cit., 1867, pp. 33-43; 47, 89; *Nuovo Bull.,* 1903, p. 199 seq. It will be taken up in its proper place.

33. Acts XII, 17.

34. "Ad locum qui vocatur naumachia iuxta obeliscum Neronis." The *Book of the Popes* has: "Sepultus iuxta locum ubi crucifixus est iuxta palatium Neronianum in Vaticanum in territorium triumphale." Cf. Grisar, *I Papi nel medio evo,* Vol. I, p. 409; Marucchi, *Le memorie etc.,* p. 75; Bosio, *Roma sotterranea,* II, c. 3. The question of the place of St. Peter's martyrdom has been the occasion for the publication of numerous works and polemics. Mons. G. B. Lugari (*Le lieu du crucifiement de Saint Pierre,* Tours, 1898; *Il Gianicolo, luogo della crocifissione di san Pietro,* Rome, 1908) has attempted to defend the claim that it was the Janiculum. For the same purpose, in 1903, Fr. Bonaventure Lauretti of Vallecorsa republished a dissertation of Fr. John Capistran dedicated to Pius VII: *Il martirio del Principe degli apostoli rivendicato alla sua sede in sul Gianicolo.* In favor of the ancient tradition of the Vatican, Fr. Grisar has written very ably in the *Civiltà Cattolica,* September 16, 1905, p. 719 seq.; cf. O. Marucchi, *La croci-*

*fissione di san Pietro in Vaticano,* in the *Nuovo Bullettino d'Arch. crist.,* 1905, p. 136-183.

35. St. Ambr., *Contr. Auxent.,* 13 (*Patr. Lat.,* Vol. XVI, col. 1011).

36. Acts XXV-XXVI.

37. Acts XXVII-XXVIII.

38. Philip. I, 13. On the possible relation between St. Paul and Seneca, cf. de Rossi, *Bull. d'Arch. crist.,* 1886, p. 62; 1867, p. 7.

39. Rom. XVI, II.

40. Rom. XVI, 8.

41. Cf. O. Marucchi, *Roma sotterranea* (New Series), fasc. 2, Vol. I.

42. *Ann.,* XIII, 32.

43. Rom. I, 8. Some authors, as Duruy (*Histoire des Romains,* IV, p. 723) have denied that Christianity was able to influence the higher levels of Roman society or attract the noble families of the Roman Empire. It is true that St. Paul (I Cor. I, 26) wrote: "Videte vocationem vestram, fratres, quia non multi sapientes secundum carnem, non multi potentes, non multi nobiles." Tertullian (*Ad uxor.,* II, 8 — *P. L.,* Vol. I, col. 1301) and Minucius Felix (*Octav.,* c. 36 — *P. L.,* Vol. III, col. 351) make the following confession: "Plerique pauperes dicimur." And St. Jerome (*In Ep. ad Gal.,* I, III, proem. — *P. L.,* Vol. XXVI, col. 400) says: "Ecclesia de vili plebecula congregata est." But the "non multi" of St. Paul does not absolutely exclude the noble; on the contrary, it indicates that there were some. The words of Tertullian must be supplemented by his own statement elsewhere (*Apol.,* 37 — *P. L.,* Vol. I, col. 462): "Hesterni sumus et vestra omnia implevimus . . . castra, tribus, decurias, palatium, senatum, forum." Cf. de Rossi, *Bullettino d'Arch. crist.,* 1888-1889, p. 57-66, and Leclercq, *Aristocratiques [classes]* in the *Dictionnaire d'Arch.* of Cabrol, Vol. I, col. 2845-2886.

44. II Tim. IV, 17.

45. Rom. XV, 28; cf. St. Clement, *I ad Cor.,* v (*P. G.,* Vol. I, col. 220); St. Athanasius, *Ad Dracont.,* IV (*P. G.,* Vol. V, 528); St. Epiphanius, *Adv. haer.,* XXVII, 6 (*P. G.,* Vol. XLI, col. 373).

## CHAPTER II

1. Tacitus, *Ann.,* XV, 38-44; Suetonius, *Nero,* 31, 38, 39; Dion Cassius, LXII, 16-18.

2. *Hist.,* V, 55.

3. "Primum correpti qui fatebantur, deinde indicio eorum multitudo ingens haud proinde in crimine incendii quam odio humani generis convicti sunt" (Tacitus, op. cit., XV, 44). We do not believe that it is necessary to defend the authenticity of this narration against the objections of Hochart. Cf. Douais, *La persécution des chrétiens de Rome en l'année 64,* in the *Rev. des questions historiques,* Vol. XXXVIII, p. 337-397.

4. I Cor. VI, (*P. G.,* Vol. I, col. 220).

5. I Petr. v, 13. Protestants have been of the opinion that this

treats of the true Babylon. But it is certain that this name, in the language of the first Christians, had a symbolical meaning. Cf. Tertullian, *Apol.*, XIV, 8. It is very unlikely that St. Peter had preached in Babylon; Christianity has never made great progress among the Parthians. Hence, the Protestant opinion is not generally accepted.

6. *Hist. des persécut.*, Vol. I, p. 64.

7. *Epist.*, LXXVIII, *ad Lucie.*

8. *Fatti e leggende di Roma antica*, 1903, p. 117-185.

9. *Les chrétiens ont-ils incendié Rome sous Néron?* Paris, 1904, p. 61.

10. *L'incendio Néroniano, le sue fonti, i suoi tempi*, 1904.

11. Cf. Allard, *Hist. des persécut.*, Vol. I, c. I, IV.

12. *De viris illustribus*, c. XII (*Patr. Lat.*, Vol. XXIII, col. 629).

13. Cf. Duchesne, *Les origines chrétiennes*, c. VII.

14. There are numerous collections of apocryphal Acts concerning the martyrdom of the two Apostles, e. g., the *Acta Lini* and the *Acta Marcelli.* There were, however, original Acts written shortly after the time of the Apostles which were later lost. It may be supposed that the *Passio Petri,* cited by the celebrated *Canon of Muratori,* was the primitive historical fund from which all the later legends were derived. The same must have happened in the case of the Acts of St. Paul.

15. The number of popes during the first century is uncertain. Cf. Duchesne, *Les origines chrétiennes,* c. XII; de Smedt, *Dissertationes selectae,* Vol. I, p. 300-312).

16. What has recently been said by Wilpert concerning the form and dimensions of the sarcophagus of St. Peter, indicated by the *Book of the Popes,* does not go beyond simple hypothesis, and presents many difficulties.

17. Some apocryphal inscriptions are to be referred to the martyrs during the time of Vespasian, as that of the architect of the Flavian amphitheatre, Gaudentius by name; others from a later period, as the inscriptions reported by Pérez (*Histoire d'Espagne*), which speaks of the destruction of Christianity under Diocletian: "Nomine Christianorum ubique deleto . . . "

18. "Permansit, erasis omnibus, hoc solum institutum Neronianum" (Tertullian, *Ad nat.*, I, 7 — *P. L.*, Vol. I, col. 567).

19. Apoc. VI, 9.

20. *I ad Cor.*, I (*P. G.*, Vol. I, col. 285).

21. Pliny, *Ep.*, X, 98.

22. *Hist. eccles.*, III, (*P. G.*, Vol. XX, col. 249).

23. *De praescript.*, 46 (*P. L.*, Vol. II, col. 49).

24. *Domit.*, 15.

25. LXVII, 13.

26. *Hist.*, III, 65.

27. On the distinction between the two Domitillas, denied by Mommsen, Gsell, etc., cf. de Rossi, *Bull. d'Arch. crist.*, 1865, p. 17-24; 1875, p. 69-77. Eusebius presumes it (*Chronic.*, 1, II — *P. G.*, Vol. XIX, col. 551), and his testimony has a particular value because it is

based on the historical Bruttius Presens, who possessed a villa near that of the Flavii.

28. Cf. Marucchi, *Le catacombe Romane secondo le piu recenti scoperte,* 1905, p. 110 seq.

29. Cf. Marucchi, ibid., p. 416 seq.

30. Cf. de Rossi op. cit., 1875, p. 37 seq.; 1888-1889, p. 15-67.

31. Eusebius, op. cit., III, 20 (*P. G.,* Vol. XX, col. 252, 256).

32. *Histoire des persécutions de l'Eglise,* c. IV.

33. *Domit.,* 17.

## CHAPTER III

1. *Epist.* X, 97, 98; cf. Variot, *Les lettres de Pline le Jeune,* in the *Rev. des questions historiques,* Vol. XXIV, p. 80-153.

2. *Apol.,* IV (*P. L.,* Vol. I, col. 285). Mommsen in his *Der Religionsfrevel nach romischen Recht,* in the *Historische Zeitschrift,* Vol. 64, p. 389, denies that there was ever a special law against the Christians. In his opinion, the ancient laws were sufficient to condemn them. Hence, when they refused to swear at the bidding of the emperor, they offended against the *majestas imperatoris* and rendered themselves guilty of the crime of high treason; in professing a foreign religion they fell under the law which made this punishable as disobedience to the fatherland, and overzealous governors were usually not lacking to apply these laws. Cf. Duchesne, *Les origines chrétiennes,* n. IX.

3. Concerning this punishment, cf. de Rossi, *Bull. d'Arch. crist.,* 1868, p. 17; 1879, p. 51-60; 1895, p. 95.

4. *Ad Rom.,* IV (*P. G.,* Vol. V, col. 689).

5. Melito in Eusebius, *Hist. eccl.,* IV, 26 (*P. G.,* Vol. XX, col. 396).

6. St. Justin, *Apolog.,* I, 68-69 (*P. G.,* Vol. VI, col. 432-435).

7. Eusebius, op. cit., IV, 3 (*P. G.,* Vol. XX, col. 308).

8. Leclercq, *Accusations contre les Chrétiens,* in the *Dictionn. d'Arch. et de Litt.,* Vol. I, col. 265-307.

9. Eusebius, op. cit., IV, 15 (*P. G.,* Vol. XX, col. 340 seq).

10. *P. G.,* Vol. VI; cf. Duchesne, *Les origines chrétiennes,* c. XIII; Batiffol, *Anciennes littératures chrétiennes; La Littérature grecque,* p. 86-98; Mgr. Freppel, *Saint Justin et les apologistes du IIe siècle.*

11. A controversy exists concerning a point of detail, an affirmation made by St. Justin. He says that he saw in Rome, on an island in the Tiber, a monument in honor of Simon Magus, with the inscription: "Simoni Deo Sancto" (*Apolog.,* I, 26 — *P. G.,* Vol. VI, col. 368). Mgr. Duchesne thinks that St. Justin made a mistake (*Les origines chrétiennes,* c. VIII). On this selfsame island there was found, in the sixteenth century, an inscription to the god of good faith: SEMONI SANCO DEO FIDIO SACRUM. St. Justin may have taken this Semo Sancus, god of the Sabines, and honored at Rome, for Simon Magus. This hypothesis, however, does not take away every difficulty. Justin was a Samaritan, and as such knew Simon Magus perfectly well; how could he have confused him with the god of the Sabines whose

cult was so celebrated? Nothing prevents us from supposing that the island in the Tiber could have contained not only the monument of Simon Magus but also the one dedicated to Semo Sancus.

12. The testimony of Apollinaris does not remove every motive of doubt. Eusebius, op. cit., V. 5 (*P. G.*, Vol. XX col. 441 seq.). Cf. Duchesne, *Les origines chrétiennes*, p. 374, note.

13. *Apol.*, 5 (*P. L.*, Vol. I, col. 295).

14. The original of this epistle is no longer extant. There is only a re-composition of a later date.

15. op. cit., 1863, p. 19; Doulcet, *Essai sur les rapports de l'Eglise chrétienne avec l'Etat romain pendant les trois premiers siècles*, p. 187 seq.

16. Führer, *Ein Beitrag zur Lösung der Felicitasfrage*, 1890; Mgr. Duchesne is practically of the same opinion (*Liber pontificalis*, Vol. I, p. CI).

17. *Serm.*, 134 (*P. L.*, Vol. LII, col. 565).

18. Thus Aubé (*Les chrétiens dans l'Empire romain de la fin des Antonins au milieu du IIIᵉ siècle*, p. 411, Paris, 1881) places the martyrdom of Cecilia between 251 and 260, under Gallus and Volusianus or under Valerian and Gallienus; Erbes contends that the martyrdom of the saint may have occurred during the persecution of Septimius Severus (202-211); Langen is of the opinion that it happened at the time of Maximinus the Thracian; Kirsch (*Das Todesjar der hl. Cäcilie*, in Στρωμάτιον ἀρχαιολογικόν, Rome, 1900) goes back to the date of 229-230, at the end of the pontificate of Urban and under the reign of Alexander Severus. This opinion is more probable than the one which places the martyrdom of St. Cecilia under Septimius Severus.

19. Cf. Aubé, *Etude sur un nouveau texte grec des Actes des martyrs Scillitains*, 1881.

20. Cf. above, p. 13.

21. XXXVII (*P. L.*, Vol. I, col. 462-465).

## CHAPTER IV

1. Eusebius, *Hist eccl.*, IX, 32; cf. de Rossi, *Bull. d'Arch. crist.*, 1864, p. 51-52; 1866, pp. 9, 40; Harnack, *Die Mission und Ausbreitung des Christenthums in den ersten drei Jahrhunderten*, Leipzig, 1902.

2. *Ad. Scap.*, IV (*P. L.*, Vol. I, col. 703).

3. *Severus*, XVII.

4. *Digest.*, L. L., tit. II, 3.

5. *Apol.*, XXXIX (*P. L.*, Vol. I, col. 470).

6. For the history of Callistus, cf. de Rossi, op. cit., 1866, pp. 1-14, 17-33, 65-72, 77-97; Duchesne, *Les origines chrétiennes*, c. XVIII, XIX; de Smedt, *Dissertationes selectae*, Vol. I, p. 83 seq.

7. *Adv. Gnost. Scorpiace, c. I* (*P. L.*, Vol. I, col. 124-125).

8. Op. cit., VI, c. I (*P. G.*, Vol. XX, col. 521).

9. "Nobis autem sunt quotidie redundantes martyrum fontes, qui nostris spectantur oculis, qui torrentur, torquentur, et capite truncantur." *Strom.* II, c. 20 (*P. G.*, Vol. VIII, col. 1070).

10. *Hist.,* VII, c. 17 (*P. L.,* Vol. XXXI, col. 1103).

11. Tertullian, *Apol.,* XVI (*P. L.,* Vol. I, col. 272-373).

12. Cf. Garrucci, *Un crocifisso grafitto da mano pagana nella casa dei Cesari sul Palatino,* 1856. Wünsche has recently tried to deny the Christian character of this inscription (graffito). In another inscription of the same nature close by, Marucchi supposed was the answer made by a Christian: BOETIA · ΕΠΙ · ΘΕΟΫ · ΒΑΣΙΛΕΥΣ ("Auxilium a Deo Rege"). Cf. Marucchi, *Le Forum romain et le Palatin,* p. 340.

13. *Ad Scap.,* C. III (*P. L.,* Vol. I, col. 701).

14. Cf. Fr. Franchi de' Cavalieri, *La "Passio Ss. Perpetuae et Felicitatis,"* Rome, 1896.

15. *Hist. Fr.,* I, 29 (*P. L.,* Vol. LXXI, col. 174-175).

16. Lampridius, *Alex. Sev.,* 50.

17. Ibid., 21.

18. Ibid., 28, 42.

19. Ibid., 48.

20. "Eo tempore Pontianus episcopus et Yppolitus presbyter exules sunt deportati in Sardinia in insula nociva Severo et Quintiano consulibus. In eadem insula defunctus est IIII kal. oct. et loco ejus ordinatus est Antheros XI kal. dec. consulibus suprascriptis" (*Liber pontificalis*).

21. Cf. Orosius, op. cit., VII, 20 (*P. L.,* Vol. XXXI, col. 1114); St. Jerome, *De viris illustribus,* 54 (*P. G.,* Vol XXIII, col. 665).

22. Op. cit., VI, 34 (*P. G.,* Vol. XX, col. 596).

23. Cf. Duchesne, *Les origines chrétiennes,* p. 381-388.

24. *Epitom.,* 29.

25. *Aurelian.,* 42. The *Historia Augusta* is still an object of important critical study. Numerous German authors hold it to be apocryphal; Dessau believes it to be a falsification of the fifth century. Generally, this advanced opinion is not admitted. All in all, it has been shown that this is a collection of true historical facts, though there are often legendary documents joined with it, as in some small measure in the Acts of the martyrs.

26. The day is even more uncertain than the year. The Martyrology of St. Jerome names them five times: *III id. febr. — XIIII kal. maj. — XVI* and *XIIII kal. iun. — XIII kal. aug.*

27. *Ep. de Basilide et Mart.* (*P. L.,* Vol. III, col. 1029-1030).

28. In the *Sitzungsberichte der Königlichen Akademie der Wissenschaften* of Berlin, 1893, p. 1007-1014; Cf. Fr. Franchi de' Cavalieri, *Due libelli originali di libellatici,* in the *Nuovo Bull. d'Arch. crist.,* 1895, p. 68-73.

29. *P. L.,* Vol. III, col. 1497-1506.

30. *Ep.,* LXXXII (*P. L.,* Vol. IV, col. 430).

31. Cf. de Rossi, *Roma sott.,* Vol. II, I, c. 3.

32. *Carm.* XVIII (*P. L.,* Vol. XIII, col. 392).

33. Cf. de Rossi, *Bull. d'Arch. crist.,* 1881, p. 25-56; 1882, p. 9-77; 1883, p. 60-65; Duchesne, *Les origines chrétiennes,* c. xx; Batiffol *Anciennes littératures chrétiennes: La littérature grecque,* p. 146-169. Mgr. Duchesne does not admit all of de Rossi's dates, but places the death of Hippolytus during a persecution prior to Valerian.

34. *Peristeph.,* XI (*P. L.,* Vol. LX, col. 547 seq).

35. Cf. de Rossi, op. cit., 1881, p. 26-55.

36. Many admit today that the author of the *Philosophumena* is Hippolytus.

37. *P. L.,* Vol. III, col. 1505; cf. Ruinart, *Acta sincera primorum martyrum.*

38. It was thought that there might be an indication of this in a motto inscribed on medals commemorating Salonina: SALONINA AVG IN PACE.

39. Op. cit., VII, c. 13 (*P. G.,* Vol. XX, col. 673-675).

40. *Critic. in Ann. eccles. Baron.,* Vol. III, p. 165.

41. *L'Eglise et l'Etat dans la seconde moitié du III^e siècle,* pp. 444, 451.

42. Allard, *Les dernières persécutions du III^e siècle,* c. v.

43. Allard, ibid., append. J.

44. Op cit., VII, 30 (*P. G.,* Vol. XX, col. 720).

45. *Interpretatio Chronic. Euseb.* (*P. L.,* Vol. XLI, col. 653-654).

46. *De civ. Dei,* XVIII, c. 52 (*P. L.,* Vol. XLI, col. 614) ; cf. Orosius, *Hist.* VII, c. 23 (*P. L.,* Vol. XXXI, col. 1122).

47. *P. L.,* Vol. VII, col. 203.

48. Οἷς ἄν οἱ κατὰ τὴν ᾿Ιταλίαν καὶ τὴν ῾Ρωμαίων πόλιν ἐπίσκοποι τοῦ δόγματος ἐπιστέλλοιεν. Eusebius, *Hist. eccl.,* VII, c. 30 (*P. G.,* Vol. XX, col. 720).

49. Cf. O. Marucchi, *Sant' Agapito Prenestino,* Rome, 1898 (also contains a study on the persecution of Aurelian).

## CHAPTER V

1. *Hist. eccl.,* VIII-IX (*P. G.,* Vol. XX).

2. *P. L.,* Vol. VII.

3. *De corona militis* (*P. G.,* Vol. II).

4. Cf. de Rossi, *Bull. d'Arch. crist.,* 1879, p. 4590.

5. Cf. de Rossi, ibid., 1869, p. 68-72.

6. "Furori ejus repugnavit" (*De mort. persecut.,* XI — *P. L.,* Vol. XII, col. 212).

7. Eusebius, op. cit., VIII, c. 2 (*P. G.,* Vol. XX, col. 744).

8. *P. L.,* Vol. XLIII.

9. De Rossi, op. cit., 1875, p. 162-175; 1876, p. 59-64. Cf. St. Octavius, *De schism. Donatist.,* III, 8 (*P. L.,* Vol. XI, col. 1017-1019).

10. An inscription of Salona says: "Herculi Augusto sacrum, Valerius Valerianus miles cum adsisterem ad capitella columnarum ad termas Licianas quae sunt Sirmium libens solvi."

11. Op. cit., IX, 7 (*P. G.,* Vol. XX, col. 809-816).

12. *C. I. G.,* Vol. III, *Suppl.,* n. 12132. Cf. de Rossi, op. cit., 1894 p. 54. Marucchi, *Un nuovo monumento della persecuzione di Diocleziano* in the *Nuova Antologia,* June, 1893.

13. St. Augustine defends him against the attacks of Petillianus: "Episcopos nominas, quos de traditione codicum soletis arguere. De quibus et nos solemus respondere: Aut non probatis, et ad neminem

pertinet; aut probatis, et ad nos non pertinet" (*Contr. litt. Petilliani,* II, c. xcii — *P. L.,* Vol. XLIII, col. 322 seq.). And in another passage he adds that he was "innocent." Cf. *Nuovo Bull. d'Arch. crist.,* 1907, n. 1-3.

14. Cf. O. Marucchi, *Nuovo Bull. d'Arch. crist.,* 1904, n. 1-4.

15. *Carm.,* XII (*P. L.,* Vol. XIII, col. 385-386).

16. For example, Dodwell, *De paucitate martyrum;* Aubé, *Les Chrétiens dans l'Empire romain de la fin des Antonins au milieu du IIIᵉ siècle,* etc.

17. J. B. de Rossi, *Mélanges,* 1892.

18. *Peristeph.,* Hymn. X, v. 818 (*P. L.,* Vol. LX, col. 506).

## Chapter VI

1. *De vita Constant.,* I, c. 28-29 (*P. G.,* Vol. XX, col. 944).

2. Ibid., c. 31 (*P. G.,* Vol. XX, col. 946).

3. Cf. Cavedoni, *Ricerche critiche intorno alle medaglie di Costantino;* Garrucci, *Le medaglie e monete di Costantino.*

4. *Roma antica* (1838), Vol. I, p. 12.

5. Ibid., Vol. I, p. 447.

6. Cf. de Rossi, *Bull. d'Arch. crist.,* 1863, p. 49-57.

7. *De vita Constant.,* Vol. I, c. 40 (*P. G.,* Vol. XX, col. 953-955).

8. Paper read before the *Pontificia Accademia d'Archeologia,* March 16, 1899.

9. *De morte persecut.,* XLVIII (*P. L.,* Vol. VII, col. 267-270). This proves that the Church already possessed some cemeteries, even before the time of Constantine.

10. Orelli-Henzen, n. 5580.

11. Cf. P. Allard, *Les esclaves chrétiens.* Some writers of the Protestant persuasion, as Pressensé (*Histoire des trois premiers siècles de l'Eglise,* Vol. VI, p. 453-486), Roller (*Les catacombes de Rome,* Vol. I, pp. 38, 271), and freethinkers like Renan (*Marc-Aurèle et la fin du monde antique,* pp. 610, 613) are forced to confess the beneficent action of the Church on the social conditions of the Roman world: "Christianity did not suppress slavery," says Renan, "but it suppressed the practices of slavery"; and again: "The new faith made slavery impossible."

12. Cf. de Rossi, op. cit., 1874, p. 41-73.

13. Cf. Héfélé, *Hist. des Conc.,* V, para. 81.

14. Cf. de Rossi, op. cit., 1883, p. 5-60; 1890, p. 123-140. The attribution of this eulogy to Pope Liberius does not seem sufficiently warranted to Mommsen, who thinks that it ought to be referred rather to Pope Felix II. This opinion, however, is not admissible. It is necessary to note especially that according to the order followed in the manuscript this poem must refer properly to a monument on the Salarian Way, where the tomb of Liberius is to be found; that of Felix II was either on the Aurelian Way or on the Portuan Way.

## Chapter VII

1. Lib. XXII, c. 5.
2. *La fin du paganisme,* 1891.
3. *Orat. IV contr. Julian.,* LXIII-LXIV, etc. (*P. G.,* Vol. XXXV, col. 585).
4. *Hom. in Juventin. et Maximin.,* I (*P. G.,* Vol. L., col. 573).
5. *Hist. eccl.,* I, c. 35 (*P. L.,* Vol. XXI, col. 503).
6. Ibid., III, c. 3, II, etc. (*P. G.,* Vol. LXXXII, col. 1092 seq.).
7. Ibid., III, c. 15-19 (*P. G.,* Vol. LXVII, col. 417 seq.).
8. Ibid., V, c. 9 seq. (*P. G.,* Vol. LXVII, col. 1238 seq.).
9. *De civ. Dei,* XVIII, c. 52 (*P. L.,* Vol. XLI, col. 615).
10. Lib. XXII, c. 12; lib. XXV, c. 2.
11. Tillemont (*Hist. eccles.* VII, p. 352) is of the opinion that it is necessary to refer the martyrs commonly ascribed to the persecution of Julian to that of Diocletian, but de Rossi (*Bull. d'Arch. crist.,* 1890, p. 45) thinks that if the date is doubtful about any of the martyrs, this is not the case with Sts. John and Paul, whom he ascribes to the persecution of Julian. Cf. *La casa Celimontana dei santi martiri Giovanni e Paolo,* discovered and illustrated by P. Germano di Santo Stanislao, Rome, 1894; P. Allard, *Etudes d'histoire et d'Archéologie,* p. 159 seq.; Mazzocchi, *Kal. Neap.,* III, p. 722 seq. Recently, Pio Franchi de' Cavalieri has denied that Sts. John and Paul were martyred under Julian, holding that they were martyred in a previous persecution and maintaining that their relics may have been moved to Mt. Coelius. But one might cite some serious difficulties confronting this opinion.
12. Sozomen, *Hist. eccles.,* VII, c. 22 (*P. G.,* Vol. LXVII, col. 1485-1488); Rufinus, *Hist. eccles.,* II, 33 (*P. L.,* Vol. XXI, col. 539-540); Theodoret, *Hist. eccles.,* V, 24 (*P. G.,* Vol. LXXXII, col. 1248-1253); Zosimus, *Hist.,* IV, 5; Prudentius, *Contra Symmach.,* V, 410 seq. (*P. L.,* Vol. LX, col. 153 seq.).
13. This tablet was found again in 1848; it is reproduced in an article of J. B. de Rossi's in the *Annali dell'Istituto Germanico,* 1849.
14. Cf. de Rossi, *Bull. d'Arch. crist.,* 1868, p. 49-75.
15. Cf. de Rossi, ibid., 1865, p. 3-8; 1866, p. 52-57; Winckelmann, *Storia delle Arti,* translated into the Italian and annotated by Fea, Vol. III, p. 267 seq.
16. *Epist.* (*P. L.,* Vol. XVIII, col. 391).
17. *Hist.,* V, 38.
18. Cf. *C. I. L.,* especially in Vol. VI.
19. "Christianity well understood that the monuments of pagan Rome formed an integral part of a glory which it could not deny, because, according to the secret designs of Providence, it had served to group the nations as one family and thus prepare them to receive the Gospel.... In general, it can be said that the Middle Ages preserved

and saved many of the records which remained of pagan antiquity"
(A. Geffroy, *Etudes italiennes,* Florence and Rome, 1893).

20. Cf. Lanciani, *La destruction de Rome antique,* translated by
D. L'Huillier, Desclée, 1905.

# PART THREE

# INTRODUCTION

1. Armellini, *I cimiteri cristiani di Rome e d'Italia,* p. 41-117;
Kaufmann, *Handbuch der christl. Arch.,* p. 111; Leclercq, *Manuel
d'Archéologie chrét.,* Vol. I, c. II; O. Marucchi, *Le Catacombe romane*
(1905).

2. A. Peraté, *L'Archéologie chrétienne,* p. 15.

3. Michael Stephen de Rossi has shown, with absolute scientific
accuracy, the original use of the Christian cemeteries in his *Analisi
geologica ed architettonica.* This scientifically exact geologic and architectonic analysis was placed at the end of Volume I of J. B. de Rossi's
*Roma sotterranea.*

## CHAPTER I

1. De Rossi, *Roma sott.,* Vol. 1 p. 83-108; *Bull. d'Arch. crist.,*
1865, p. 89.

2. *Act.,* VIII, 2.

3. *P. G.,* Vol. V, col. 1043.

4. Cf. Cabrol, *Dictionn. d'Arch. chrét.,* Vol. I, 479-509: "Ad
Sanctos."

5. During the excavations made in recent years in the cemetery of
Commodilla, numerous inscriptions of the fifth and even of the sixth
century have been found. However, the general rule still holds good
for the great majority of the tombs.

6. The graffiti will receive special attention in Part IV, which
treats of inscriptions, etc.

7. *Hom.* XXVIII, given at the Basilica of Sts. Nereus and Achilleus (*P. L.,* Vol. LXXVI, col. 1212).

8. Cf. Grisar, *Storia di Roma e dei Papi nel medioevo,* Vol. I, 3,
*The Pontificate of St. Gregory the Great.*

9. *Itin. d'Einsiedeln;* cf. de Rossi, *Inscript. Christ.,* II, p. 24.

10. *Itin. Salisburgense;* cf. Marucchi, *Il cimiterio e la basilica di San
Valentino,* p. 115.

11. Cf. de Rossi, *Roma sott.,* Vol. I, p. 144.

12. *Hist. eccles.,* V, c. 7 (*P. L.,* Vol. XCV, col. 237).

13. *Itin. Salisburg.* The author wrote "tamen quiescunt," but the
sense is clear and leaves no doubt as to the meaning.

14. *P. L.,* Vol. LV, col. 48.

15. "There were two categories of churches, the ordinary churches
which were nothing more than places for liturgical assemblies, and
churches where rested the bodies of the saints. . . . The second type was
represented by a small number of sacred edifices, limiting itself to those

churches really built on the tombs of the martyrs, relatively few in number, of whom there was still preserved the memory and cult.

"But, by a species of legal fiction, it soon became the practice that one saint could have a great number of tombs. Any sort of relic, a small piece of cloth soaked in the blood of the martyr, a vial of oil taken from the sanctuary lamp, a fragment of material cut from the veil which covered the sarcophagus, was sufficient to represent him at a distance. To possess an object of this kind was to possess the body of the saint itself; and to transfer it and deposit it in a church was similar to burying the very body of the saint.

"There were thus tombs representative of saints without number or limit. In this manner, churches with relics became as numerous as the others; and even more numerous when these churches came to enjoy a prestige greater than all others. It was then impossible to conceive of a church which did not have relics in its altar" (Duchesne, *Origines du culte chrétien,* c. XII, para. 1). This explanation makes us understand how it was possible to find, in Africa, inscriptions of the fifth century mentioning at Megroun, a "memoria domni Petri et Pauli"; at Orléansville, a Christian buried "aput (Sanctos) Petru et (Paulu)"; at Setif, "reliquiae sancti Laurenti martyris." Cf. St. Greg. the Great, *Epist.,* IV, 30 (*P. G.,* Vol. LXXVII, col. 702); de Rossi, *Bull. d'Arch. crist.* 1877, p. 97.

16. Cf. Fr. Fabre, *De patrimoniis S. Romanae Ecclesiae,* Paris, 1892, and *Les colons de l'Eglise Romaine au VIᵉ siècle,* in the *Revue d'histoire et de littérature religieuses,* 1896.

17. Cf. *Mon. Germ. Hist., Script.,* XV; Guiraud, *Le commerce des reliques* in *Mélanges,* J. B. de Rossi, 1892.

18. Cf. Paschalis pp. I, *Ep.* (*P. L.,* Vol. CII, col. 1085-1088).

19. The celebrated inscription of this translation, according to Grossi-Gondi, is a copy of an ancient exemplar.

20. *Liber pontificalis.*

21. Mabillon, *Vet. analecta,* p. 350 seq.; cf. Marucchi, *Il cimitero e la basilica di S. Valentino,* p. 132 seq.

22. Cf. de Rossi, *Roma sott.,* Vol. I, p. 101-108; *Bull. d'Arch. crist.,* 1864, p. 25-32; 1865, p. 89-99; Allard, *Hist. des perséc.,* Vol. II, c. I and append. *A* and *B;* Duchesne, *Les origines thrétiennes,* c. XXIII, para. 4.

23. See above, Part II, c. VI.

24. Eusebius, *Hist. eccl.,* IX, 10 (*P. G.,* Vol. XX, col. 832-836).

25. Eusebius, *ibid.,* VII, 13 (*P. G.,* Vol. XX, col. 675).

26. In *Aurelian.,* XX.

27. *Sever.,* XLIV. In the same manner the phrase of Tertullian: "de areis sepulturarum nostrarum" (*ad Scap.,* c. III (*P. L.,* Vol. I, col. 701) seems to indicate a collective ownership.

28. The question has been very well treated by Allard, *Le Christianisme et l'Empire Romain de Néron à Théodose,* p. 76-89.

29. Cf. Williams, *Exempla inscript. Lat.,* Vol. I, p. 116.

30. "It is enjoined on the heads of provinces by special regulations that they do not permit societies, organizations nor associations of

soldiers in the camps; but it is permissible for those of slender means to give a monthly stipend provided they come together only once a month. It should be seen to, that this be not used as an excuse to organize illegal societies, which the divine emperor Severus has forbidden not only in the city but also in the provinces. It is not prohibited to persons to come together for religious purposes, but only so long, however, as these do not perform anything which has already been forbidden by the decree of the senate" (*Digest.*, XLVII, tit. 22, n. I).

31. Cf. Mommsen, *De collegiis et sodaliciis Romanorum.*
32. *Apol.*, 39 (*P. L.*, Vol. I, col. 570).
33. This beautiful inscription is no longer at Civita-Lavinia, but has been carried to Rome where it is preserved in the Museum delle Terme.
34. Williams, op. cit., p. 100-112.
35. Cabrol, *Dictionn. d'Arch. chrét.*, Vol. I, col. 775-848: "Agape."
36. Renier, *Inscript. de l'Algérie*, n. 4025.
37. Cf. de Rossi, *Bull. d'Arch. crist.*, 1864, p. 28.
38. *Les origines chrétiennes*, XXIII, para. IV.
39. *Apol.*, 39 (*P. L.*, loc. cit.).
40. *Ep. de Basilide et Martiali* (*P. L.*, Vol. III, col. 1030).
41. Loc. cit., p. 401-403. The author maintains this theory in his recent book, *Histoire ancienne de l'Eglise* (1906), Vol. I.
42. De Rossi, *Roma sotterr.*, Vol. III, III.

## CHAPTER II

1. Cf. de Rossi, *Roma sotterr.*, Vol. III, III.
2. To render these notions of the nomenclature employed in the early Christian cemeteries clearer, a plan of the general lay-out of a cemetery and several reproductions of galleries, corridors, *arcosolia* and burial will be given in the following pages.
3. Kaufmann, *Handbuch der christlichen Archäologie*, p. 117; Leclercq, *Manuel d'Arch. chrét.*, Vol. I, V, "Definitions," p. 79-100.
4. Cf. O. Marucchi's observations in the *Nuovo Bull. d'Arch. crist.*, 1904 p. 207 seq.
5. Cf. Cabrol, *Dictionnaire d'Arch. et de Litt. chrétienne*, art. "Arcosolium," Vol. I, col. 2774-2787.
6. Marchi, *I monumenti delle arti crist. prim.*, p. 85.
7. *De corona militis*, III (*P. L.*, Vol. II, col. 79).
8. *Comm. in Job.*, III (*P. L.*, Vol. XVII, col. 517).
9. *Contr. Faust.*, XX, 21 (*P. L.*, Vol. XLII, col. 384-385).
10. *Confess.*, IX, 12 (*P. L.*, Vol. XXXII, col. 777).
11. *De cura pro mortuis gerenda*, written about 421 (*P. L.*, Vol. XL, col. 591, seq).
12. *Cathemer.*, hymn II; *Peristeph.*, hymn III (*P. L.*, vol. LIX, col. 880 seq.; Vol. IX, col. 353 seq.).
13. *Contr. Faust.*, XX, 20 (*P. L.*, Vol. XLII, col. 383).

14. *Acta s. Cyprian.* V (*P. L.,* Vol. III, col. 1505).

15. *Peristeph.,* hymn XI (*P. L.,* Vol. LX, col. 545). And elsewhere (Hymn V, loc. cit., col. 398):

> "Plerique vestem linteam
> Stillante tingunt sanguine
> Tutamen ut sacrum suis
> Domi reservent posteris."

16. *Serm.,* XVIII (*P. L.,* Vol. XX, col. 963).

17. Cf. De Buck, Bolland, *De phialis rubricalis quibus martyrum Romanorum sepulcra dignosci dicuntur,* Brussels, 1855; F. X. Kraus, *Die Blutampullen der römischen Katacomben,* Frankfurt, 1868; also Cabrol, *Dictionnaire d'Arch. chrét.,* "Ampoules de sang," by H. Leclercq, Vol. I, col. 1747-1778.

## CHAPTER III

1. *Roma sotterr.,* Vol. III, III. Cf. de Rossi, *Bull. d'Arch. crist.,* 1864, p. 25-32.

2. De Rossi, *Bull. d'Arch. crist.,* 1874, p. 88-90; Bertolini, *Scavi di antichità nell'area dell'antica Julia Concordia Colonia,* Rome, 1881.

3. Cf. Bulic-Jelic, *Guida di Spalato e Salona,* 1894.

4. Cf. Le Blant, *Epigraphie de la Gaule.*

5. Cf. O. Marucchi, *Guida archeologica della città di Palestrina,* 1912, p. 161.

6. Cabrol, *Dictionn. d'Arch. chrét.,* under the word "Area," by Leclercq, Vol. I, col. 2787-2802.

7. This basilica was located near the cemetery of Callistus.

8. The meaning of the word *memoria* in epigraphic and sepulchral language is determined by the title (*titulus*) written on the commemorative inscriptions of the deceased: MEMORIAM POSVIT, FECIT. The Christians applied this word in an especial manner to the tombs which contained relics. Within the confines of a basilica or of an oratory, the *memoria martyris* is composed of two essential parts: the lower is the confession, a reduced copy of the underground chapel; the upper is the altar with its *ciborium.* Cf. de Rossi, *Roma sotterr.,* Vol. III, p. 425-426; *Bull. d'Arch. crist.,* 1877, p. 97 seq.; Martigny, *Dictionnaire des antiq. chrét.,* under the word "Confessio"; Cabrol, *Dictionn. d'Arch. chrét.,* under the word "Apse," by H. Leclercq, Vol. I, p. 183-197.

9. Cf. de Rossi, *Roma sotterr.,* Vol. III, III.

## CHAPTER IV

1. It is called *Liberian* and was published for the first time by Bucher, *De doctrina temporum* (Antwerp, 1634), for which reason it is also known as the Bucherian calendar.

2. This indicates the difference between the two adjoining catacombs.

3. Feast of the Primacy of Peter.

4. Cf. Urlichs, *Codex urbis Romae topographicus,* p. 1 seq.

5. It is very noticeable that the Greater Cemetery of St. Agnes on the Nomentan Way, where St. Emerentiana was interred, is omitted from this calendar: a thing that would not have happened had it been as important as some suppose it to be who identify it with the *Ostrian Cemetery.*

6. Consult the important article of Schneider-Graziosi, published in the *Nuovo Bullet. di Arch. crist.,* 1909, p. 79 seq.

7. Urlichs, op. cit., p. 86 seq.

8. *Vetera analecta,* Vol. IV; cf. Urlichs, op. cit., p. 59 seq.

9. Urlichs, op. cit., p. 59 seq.

10. *P. L.,* Vol. CI, col. 1359 seq.

11. A reprint of these documents will be given further on.

12. This catalogue, very much mutilated, was transcribed after the *Notitia regionum Urbis Romae* which forms Ms. 3851 of the Vatican Library.

13. Cf. de Rossi, *Bull. d'Arch. crist.,* 1878, p. 44 seq.; Urlichs, op. cit., p. 91 seq.

14. Published by Marini, *Papiri diplomatici,* Rome, 1805, p. 208-209. Another publication was made of it recently by Sepulcri, *I papiri di Monza,* Milan, 1903.

15. Marucchi, *Il valore topografico della silloge de Verdun e del papiro di Monza* in the *Nuovo Bull. d'Arch. crist.,* 1903, n. 4.

16. Cf. de Rossi, *Roma sotterr.,* I, p. 175 seq.

## CHAPTER V

1. Those who wish to go into this matter more deeply should consult Marucchi's *Le Catacombe romane,* Rome, Desclée, 1905. The remarks here are a compendium of the above volume which, in its turn, is a synopsis of the *Roma sotterranea.*

2. Cf. above, the tables of the Itineraries: Cornelian Way; Armellini, *Gli antichi Cimiteri crist.,* p. 258; Marucchi, *Le Catacombe rom.,* p. 31.

3. Tacitus, *Annal.,* XV, 44.

4. Cf. above, Part II.

5. *Book of the Popes* on "Anacletus."

6. Cf. Barnes, *St. Peter in Rome and His Tomb on the Vatican Hill,* London, 1900.

7. The plan of these ruins found in the sixteenth century was designed by Benedetto Drei and published by de Rossi (*Inscript. christ.,* Vol. II, p. 235).

8. Eusebius, *Hist. eccl.,* Vol. II, c. 25.

9. Cf. Marucchi, op. cit., p. 46.

10. Cf. *Liber pontif.,* under the biography of Sergius II, 846 A.D.

11. Cf. Middleton, *Remains of Ancient Rome,* 1892; Grisar, *Civiltà cattol.,* 1859, fasc. I, p. 202 seq; Marucchi, *Basiliques et églises de Rome.*

12. Cf. Dufresne, *Les chryptes Vaticanes,* 1902.

13. Op. cit.

14. Cf. above, tables of the Itineraries: Aurelian Way.

15. Cf. Armellini, op. cit., p. 513; Marucchi, op. cit., p. 53.

16. *Liber pontif.,* under "Symmachus."

17. Cf. Urlichs, *Cod. Urb. Rom. topogr.,* p. 63.

18. Cf. Armellini, op. cit., p. 520; Marucchi, op. cit., p. 56.

19. *Hom. in Evangel.,* II, hom. 32 (*P. L.,* Vol. LXXVI, col. 1237).

20. In *Vita Symmachi*: "In fundo Lardario, basilica B. M. Agathae."

21. Cf. Armellini, op. cit., p. 542; Marucchi, op. cit., p. 61.

22. *Roma sotterr.,* II, 13.

23. Cf. Armellini, op. cit., p. 522; Marucchi, op. cit., p. 62.

24. Cf. *Liber pontif.,* under the biography of Julius I.

25. Cf. above, tables of the Itineraries, Portuan Way.

26. Cf. Armellini, op. cit., p. 503; Marucchi, op. cit., p. 66.

27. Cf. Marchi, *I monumenti delle arti cristiane primitive,* etc., pp. 17-32, 220-223.

28. Armellini, op. cit., p. 512; Marucchi, op. cit., p. 73.

29. Cf. article by Prof. Tomassetti published in the *Nuovo Bullet. di Arch. crist.,* 1889, p. 77.

30. Cf. de Rossi, *Roma sotterr.,* Vol. III; *Bull. di Arch. crist.,* 1868, pp. 25, 31, 48, 84; 1869, p. 1; 1874, p. 131.

31. This sarcophagus is preserved in the palace of St. Mary Major.

32. Cf. de Rossi, op. cit., Vol. III.

33. Cf. above, tables of the Itineraries: Ostian Way.

34. Cf. Stevenson, *Osservazioni sulla topografia della via Ostiense e sul cimitero ove fu sepolto l'apostolo san Paolo. L'area di Lucina sulla via Ostiense* in the *Nuovo Bull. di Arch. crist.,* 1897, p. 283, and 1898, p. 60 seq.; Cf. also Armellini, op. cit., p. 479; Marucchi, op. cit., p. 86.

35. Cf. above, Part II.

36. Baronius, *Ann.,* 386 A. D.

37. *Roma sotterr.,* III, 2.

38. Stevenson, in the *Nuovo Bull.,* loc. cit.

39. Armellini, op. cit., p. 486; Marucchi, op. cit., p. 98.

40. Delehaye, *Les saints du cimitière de Commodille* in *Analecta Bolland.,* 1897, Vol. I, p. 17. According to this author, the word *Degna* was derived from the false reading of an inscription.

41. Boldetti, *Osservazioni sopra i Cimiteri,* p. 542.

42. *Acta Sanctorum,* August 30, Vol. VI.

43. Wilpert, *Di tre pitture recentemente scoperte nella basilica dei Santi Felice e Adautto nel cimitero di Commodilla,* in *Nuovo Bull. d'Arch. crist.* 1904, p. 1-10.

44. For a complete illustration of the monuments so far found in the cemetery of Commodilla, see Marucchi, *Nuovo Bull.,* 1904 and 1905.

45. Armellini, op. cit., p. 491; Marucchi, *Le Catacombe rom.,* p. 103.

46. De Rossi, *Bull. d'Arch. crist.,* 1872.

47. Armellini, *Das wieder gefundene Oratorium der H. Thecla an der via Ostiense,* in the *Römische Quartalschrift,* an. I; Armellini, op. cit., p. 498; Marucchi, op. cit., p. 104.

48. Cf. above, tables of the Itineraries: Ardeatine Way.

49. Cf. de Rossi, *Bull. d'Arch. crist.,* 1865, 1874, 1875; Armellini, op. cit., p. 433-439; Marucchi, op. cit., p. 110-145.

50. De Rossi, *Bull. d'Arch. crist.,* 1865, p. 33-46.

51. Cf. above, Part II.

52. De Rossi, *Bull. d'Arch. crist.,* 1881.

53. Cf. above, Part II.

54. Cf. above, tables of the Itineraries: Appian Way.

55. Cf. de Rossi, *Roma sotterr.,* 1864-77; Armellini, op. cit., p. 359; Marucchi, op. cit., p. 148.

56. Cf. *Römische Quartalschrift,* 1901; *Nuovo Bull. d'Arch. crist.* 1903, p. 43 seq.; 1905, p. 191 seq.

57. Cf. above, Part II.

58. Wilpert, *Die Malereien der Sakramentskapelten, in der Katakombe des hl. Callistus,* Freiburg, 1897.

59. Armellini, op. cit., p. 409; Marucchi, op. cit., p. 202.

60. *Silloges,* Ihm, number 26.

61. Cf. *Nuovo Bull. d'Arch. crist.,* 1916, 1919, 1920, 1921.

62. Cf. de Rossi, op. cit., Vol. I, p. 235 seq.

63. Armellini, op. cit., p. 396; Marucchi, op. cit., p. 216.

64. *Scoperta di un graffito nel cimitero di Pretestato sulla via Appia,* Rome, 1874.

65. Kanzler, *Restaurazione architettonica della cripta dei Ss. Felicissimo e Agapito* in the *Nuovo Bull. d'Arch. crist.,* 1895, p. 172.

66. Cf. above, tables of the Itineraries, Latin Way; Armellini, *I Cimit. crist. della via Latina,* Rome, 1874; Marucchi, op. cit., p. 248.

67. *Nuovo Bull. d'Arch. crist.,* 1911.

68. Ibid., 1921.

69. Cf. above, tables of the Itineraries: Labican Way.

70. Armellini, *Gli antichi Cimit. crist.,* p. 323; Marucchi, op. cit., p. 258.

71. Cf. Iozzi, *Il cimitero di San Castulo sulla via Labicana,* Rome, 1904.

72. Armellini, op. cit., p. 327; Marucchi, op. cit., p. 260.

73. Cf. Marucchi, *La cripta storica dei Santi Pietro e Marcellino recentemente scoperta sulla via Labicana* in the *Nuovo Bull. d'Arch. crist.,* 1898, p. 137.

74. Cf. above, tables of the Itineraries: Tiburtine Way.

75. Cf. Armellini, op. cit., p. 293; Marucchi, *Le Catacombe rom.,* p. 299.

76. Cf. above, Part II.

77. Cf. Armellini, op. cit., p. 312; Marucchi, op. cit., p. 320.

78. Cf. above, Part II.

79. Cf. de Rossi, *Bull. d'Arch. crist.,* 1881-1883.

80. Cf. above, tables of the Itineraries: Nomentan Way.

81. Cf. Armellini, op. cit., p. 248; Marucchi, op. cit., p. 341.

82. Cf. Armellini, *Il cimitero di Sant'Agnese sulla via Nomentana descritto ed illustrato,* Rome, 1880; Marucchi, op. cit., p. 347; Jubaru, *Sainte Agnès d'après de nouvelles recherches,* Paris, 1907.

83. A learned monograph, *Sant'Agnese nella storia e nella leggenda,* Rome, 1899; was published by Pio Franchi de' Cavalieri.

84. Armellini, *Gli antichi cimit. crist.,* p. 273; Marucchi, op. cit., p. 366.

85. Cf. Marucchi's articles in the *Nuovo Bull. d'Arch. crist.* for the year 1901 and following.

86. Armellini, op. cit., p. 544; Marucchi, op. cit., p. 379.

87. O. Marucchi, *Il cimitero e la basilica di Sant'Alessandro,* published by the Propaganda in 1922.

88. Cf. above, tables of the Itineraries: New Salarian Way.

89. Cf. Armellini, op. cit., p. 195; Marucchi, *Le Catacombe rom.,* p. 388.

90. Cf. above, Part II.

91. Armellini, op. cit., p. 209; Marucchi, op. cit., p. 400.

92. Ihm, *Damasi epigrammata,* 40.

93. Cf. Armellini, op. cit., p. 209; Marucchi, op. cit., p. 404.

94. Cf. de Rossi, *Bull. d'Arch. crist.,* 1873, pp. 6 seq., 37 seq.

95. Cf. Armellini, op. cit., p. 221; Marucchi, op. cit., p. 416.

96. Wilpert, *"Fractio panis," die älteste Darstellung des eucharistichen Opfers,* Freiburg, 1895. An illustration of this and of other important paintings of the catacombs will be found in Part V, which treats of Christian art.

97. Cf. de Rossi, *Bull. d'Arch. crist.* 1888, 1889.

98. Cf. above, Part II.

99. Cf. Marucchi's article: *Il sepolcro del papa Marcellino nel cimitero di Priscilla,* in the *Nuovo Bull. d'Arch. crist.,* 1907, p. 115.

100. Cf. above, tables of the Itineraries: Old Salarian Way.

101. Cf. de Rossi, op. cit., 1865, p. 1; Armellini, op. cit., p. 171; Marucchi, *Le Catacombe rom.,* p. 525.

102. Cf. above, Part II; de Rossi, op. cit., 1891, p. 58.

103. This cemetery was especially explored by Dr. E. Iosi, whose findings have been published in the *Rivista d'Archeologia cristiana,* 1924, 1926.

104. Cf. *Nuovo Bull. d'Arch. crist.,* 1920, p. 60.

105. Cf. Armellini, op. cit., p. 177; Marucchi, op. cit., p. 323.

106. Cf. Armellini, op. cit., p. 192; Marucchi, op. cit., p. 537.

107. Cf. above, tables of the Itineraries: Flaminian Way; Marucchi, *Il cimitero e la basilica di San Valentino,* Rome, 1890.

## Chapter VI

1. Cf. Armellini, *Gli antichi Cimit. crist.,* p. 541; Marucchi, *Le Catacombe rom.,* p. 639.

2. Cf. de Rossi, *Bull. d'Arch. crist.,* 1875, p. 107; Armellini, op. cit., p. 616.

3. Cf. de Rossi, op. cit., 1894, p. 133.
4. Cf. Armellini, op. cit., p. 615; de Rossi, op. cit., 1875, p. 105.
5. Cf. Nibby, *Analisi della carta dei dintorni di Roma,* p. 607; Armellini, op. cit., p. 609; Marucchi, op. cit., 696.
6. Cf. de Rossi, op. cit., 1866.
7. Cf. Bosio, *Roma sotterr.,* p. 233; Armellini, op. cit., p. 597; Marucchi, op. cit., p. 696.
8. Lateran Museum, Part XXI.
9. Cf. de Rossi, op. cit., 1877, p. 136.
10. Cf. Armellini, op. cit., p. 596.
11. Cf. Boldetti, *Osservazioni,* p. 558; Armellini, op. cit., p. 582.
12. Cf. de Rossi, op. cit., 1869, p. 65; 1873, p. 83; Armellini, op. cit., p. 584; Marucchi, op. cit., p. 645.
13. Armellini, op. cit., p. 590.
14. Cf. de Rossi, op. cit., 1869, p. 79; 1894, p. 96.
15. Cf. de Rossi, ibid., 1873, p. 107; Schneider, *Nuovo Bull. d'Arch. crist.,* 1901, p. 269.
16. Cf. de Rossi, op. cit., 1876, pp. 32 and 153.
17. Cf. de Rossi, ibid., 1872, pp. 85 and 125; 1873, p. 83.
18. Boldetti, op. cit., p. 566; Armellini, op. cit., p. 574.
19. Boldetti, op. cit., p. 564; Stevenson, *Il cimitero di Zotico al X miglio della via Labicana,* 1876.
20. Cf. de Rossi, op. cit., 1873, p. 115; Armellini, op. cit., p. 561.
21. Cf. Marucchi, op. cit., p. 665; *Sant' Agapito Prenestino,* Rome, 1898.
22. Cf. Stevenson, *La basilica di Santa Sinforosa e dei suoi sette figli,* 1877.
23. Cf. Armellini, op. cit., p. 557.
24. Cf. Boldetti, *Osservazioni,* p. 575; Armellini, op. cit., 542.
25. Cf. Armellini, ibid., p. 543.
26. Cf. de Rossi, op. cit., 1883, p. 115 seq.; Armellini, op. cit., p. 622.
27. Cf. de Rossi, op. cit., 1883, p. 143 seq.; Armellini, op cit., p. 631.
28. Cf. de Rossi, op. cit., 1875, p. 142 seq.; Armellini, op. cit., p. 626.
29. Cf. *Nuovo Bull. d'Arch. crist.,* 1921, pp. 44 and 83.

## Chapter VII

1. Müller, *Koimeterien,* p. 13 seq.; Armellini, op. cit., p. 619-763; Kaufmann, *Handbuch der christl. Archäol.,* p. 90; Leclercq, *Manuel d'Arch. chrét.,* I, p. 460.
2. Cf. de Rossi, *Bull. d'Arch. crist.,* 1876, p. 69; 1879, p. 128; Armellini, *Gli antichi Cimit. crist.,* p. 669; Cabrol, *Dictionn. d'Arch. chrét.,* Vol. I, col. 1993.
3. Boldetti, *Osservazioni,* p. 603; Armellini, op. cit., p. 687; Marucchi, in the *Nuovo Bull. d'Arch. crist.,* 1892, p. 259; Bevignani, ibid., 1903, p. 187.

4. Cf. de Rossi, op. cit., 1882, p. 89; Armellini, op. cit., p. 668.
5. Armellini, op. cit., p. 762.
6. Armellini, ibid., p. 711; Galante, *Il cimitero di Sant' Ipolisto, martire in Atripalda,* Naples, 1893; Cabrol, op. cit., Vol. I, col. 3115.
7. Taglialatela, *Dell'antica basilica e della catacomba di Prata.* 1878; Armellini, op. cit., p. 710.
8. Boldetti, op. cit., p. 609; Armellini, op. cit., p. 716.
9. P. Germano, *Gli Atti e il cimitero di Sant' Eutizio di Ferento.* p. 331.
10. Armellini, op. cit., p. 692; Bevignani, op. cit., 1903, p. 187.
11. Cf. de Rossi, *Bull. d'Arch. crist.,* 1887, p. 94; Armellini, op. cit., p. 651.
12. Armellini, ibid., p. 671.
13. De Rossi, op. cit., 1880, p. 71; 1894, p. 120; Stevenson, *L'ipogeo cristiano di Santa Cristina a Bolsena,* Rome, 1881; *Römische Quartalschrift,* 1880, p. 327; 1889, p. 79; *Bull. della Società storica Volsiniese,* 1892, p. 97.
14. Armellini, op. cit., p. 652.
15. Boldetti, op. cit., p. 559; Odorici, *Antichità cristiane di Brescia,* 1848-1868; Armellini, op. cit., p. 678.
16. De Rossi, op. cit., 1892, p. 130; Pinza, *Nuovo Bull. d'Arch. crist.,* 1901, p. 61.
17. Cf. de Rossi, op. cit., 1884, p. 105-125; Armellini, op. cit., p. 694.
18. De Rossi, op. cit., 1884, pp. 36, 118-127; G. Cosenza, *Il cimitero e la cappela stabiana di San. Biagio, Naples,* 1898; F. S. Kraus, *Roma sotterranea,* p. 602 seq.
19. De Rossi, op. cit., 1868, p. 75; *Notizie degli scavi,* 1895, p. 385; Armellini, op. cit., p. 736.
20. De Rossi, op. cit., 1874, p. 84; Armellini, op. cit., p. 621.
21. Bartolini, *Le nuove catacombe di Chiusi,* 1852; Liverani, *Le catacombe di Chiusi,* 1872; de Rossi, op. cit., 1865, p. 51; 1876, p. 91 seq.
22. De Rossi, op. cit., 1887, p. 104; Armellini, op. cit., p. 636.
23. Armellini, op. cit., p. 664; de Rossi, op. cit., 1874, p. 81-118.
24. De Rossi, op. cit., 1880, p. 70; Armellini, op. cit., p. 630.
25. Armellini, op. cit., p. 945.
26. P. Germano di Santo Stanislao, *Sant'Eutizio di Ferento,* 1881.
27. Picone, *Memorie storiche agrigentine,* 1866-80; de Rossi, op. cit., 1875, p. 83; *Notizie degli scavi,* 1901, p. 20 seq.
28. Armellini, op. cit., p. 734.
29. Boldetti, *Osservazioni,* p. 596; Armellini, op. cit., p. 668.
30. Armellini, op. cit., p. 733.
31. Cavallari, *Appendice della topografia archeol. di Siracusa,* 1891.
32. Boldetti, op. cit., p. 624; Armellini, op. cit., p. 734.
33. Boldetti, *Osservazioni,* p. 615; Polidori, *Una catacomba dei primi secoli scoperta in Milano,* and also *Sopra alcuni sepolcri antichi e*

*cristiani,* 1845; de Rossi, *Bull. d'Arch. crist.,* 1864, p. 29 seq.; Armellini, op. cit., p. 673 seq.

34. Cf. de Rossi, op. cit., 1867, p. 72; 1871, pp. 37 and 155; 1883, p. 85; 1887, p. 122; Galante, *Guida sacra della città di Napoli,* Naples, 1873; Scherillo, *Archeologia sacra,* Vol. I, Naples, 1875; Armellini, op. cit., p. 697 seq.; Galante, *Relatazione sulle catacombe di San Gennaro,* in the *Rendiconti della Reale Accad. di Napoli,* 1900; *Nuovo Bull. d'Arch. crist.,* 1900, p. 177.

35. Cf. de Rossi, op. cit., 1867, p. 30; Armellini, op. cit., p. 647.

36. Boldetti, op. cit., p. 579; de Rossi, op. cit., 1874, p. 113; *Römische Quartalschrift,* 1893, p. 84; Armellini, op. cit., p. 635.

37. Boldetti, op. cit., p. 586; de Rossi, op. cit., 1871, p. 83; Armellini, op. cit., p. 620.

38. Boldetti, op. cit., p. 597; Armellini, op. cit., p. 684.

39. Di Giovanni, *La topografia antica di Palermo,* 1890, p. 133-169; Armellini, op. cit., p. 729 seq.

40. De Rossi, op. cit., 1876, p. 77 seq.; Armellini, op. cit., p. 677; Lugari, *San Siro, il primo vescovo di Pavia,* Rome, 1895.

41. De Rossi, op. cit., 1873, p. 80; 1874, p. 133; 1879, p. 27; Armellini, op. cit., p. 685.

42. Boldetti, op. cit., p. 609; Armellini, op. cit., p. 708.

43. De Rossi, op. cit., 1878, p. 85-99; Armellini, op. cit., p. 692.

44. Pennavaria, *Ricordi archeologici e paleontologici,* Palermo, 1891; Armellini, op. cit., p. 728.

45. De Rossi, op. cit., 1879, p. 98-117; Armellini, op. cit., p. 682.

46. *Archivio storico Siciliano,* 1883, p. 126-135; *Notizie degli Scavi,* 1885, p. 288-298; Armellini, op. cit., p. 735.

47. *Nuovo Bull. d'Arch. crist.,* 1897, p. 140 seq.; Di Lella, *L'antica basilica cristiana di Sesse Aurunca ed i suoi monumenti,* Canino, 1901.

48. De Rossi, op. cit., 1872, p. 81; 1875, p. 83; 1879, p. 39; 1881, p. 118; 1894, p. 125; Cavallari and Holm, *Topografia archeologica di Siracusa,* Palermo, 1893; Cavallari, *Appendice della Topografia archeologica di Siracusa,* 1891; Führer, *Forschungen zur "Sicilia sotterranea,"* Munich, 1897; Strazzulla, *Studio critico sulle iscrizione cristiane di Siracusa,* Palermo, 1898; Carini, *Le catacombe di San Giovanni in Siracusa,* 1890; Armellini, op. cit., p. 720 seq.

49. P. Germano di Santo Stanislao, *Memorie archeologiche e critiche sopra gli Atti e il cimitero di Sant'Eutizio di Ferento,* Rome, 1886.

50. Orioli, *Viterbo e il suo territorio,* Rome, 1849, pp. 13, 34 seq.; de Rossi, op. cit., p. 85; Armellini, op. cit., p. 663.

51. Boldetti, *Osservazioni,* p. 593 seq.; de Rossi, op. cit., 1871, pp. 88, 94-114; Armellini, op. cit., p. 642 seq.

52. De Rossi, op. cit., 1881, p. 108; Armellini, op. cit., p. 619.

53. Boldetti, op. cit., p. 581; de Rossi, op. cit., 1865, p. 28; Armellini, op. cit., p. 627; *Römische Quartalschrift,* 1902, p. 244.

54. Armellini, op. cit., p. 740.

55. Boldetti, op. cit., p. 593; de Rossi, op. cit., 1871, p. 85 seq.;

1876, p. 71; 1880, p. 58; *Römische Quartalschrift,* 1889, p. 25 seq.; Armellini, op. cit., pp. 638 and 646.

56. Armellini, op. cit., p. 693.

57. De Rossi, op. cit., 1877, p. 85 seq.; *Nuovo Bull. d'Arch. crist.,* 1900, p. 271; Armellini, op. cit., p. 716.

58. Orioli, op. cit., p. 32; Armellini, op. cit., p. 655.

59. *Bull. dell'Ist. di Corr. arch.,* 1835, p. 177 seq.; de Rossi, op. cit., 1874, pp. 84, 112-114; 1887, p. 107.

## CHAPTER VIII

1. Cf. Müller, *Koimeterien,* p. 12 seq.; Kaufmann, *Handbuch der christ. Archäolog.,* p. 74 seq.; Leclercq, *Manuel d'Arch. chrét.,* I, p. 434 seq.

2. Armellini, *Gli antichi Cimit. crist.,* p. 738 seq.; Carnana, *Ancient Pottery from the Pagan Tombs and Christian Cemeteries in the Islands of Malta,* Malta, 1899; Mayr, *Die altchristlichen Begräbnistätten auf Malta,* in *Römische Quartalschrift,* 1901, pp. 216-244, 352-385.

3. De Rossi, *Bull. d'Arch. crist.,* 1874, p. 134.

4. Cf. above, Part III; de Rossi, op. cit., 1878, p. 100-114; *Nuovo Bull. d'Arch. crist.,* 1900, p. 275-283; Yelic and Rutar, *Guida di Spalato e Salona,* Zara, 1894; *Bull. d'Arch. e Storia dalmata,* passim.

5. Hytrek, in *Ephem. Salonit.,* 1894, p. 5 seq.

6. De Rossi, op. cit., 1874, p. 144-149; Cabrol, *Dictionn. d'Arch. chrét.,* Vol. I, col. 1211-18.

7. Whenever the word "cemetery" alone is used, we are to understand the whole "burial area."

8. Boldetti, *Osservazioni,* p. 640 seq.

9. Hübsch, *Die altchristl. Kirchen,* 1858, p. 108.

10. De Rossi, op. cit., 1863, p. 31.

11. De Rossi, op. cit., 1880, p. 87.

12. Boldetti, op. cit., p. 641; de Rossi, op. cit., 1865, p. 48; Eulart, *Manuel d'Arch. franc.,* Vol. I, p. 115.

13. Boldetti, op. cit., p. 642 seq.

14. Boldetti, op. cit., p. 647; Kraus, *Roma sotterr.,* p. 611.

15. Cabrol, op. cit., Vol. I, col. 3084.

16. *Römische Quartalschrift,* 1890, p. 2.

17. Boldetti, op. cit., p. 635.

18. Boldetti, op. cit., p. 633.

19. Cf. Prudentius, Περὶ στεφάνων, Bk. I, v. 105-8.

20. Boldetti, op. cit., p. 637.

21. Boldetti, op. cit., p. 641; Bourban, *Saint-Maurice d'Agaune et ses fouilles,* in the *Nuovo Bull. d'Arch. crist.,* 1898, p. 194; Cabrol, op. cit., Vol. I, col. 850-71.

22. Strzygowski, *Kleinasien,* Leipzig, 1983, p. 51.

23. De Rossi, op. cit., 1864, p. 32; Cavedoni, *Opuscoli religiosi,* Modena, 1860, p. 176.

24. Duchesne, *Les nécropoles chrét. d'Isaurie,* in *Bull. de Corres. hellénique,* Vol. IV, p. 195 seq.; Strzygowski, op. cit., p. 91.

25. *Bull. de Corresp. hellénique,* 1880, p. 195 seq.; 1883, p. 230 seq.

26. Fellows, *Ausflug nach Kleinasien,* Leipzig, 1853, p. 197.

27. *Zeitschrift des deutschen Palästina Verein,* 1890, p. 175 seq.

28. Leclercq, *L'Afrique chrétienne,* 2 vols., Paris, 1904.

29. De Rossi, op. cit., 1884, p. 44; *Nuovo Bull. d'Arch. crist.,* 1895, p. 116 seq.; 1896, p. 92 seq.; 1899, p. 296; 1902, p. 544; Audollent, *Carthage romaine,* Paris, 1901.

30. Gsell, *Monum. antiq. de l'Algérie,* Paris, 1901, Vol. II, p. 190 seq.

31. De Rossi, op. cit., 1864, p. 28; 1876, p. 64; Gsell, op. cit., Vol. II, p. 409.

32. Leynaud, *Les catacombes d'Hadrumète, deuxième campagne de fouilles,* Sousse, 1906.

33. *Nuovo Bull. d'Arch. crist.,* 1898, p. 212 seq.; *Mélanges d'Arch. et d'Hist.,* 1898, p. 470-480.

34. Gsell, op. cit., Vol. II, p. 400.

35. Ibid., p. 227.

36. *Bull. Arch. du Comité des trav. histor.,* 1891, p. 371 seq.

37. De Rossi, op. cit., 1887, p. 124.

38. Gsell, op. cit., Vol. II, pp. 294 and 401.

39. Gsell, *Cherchel, Tipasa,* Algiers, 1896.

40. Cabrol, op. cit., Vol. I, col. 1042-58.

41. Cabrol, op. cit., Vol. I, 1098-1156.

42. Karabacek in Στρωμάτιων 'Αρχαιολογικόν, Rome, 1900; Cabrol, op. cit., Vol. I, col. 2326-2559.

43. Rohlfs, *Von Tripolis nach Alexandrien,* Bremen, 1871, p. 152.

44. Clédat, *Le monastère et la nécropole de Baouït,* in *Mémoires de l'Institut franc. d'Arch. orient.,* Vol. XII; Cabrol, op. cit. *(Baoüit),* Vol. II, col. 203-251, by Clédat.

45. De Bock, *Matériaux pour servir à l'archéologie de l'Egypte chrétienne,* 1901; Cabrol, op. cit. *(El Bagaouât),* Vol. II, col. 31-62, by Leclercq.

46. Kaufmann, *Zweiter Bericht über die Ausgrabung der Menas-Heiligthümer,* Cairo, 1907. His last work bears the title *Menastadt* (City of St. Menna), Leipzig, 1910.

# PART FOUR

## CHAPTER I

1. *Vivens* ("Living"); θανῶν, *mortuus* ("Dead"); *In fronte pedes* ("so many feet in front"); *Hoc monumentum haeredem non sequitur* ("This monument does not follow the inheritor, i.e., cannot be inherited").

2. Lib. VI, x, 429.

3. Cf. Ludwig, *Commodiana carmina,* Leipzig, 1877-78; Msgr. Freppel, *Commodien,* I.

4. Cf. above, Part III.

5. Aringhi, *Roma sotterr.,* Vol. II, p. 174.

6. "Sed nos pisciculi sumus secundum ΙΧΘΥΝ nostrum Jesum Christum," Tertullian, *De baptismo,* c. I (*P. L.,* Vol. I, col. 1198).

7. Luke, VI: 38.

8. II Timothy, IV: 7; I Cor., IX: 24.

9. See below.

## CHAPTER II

1. Cf. de Rossi, *Inscriptiones Christianae urbis Romae VII saeculo antiquiores,* Vol. I, 1861.

2. Ibid., Vol. I, n. 139, 190. Recently the following was also found: SVB IVLIO A(*ntistite*), "in the reign of Pope Julius I."

3. Innocent I (402-417). The inscription stood in St. Sebastian's, and today may be seen in the Lateran Museum.

4. Celestine I (423-432).

5. Cf. de Rossi, *Inscript. christ.,* Vol. I, p. 22-23.

6. Boldetti, *Osservazioni,* pp. 69, 78; de Rossi, loc. cit. Some have expressed doubt as to the authenticity of these inscriptions.

7. *P. L.,* Vol. LXXIV, col. 703 seq.

8. Cf. Marucchi, *Epigrafia cristiana* (Hoepli Edition), p. 259 seq.

9. Cf. P. Allard, *Etudes d'histoire et d'archéologie,* 1899, pp. 404, 405; Le Blant, *Inscriptions chrétiennes de la Gaule,* Introd., p. 101.

## CHAPTER III

1. Cf. de Rossi, *Bull. d'Arch. crist.,* 1876, p. 26.

2. Lactantius, *Divin. Institut.,* V, c. II (*P. L.,* Vol. VI, col. 587).

3. "If the first letters of the five words Ἰησοῦς Χριστὸς Θεοῦ Υἱὸς Σωτήρ are joined together, they will make the word ἰχθύς, which means 'fish,' which was mystically interpreted as Christ." St. Augustine, *De Civit. Dei,* XVIII, c. 23.

4. See above.

5. *Peristeph.,* hymn II (*P. L.,* Vol. LX, col. 330). Cf. de Rossi, *Bull. d'Arch. crist.,* 1869, p. 65 seq.

6. Many archeologists had been under the impression that the *dies martyrum* mentioned in the inscription of *Pecorius* might be the feast-day of St. Felicitas and her sons. Marucchi believes that it refers rather to the octave of Sts. Processus and Martinianus, which actually falls on July 9. It was but natural to record the feast of these two saints in the place where they were buried and where their tombs were to be found.

7. Cf. above, Part II.

8. *Lateinische und griechische Messen aus dem zweiten bis IV Jahrhundert,* Frankfort, 1859.

9. Cf. de Rossi, *Bull. d'Arch. crist.,* 1869, p. 21; *Nuovo Bull.,* 1899, p. 279-281.

10. Cf. O. Marucchi, *Di una pregevole ed inedita iscrizione cristiana,* in *Studi in Italia,* 1883.

## CHAPTER IV

1. Cf. G. Schneider, *Osservazioni sopra la triplice deposizione del papa Gaio nel cimitero di Callisto,* in the *Nuovo Bull. d'Arch. crist.,* 1907, p. 147.

2. Cf. de Rossi, *Bull. d'Arch. crist.,* 1874, p. 49-56; 1876, p. 85-95; *Roma sotterr.,* Vol. II, p. 31.

3. Cf. *Nuovo Bull. d'Arch. crist.,* 1903, n. 1-3.

4. Cf. Duchesne, *Origines du culte chrétien,* c. X, para. I.

5. Cf. de Rossi, op. cit., 1871, p. 32.

6. Cf. Duchesne, op. cit., c. XIII, para. I; de Rossi, op. cit., 1863. pp. 23, 32, 72, 80; Wilpert, *Die Gottgeweihten Jungfrauen,* Freiburg, 1892.

7. Cf. Duchesne, op. cit., c. V, para. I; de Rossi, op. cit., 1886, p. 90; Thomassin, *Discipline de l'Eglise,* I, I, 52; II, I, 43.

8. A reference to I Timothy, V, 16.

9. Cf. above, Part II.

## CHAPTER V

1. Cf. Marucchi, *La santità del matrimonio confermata dagli antichi monumenti cristiani,* published in the *Nuovo Bull. d'Arch. crist.* 1902.

2. Cf. Cabrol, *Dictionn. d'Arch. chrét.,* under the word "Alumni" (Leclercq), Vol. I, col. 1288-1306.

3. *Divin. Instit.*

4. Tertullian, *Apolog.* 37 (*P. L.,* Vol. I, col. 462).

## CHAPTER VII

1. Cf. de Rossi, *Bull. d'Arch. crist.,* passim, especially for the year 1884, p. 8-31; *Roma sotterr.,* Vol. I, p. 118-122; *P. L.,* Vol. XIII; Max. Ihm, *Damasi epigrammata,* Leipzig, 1895.

2. *De scriptoribus eccles.,* CIII (*P. L.,* Vol. XXIII, col. 701).

3. *Damasus et Laurentius Hispanis asserti et vindicati* (*P. L.,* Vol. LXXIV, col. 533 seq.).

4. Cf. *Nuovo Bull. d'Arch. Crist.,* 1903, n. 1-3.

5. *Carm.,* XXXV (*P. L.,* Vol. XIII, col. 409).

6. Ibid., XVI (*P. L.,* loc. cit., col. 290).

7. Op. cit., CIII, (*P. L.,* Vol. XXIII, col. 701).

8. *Carm.,* XXIII (col. 396).

9. Ibid., XXIX (col. 402).

10. Eulogy of St. Hippolytus; cf. *Bull. d'Arch. crist.,* 1881, p. 26. According to Dufourcq, the reserve of Damasus and the few notices he

gives concerning the martyrs show that, by the fourth century, very little was known of the authentic history of the martyrs (*Etude sur les "Gesta martyrum" romains*, 1900, p. 24-28).

11. *Damasi papae opuscula et gesta*, Rome, 1754.

12. Cf. Stornaiolo, *Osservazioni letterarie e filologiche sugli epi-grammi Damasiani*, Rome, 1886.

13. Hertz, *Analecta ad Horatium*, IV, p. 19.

14. *Carm.*, XXXV (col. 410).

15. Ibid., XII (col. 385).

16. Ibid., XXXVII (col. 414). Damasus himself has had numerous imitators. Cf. Weymann, *De carminibus Damasianis et pseudodamasi-anis observationes*, published in the *Revue d'hist. et de littérat. ré-ligieuses*, 1896, p. 58 seq.

17. Cf. Carini, *Epigrafia e paleografia del papa Damaso*, Rome, 1889.

18. Cf. page 161 for a reproduction of the poem placed by Damasus on the crypt of the popes.

19. Cf. above pp. 144-183.

20. Cf. de Rossi, op. cit., 1881, p. 26 seq.; cf. above pp. 171-172.

21. Cf. de Rossi, op. cit., 1883, p. 60 seq.

22. Cf. de Rossi, *Inscript. christ.*, Vol. II, p. 136.

23. *Bull. d'Arch. crist.*, 1881.

## CHAPTER VIII

1. Northcote-Allard, *Rome souterraine*, p. 177-178. "The sub-lime 'Till we meet again,' not the eternal 'Farewell' of the pagans, but Christian hope and confidence: 'Semper vives in Deo!' — 'May you always live in God' " (de Rossi, *Roma sotterr.*, Vol. II, p. 15).

2. Above, pp. 262-263.

3. *Nuovo Bull. d'Arch. crist.*, 1916-1921.

4. Cf. de Rossi, op. cit., Vol. I, p. 167.

# PART FIVE

## CHAPTER I

1. Cf. Marchi, *I monum. delle arti crist. primit.*, 1844; Garrucci, *Storia dell'arte cristiana*, 1873-1881; Grimouard de Saint-Laurent, *Guide de l'art chrétien*, 1872; Kraus, *Die christl. Kunst, in ihren frü-hesten anfängen*, 1873; *Geschichte der christ. Kunst*, 1895; Müntz, *Etudes sur l'hist. de la peinture et de l'iconographie chrétienne*, 1886; Lefort, *Etudes sur les monuments primitifs de la peinture chrétienne*, 1885. Peraté, *L'Archéologie chrétienne*, 1892; Wilpert, *Le pitture delle catacombe romane*, Rome, 1903; Von Sybel, *Christliche Antike. Ein-führung in die altchristliche Kunst*, Marburg, 1606; Venturi, *Storia dell' arte*, Vol. I.

2. Peraté, op. cit., p. 43.

3. Cf. Wilpert, op. cit., Kaufmann, *Handbuch der christl* *Archäolog.,* p. 275-486; Leclercq, *Manuel d'Archéol. chrét.,* Vol. II, p. 133-192.

4. I Cor., X, 4.

5. Cf. Kaufmann, op. cit., p. 487-542; Leclercq, op. cit., Vol. II, 245-326.

6. Peraté (op. cit., p. 205-307) believed that he had discovered both Christian and pagan figures on the same sarcophagus, but what he took to be a seated divinity is merely the figure of a philosopher in conversation with another person, a representation which is repeated on many sarcophagi.

7. Schultze, *Archäologische Studien,* 1880; *Die Katakomben,* 1882; Roller, *Les catacombes de Rome,* 1881.

8. Tertullian, *De resurrect. carnis,* c. I (*P. L.,* Vol. I, col. 795).

9. Kaufmann, *Die sepulcralen Jenseitsdenkmäler der Antike und der Urchristentums,* 1900.

10. *Etudes sur les sarcophages chrétiens antiques de la ville d'Arles,* 1878; *Les sarcophages chrétiens de la Gaule,* 1886.

11. Cf. Wilpert, *Sulla tecnica delle pitture cimiteriali e sullo stato di loro conservazione,* Rome, 1894.


## CHAPTER II

1. Cf. Wilpert, *Le pitture delle catacombe romane,* c. II, I, p. 21-36.

2. John, XV, 1 seq.

3. Cf. de Rossi, *Bull. d'Arch crist.,* 1863, p. 3.


## CHAPTER III

1. Cf. Martigny, *Etude archéologique sur l'agneau et le Bon Pasteur;* Veyries, *Les figures criophores.*

2. John I, 29, 36.

3. *Ep. XXXII ad Severum,* 10, 17 (*P. L.,* Vol. LXI, col. 336, 339).


## CHAPTER IV

1. Cf. pages 92 and 309.


## CHAPTER V

1. I Cor., X, 4. Concerning the Christian symbolism of water, see de Rossi, *Bull. d'Arch. crist.,* 1867, p. 78.

2. Cf. de Rossi, op. cit., 1868, p. 1 seq.; 1874, p. 174; 1877, p. 77 seq.

3. *De baptismo,* c. I (*P. L.,* Vol. I, col. 1198).

4. This subject has been represented twice. Wilpert noted that in one of the pictures, the minister who confers the sacrament is dressed

in a tunic and pallium, while in the other, he wears only a loin cloth. This last might properly represent the baptism of Jesus Christ, as indicated by a picture of the dove, traces of which were recognized at the left by Wilpert. Cf. *Nuovo Bull. d'Arch. crist.*, 1897, p. 132.

5. Cf. above, p. 276.

6. Cf. de Rossi, op. cit., 1876, pp. 7-16. Before Baptism, there occurred a Christian initiation. This consisted of a reading of some tracts from the Gospels, followed by the Creed and the Our Father. Duchesne believes that "we possess an artistic representation of this rite in the celebrated scene of the *traditio legis* ("giving of the law") which figures on so many Christian monuments, paintings and sarcophagi, glass vases and especially in the mosaics of the apses of the basilicas. The Redeemer is seated on a throne on a mountain top whence flow the four streams of Paradise. Surrounding Him are the apostles. St. Peter, their leader, receives from the hands of the Saviour a volume, symbol of the Christian law, on which is written: DOMINVS LEGEM DAT or some equivalent phrase. Above this group may be seen, in the firmament of the heavens, the four symbolical animals with the four books of the Gospels. I do not attempt to claim that this scene was composed expressly according to the ritual of the *traditio legis Christianae* (giving of the Christian law), but between them there is an agreement so evident that it does not escape observation. Many of the faithful, casting their eyes on the paintings which adorned the apses of their churches, could not but be reminded of one of the most beautiful ceremonies of their initiation" (*Les origines du culte chrétien*, c. IX).

7. The funeral banquets or agapes, which are an entirely different institution from this, continued until the fourth or even the fifth century.

8. St. Paul alludes to this usage in I Cor., XI.

9. Pliny, *Epist. ad Traian.*, X, 97.

10. *Epist. ad Smyrn.*, VIII (*P. G.*, Vol. V, col. 713).

11. *De idol.*, VII (*P. L.*, Vol. I, col. 669).

12. *De spectacul.*, XXV (ibid., col. 637).

13. *Contra haeres.*, part I, col. 13 (*P. G.*, Vol. VII, col. 580).

14. Cf. *Nuovo Bull. d'Arch. crist.*, 1897, p. 131.

15. *Epist.* XIII (*P. L.*, Vol. LXI, col. 213).

16. St. Jerome, *Epist. CXXV ad Rustic* (*P. L.*, Vol. XX, col. 1085).

17. Cf. above, 216, 291; de Rossi, *De christianis monumentis "ichthus" exhibentibus*, in the *Spicilegium Solesm.*, Vol. III, p. 544-577; Wilpert, *Principienfragen der christl. Archäol.*, p. 37. Concerning the dolphin employed as an image of the Saviour, see de Rossi, op. cit., 1870, p. 61-88. See also the recent work of Dolger, *Das Fischsymbol in früherchristlicher Zeit.*

18. Wilpert, *"Fractio panis," die älteste Darstellung des eucharistischen Opfers*, Freiburg, 1895.

19. St. Augustine, *In Johann.*, tract. 123 (*P. L.*, Vol. XXXV, col. 1966).

20. *De promissionibus et praedictionibus Dei*, 2, col. 39 (*P. L.,* Vol. LI, col. 816).

21. Wilpert, *Le pitture recentemente scoperte nel cimitero dei Santi Pietro e Marcellino*, in the *Nuovo Bull. d'Arch. crist.*, 1900, p. 85.

22. Luke, XXII, 29.

23. Wilpert, *Die Gottgeweheiten Jungfrauen*, p. 69, sees in this a picture of the Wise Virgins on one side and the Foolish Virgins on the other.

24. Cf. above, pp. 277, 278.

25. John, VI, 59.

26. Cf. Pitra, *Spicil. Solesm.*, III, p. 554-564; de Rossi, *Inscript. christ.*, Vol. II, part 1, p. xx; Pohl, *Das Ichtysmonument von Autun*, Berlin, 1880.

27. Probably it was Abercius Marcellus himself of whom Eusebius speaks (*Hist. Eccl.*, V, 19), and who was celebrated for a treatise against the Montanists. Cf. de Rossi, op. cit., Vol. II, p. 1.

28. Cf. Ramsay's article in the *Bulletin de correspondence hellénique*, July, 1882.

29. Other archeologists maintain that it was placed entirely on one side.

30. A large photograph of this precious fragment was published by Marucchi in the *Nuovo Bull. d'Arch. crist.*, 1895, n. 1.

31. John, X, 11.

32. *De baptismo*, c. I (*P. L.,* Vol. I, col. 1198).

33. Rom., I, 8.

34. Origen who was almost a contemporary of Abercius, also says: "Novit qui mysteriis imbutus est" (*Hom. in Levit.*, IX, 10); "Quae norunt qui initiati sunt" (*In Exod.*, VIII, 4).

35. Cf. de Rossi, *Bull. d'Arch. crist.*, 1879, p. 102.

36. Cf. Duchesne, *Bullett. critiq.*, 1897, p. 101-107; De Sanctis, *Theolog. Zeitschrift, Innsbrück,* 1897, p. 673 seq.; Zaccherini, *L'iscrizione d'Abercio,* Rome, 1898; Rocchi, *L'epitaffio di sant'Abercio vescovo di Geropoli in Frigia,* Rome, 1907.

37. Cf. de Rossi, op. cit., 1894; Duchesne, op. cit., March, 1894; Marucchi, *Nuovo Bull. d'Arch. crist.*, 1895, p. 1-41.

38. A vast literature has accumulated about the inscription of Abercius. For an extended bibliography, consult the *Dictionn. d'Arch. chrét.* of Cabrol under the article "Abercius" by Leclercq, Vol. I, col. 67-87.

## CHAPTER VI

1. Cf. Kaufmann, *Handbuch der christl. Archäol.,* p. 525 seq. and especially the synoptic tables on pages 226-330, reproducing the various passages of the Scriptures taken from the paintings of the first centuries.

2. I Peter 20, 21.

3. Wilpert, *Das Opfer Abrahms in der altchristlichen Kunst,* in the *Römische Quartalschrift,* 1877.

4. Cf. Mitius, *Jonas auf Denkmäler des christlichen Altertums,* Freiburg, 1897.

5. Matthew, XII, 40.

6. Cf. St. Jerome, *Epist.,* CXII (*P. L.,* Vol. XXII, col. 930).

7. Cf. *Nuovo Bull. d'Arch. crist.,* 1921, p. 83.

8. This scene is also found on some African lamps. Cf. Toulotte, *Le roi Nabuchodonosor sur les monuments Africains,* in the *Nuovo Bull. d'Arch. crist.,* 1900, p. 113 seq.

9. Wilpert, *Die malerein der Sacramentskapellen,* 1897, p. 11.

10. Luke, XIII, 11 seq.; cf. Iosi in the *Nuovo Bull. d'Arch. crist.,* 1918-1919, p. 82.

11. Cf. Peraté, *La résurrection de Lazare dans l'art primitif,* in the *Mélanges J. B. de Rossi,* 1892, p. 271-280.

12. Wilpert, *Di un ciclo di rappresentanze cristologiche nel cimitero dei Santi Pietro e Marcellino,* Rome, 1892.

13. John, XIV, 2.

14. Psalm CXVIII, 105.

## Chapter VII

1. Cf. Gabler, *De authentia epistolae Publii Lentuli ad senatum Romanum de Iesu Christo scriptae,* Jen. 1809; Fabricius, *Codex apocryphus Novi Testamenti.*

2. Wilpert, *L'Acheropita, ossia l'immagine del Salvatore nella cappella del "Sancta Sanctorum"* (*L'Arte,* year X, 1907, fascicles III and IV).

3. Eusebius, *Hist. eccles.,* I, 13 (*P. G.,* Vol. XX, col. 120 seq.). It appears that Christianity under the Abgar dynasty began under Abgar VIII (176-213).

4. *P. L.,* Vol. LIX, col. 164.

5. *Hist. eccles.,* IV, 26 (*P. G.,* Vol. LXXXVI, col. 2748).

6. Ibid., VII, 18 (col. 680).

7. Cf. Wilpert, *Pitture delle catacombe,* tab. 187.

8. Cf. *Nuovo Bull. d'Arch. crist.,* 1909, p. 157 seq.

9. Cf. pages 333, 334.

10. Cf. Wilpert, *La croce sui monumenti delle catacombe,* in the *Nuovo Bull. d'Arch. crist.,* 1902, p. 5.

11. Cf. above, p. 44.

12. *Roma sotterr.,* III, col. 65; cf. Marucchi, *La cripta sepolcrale di San Valentino,* 1878; idem, 1890.

13. *De gloria martyrum,* I, col. 6 (*P. L.,* Vol. LXXI, col. 710).

14. Cf. Vigouroux, *Dictionn. de la Bible,* art. "Croix," by Marucchi; Jaugey, *Dictionn. apol.,* art. "Croix," by Harlez; de Rossi, *Bull. d'Arch. crist.,* 1868, p. 88-91; Forrer and Müller, *Kreuz und Kreuzigung Christi in ihrer Kustentwickelung,* Strasburg, 1894; Bréhier, *Les origines du crucifix,* Paris, 1904.

15. This is the opinion of Grimouard de Saint Laurent (*Guide de l'art chrétien.,* Vol. III, p. 59), which is not contradicted by de Rossi.

16. St. Ambrose, *De instit. Virg.,* c. XIV (*P. L.,* Vol. XVI, col. 326).

17. *De Trinitate,* XIII, col. 5 (*P. L.,* Vol. XLII, col. 952).

18. Cf. de Rossi, *Immagini scelte della beata Vergine Maria tratte dalle catacombe romane,* Rome, 1863.

19. Cf. above, pp. 178-319.

20. Isaias, IX, 2; XLII, 6; Micheas, V, 2; Numbers, XXIV, 17.

21. Cf. above, p. 156.

22. Cf. above, p. 169.

23. Cf. above, p. 159.

24. Cf. above, p. 175.

25. Marchi, *I Monumenti delle arti cristiane primitive,* etc., p. 152 seq.

26. Cf. above, p. 154.

27. Cf. above, p. 183.

28. Cf. Marucchi, *Le catacombe rom.,* p. 560-561.

29. Cf. above, p. 308 seq.

30. Cf. above, p. 308 seq.

31. Cf. *P. L.,* Vol. LX.

32. *Poem.* XXVIII (*P. L.,* Vol. LXI, col. 663).

33. A painting of this kind has been discovered in the catacombs of Domitilla. Cf. Marucchi, *Nuovo Bull. d'Arch. crist.,* 1899, p. 8-9.

## Chapter VIII

1. Grousset, *Etude sur l'histoire des sarcophages chrétiens,* Paris, 1885. Garrucci, *Storia dell'arte cristiana* (sculpture). The sarcophagi preserved in the Lateran Museum were reproduced by Marucchi in a special volume entitled, *I monumenti del museo cristiano Lateranense,* 1910.

2. Cf. Marucchi, op. cit., and *Guida del Museo cristiano Lateranense,* Rome, 1922.

3. "The imprisonment of St. Peter, followed by his miraculous delivery, was the cause of his voyage to Rome; it was for this reason that the Romans delighted to reproduce this scene on their tombs" (Northcote and Brownlow, translated by Allard, *Rome souterraine,* p. 437).

4. Cf. Marucchi, *Guida* etc.

5. Cf. de Rossi, *Bull. d'Arch. crist.,* 1871; Dufresne, *Les cryptes Vaticanes,* p. 111; De Waal, *Der Sarkophag des Junius Bassus,* Rome, 1900.

6. Kondakoff, *Les sculptures de la porte de Sainte-Sabine,* in the *Revue archéologique,* 1877; Berthier, *La porte de Sainte-Sabine à Rome,* Freiburg, 1892; Grisar, *Kreuz und Kreuzingung auf der altchristlichen Thüre von S. Sabina in Rom,* Rome, 1894; and the *Analecta romana,* Vol. I, x.

7. Cf. above, p. 338.

8. In the Lateran Museum, near this statue, may be seen another which resembles very much statues of the second type.

9. *De vita Constant.,* III, 49 (*P. G.,* Vol. XX, col. 1109).

## Chapter IX

1. Cf. Buonarroti, *Osservazioni sopra alcuni frammenti di vasi antichi di vetro*, Florence, 1716; Garrucci, *Vetri ornati di figure in oro, trovati nei cimiteri dei Cristiani primitivi in Roma*, Rome, 1858; de Rossi, *Bull. d'Arch. crist.*, 1864, p. 81-82; 1868, p. 1-5; 1883, p. 134; 1884, p. 80-95; Armellini, *I vetri cristiani della Collezioni di Campo Santo* in *Römische Quartals.*, 1862; Vopel, *Die altchristlichen Goldgläser*, 1899; Fröhner, *Verres chrétiens à figures d'or*, Paris, 1899.

2. The object known as the Plate of Podgoritza is reproduced on page 285. Cf. de Rossi, op. cit., 1874, p. 174 seq.

3. Apoc., V, 8.

4. Cf. Sante Bartoli, *Lucernae veterum sepulcrales iconicae cum observationibus Petri Bellorii*, 1720; de Rossi, op. cit., passim; Garrucci, *Storia dell'arte cristiana*, Vol. VI; De Waal, *Die figurlichen Darstellungen auf altchristlichen lampen*, in the *Congr. scient. int. des cathol. à Fribourg*, Paris, 1898; Leclercq, *Manuel d'Arch. chrét.* Vol. II, p. 509 seq.

5. *Nuovo Bull. d'Arch. crist.*, 1895, p. 165.

6. St. Augustine, *Contra Faust., Manich.*, XII, 42 (*P. L.*, Vol. XLII, col. 276).

7. *Altercatio inter Teop.*, etc., (*P. L.*, Vol. XX, col. 1175).

8. *Liber formularum spirit. intell.*, c. IV (*P. L.*, Vol. L, col. 744).

9. A reproduction is given in Part VI, where the form of ancient Christian basilicas is treated.

10. Cf. de Rossi, *Le medaglie di devozione dei primi sei o sette secoli della Chiesa*, in *Bull. d'Arch. crist.*, 1869, p. 33-43; 1871, p. 150.

11. Cabrol, *Dictionn. d'Arch. chrét.*, under the word "Amulette" by Leclercq, Vol. I, col. 1784-1860.

12. Cf. de Rossi, *Bull. d'Arch. crist.*, 1868, p. 33-45, p. 79-84; 1881, p. 75-85, p. 125-146; 1890, p. 29-47.

13. Cf. de Rossi, *Roma sotterr.*, Vol. III, tab. XVII, n. 4.

14. Cf. de Rossi, *Bull. d'Arch. crist.*, 1876, p. 7-15 and tab. I.

15. Cf. de Rossi, *Bull. d'Arch. com.*, 1884; *Bull. d'Arch. crist.*, 1884, p. 86-94, tabs. V, VI.

16. Cf. de Rossi, op. cit., 1888-1889, p. 77; Le Blant, *Mélanges d'Arch. et d'Hist.*, 1888, p. 213 seq.

17. Odorici, *Antichità cristiane di Brescia*, Brescia, 1844.

18. *Bull. d'Arch. crist.*, 1873, p. 21, tab. III.

19. Cf. de Rossi, *Vasi di vetro diatreti*, in the *Bull. dell'Istituto*, 1874, p. 9-10; *Roma sotterr.*, Vol. III, p. 328-329.

20. Martigny, *Des anneaux chez les premiers chrétiens et de l'anneau épiscopal en particulier*, Mâcon, 1858; de Rossi, *Bull. d'Arch. crist.*, 1874, Vol. II; 1880, Vol. VII; 1881, p. 113 et passim; Cabrol, op. cit., under the word "Anneaux" by Leclercq, Vol. I, col. 2174-2223.

# PART SIX

## CHAPTER I

1. Holtzinger, *Die altchr. Architektur in systematicher Darstellung,* Stuttgart, 1889; Dehio, *Die Kirchliche Baukunst des Abendland,* I, Stuttgart, 1892; Crostarosa, *Le basiliche cristiane,* Rome, 1892; Kirsch, *Die christlichen Kultusgebäude in Altertum,* Cologne, 1893; Kraus, *Geschichte der christl. Kunst,* I. p. 257 seq., Freiburg, 1896; Marucchi, *Basiliques et églises de Rome,* Rome, 1902; Kaufmann, *Handbuch der christl. Archäol.,* p. 145-167; Leclercq, *Manuel d'Arch. chrét.,* Vol. I, p. 335-428; Cabrol, *Dictionn. d'Arch. chrét.,* art. "Basilique" by Leclercq, Vol. II, col. 525-602.

2. Cicero, *Contr. Verr.,* II, v, 58; *Ad Attic.,* II, 14.

3. XXVI, 27.

4. Marucchi, *Description du Forum Romain et du Palatin,* Rome, 1902; Thédenat, *Le Forum Romain.*

5. Cf. Hübsch, *Monumenti dell'architettura cristiana da Costantino a Carlo Magno.*

6. *From Schola to Cathedral,* Edinburgh, 1886.

7. Besides the authors cited at the beginning of this section, cf. also: Dehio, *Die Genesis der Basilika;* Duchesne, *Origines du culte chrétien,* c. XII.

8. Book VI, c. 5.

9. Cf. Marucchi, *Le Catacombe romane,* p. 370; Holtzinger, *Altchristliche Basiliken in Rom und Ravenna,* 1898; also *Die altchristliche und byzantinische Baukunst,* 1898. A few years ago, a subterranean edifice was discovered near the Porta Maggiore in Rome which has the form of a basilica, but this structure is certainly pagan.

## CHAPTER II

1. That of Damous-el-Karita, near Carthage, had nine naves; cf. *Nuovo Bull. d'Arch. crist.,* 1898, p. 220 seq.

2. Cf. de Rossi, *Roma sotterr.,* Vol. III, p. 488-495; Rohault de Fleury, *La Messe. Etudes archéol. sur ses monuments,* Paris, 1883, Vol. I; Sacco, *L'arte nel culto e specialmente nell'altare,* Florence, 1901; Cabrol, *Dictionn. d'Arch. chrét.,* article "Autel" by Leclercq, Vol. I, col. 3155-3189.

3. Cf. *Liber pontif.,* under the life of Gregory III; Mazzanti, *La scultura ornamentale romana nei bassi tempi,* in *Archivio storico dell'arte,* 1896; Rohault de Fleury, *La Messe,* p. 240.

4. *Nuovo Bull. d'Arch. crist.,* 1895, p. 122 seq.

5. Cf. Marucchi, *Le Catacombe romane,* p. 607.

6. Ibid., p. 370.

7. Ibid., p. 48.

8. Crostarosa, *Le basil. crist.,* p. 64 seq.

## CHAPTER III

1. Esther, I, 6.
2. *Nat. Hist.,* XXXVI, 25. Numerous archeologists have believed that this text treats of the celebrated mosaic of the temple of Fortune, representing the inundation of the Nile. But this mosaic is formed of small cubes similar to those of the imperial age; for that reason, it does not correspond to the description of Pliny and must be ascribed more correctly to the period of Hadrian. Cf. Marucchi, *Guida archeologica della città di Palestrina,* Rome, 1912, p. 79 seq.; idem *Nuove osservazioni sul mosaico di Palestrina,* in the *Bull. della Commiss. arch. commun. di Roma,* 1904.
3. Cf. Furietti, *De Musivis,* Rome, 1752; Ciampini, *Vetera monumenta,* Rome, 1747; Barbet de Jouy, *Les mosaïques chrétiennes des basiliques et des églises de Rome,* Paris, 1857; de Rossi, *Musaici cristiana e saggi dei pavimenti delle chiese di Roma anteriori al secolo XV,* Rome, 1872 seq.; Gerspach, *La mosaïque,* Paris, 1882, 1886; Peraté, *L'Archéologie chrét.,* Paris, 1892, p. 169-269; Clausse, *Basiliques et mosaïques chrétiennes d'Italie,* Paris, 1893; Wilpert, *Mosaiken,* 1918.
4. Cf. Marangoni, *Acta sancti Victorini,* p. 99.
5. Cf. Marucchi, *Le catacombe romane,* pp. 278, 357, 361, 533.
6. Eusebius, *De vita Constant.* (*P. G.,* Vol. XX, col. 1209).
7. *Nuovo Bull. d'Arch. crist.,* 1896, p. 14 seq.; p. 122 seq.
8. Ibid., 1897, p. 45 seq.
9. Cf. de Rossi, *Bull. d'Arch. crist.,* 1880, pp. 65, 153; Gerspach, *La mosaïque,* pp. 34, 72.
10. Cf. Diehl, *Ravenne,* Paris, 1903.
11. In these mosaics may be seen the picture of Pope Paschal I with the squared nimbus which, according to John the Deacon (*Vita Sancti Gregorii,* IV, c. 84; *P. L.,* Vol. LXXV, col. 281), is the distinctive mark of a person still living.
12. Cf. above, p. 327.
13. Cf. Boito, *L'Architettura cosmatesca,* Milan, 1860.
14. Cf. Faloci-Pulignani, *Del chiostro di Sassovivo,* Foligno, 1879.
15. Cf. de Rossi, op. cit., 1875, p. 110 seq.; 1888-1889, p. 156 seq.; 1891, p. 73 seq.
16. Cf. de Rossi, op. cit., 1875, p. 110 seq.
17. Ms. Menestrier, (Coll. de Rossi, Vatican Library), fol. 222.
18. Chigi Library, I, V, 167, fol. 322.
19. Panvinio, *Cod. Vat.,* 6781, fol. 122.
20. Cf. de Rossi, *Inscript. christ.,* Vol. II, p. 433.
21. Forcella, *Iscrizioni delle chiese di Roma.*
22. National Library of Paris, *Cod. suppl. Lat.,* 1420, fol. 29. Cf. also de Rossi, op. cit., 1891, p. 90-93.
23. *Bull. dell'Ist. di corrisp. archeol.,* 1881.
24. *Una scuola di marmorari medioevali,* in the *Nuovo Bull. d'Arch. crist.,* 1895, p. 42 seq.; p. 127 seq.
25. Forcella, *Iscr. delle chiese di Roma,* I, II, p. 5, n. 10.

26. Suarez, *Cod. Vat.*, 9040.
27. Cf. de Rossi, *Inscript. christ.*, Vol. I, p. 105, n. 202.

## CHAPTER IV

1. Duchesne, *Origines du culte chrétien*, Paris, 1899.
2. Cf. Cabrol, *Dictionn. d'Arch. chrét.*, article "Baptistère," by Leclercq, Vol. II, col. 382-469.
3. *Acta Apost.*, XX, 6, 7.
4. Cor., I, II, 20.
5. Cf. above, p. 288 seq.

## CHAPTER V

1. Cf. Wilpert, *Un capitolo di storia del vestiario*, Rome, 1898-1899; Duchesne, *Origines du culte chrétien*, Paris, 1903; Semeria, *La Messa nella sua storia e nei suoi simboli*, 2nd edit., 1907, p. 249-280; Braun, *Die liturgische Gewandung in Occident und Orient*, Freiburg, 1907.

## CHAPTER VI

1. Cf. Kirsch, *Die römischen Titelkirchen*, 1918. For a description of the churches of Rome, see Armellini, *Le chiese di Roma*, 1891; Marucchi, *Basiliques et églises de Rome*, 2nd edit., 1909; A. D. Tani, *Le chiese di Roma*, 1922.
2. Acts, I, 13.
3. Ibid., X, 9; XX, 8.
4. Romans, XVI, 5; I Corinthians, XVI, 19.
5. Cf. Duchesne, *Les origines chrét.*, p. 85.
6. Ciaconius, *Cod. Vat.*, 5409.
7. Cf. above, pp. 23, 178.
8. Cf. *Gesta apud Zenophilum* (*P. L.*, Vol. VIII, col. 731).
9. Duchesne, *Origines du culte chrétien*, c. XII, p. 1; de Rossi, *Bull. d'Arch. crist.*, 1856, p. 38-53.
10. The number of the clergy of Rome in relation to the churches or titles during the third century is given in a letter of Pope Cornelius (*Epistola IX ad Fabium*), recorded also by Eusebius. The number indicated was 44 priests and 7 deacons.
11. Cf. Mansi, *Coll. Conc.*, VIII, 235; *P. L.*, Vol. LXXVII, col. 1338; Vol. LXXVIII, col. 858 seq.; Duchesne, *Les titres presbytériaux et les diaconies* in the *Mélanges de l'Ecole francaise*, 1887.
12. According to Duchesne, we should say "Romanus tituli Marcelli," instead of "Marcellus tituli Romani," although this and some other names are doubtful.
13. *Hist. eccl.*, X, col. 5 (*P. G.*, Vol. XX, col. 884).
14. Cf. above, p. 95.
15. *Ep. XVIII, P. L.*, Vol. IV, col. 272.
16. Mabillon, *Mus. Ital.*, II, p. 16.
17. Marucchi, *Le catacombe romane*, p. 54.

## Chapter VII

1. Rome, 1666.
2. *Roma nel 1838.*
3. *Roma sotterr.,* Vol. III, c. XVII.
4. Cf. Duchesne, *Les circonscriptions de Rome pendant le moyen-âge* in *Revue des quest. histor.,* Vol. XXIV, p. 217 seq.

## Chapter VIII

1. The number of ancient Christian basilicas in Europe, Asia and Africa is great, and this list refers only to the most outstanding. For further information, consult the following: Kraus, *Real. Encyclop. der christlichen Alterthümer,* Freiburg, 1882, Vol. I, p. 136-145; Kaufmann, *Handbuch der christlichen Archäologie,* p. 74-107; Leclercq, *Manuel d'Archéologie chrétienne,* Vol. I, p. 434-493.
2. *Bull. d'Arch. crist.,* 1869, p. 76; 1873, p. 103; Franconi, *La catacomba e la basilica Costantiniana di Albano Laziale,* Rome, 1877.
3. Volpi, *Vetus Latium,* Vol. VII, p. 141; *Bull. d'Arch. crist.,* 1869, p. 79; 1875, p. 101.
4. Hübsch, *Die altchristl. Kirchen,* p. 81.
5. *Römische Quartalschr.,* 1893, p. 84 seq.
6. *Bull. d'Arch. crist.,* 1871, p. 147; Grisar, in *Nuovo Bull. d'Arch. crist.,* 1895, p. 42 seq.
7. *Bull. d'Arch. crist.,* 1864, p. 40 seq.
8. Ibid., 1872, pp. 9, 111 seq.
9. Armellini, *I cimit. crist. di Roma e d' Italia,* p. 669.
10. *Bull. d'Arch. crist.,* 1872, p. 90 seq.
11. Ibid., 1863, p. 40; 1864, p. 6 seq.; Savio, in the *Nuovo Bull. d'Arch. crist.,* 1896, p. 163 seq.; Hübsch, op. cit., p. 91 seq.
12. Hübsch, op. cit., n. 95.
13. Galante, *Guida sacra della città di Napoli,* Naples, 1873; *Nuovo Bull. d'Arch. crist.,* 1900, p. 99 seq.
14. *Bull. d'Arch. crist.,* 1871, p. 61; 1875, p. 24 seq.
15. Ciampini, *Vet. monument.,* p. 139; *Bull. d'Arch. crist.,* 1864, p. 40; 1866, p. 44.
16. Scognamiglio, *Della primitiva basilica del martire Sant' Agapito,* 1865; Marucchi, in the *Nuovo Bull. d'Arch. crist.,* 1898, p. 43-97 seq.; 1899, p. 225-244; 1900, pp. 68 seq.
17. Amoroso, *Le basiliche cristiane di Parenzo,* 1898; Marucchi, in the *Nuovo Bull. d'Arch. crist.,* 1896, p. 14-26; 122-138; Neumann, *Der Dom von Parenzo,* 1902.
18. *Bull. d'Arch. crist.,* 1866, p. 49-170 seq.
19. Hübsch, op. cit., nn. 29, 31, 49, 63, 65; Ricci, *Ravenna,* Bergamo, 1901.
20. The names of the basilicas already mentioned in connection with the catacombs have been omitted from this list. Only those churches are mentioned which preserve some ancient or monumental characteristic. A description of the particular churches of Rome may

be found in Armellini, *Le chiese di Roma dalla loro origine sino al secolo XVI,* 2nd edit., Rome, 1891; Marucchi, *Basiliques et églises de Rome,* Rome, Desclée, 1902.

21. *Bull. d'Arch. crist.,* 1871, p. 116 seq.
22. Ibid., 1874, p. 81-118.
23. Ibid., 1873, p. 129-139.
24. Hübsch, op. cit., Vol. XXVII.
25. Hübsch, op. cit., n. 91.
26. Ibid., n. 92.
27. *Bull. d'Arch. e Stor. dalmata,* 1876-1908 passim; Jelic, *Guida di Spalato e Salona,* 1894, p. 234 seq.
28. Cabrol, *Dictionn. d'Archéol. chrét.,* article, "Arles," by Leclercq, Vol. I, col. 2889-2913.
29. *Bull. d'Arch. crist.,* 1872, p. 45; Enlart, *Manuel d'Arch. franç.,* Vol. I, p. 115.
30. Hübsch, op. cit., p. 106.
31. Le Blant, *Inscriptions,* Vol. II, 454 seq.
32. *Mémoires de la Soc. archéol. du midi de la France,* 1897, Vol. II, p. 250-254.
33. Hübsch, op. cit., n. 108.
34. *Bull. d'Arch. crist.,* 1865, p. 48; Enlart, op. cit., Vol. I, p. 115.
35. F. Guerra y Orbe, *Deitania y su cathedral episcopal de Begastri,* Madrid, 1879.
36. Cabrol, op. cit., article, "Baléares," by Leclercq, Vol. II, col. 161-164.
37. *Bull. d'Arch. crist.,* 1878, p. 37-43.
38. Audollent, *Carthage Romaine,* Paris, 1901; *Bull. d'Arch. crist.,* p. 44 seq.
39. Gsell, *Monuments antiques de l'Algérie,* Vol. II, p. 192.
40. *Mélanges d'Arch. et d'Hist.,* 1894, p. 59.
41. *Atti del II Congr. intern. d'Arch. crist.,* 1902, p. 225 seq.
42. *Nuovo Bull. d'Arch. crist.,* 1898, p. 212-218.
43. Gsell, op. cit., Vol. II, p. 236-241.
44. *Bull. d'Arch. crist.,* 1886, p. 26-28.
45. Gsell, op. cit., 1901, Vol. II, p. 265-291, n. 138, pl. LXXXVI-XC.
46. *Mém. de l'Acad. des Inscr. et Bell. Lettr.,* Vol. XIII, fasc. ii.
47. Kyrillos II, *Le temple du "Caesareum" et l'église patriarc. d'Alexandrie,* Cairo, 1892.
48. Cabrol, op. cit., article, "Antinoe," Vol. I, col. 2326-2359, by Leclercq.
49. Ibid., article, "Bagaouât," Vol. II, col. 31-62, by Leclercq.
50. Ibid., article, "Baouït," Vol. II, col. 203-251, by Cledat.
51. De Bock, *Matériaux pour servir à l'histoire de l'Egypte chrétienne,* p. 85.
52. Edwards, *The Early Christian Church at Philae,* in *The Academy,* 1882, p. 107 seq.
53. Strzygowski, *Kleinasien,* p. 44; Cabrol, op. cit., Vol. I, col. 191-193.

54. Strzygowski, op. cit., p. 67.
55. *Bull. d'Arch. crist.*, 1868, p. 32; Strzygowski, op. cit., pp. 45, 115-171.
56. Cabrol, op. cit., article, "Antioche," Vol. I, col. 2359-2427.
57. Ciampini, *De aedificiis Constantini Magni*, 1693, p. 178.
58. Ibid.
59. *Bull. d'Arch. crist.*, 1872, p. 139.
60. Strzygowski, *Orient oder Rom*, Leipzig, 1901.
61. *Nuovo Bull. d'Arch. crist.*, 1901, p. 145 seq.; 1902, p. 184-185.
62. Ibid., 1901, p. 149-151.
63. Sakau, *Reise in Syrien und Mesopotamien*, p. 134.
64. Texier et Pullan, *Architecture byzantine*, p. 189.
65. Butler, *Architecture and other Arts*, p. 209.
66. Ibid.
67. De Vogüé, *Syrie centrale*, 102.
68. Butler, op. cit., 209.
69. De Vogüé, op. cit., p. 69 seq.
70. Ibid., p. 141 seq.; Butler, op. cit., p. 184-193; Cabrol, op. cit., Vol. I, col. 2380-2388.
71. Pulgher, *Les anciennes églises byzantines de Constantinople*, Vienna, 1878.
72. *Bull. d'Arch. crist.*, 1864, p. 5-6; *The Academy*, 1879, p. 292.

# Bibliography
# and Index

# PRINCIPAL WORKS

## To Be Consulted in a Study of Christian Archeology

### I. For the General Part of the Present Work and for the Christian Cemeteries

Aringhi, *Roma subterranea Antonii Bosii,* Rome, 1651.

Armellini, *Lezioni di Archeologia cristiana,* Rome, 1898.

— *Gli antichi cimiteri cristiani di Roma e d' Italia,* Rome, 1893.

Bardenhewer, *Patrologia* (three volumes), Desclée, 1903.

Batiffol, *Anciennes littératures chrétiennes: Littérature grecque,* Paris, 1897.

Boldetti, *Osservazioni sopra i cimiteri de' santi martiri ed antichi cristiani di Roma,* Rome, 1720.

Bosio, *Roma sotterranea,* Rome, 1632.

Cabrol, *Dictionnaire d' Archéologie chrétienne et de liturgie,* Paris, 1903.

Catalano, *Corso fondamentale di Archeologia cristiana,* Naples, Vol. 1, 1904; Vol. II, 1906.

— *Corpus scriptorum ecclesiasticorum Latinorum,* Vienna, 1866 seq.

De Rossi, *Roma sotterranea cristiana* (three volumes), Rome, 1864-1877.

— *Bullettino di Archeologia cristiana,* Rome, 1863-1894. A French translation was made during the years 1867-1882 under the direction of Martigny and Duchesne.

Kauffmann, *Handbuch der christlichen Archäologie,* Paderborn, 1905.

Kraus, *Realencyklopädie der christlichen Alterthümer,* Freiburg, 1880-1886.

— *Roma sotterranea,* Freiburg, 1873.

Leclercq, *Manuel d' archéologie chrétienne,* Paris, 1907.

Lowrie, *Monuments of the Early Church,* New York, 1901.

Marangoni, *Acta s. Victorini,* Rome, 1740.

Marchi, *I Monumenti delle arti cristiane primitive,* Vol. I, Rome, 1844.

Martigny, *Dictionnaire des antiquités chrétiennes,* 2nd edit., Paris, 1877.

Marucchi, *Elements d' Archéologie chrétienne: I. Notions générales; II. Itinéraire des catacombes; III. Les basiliques,* Rome, 1900-1903.

— *Le catacombe romane,* Rome, 1905.

— Continuation of *Roma sotterranea.* Description of the cemetery of Domitilla (two fasicles up to the present; the continuation was interrupted by the war).

Migne, *Patrologiae cursus completus,* Paris, 1884 seq.

Müller, *Koimeterien. Die altchristlichen Begräbnitzstätten,* Leipzig, 1902.

Northcote and Brownlow, *Rome souterraine,* translated by Allard, Paris, 1872-1874.

*Nuovo Bullettino di Archeologia cristiana,* Rome, 1895-1920; the continuation of de Rossi, begun by M. Armellini, M. S. de Rossi, O. Marucchi and E. Stevenson, and continued to 1899 by G. Bonavenia, D. Franchi de' Cavalieri, G. Gatti, R. Kanzler, O. Marucchi and G. Wilpert; new series continued by Alfieri and Lacroix in 1921.

Perret, *Catacombes de Rome,* Vols. I-VI, Paris, 1851-1855.

Roller, *Les catacombes de Rome* (two volumes), Paris, 1881.

Smith, *A Dictionary of Christian Antiquities,* London, 1876-1880 (Protestant).

Wilpert, *Principienfragen der christlichen Archäologie,* Freiburg, 1889.
— *Nochmals Principienfragen der christlichen Archäologie,* Rome, 1890.
— *La cripta dei Papi e di S. Cecilia,* 1909.

## II. On the History of the Persecutions; Hagiography

Allard, *Histoire des persécutions,* Paris, 1885-1890.
— *Le Christianisme et l'empire romain de Néron à Théodose,* Paris, 1897 (compendium of the preceding).
— *Dix leçons sur le martyre,* Paris, 1906.

Aube, *Les chrétiens dans l'empire romain,* Paris, 1881.

*Augusta historia,* Paris, 1620; Leipzig, 1865.

Boissier, *La fin du paganisme,* Paris, 1891.

Bollandists, *Acta sanctorum,* Anvers-Paris, 1643-1897.
— *Analecta Bollandiana,* Brussels, 1882 seq.

Delehaye, *Légendes hagiographiques,* 1905.

Doulcet, *Essai sur les rapports de l'Eglise chrétienne avec l'état romain,* Paris, 1882.

Duchesne, *Le "Liber pontificalis,"* Paris, 1886-1892.
— *Les origines chrétiennes,* two lithographed volumes, Paris.
— *Histoire ancienne de l'Eglise* (two volumes), Paris, 1906-1907.

Dufourcq, *Etudes sur les "Gesta martyrum" romains* (two volumes), Paris, 1900-1907.

Eusebius, *Historia ecclesiastica et chronicon* (edit. Heinichen, Leipzig, 1868, and Migne, P. G., Vol. XIX-XX).

Franchi de' Cavalieri, *La "Passio Ss. Perpetuae et Felicitatis,"* Rome, 1896, and other hagiographic monographs of St. Agnes, etc.

Friedländer, *Civilisation et moeurs romaines du règne d' Auguste à la fin des Antonins* (Vogel translation), Paris, 1865-1874.

Funck, *Histoire de l'Eglise,* translated by Hemmer, Paris.

Grisar, *Storia di Roma e dei Papi nel medio evo,* Rome, 1899.

Harnack, *Geschichte der altchristlichen Litteratur bis Eusebius,* Vols. I, II, Leipzig, 1893-1897.

Krüger, *Geschichte der altchristlichen Litteratur in den ersten drei Jahrhunderten,* Freiburg, 1895.

Ruinart, *Acta primorum martyrum sincera et selecta,* Paris, 1689.

Tillemont, *Mémoires pour servir à l'histoire ecclésiastique des six premiers siècles,* Paris, 1693-1712.

## III. On Christian Inscriptions

Bayet, *De titulis Atticae Christianis antiquissimis commentatio his-torica et epigraphica,* Paris, 1878.

Bruzza, *Iscrizioni antiche Vercellesi pagane e cristiane,* Rome, 1874.

Caesar, *Observationes ad aetatem titulorum Christianorum definiendam spectantes,* Bonn, 1896.

*Corpus inscriptionum Graecarum,* Berlin, 1828-1877.

*Corpus inscriptionum Latinarum,* Berlin, 1863 seq.

De Rossi, *Inscriptiones Christianae urbis Romae VII saeculo antiquiores,* Vol. I, parts I and II, Rome, 1861-1888.

— *Il museo epigrafico cristiano Pio-Lateranense,* Rome, 1878.

Fabretti, *Inscriptionum antiquarum quae in aedibus paternis asservantur explicatio,* Rome, 1699.

Forcella and Seletti, *Iscrizioni cristiane in Milano anteriori al IX secolo,* Cologne, 1897.

Gatti, *Inscriptiones Christianae urbis Romae,* 1915.

Grossi-Gondi, *Trattato di epigrafia cristiana,* 1920.

Hübner, *Inscriptionum Hispaniae Christianarum supplementum,* Berlin, 1900.

— *Inscriptiones Britanniae Christianae accedit supplementum in-scriptionum Christianarum Hispaniae,* Berlin and London, 1876.

Kauffmann, *Handbuch der christlichen Epigraphik,* 1917.

Kraus, *Die altchristlichen Inschriften der Rheinland,* Vols. I and II, Freiburg and Leipzig, 1890-1894.

Le Blant, *Inscriptions chrétiennes de la Gaule,* Paris, 1856-1865.

— *Manuel d'épigraphie chrétienne,* Paris, 1869.

— *L'épigraphie chrétienne en Gaule et dans l'Afrique romaine,* Paris, 1890.

— *Nouveau recueil des inscriptions chrétiennes de la Gaule anté-rieures au VIIIᵉ siècle,* Paris, 1892.

Lupi, *Dissertatio et animadversiones ad nuper inventum Severae mar-tyris epitaphium,* Palermo, 1734.

Mai, *Scriptorum veterum nova collectio,* Vol. V, Rome, 1831.

Marucchi, *Manuale di epigrafia cristiana,* Hoepli, 1910.

Migne, *Dictionnaire d'épigraphie chrétienne,* Vols. I and II, Paris, 1852.

Millet, *Recueil des inscriptions chrétiennes de l'Athos,* Paris, 1904.

## IV. On Ancient Christian Art

Bottari, *Sculture e pitture sacre estratte dai cimiteri di Roma,* Rome, 1737-1754.

Buonarroti, *Osservazioni sopra alcuni frammenti di vasi antichi di vetro,* Florence, 1716.

De Rossi, *Musaici delle Chiese di Roma anteriori al secolo XV,* Rome, 1872 seq.

Garrucci, *Storia dell' arte cristiana,* Prato, 1873-1881.
— *Vetri ornati di figure in oro trovati nei cimiteri dei Cristiani primitivi di Roma,* Rome, 1858.
Kraus, *Geschichte der christlichen Kunst,* Freiburg in B., 1895-1897.
Lefort, *Etudes sur les monuments primitifs de la peinture chrétienne en Italie,* Paris, 1885.
Marchi, *I monumenti delle Arti cristiane primitive nella Metropoli del Cristianesimo,* Rome, 1844.
Marucchi, *I monumenti del Museo cristiano Lateranense,* Hoepli, 1910.
Pératé, *L'Archéologie chrétienne,* Paris, 1892.
Sybel, *Christliche antike, Einführung in die altchristliche Kunst,* Marburg, 1906.
Venturi, *Storia dell' Arte italiana,* Vols. I and II.
Wilpert, *Le Pitture delle Catacombe Romane* (text and tables), Rome, Desclée, 1903.
— *Mosaiken und malereien,* 1918.

## V. On the Primitive Liturgy

Batiffol, *Histoire du Bréviaire romain,* Paris, 1904.
Baudot, *Notions générales de liturgie,* Paris, 1908.
Baumer, *Histoire du Bréviaire,* Paris, 1905.
Baumstark, *Liturgia romana e liturgia dell' Esarcato,* Rome, 1894.
Braun, *Die liturgische Gewandung in Occident und Orient nach Ursprung und Entwickelung, Verwendung und Symbolik,* Freiburg, 1907.
Cabrol, *Le livre de la prière antique,* Paris, 1903 (third edition).
— *Les origines liturgiques,* Paris, 1906.
— *Introduction aux études liturgiques,* Paris, 1907.
De Herdt, *Sacrae liturgiae praxis,* Vol. III, Van Linthout, 1902-1904.
Duchesne, *Origines du culte chrétien,* Paris, 1903.
Kellner, *L'anno ecclesiastico e le feste dei Santi nel loro svolgimento storico,* ΕΟΡΤΟΛΟΓΙΑ, Rome, 1906.
Menghini, *Elementa iuris liturgici,* Rome, 1907.
Semeria, *La Messa nella sua storia e nei suoi simboli,* Rome, 1907 (second edition).
Vandeur, *Notes sur la liturgie de la Messe.*
Wilpert, *Un capitolo di storia del vestiario,* two volumes, Rome, 1898-1899.

# INDEX

Abercius, Bishop of Hieropolis in Phrygia, 42, 206, 216
Acilii Glabriones, 217
Acilius Glabrio, 34
Acrostic, pseudo-damasian, 256
Acts, apocryphal, 153; of martyrs, as scholastic exercises, 9; of Processus and Martinianus, 25; of St. Cyprian, 51, 53; of St. Felicitas, 40; of Sts. Nereus and Achilleus, 9; of St. Perpetua, 45; of Sts. Perpetua and Felicitas, 9; of St. Peter, 25; of St. Polycarp, 9; of St. Victor, 18; of the Apostles, 1, 25, 77, 380; of the Greek martyrs, 54; of the martyrs, 8, 56; of the Roman Church, 9; of the Roman Councils, 382; Proconsular, 9; solemn Christian, 212
Aderchius, 348
*Ad martyres,* 4
*Ad nationes,* 4
Adoration of Sacred Species, 378
Adrian I, pope, 14, 87
*Adversus haereses* of St. Irenaeus, 4
Aeneid, 197, 255
Africa, Church of, 7; Roman, 388
Agape, 104, 288, 376
Alb, 379
Albano, 386
Alexander Severus, favorable to Christians, 46, 358
Alexandria, 389
Allard, 27, 28, 29, 54
Allegory of Orpheus, 274
*Alumni,* 242
Altar, in ancient times, 377; modern, 354; of early Christians, 376; of pagan divinity, 350
Ambones, for Epistle and Gospel, 354
Ampliatus, 26
Amphitheater, Flavian, 351
*Analisi geologica ed architettonica della Roma sotterranea,* 96
Anastasius Bibliothecarius, 12
Anastasius, pope, 113, 151
Anatolius, 221
Ancona, 186
Angilsperga, 348
*Annales* of Baronius, 16

Anniversaries of the dead, 74
Annunciation, 306
Anterus, pope, 48, 232
Anthony, 20
Antioch, 389
Apocalypse, 32
Apocalyptic letters, 349
Apollinaris, Claudius, Bishop of Hieropolis, apologete, 3, 40
*Apologeticum,* 4
Apologetes of Christianity, 3
Apology, of St. Justin, 38; of Tertullian, 41
Appian Way, 204
Apostates, Christian, 49; referred to by St. Clement, 32
Aquila, 24, 186
Aquileia, 186, 219; pavement of, 359
Aquitania, 210
Ara Coeli, 371
Arcadius, 208
Archeology, Christian, 1; at time of Renaissance, 15; foundations of, 1, 11; general bibliography, 434; general sources of, 1, 3; manual of, 1; special and general documents of, 1; special sources, 8; study of, 432
Architecture, pagan temple, 350
Arch of Septimius Severus, 351
Archives of Roman Church, burnt, 9
*Arcosolium,* cemetery of Callistus, 82, 97
*Area,* 45
Arezzo, 187
Aristides, Athenian apologete, 3, 38
Arles, 388
Armellini, 19
Art, ancient Christian, 11, 266, 436; decadence, 266; historical remarks on, 267; iconographic, 268; in Occident, 266; in Orient, 266; Roman, 266
Artists, independent, 373; Roman, 366
Ascoli, 187
Asia, 206
Asia Minor, 191, 389
Athalaric, 206
Athenagoras, apology, 4
Atripalda, 187

438

Persecutions, history of, 11; General, 37; in Egypt, 50; of Claudius and Aurelian, 37; of Decius, 37; of Diocletian, 37; of Domitian, 32; of Hadrian, 37; of Julian the Apostate, 68; of Marcus Aurelius, 38; of Maximian, 37; of Nero, 27; of Septimius Severus, 37; of the second century, 35; of the third century, 42; of Trajan, 35; of Valerian, 37
Peter, St., the Apostle, 22; bust of, 347
Philo, 20
*Philosophumena,* 6, 41, 43, 93
Piazza of the Signoria, 351
Pitcher, with milk, 296
Pictures, of the Saviour, 312; of the saints, 312; of Christ Crucified, 315; of the Blessed Virgin, 319; in ancient Christian basilicas, 377
Pilgrimage, 85
Pilgrims, their prayers to martyrs, 109
Piperno, 188
Pius, VI, pope, 25; VII, pope, 18; IX, pope, 18
Pius, Antoninus, Roman emperor, 3
Pluvial, 380
Pliny, 358; the Younger, letter to Trajan, 35
Podgoritza, plate of, 285, 348
Polycarp, Bishop of Smyrna, 4
Polytheism, negation of, 212
Pompeii, 352
Pompey, 20
Pontian, pope, 47; abdicates papacy, 48
Pontine region, 390
Popes, 232
Porticoes of the temple, 350
Porto, 387; excavations at, 348
Portogruaro, 188
Pozzuoli, 188
Prayers, ancient liturgical, 227; of the graffiti, 262
Preachers, the first of Christianity, 22
Prefects of Rome, 210
Priests, 235
Primacy of the Roman Church, 301
Principles, Christian, 39
Prisca, 24
Priscilla, 16
Prison, Mamertine, 24
Professions, 245
Property, corporative, 89; collective, of the Church, 95
Prophet Habacuc, 304
Protestants, 22
Protomartyrs under Nero, 30; of Rome, 144

Protus, 217
Prudentius, poet, 8, 23, 30, 220
Pudens, 24

Quadratus, Bishop of Athens, 3; apology to Hadrian, 3; apologete, 38
*Quattuor Coronati,* 57, 170

Rabanus Maurus, 11
Ragusa, 188
Rahmani, Patriarch of Antioch in Syria, 2
Raoul, Rochette, 18
Ravenna, 188, 387; basilica of, 359
Redemption, 216
*Refrigerium,* 105
Refutation of heresies, 6
Region of the Madonna, 158; of Liberius, 159; ancient ecclesiastical, of Rome, 384
Regimont, 388
Relics, selling of, 87; of glass, 348
Religion, Christian, amidst Jewish communities, 21
Remission of sins, power of, 62
Representations, Christian, 348
Resurrection, concept of, 211; dogma of, 163
Reunions, liturgical, 79, 223; on Sundays, 375
Rings, of glass, 349; of gold, 349; of iron, 349; of pewter, 349; of silver, 349; with Christian symbols, 348
Rites, funeral, of the catacombs, 96; among the Greeks, 355; Oriental, 355
Rome, ancient Christian cemeteries, 144; ancient ecclesiastical regions of, 384; basilicas of, 359; chronological signs, 205; depopulated, 86; division into regions, 385; founding of, 210; restoration of, 86; sacking of, 85
Rufinus, 68, 69
Ruinart, 45, 54
Rule of Constantine, 214

Sacramentaries, ancient missals, 13; Gelasian, 14; Gregorian, 14; Leonine, Gelasian, Gregorian, 13
Sacraments, 284; of Baptism and Holy Eucharist, 218, 228; of Penance, 229
Sacred Species, 355
Sacrifice, of Abraham, 302; of the liturgy, 375
*Sacrificarii,* 50
Sailor, 246
Saints, pictures of, 326
Salona, 388